THE GAMES THEY PLAYED

Sports in American History, 1865-1980

Douglas A. Noverr

Lawrence E. Ziewacz

NELSON-HALL nh CHICAGO

Library of Congress Cataloging in Publication Data

Noverr, Douglas A.
  The games they played.

  Bibliography: p.
  Includes index.
  1. Sports–United States–History. 2. Sports–
Social aspects–United States–History. I. Ziewacz,
Lawrence E. (Lawrence Edward) II. Title.
GV583.N68 1983   796'.0973   83–5647
ISBN 0–88229–728–7 (cloth)
ISBN 0–88229–819–4 (paper)

Manufactured in the United States of America

10 9 8 7 6 5 4 3 2

The paper in this book is pH neutral (acid-free).

85 - 1294

Contents

Illustrations

Introduction

This book examines the origins, evolution, and expansion of American sports within the context of historical and cultural developments. Sports have been thought of as a "special place" where fair competition could mold character and provide a lineage of heroes worthy of worship and emulation. For this reason the sports world has always enjoyed and been granted special exemptions so that it could function as a model of clean and pure competition and in order that it could avoid the stigma of being only a commercial enterprise. These exemptions have ranged from the reserve clause, the league monopolies, and control over access to franchises that the established owners in baseball enjoy, to the concessions granted "amateur" athletes in order to insure amateur status but keep them active in a sport, and finally to the autonomy and power enjoyed by athletic departments in higher education.

The theory was that in return for this trust sports would exemplify and reinforce cherished American values: the need for strength and readiness to face any physical challenge, democratic fairness of play and equal opportunity of participation, character tested under stress, and leadership by the physically fit. American sports became a key element in the national dream of success and mobility through mental readiness, individual aspiration, and physical toughness. Andrew Jackson symbolized this complex of virtues for the nineteenth century, while the "Rough Rider" Teddy Roosevelt carried them into the twentieth century. After the disappearance of initial negative reactions toward sports and games as frivolous and dissipating play, sports began to take on meanings and social roles far beyond the need for exercise, peer group companionship, and structured play. Coaches began to assume the role of "builders of character" and teachers of democratic values and attitudes, thus becoming as important to players as the minister and parents. Competition and play by the rules became the training ground for later participation in the economy and democracy, and this was important in a society where prolonged adolescence and delayed entry into full participation were necessary realities. As American society saw its needs change, it increasingly saw sports as an island of stability, an ongoing tradition that carried the unique American outlook and core values intact from one era or generation to the next.

Sports were not immune to the pressures of such historical exigencies as war, economic disruptions like depressions and recessions, internal problems of the nation, and shifts in dominant cultural and social values. Amateur sports moved gradually toward business organization and commercialization as soon as entrepreneurs could see profit or enhanced social status coming from ownership or when athletes could see mobility or opportunity deriving from "professionalism." The Great Depression introduced a new breed of hungry, aggressive baseball players who contrasted greatly with the fast set heroes of the Golden Age of Sports in the 1920s. Wartime play introduced concerns for the quality and level of play, and the return of established players and stars produced a postwar boom. In the 1960s and 1970s athletes underwent the same confusion and disorientation that society was convulsed with, producing new questions about the purposes and ends of sport or the excesses of violence and commercialization that had become permanent features of the sports world.

A tension has always existed between sports and American society as the culture has reevaluated and assessed the meaning and value of organized sports. Historical eras and periods each have their own unique consciousness or mind set, and circumstances have often changed dramatically and substantially between succeeding generations. Thus, discontinuities have been as prevalent in American history as continuities and intact traditions. Each generation discovers its own identity and purpose, its place in the culture and ongoing history. Sports provide a focus for this process of exploration and maturation because rules can and do change, conditions and circumstances of play shift, new styles of performance and levels of skill evolve, and new meanings of participation emerge. The act of winning can assume varied significance or serve different social and psychological purposes, depending on the specific historical context. As sports have expanded and involved more people, and as sports have become more varied, the act of participation assumes more diffused meanings.

This book attempts to show the unique qualities of the major American sports in definite eras and decades of American history. The first two chapters cover the periods of 1865 to 1900 and 1900 to 1920 with an analysis of the major features, developments, and trends within those eras. The next six chapters present a detailed coverage of the sports record and salient features in sports with a chapter devoted to each of the decades from 1920 through 1980. The final chapter offers a view of the possible and probable future of American sports given the current situation and the trends established in the 1970s.

The discussion and analysis are restricted to those sports that have involved the largest numbers of participants and spectators, have developed in uniquely American ways or had American origins, and have been most consistently in the popular consciousness. Therefore, treatment of such sports as bowling, horse racing, soccer, and hockey has been omitted. Consideration is given to baseball, basketball, boxing, golf, tennis, and track and field, including the Olympics. The treatment is necessarily selective because the focus is on the overall historical and cultural context and because the concern is with those sports that have experienced their unique development and major evolution in the United States.

1

Sports in the Gilded Age: The Nineteenth-Century Experience of Sports

The period from 1865 to 1900 is most commonly described as the "Gilded Age," a term used by Mark Twain and lawyer-editor Charles Dudley Warner to title a novel published in 1873 that took a sardonic look at the American drive for success and profits and the often unscrupulous activities of businessmen and politicians to grab a share of the largess. Although these activities did occur, the term "Gilded Age" is far too shallow and inadequate to depict the period correctly and accurately. In his superb analysis, *The Response to Industrialism, 1885–1914* (1957), Samuel Hays argues that the basic thrust of social, economic, and political movements during this era constituted not only a reaction to corporate control but "also against industrialism and the many ways in which it affected the lives of Americans." He further contends that to interpret the period as a time when "the discontented poor" were "struggling against the happy rich does violence to the complexity of industrial innovation and to the variety of striving that occurred in response to it." In other words, it was a period of revolutionary change that profoundly altered the total fabric of American life—for better or for worse.

In examining a bit more closely and specifically the challenges facing the nation in the post-Civil War period, one finds that they were many and varied. In the first place, the Civil War is a far less perplexing field of study than the "Era of Reconstruction." The Civil War was the ultimate human solution, a physical confrontation between two opposing sides. It was a time for heroism, valor, and glory. Reconstruction, on the other hand, was a healing process, a time for mending of wounds and for forgetting bitter memories. Yet this convalescence of a nation could not go on in the sterile confines of a hos-

1

pital ward or within the boundaries of some timeless vacuum. The war, time, and progress had irrevocably altered the world so that little reliance could be placed upon antebellum principles, customs, and mores. They had little relevance in a world that required constant adjustments to continuously changing situations.

The post-Civil War period presented many questions for each southerner. The southern planter could no longer watch over his fields with mint julep in hand as the slaves toiled away. He had to adjust to plantation life without slaves—if he still had a plantation left. What was to be done with the former slaves? Did cooperation with the Union forces mean that a southerner was a despised "scalawag" or a pragmatic realist who saw that a "New South" could be created only through a new economic foundation? Was every northerner who moved south a "carpetbagger" or was he sometimes an idealistic schoolteacher or an earnest preacher? Were the new state legislatures to be filled with freed blacks and their spendthrift white allies? Or were they representative assemblies now forced to make larger expenditures than had been previously necessary in order to provide for legitimate projects such as providing schools for black children and rebuilding devastated cities, industry, and plantations? Thus, for the average southerner, Reconstruction was a time of new decisions and new judgments, a period of readjustment to a society that had undergone profound changes.

The North did not escape from the problems of Reconstruction. As the winner, the North was confronted with the perplexing problem of developing a policy to deal with the conquered foe. The basic question that faced the North was how magnanimous should the Union be in its peace overtures. Should the South be welcomed back into the Union and pardoned for its transgression or should the South be treated as a vanquished enemy whose treatment would be guided by the maxim, "To the victor belongs the spoils"?

Unfortunately, the only man who could possibly have settled the controversy with the minimum amount of disturbance was killed. Lincoln's politically inept successor, Andrew Johnson, himself a former southerner, proved to be unsatisfactory to most politicians, no matter what their political allegiance. Johnson alienated northern Republicans to the point that they sought to impeach him and to institute a harsh and punitive congressional plan of Reconstruction.

Perhaps the greatest tragedy of Reconstruction is that it never settled the central question and the fundamental problem of the post-Civil War society—the role of the black person in that society. The politicians, the federal government, and the state governments could not come to an agreement as to what civil and human rights the emancipated Negro was legally entitled. Although the radicals in Congress attempted to guarantee civil rights for all by amending the Constitution, they were woefully inadequate to the task of making their ideals a living reality. Thus, the problem of civil rights has been a problem faced by each generation of Americans since that time.

Although the Industrial Revolution had made its impact on the United States prior to the Civil War, it was in the post-Civil War era that the United States underwent the widespread industrialization that transformed it economically from a primarily rural and agricultural society to an urban and industrial giant. Many factors were responsible for this industrial explosion: an abundance of natural resources, a growing labor force, and the development of new explosive techniques necessary to mine and refine these raw materials, among others. Perhaps the most important ingredients for industrial growth were the development of a nationwide network of railroads and the concomitant development of heavy industry such as steel, combined with the expansion and development of the fuel industries such as oil and coal. This simultaneous development of industrial capacity created competition and financial dealings which had not been witnessed heretofore on the North American continent. The drive for national markets was made possible because the railroads' expansion resulted in unprecedented consolidation and integration of manufacturing and industrial enterprises.

The high cost of industrial expansion and the need to control a substantial portion of the consumer market often resulted in ruthless competitive practices among business rivals as they eagerly sought to outmaneuver each other by any means available in order to attain the lion's share of the market. Robert L. Heilbroner, in *The Economic Transformation of America* (1977), has noted that "the most important immediate effect was a devastating new form of competition." He found that "not just in steel, but in virtually all industries with heavy fixed costs—railroads, coal, copper—'cutthroat' price wars broke out repeatedly as producers desperately struggled to find markets for their products when business was slack." The result, Heilbroner notes, was that "this cutthroat competition soon forced smaller firms with less wealth against the wall." Heilbroner states that an examination of the statistics of the iron and steel industry between 1870 and 1900 indicates there were "fewer firms in operation in 1900 than 1870, even though the industry's output had increased enormously." In some industries, giant enterprises, like Standard Oil, the American Sugar Refining Company, United States Steel, International Harvester, and Armour and Company, controlled 50 percent or more of the total production.

It was an era where capitalists and opportunists thrived, amassing great wealth and displaying it ostentatiously. Their taste was often vulgar and gaudy, and they were often haughty and arrogant. Yet there was a popular fascination with the wealthy. And at the Marlborough-Vanderbilt marriage in 1895, the *New York Times* stated that "women and children threw themselves under the feet of the horses in their desire to get a look at the occupants of vehicles." This fascination with the elite was pandered to by newspapers as they instituted the "Society Page." Since the wealthy social elite lived in isolated enclaves and moved in exclusive circles of leisure and entertainment, the middle class and poor could only imagine the scale of upper class affluence and the comforts they enjoyed.

The impact of industrialism was not limited to the business sector. Every level of American society was affected by the changes wrought by industrialism. Although most Americans enjoyed the fruits of economic progress such as faster transportation, quicker communication, and a plethora of consumer goods, the price of the new cornucopia was not cheap. Industrialization had expanded the labor force, stimulated large-scale immigration from abroad, which provoked nativist resentment, and spawned large urban centers that created new problems demanding amelioration or solution. These problems included homeless and delinquent children, domestic violence and street crime, sanitation and disease, and antagonisms between racial and ethnic groups.

The technical advances and mechanical innovations responsible for wide-scale industrialization made almost obsolete the craftsmanship of the individual artisan. Men operating machines could produce greater quantities and at a cheaper price than a single individual working in his own shop. Yet the men working in the factories could not take a great deal of pride in their work. They performed repetitive tasks that required largely unskilled labor. Their hours were long (an eleven-hour day was common) and their working conditions were invariably unsafe and unsanitary. In an effort to better their status, the workers attempted to organize, and the modern American labor union movement was thus conceived. The birth of the labor union was not accomplished without considerable "labor" pains. Strikes, riots, strikebreaking retaliations, and other outward manifestations of labor discontent were numerous in the period from 1870 through 1900.

The nation's growth rate was phenomenal during this period. The population of the country totaled approximately 47 million in 1877 and had increased to 67 million in 1893. In the eighties, nearly 5.25 million immigrants arrived and in the nineties about 3.75 million landed. Most of these immigrants in the latter part of the nineteenth century were from central and eastern Europe and tended to cluster in the large eastern cities. Generally they were Catholic or Jewish and possessed clothing, habits, food, and customs which made them "different" from those already settled here. "Old stock" Americans, in many cases, came to resent this "new immigration" because the newcomers were perceived as a threat to job security. In fact many immigrants were used by unscrupulous business owners as cheap labor to cut wages and undermine threats of strike, and their potential votes were a power often mobilized with much success by urban political machines such as the infamous Tweed Ring in New York.

Such resentment of immigrants was even used as a reason for supporting women's suffrage. In 1885 Senator Thomas W. Palmer of Michigan gave the first public speech in the U.S. Senate in defense of women's suffrage. In his address, he emphasized that the greatest reason for the enfranchising of women was that it would provide a bulwark of voters to counteract the flood of immigrants, who, without restrictions as to "intelligence, character or patriotism," were allowed to vote. Since American women had been raised and educated under the "American system," they would be an effective counterbalance to this questionable foreign element.

In 1887 the Michigan Republicans, at their meeting to select delegates to the national convention, were divided on many issues, but on one topic they were unanimous in their opinion—that of restricting immigration. It was the consensus of the delegates that no foreigner should be welcome to American shores who lacked a certificate attesting to his or her good character and who would not promise obedience to the American Constitution and its form of government. The *Detroit Tribune* lauded the Republicans for their stand and asserted that such laws would probably have prevented the 1886 Haymarket Square riot that occurred in Chicago and caused the deaths of seven policemen and four others. The Detroit paper further commented: "It is time that this gross abuse of American kindness and liberty was stopped. They ought to be prevented from landing on our shores. We demand a clean bill of health when immigrants come from infected districts abroad. Let these jail birds and professional agitators bring proofs of their previous good behavior and in default be shipped back without ceremony. That prescription for a great and growing evil we feel sure will meet with the hearty endorsement of the American people." Antiforeignerism was a problem that was deep-rooted and would always be present to a greater or lesser degree in the American character.

Perhaps the greatest problems were the new urban centers, which were often doubling and quadrupling their population within a decade (by 1893 Chicago contained 70,000 Bohemians, one of the largest urban concentrations of Bohemians in the world). Too often the cities grew without much planning and foresight. Sanitation, transportation, and communication in a large urban community presented problems of an unprecedented nature to beleaguered city officials. The constant influx of immigrants meant that there was little respite from these problems as tenements multiplied.

Great discrepancies developed between the rich and poor. In testimony taken by the Senate Committee upon the Relations between Labor and Capital in 1883, Thomas O'Donnell of Fall River, Massachusetts, testified that he supported a wife and two children on $133 per year and that he knew of a thousand others who lived on less than $150 per year. John Spargo, in his *Bitter Cry of Children* (1906), gave an example of the meal menus of six city families in which the food provided included only bread, jam, coffee, tea, and soup. Contrast this scarcity with a luncheon given by one Mrs. Stanford, which took two and a half hours to serve. "Its twelve courses consisted of raw oysters, consumé in cups, baked bass and potatoes, macaroni, roast beef and tomatoes, Roman punch, brown squab, salad, olives and cheese, fresh strawberries and cream, charlottes, ices, coffee and sweets." A Bradley Martin costume ball at the Waldorf Hotel in February of 1897 cost a tidy sum of $368,200. The Vanderbilts owned a mansion which required the labor of thirty servants to maintain it. Likewise, *Munsey's Magazine* could report in 1901 that four members of the New York Yacht Club—including August Belmont, Cornelius Vanderbilt, W. K. Vanderbilt, Jr. and H. Payne Whitney—agreed to build identical steam yachts which each cost $26,000. Each had a $18,000 steamer built as well to act as a coal tender for the yacht. All these expenses were incurred so that the four gentlemen could race each other.

The immigrants, clustered in tenement slums and trapped by economic conditions, reflected an image of a new America that was more of a mosaic than a "melting pot." Exploited by business entrepreneurs, slum landlords, and local political bosses, the new immigrants and the urban poor in general were victimized. Yet the business philosophy of the day mitigated against any large-scale social reform or welfare. When Jefferson wrote the Declaration of Independence, he was interested in establishing the principle that all men were equal on a moral and a spiritual level. Thus, for Jefferson and those who later upheld the Jeffersonian tradition, the basic human freedoms were superior to economic freedom. Sometime between 1776 and the latter part of the nineteenth century this ideological position or credo underwent a substantial transformation. The idea of property rights was assigned to an equal or superior plane to human rights. This shift can probably be explained by the fact that an encroachment upon property rights is more readily discerned and can bring swifter and more efficacious reaction than a similar encroachment upon human rights.

When the materialistic post-Civil War generation looked back upon the democratic value system, they found it malleable enough so that they could hammer out a philosophy by which they could easily justify their actions. For industrialists and businessmen in particular, according to Robert Green McCloskey, *American Conservatism in the Age of Enterprise 1865–1910* (1951), "liberty was translated as the freedom to engage in economic enterprise, while the more basic and humane significance of the term was gradually submerged." Thus, the new American belief system became centered around the paramount rights of property and the transformation of "personal worth into an exchange value." Within this transformation of democratic political philosophy, capitalistic entrepreneurs could carry out their endeavors under the banner of economic freedom and raise their hackles in moral indignation when they perceived any threat of restriction on their activities.

The philosophical rationale necessary to calm any remaining uneasy conscience was conveniently provided by the doctrines of Social Darwinism. The chief spokesmen for this new socioeconomic philosophy was the English philosopher Herbert Spencer, who managed to transfer Darwinian biological principles of evolution into the social sphere. From Spencer's standpoint, the biological principles of the "struggle for existence," "natural selection" and "survival of the fittest" came to be represented by "business competition," "laissez-faire," and the "giant corporation."

In the United States, the chief disciple of Social Darwinism was a professor at Yale, William Graham Sumner. Sumner believed that life was essentially a grim struggle. Those who were fit would survive, and those who weren't fit would perish. The weak and indigent should not be helped because any aid contributed only to the degeneration of society. The rich should not aid the poor because the wealthy would be doing a "moral" wrong if they helped the "unfit" to survive.

Industrial leaders could applaud with enthusiasm when they read in Sumner's *What Social Classes Owe to Each Other* (1883), that people had to accommodate themselves to the "great inequality of environment, the concentration of business, industrial, and commercial wealth in the hands of the few, and the law of competition between these, as being not only beneficial but essential for the future progress of the race.''

Sumner offered further comfort to the capitalists by revealing that any movement for reform presented a clear and present danger to society and that the ''socialist or anarchist who seeks to overturn present conditions is to be regarded as attacking the foundations upon which civilization itself rests.''

If the Carnegies and the Rockefellers were satisfied with those doctrines, they probably went into ecstasy when they heard a distinguished member of the cloth, the Reverend Russell H. Conwell, give his much repeated sermon (over six thousand times) titled ''Acres of Diamonds,'' in which he declared it was every man's duty to become wealthy and ''to make money honestly is to preach the gospel.'' Conwell exhorted that piety could not be equated with poverty, and every man should ''trust in God and in business for everything that is worth living for on earth.'' For those who could still trust God but not their fellow man and who were being exploited by the new industrialism, the claxon trumpeting of the Social-Darwinian philosophy fell upon deaf ears.

For those who sought to turn to the government for help, politicians were extremely reluctant to discard precipitously and completely the Jeffersonian-Jacksonian theory of limited government. Also there was the matter of ''realpolitik''—the sustaining of political power. After 1872 the Democratic party was always competitive in presidential contests and often controlled the House of Representatives. The U.S. Senate was continuously in Republican control, but rarely did the victorious party have more than a three-vote margin. Because of the closeness of party strength, both major parties relied on emotional speeches, bands, and parades rather than issues to bring the faithful to the polls. Avoidance of controversial policy questions was common, as party leaders feared alienating any segment of voters. Consequently, many groups felt left out of the political process and created their own parties in the hope of mustering enough support to convince a major party to adopt their platforms to gain more votes.

But was not the American dream possible for all? Would not hard work and a little bit of luck—the formula for Horatio Alger's myriad of novels concerning young boys making good—bring rewards for everyone who worked hard? Hadn't Andrew Carnegie proven that a Scottish bobbin boy could become a ''captain of industry''? Recent historical studies have amassed evidence to the contrary. William Miller, in an article published in the *Journal of Economic History* (1949), entitled ''American Historians and the Business Elite,'' concludes from this study of the background of two hundred late-nineteenth-century business leaders that most "came from well-to-do or middle-class families of old American stock. Poor immigrant boys and poor farm boys together actually make up no more than 3 percent of the business leaders." Similarly, John N. Ingham, in his article, "Rags to Riches Revisited: The Effect of City Size and Related Factors on the Recruitment of Business Leaders," in the *Journal of American History* (1976), studied the leaders in the iron and steel industry during the period and made this summary of his findings: "The situation for the recruitment of officers for the iron and steel industry in the nineteenth century is more complex than has been recognized by previous students of the American economic and social order. The size and age of the city, along with its degree of economic and social autonomy, did much to determine the kinds of men recruited to executive ranks. Despite these variations, however, it can be stated with some confidence that iron and steel manufacturers generally were not alien men operating on foreign soil, but came from the 'first families' of their communities. This strongly implies that the Industrial Revolution, whatever the changes it wrought in the economic and technological spheres, did little to disturb the hegemony of the antebellum social upper classes over economic affairs." Economic and social mobility seems not to have accelerated during this period.

With many avenues of advancement denied them, the majority of the American people had to make do the best they could. It was still a time of great promise—a time when the settlement of the nation stretched from coast to coast and transportation and communication technology helped to link the nation. Despite these difficulties, it is evident that in these thirty-five years following the Civil War, the nation grew from youth to adulthood, attaining its full growth. As adolescence is a period when a human being undergoes certain changes which produce an adult, so too during this period did the United States undergo the changes that transformed it into a mature nation and a world power.

What does this have to do with sports? A great deal! As the late John Betts, author of one of the major works on American sport history, *America's Sporting Heritage: 1850–1950* (1974), has amply demonstrated, the post-Civil War period witnessed an athletic revolution. According to Betts, "the roots of our sporting heritage lie in the horse racing and fox hunting of the colonial era, but the main features of modern sport appeared only in the middle years of the nineteenth century." Acknowledging that such factors as the decline of rural influence, the decline of the Puritan orthodoxy, the rise of the English athletic movement, the impact of immigrants and frontier traditions, and the enthusiastic promotion of energetic sportsmen aided in promoting sports, Betts stated further that "the technological revolution is not the sole determining factor in the rise of sport, but to ignore its influence would result only in a more or less superficial understanding of the history of one of the prominent social institutions of modern America."

Betts gave many examples to demonstrate his contention. The development of the railroad and telegraph, which made possible long distance team travel as well as the instantaneous transmission of scores, meant that newspapers could more quickly report the results of sporting events and thus generate interest among the public. The electric light which eventually made possible night contests, the bicycle safety frame which gave mobility to both sexes, the Kodak camera which captured sports highlights for all time, the engraving of printing plates by the halftone process which slashed the price of print illustrations by ninety percent, the sewing machine and the factory system which meant that it was easier to make uniforms and equipment—all played vital roles. The development of such journals as *Outing* (published from 1882 to 1923) and others which featured many articles concerning athletics and sports helped to popularize athletics.

The sports that are most popular today were not even in existence then, or were virtually unknown. These include such favorites as baseball, basketball, football, ice hockey, track and field, golf, and tennis. A more scientific study than that of Betts also tends to confirm that the mid to late nineteenth century was a time of athletic revolution. In an article entitled "Origins of Contemporary Sports" in the *Research Quarterly* (1961), Marvin H. Eyler studied a total of ninety-five sports and concluded: "The evidence shows that there was a substantial increase in the number of sports introduced during the nineteenth century. A close relationship seems to exist between the increase of leisure time in part induced by the Industrial Revolution, and this development. Of the 95 sports covered, 49 or 52 percent came into being during the nineteenth century. A combination of the figures for the nineteenth and the twentieth centuries reveals that 65 or 68 percent of the sports reported originated during this period." Eyler discovered that England and the United States were the sites of origin for 56, or 59 percent, of the sports analyzed and found that of those sports originating in the United States, 17, or 71 percent, were created after 1890.

An examination of the records of sports originations and formations also tends to confirm this period as crucial to American sports development. For example, in 1871 the Rowing Association of American Colleges was formed; 1876 saw the Intercollegiate Football Association and the ICAAA (Intercollegiate track and field); 1881, the U.S. Lawn Tennis Association; 1887, the American Hockey Association; 1894, the U.S. Golf Association; in 1891 basketball was invented; and in 1892 the first heavyweight championship with gloves was held.

In addition, contemporaries of the period believed that society was undergoing a sports revolution. Albert Bushell Hart, writing in the *Atlantic Monthly* in 1890, commented that athletics had become so popular in college that "the popular caricature of the college student is no longer the stoop shouldered, long-haired grind but a person of abnormal biceps and rudimentary brains." The *Nation* in its March 29, 1883, issue defended colleges from criticism because of their sports orientation and stated: "It must be remembered that the enthusiasm for sport is not confined to college students but is a feature of modern life outside as well as inside the colleges, and as a matter of fact runs a much wider riot outside of them than it does inside." The *Nation* declared that it was "not the college students who are responsible for the profound interest taken by the public at large and stimulated by the press, not merely in races or baseball matches, but in six-day walking matches, quail eating against time events which are of positive injury to the human body, and are, in fact, merely got up to furnish an opportunity for betting." The *Nation* article could only conclude that "the craze for sports, contests, and 'events' is a feature of the modern world, and to expect the enthusiasm not to show itself in the colleges would be absurd."

Anne O'Hagan, writing in *Munsey's Magazine* in 1901 in an article entitled "The Athletic Girl," declared that "absolutely no other social achievement on the behalf of women is so important and so far reaching in its results. . . . With the single exception of the improvement in the legal status of women, their entrance into the realm of sport is the most cheering thing that has happened to them in the century just past." O'Hagan believed that "the adoption of athletic sports meant the gradual disappearance of the swooning damsels of old romance, and of that very real creature, the lady, who delighted a decade or so ago to describe herself as high strung, which, being properly interpreted meant uncontrolled and difficult to live with." The author also believed the "revolution meant as much psychologically as it did physically."

In terms of dress, O'Hagan believed that tennis and golf devotees who pioneered in looser, more informal wearing apparel created a benefit for all women. According to her article, "no boon has been granted so great as the privilege of wearing shirt waists and short skirts" and the woman who plays golf has made it possible for the woman who cannot distinguish between a cleek and a broom handle to go about her marketing in a short skirt; she has given the working girl, who never saw a golf course, freedom from the tyranny of braids and bindings; she has made wet ankles an unnecessary evil, and restored to the street sweeping department entire responsibility for the condition of the thoroughfare.''

The *Munsey's Magazine* article concluded that besides improving ''half the race in health, disposition, and dress,'' athletics have additionally ''robbed old age of some of its terrors for women and they promise to rob it of more.'' The ''golfing grandmother,'' O'Hagan strongly asserted, ''was no longer someone to be laughed at.'' Undoubtedly, the writer was a bit excessive in her claims concerning sports' positive and liberating influences on women, but some degree of change was experienced. Some scholars have given most of the credit for greater sports interest to increased income and the availability of more discretionary income. It is true that per capita income in the United States almost doubled during the period 1870–1900, going from $779 to $1,164. The workday decreased from twelve to ten hours with Saturday becoming for many a half-holiday. But just because there was increasing leisure time, a lot of people in urban areas did not necessarily turn to sport. Many still viewed sport as a waste of time or a questionable activity that would only increase the desire for play and dissipation.

Despite the statistics, many workers earned less than a thousand dollars a year and did not have the time, money, or energy to participate in or view sports. (Andrew Carnegie estimated that over 90 percent of the pig iron produced was done by two shifts of men, each working twelve hours a day.) During this period there would be a conflict between workers who wanted to reduce their working days, and employers who wanted to maintain high production output and low costs.

Gerald Grob, writing about the development of the labor movement in his work entitled *Workers and Utopia* (1961), commented that industrial society ''destroyed the earlier habits and customs that had held the community together. Each individual was thrown upon his own resources, and the rise of the wage payment completed the isolation of the individual from the group.'' Grob further asserted that ''the workers' loss of identity and status prepared the ground for the rise of trade unionism. While accepting industrial society, the unions set to work to replace the community that had disintegrated.'' Sports could also play a role in promoting social reintegration and new connections with the community.

Benjamin G. Rader, in his article ''The Quest for Subcommunities and the Rise of American Sport" published in the *American Quarterly* (1977), supports this contention. He contends that as older geographic communities were displaced, "Americans turned to new forms of community. Sport clubs, as one type of voluntary association, became one of the basic means by which certain groups sought to establish subcommunities within the larger society."

Rader further asserts that two types of subcommunities developed: ethnic and status. As he notes, "The ethnic community usually arose from contradictory forces of acceptance and rejection of the immigrant by the majority society. The status community, by contrast, was a product of status equals who wanted to close their ranks from those they considered inferior." The sport club, Rader found, served multifaceted purposes—"an instrument for social exclusion, for the socialization of youth, and for disciplining the behavior of its members. In short, the sport club assumed some of the traditional functions of the church, the state, and the geographic community. Almost incidentally the sport club of the nineteenth century provided a tremendous impetus to the growth of American sport."

Rader documents the formation of such clubs as the Scottish Caledonian clubs, which sponsored such events as footracing, tug-of-war, hurdling, pole-vaulting, hammer-throwing and shot-putting, and the German Turner society—"utopian, free-thinking and socialistic"—which espoused universal education and gymnastics. Long after the ideological purposes of the clubs had disappeared, the athletic influences had been perpetuated to the public. For example, Caledonian clubs soon found that crowds of up to 20,000 viewed their games, which were soon opened to the public and became the foundation of track and field in America. Similarly, the Turners continued to promote gymnastics long after they "abandoned most of their radical political program." Rader cites the U.S. commissioner of education who "declared that the introduction of school gymnastics in Chicago, Kansas City, Cleveland, Denver, Indianapolis, St. Louis, Milwaukee, Cincinnati, St. Paul, and San Francisco was due to the Turners. . . ."

On the other hand, Rader found that among the nouveau riche, a movement toward exclusive athletic clubs dramatically increased as "automatic social deference declined in the nineteenth century." Of course, this is not exactly a new theory. Thorstein Veblen, the eccentric but brilliant turn-of-the-century economist, had scathingly noted such elitist behavior in his *Theory of the Leisure Class* (1899). He theorized that "the upper classes in society established and maintained their social station by being removed from the necessities of productive toil. By devoting themselves to activities which were obviously nonproductive, they were able to inspire, under the prevailing system of social values, a competition in emulation in which victory passes to those who could spend the most money and do the least work." Therefore, "as indulgence in sports increased in expense, it increased also in social prestige." Thus Veblen found that the upper class sought to establish their elite status position through "conspicuous consumption," "conspicuous leisure," and "conspicuous waste." When one examines the protest of amateur baseball players against professionalism and the expenses involved in such sports which became popular at the gentlemen's clubs such as polo, yachting, and the adoption by exclusive country clubs of golf and tennis, these protests certainly seem to support further this argument of Rader and Veblen.

Yet, as Daniel T. Rodgers has noted in his *Work Ethic in Industrial America, 1850–1920* (1978), there was a bitter irony in the middle-class and upper-class acceptance of increased leisure for American businessmen, for they had thrived on the "work ethic," which had been derived largely from the Calvinist fear of idleness, from the anxiety caused by uncertainty over being a member of the elect, and from the acceptance of the idea that economic prosperity was one denotation of salvation. How could one enjoy leisure and still espouse the work ethic and preach it to one's employees? Rodgers points out that "the achievement of two generations of boundlessly individualistic and ambitious entrepreneurs was to eclipse the old, individualistic workshop economy with a new faceless world of system, large-scale enterprise, and intricate bureaucracies." The result of separating "work" from the "haphazardness of life was ultimately to turn" the essential allegiance of most Americans away from their jobs and into the more satisfying, work-free business of leisure. In the service of the work ethic, in short, Northerners built a world in which its values were no longer at home."

How could this dilemma be resolved? For many years prior to the Civil War, various writers had espoused the value of sports in promoting health and mental well-being. Other writers and medical authorities continued to do so after the Civil War. This health movement was given impetus by the "muscular Christianity" movement which led to the formation of the YWCA and the YMCA and to the development of health food advocates such as C. W. Post and the Kellogg brothers, who would found breakfast food empires upon what was originally a health food and exercise oriented industry. Was it not easier to accept the arguments that sports were a healthy diversion? And could not sports be used (as some have suggested) as opiates for the masses through which they could escape from the realities of their everyday world? For some temperance advocates of the day, sports activity was better than hanging out at the corner saloon, and for businessmen it was better than having labor unrest. Joel S. Spring, in an article entitled "Mass Culture and School Sports" published in *History of Education Quarterly* (1974), studied the "ideological arguments for support of modern recreation movements and the development of athletics in the public schools and universities in the United States." He found that the ultimate result of these movements was "mass spectatorship" even though the primary goal was "mass participation." After an extensive examination of the literature of recreation and sport, Spring's conclusion is that "the ideology which supported the rise of athletics in American life argued that it would relieve the monotony and tedium of work in an industrial society, end social unrest and crime, provide worthy use of leisure time and build a corporate democracy."

Another factor that must be considered in the growth of sport in the period from 1865 to 1900 is the role of betting. Americans had been notorious for betting on cockfights, bullbaiting, and ratbaiting (a weasel or another animal would be thrown into a ring with a number of rats and bets would be placed as to how quickly the animal could dispatch the rats). With the development of baseball, a legitimate sport, one could now bet on an event without the fear or threat of arrest. Bets could be placed in any number of places, such as saloons, cigar stores, factories, and ballparks. Betting on sports was a natural extension for urban subcommunities that were rife with gambling. It was a lower-class version of business speculation carried on by investors and financial power brokers.

Another point that needs further exploration is the role of democratic theory and the role of Social Darwinism theory working together to aid in the development of sports. Sam Bass Warner has written in his *Urban Wilderness: A History of the American City* (1972) that "the gulf between respectability and poverty in the corporations established the major segregation of the city, but this class separation was subdivided by further segregation within the neighborhoods of the city by race, national origin, and church affiliation." Did not democratic theory call for political equality? Were we not one people? Could not sports help cut through class structure to overcome stratification? Did not Social Darwinian philosophy call for competition to determine who was the best or fittest? Certainly the cities and towns of America were used to competing for railroad lines, grain mills, and government monies. Was not the pride they took in their ball clubs a part of this Social Darwinism spirit?

Stephen Freedman, in his article "The Baseball Fad in Chicago, 1865–1870: An Exploration of the Role of Sport in the Nineteenth-

Century City" in the *Journal of Sport History* (1975), noted that the failure of Chicago's amateur club to compete successfully with professional clubs necessitated the formation of a professional club. He concluded: "The game of baseball, then, symbolized the middle-class conception of the city in an era when a city like Chicago was undergoing a rapid transformation from a small, manageable unit to a giant metropolis. On the one hand, the game's associations with a rural setting and the American rural values underscored the reluctance of the city dweller to part with the best elements of the staid and known world of the small town. Yet the display of speed, power, and organization which the urbanite came to look for in the teams which represented his city came out of a vision of vaster, richer, more productive forms of enterprise which the entrepreneur, as leader of the community, hoped to command and control." The sponsorship of sports could only enhance the public image and reputation of business or civic leaders.

Most immigrant youths did not need an academic study or survey to reveal to them the harsh facts of life that the chances of their becoming a "captain of industry" were extremely remote. When it became apparent that sport, specifically professional sport, might provide them with travel, some extra income, and a chance for fame and adulation, they seized upon it. The Pro Football Hall of Fame in Canton, Ohio, notes that it was among the mill and mine hands of Pennsylvania, most of them immigrants from central Europe, that pro football got its start. One has only to glance briefly at the history of boxing to see how certain sports were considered avenues of immigrant mobility and opportunity. The Irish, then the Jewish, Italian, black, and Hispanic fighters sought the ring as a means to acquire fame and fortune.

Finally comes the matter of heroes. Each generation has to have heroes. America's traditional heroes have been men of action—military men—but in the post-Civil War era America's greatest military hero had been President Grant. His whole administration had been tainted by a series of scandals. Every year that passed meant another year without warfare and without new military heroes. The young need people whom they can see and read about. Dixon Wecter, in his work *The Hero in America* (1966), states that American heroes must "be self-respecting, decent, honorable, with a sense of fair play." In addition, the hero must demonstrate "firmness and self-confidence in leadership . . . hard work, tenacity, enterprise and firmness in the face of odds. . . . They translate the dream into act."

During the Gilded Age the men most admired and envied were those in business. But did they make good heroes? Corpulence, not a slim, well-maintained body, was a mark of financial success. Flamboyance and profligacy were characteristics of the "robber baron." Thomas Nast, the most famous political cartoonist of the day, used a bloated figure to represent "profiteers" while the figure of a blacksmith represented the "common working man." Thomas Bailey, a well-known historian, described Mr. James Fisk, one of the financial demons of the period: "The corpulent Fisk—bold, impudent, unprincipled—was often seen in public with 'cuddlesome women' behind a span of fast horses. He succeeded in plundering the Erie Railroad of millions." Fisk's death also was a racy affair. His mistress, Josie Mansfield, had been blackmailing Fisk over letters that he had written her. When Fisk finally refused to pay any more, one Ned Stokes, whom Fisk had aided (at Miss Josie's request), sued Fisk for libel. The court dismissed the suit, and Stokes and Miss Mansfield were indicted for blackmail by a grand jury on January 6, 1872. On that same day as Fisk was entering the parlor of the Grand Central Hotel on lower Broadway, Ned Stokes appeared and emptied a pistol at Fisk. Two of the bullets hit Fisk, who fell mortally wounded.

This was not the type of hero Victorian American fathers and mothers wanted for their children. Even if most financial entrepreneurs were not as scandalous as Fisk, the Rockefellers, Vanderbilts, and Goulds did not play and win by the rules. But the athletic hero, whose heroics were done within the framework of a carefully prescribed formula, could not violate the rules without incurring a penalty. With his clean limbs, power, and speed unleashed to hammer out a hit, smash a serve, or gallop for a touchdown, and playing fair all the while, he better reflected attributes to which middle-class Americans, heirs to the Puritan code of ethics, could relate. As Americans sought viable heroes who symbolized fair and clean play as well as exemplary character, the professional sports enterprise realized that certain sports had to be "cleaned up" of a negative image and that in the process the sports could gain in popularity and fan support. This would not be an easy task.

Baseball

In 1907 a special commission decided that Abner Doubleday, a Civil War hero who had fired the first Union shot at Fort Sumter, was responsible for the origins of baseball, having supposedly done this in 1839 in Cooperstown, New York, now home of the Baseball Hall of

Fame. One scholar has stated that Doubleday, a West Point cadet at the time, would have had to have been AWOL in order to do so. Most scholars believe that baseball was derived from an English game called rounders, which had been described in a popular children's book as early as 1744. The game spread to America, and various versions such as Town Ball, the Massachusetts Game, One Old Cat, and Baseball were popular. A game called "base" was played at Valley Forge, and a game called "baste ball" was played at Princeton University in 1786.

By 1845 a number of different "ball" games were being played in America. Usually there were five bases laid out in "the shape of an open sided square. After hitting, the batter had to go 48 feet to first, 60 feet to second, 72 feet to third, and 72 feet to home base. An out was referred to as a "handout." There were two catchers—one about 50 feet behind the batter who caught the ball on the bounce and a second catcher who backed him up. A batted ball could be an out by being caught in the air or on the first bounce. Pitching was underhand, and if the batter hit the ball, he could not simply concentrate on running since he could be put out by "burning" or "soaking"—that is, by being hit by the ball. An uncertain number of players—generally ranging from twelve to twenty—composed a team. Runs were called aces, and the winning team was the one which first reached an agreed upon number of "aces." Sometimes this number was as much as 60 or more.

Modern baseball probably could be said to be founded in 1845 when Alexander Joy Cartwright, a draftsman, was appointed by his "social and baseball club" to draft a set of rules for the game. One of his basic rules was that "in no instance is a ball to be thrown at a player." Players were reduced in number from eleven to nine; the square was made a diamond with bases 90 feet apart. Cartwright had calculated that at that distance a fielder should be able to field a grounder and throw a runner out by a "fraction of a second." A game was finished when 21 aces were achieved by one team. On June 19, 1846, Cartwright's club, the New York Knickerbockers, played another team at the Elysian Fields in Hoboken, New Jersey, with Cartwright officiating. Since that time, Cartwright has been known as the "Father of Organized Baseball."

In the beginning, baseball was a game played by gentlemen, and many wished to keep it an upper-class sport. Freedman's study of the development of baseball in Chicago indicated that it was originally played by "young men of greater wealth and standing." Baseball diamonds were generally located on the perimeter of the town. It took longer for workers who lived clustered around their places of employment to reach the field, and they "would lose wages if they took time off to play." Games were held in the afternoon in Chicago, and generally not on Sunday—the traditional day off for workers. Even company teams were "recruited . . . from the upper ranks of the work force."

Baseball, whose only expense was a bat and ball (no gloves were used initially) and an empty field, proved to be a popular undertaking and soon spread throughout the land. Ball clubs generally were found in the East and Midwest, but baseball was played in California in 1869, and by the end of 1859 there were seven teams playing ball in New Orleans.

In 1859 the first baseball league was formed and was called the National Association of Baseball Players. In 1860 the Excelsiors of Brooklyn became the first team to go on the road. After whipping several in-state teams, they then played "nines" in Philadelphia, Wilmington, and Baltimore. Their star was Jim Creighton, a nineteen-year-old pitcher who was the first pitcher who threw with real speed and control. He also featured a curve ball. The Excelsiors' games often drew as many as 3,000 spectators, and this early professional team did much to help popularize the game.

The Civil War did not stop baseball. Some 40,000 troops watched a game on Christmas Day in 1862, and Union prisoners played the game in prison camps. Albert Spaulding purportedly was taught the game by a returning veteran in 1863 in his hometown of Rockford, Illinois.

After the war, the popularity of baseball continued to grow. The game seemed to fit the upbeat tempo of the times. It was much faster than cricket. As Stephen Freedman has noted in "The Baseball Fad in Chicago, 1865–1870: An Exploration of the Role of Sport in the Nineteenth Century" (*Journal of Sports History*, Summer 1978), "In an era when the fastest means of getting downtown was a horsecar traveling little better than three or four miles an hour, baseball was a game of fast-paced action and featured a display of speed and power." Freedman also appropriately notes that Mark Twain called baseball "the very symbol, the outward and visible expression of the drive and push and rush and struggle of the raging, tearing, booming nineteenth century."

By 1867 sparsely populated Minnesota was already featuring a state baseball tournament—the telegraph and railroad making the schedule and logistics possible. In 1882 the Leadville Blues could call themselves the baseball champs of Colorado. The development of professionalism in baseball was gradual. Some of the clubs began to divvy up the receipts and pay some of the star athletes. Crowds still gathered, as many spectators preferred to go where the outstanding players were displaying their skills.

By the late 1860s many baseball squads were composed of professionals (many with working-class backgrounds), and they included such teams as the Haymakers, the Atlantics, the Athletics, the Mutuals, the Chicago White Stockings, the Unions of Lansingburgh, New York, the Buckeyes of Cincinnati, and the Marylands of Baltimore. The Cincinnati Red Stockings of 1869 would be granted the title of the first "professional team" because they were the first team to have all members paid a specified wage. The team, first organized in 1867, was reorganized by a Cincinnati lawyer, Aaron Champion, in 1869, and he hired as their manager Harry Wright, an ex-cricketeer turned baseball player. A team of good players was gathered, and they set out on tour, playing teams in Boston, Pittsburgh, Louisville, St. Louis, and San Francisco on the West Coast, made possible by the new transcontinental railroad. The team won fifty-six games without a loss and returned home to a hero's welcome. They were feted by the city and presented with a 27-foot bat, emblematic of their victory skein.

Champion would be quoted as stating that he "would rather be president of the Cincinnati baseball club than president of the United States." Players took pride in taking part in a game that required mental and physical courage, as broken or dislocated fingers or other injuries were common. To face these unflinchingly was manly.

The impact of the Cincinnati team was tremendous. Many cities sought to compete for players and turn out teams that would reflect well on their own cities. As a consequence, amateur players were losing control of the sport. In Chicago, where the local team was sustaining losses by scores such as 49-4, the *Chicago Tribune*, smarting from nasty comments from rival newspapers who spoke disparagingly of the city and its baseball team, called in its July 22, 1868 edition for "a representative club; an organization as great as her enterprise and wealth, one that will not allow the second rate clubs of every village in the Northwest to carry away the honors in baseball. . . ."

In 1871 ten clubs joined together to create the National Association of Professional Baseball Players. Included were the Philadelphia Athletics, Washington Olympics, Washington Nationals, New York Mutuals, Troy Unions, Boston Red Stockings, Forest Citys of Rockford, Forest Citys of Cleveland, Chicago White Stockings, and the Fort Wayne Kekongas. The league was run largely by the players, who were able to jump clubs with impunity, moving on to the highest bidder. In this case the Boston Red Stockings was the club which was able to corral the best talent, paying salaries of $2,000 per man, a large sum for those days.

The association had numerous other difficulties. Teams were located in cities of different sizes and thus had greatly disparate populaces from which to draw fans and provide financial stability. The league lacked specific scheduling but did provide a tournament which cost $10 to enter. Betting was heavy, with bookmakers often having their booths out in the open. Players were often accused, and sometimes rightly so, of dropping games because of bribes. Rhubarbs and controversies were frequent and often heated, with fights and near riots resulting.

Despite its problems, the association was responsible for important changes in the game. The bunt was perfected, the infield fly rule was introduced to prevent the deliberate dropping of fly balls to achieve a double play, and such niceties of the game as cutoffs and relays and proper base-running techniques were developed.

In 1876, in order to salvage the professional game, William A. Hulbert and Albert Spalding of the Boston team called a meeting of eight association members for the purpose of forming a new league free from gambling. This organization was accomplished on February 2, 1876. Teams from Boston, Chicago, Cincinnati, Louisville, Hartford, St. Louis, Philadelphia, and New York were included in the league. The National Baseball Hall of Fame, in its description of the National League's formation, described it "as the time of the Industrial Revolution and these baseball pioneers decided the game, to prosper, needed a similar business-like approach." Certainly no captain of industry directed his industry into a monopoly better than did these National League owners, who by the 1890s held a monopoly on the professional game, beating back challenge after challenge of rival leagues. Albert Spalding himself became a wealthy man from baseball by following "sound" business tactics. In 1876 his athletic goods store received the contract to supply the leagues with baseballs and to "publish the official league organ." His business success allowed him to gradually retire from active playing and concentrate on his sporting goods interests, where he became successful by using the same techniques that Rockefeller had in climbing to the pinnacle of success—driving rivals out of business.

The 1870s were a time of economic depression, having been started by what was called the "Panic of '73." Economic times were hard, and many of the teams lost money. Fans found it difficult to pay the agreed upon admission price of fifty cents per game.

Team owners believed that high salaries were responsible for this problem. In 1879 they adopted a controversial policy—that of "reserving" players. These players could only play for the team that first signed them. By 1887, the number of players who could be put on reserve was fourteen, and the reserve clause was generally a part of a player's contract.

In 1881 a new league, the American Association, challenged the National League. Introducing Sunday play, reduced admission prices, and the serving of liquor, the new league offered formidable opposition. The National League was forced to drop several small city franchises and add teams in New York and Philadelphia in order to provide competition against American Association teams located in those cities. In 1883 an agreement was made between the two rival leagues.

That same year another league was formed and called the Union Association, which did not respect the National League's reserve clause. The National League responded by blacklisting National League players who jumped to the Union League. The proliferation of teams caused lack of attendance everywhere, and the Union Association was too weak to survive. It folded after a season, but the St. Louis franchise was allowed into the National League.

The last major challenge to the National League came with the revolt of the Brotherhood of Professional Baseball Players, which was formed in 1885 with John M. Ward, a college graduate and future lawyer, as its president. The brotherhood protested against the player salary limit of $2,000 and the development in the 1888 season of the so-called classification plan by which players would be paid according to ability. When the owners proved obdurate to these and other complaints, the players formed on November 4, 1889, the Players National League of Base Ball Clubs. The league was to be run by a "senate" of sixteen player representatives. Each team had to contribute $2,500 into a prize fund which would be distributed to the teams after the season, with $7,000 going to the first-place team.

In operation during the 1890 season, the upstart Players' League actually attracted more fans than the established National League. However, each league lost hundreds of thousands of dollars. Financial backers for the league, ignoring the opposition of the players, negotiated a peace settlement. Most of the teams were simply merged with other National League teams located in the same cities as the Players' League. After this opposition had collapsed, the owners were able to control baseball for a decade without major challenge to their domination. Players' salaries decreased by 30 percent as the owners exacted revenge much like any industrial owner who slashed the wages of beaten strikers who came back to work.

Despite the problems with league organization and affiliation which plagued professional baseball during the last quarter of the century, great players played the game. Baseball modernized itself so that by the dawn of the twentieth century it had come to resemble the game fans are so familiar with today.

Many changes in the game occurred. For example, in 1880 eight balls gave the player a base on balls, but this was changed in 1889. Pitchers were moved from 45 feet to 50 feet from home plate in 1881 and then in 1893 to the current 65 feet 6 inches. A flat-sided bat was introduced and then declared illegal. In 1884 pitchers were allowed to pitch overhand and in 1887 a player could no longer call for a high or low pitch so that the batter could have an advantage. Also the same year a rule was passed prohibiting a pitcher from running and jumping before pitching. And as early as 1884 the Providence Greys of the National League and the New York Metropolitans of the American Association played a three-game series to determine the better team after the season had ended. Providence swept all three games, and this confrontation established a pattern for what would eventually become the World Series.

Outstanding players abounded during the 1870s, 1880s, and 1890s. The top pitcher during the 1870s was Albert G. Spalding, who later became the sporting goods entrepreneur. Using the underhand delivery, he pitched the Boston team to four consecutive pennants from 1872 to 1875. Spalding pitched every game in the 1874 season and he and his team were 52 and 18.

During the 1880s the Chicago White Stockings were the dominant team. They captured six titles during the first eleven years of National League play. Adrian Constantine Anson, better known as "Cap," was manager of the Chicago team for nineteen years. He was a major leaguer for twenty-seven years and twice batted over .400. At the age of forty-six he batted .302. He was the first player to collect over 3,000 hits, and his .421 average in 1887 included walks that then counted as hits.

Other formidable Chicago White Stockings members included Billy Sunday, who would become a famous revivalist preacher; Ed Williamson, who slammed 27 home runs in 1884, a record that would not be broken until thirty-five years later when Babe Ruth did it; and King Kelly, the derring dasher of the base paths whose nimbleness caused a song writer to pen the famous "Slide, Kelly, Slide." So enamored were the Chicago fans with these doughty six-footers that they nicknamed them the "Heroic Legion of Baseball."

The 1880s saw the dominance of the Boston and Baltimore teams. Boston won pennants from 1891 to 1893 and then in 1897–98. Baltimore triumphed in 1894 to 1896. Boston included in its lineup such future Hall of Famers as Hugh Duffy, Tom McCarthy, Charles A. "Kid" Nichols, and Jimmy Collins. Another member of the team,

Bobby Lowe, became the first man ever to hit four home runs in a game. Approving fans threw Lowe coins and folding money that amounted to $160.

Ned Hanlon managed the Baltimore Orioles, a team that became known as an earlier day version of the later St. Louis Cardinals "Gashouse Gang." Hanlon developed such Hall of Famers as John McGraw, Willie Keeler, Wilbert Robinson, and Hughie Jennings. Hanlon's teams were known for their intelligent and aggressive style, becoming innovators of such baseball strategy as the bunt, the hit-and-run, the squeeze, and the double steal, all of which have since become standard repertoire in the arsenal of baseball tactics.

A key player for Hanlon was 5 foot 4 inch Wee Willie Keeler, known as the "greatest place hitter of all time." Sometimes teams would play as many as seven men in the infield, but Willie would still manage to hit it through. When asked the secret of his success, Will replied, "I hit 'em where they ain't." With his light bat and keen eye, Keeler hit over .300 for thirteen consecutive seasons, and in 1897 hit in 44 straight games and collected 243 hits, records that stood until Joe DiMaggio hit in 56 straight games in 1941 and George Sisler pounded out 257 hits in the 1920 season.

Baseball even broke the "color barrier"—but only briefly—during the period. In 1884 Moses Fleetwood Walker and his brother Welday signed with the Toledo club of the American Association. Welday played only 5 games while Fleetwood played a total of 42 games, 41 of them as a catcher.

Prejudice was often leveled at them. Fleet Walker had to sit in the stands in a game in Louisville because a player from the opposing side had said he wouldn't play if a black man was on the opposing team. The manager also received letters threatening the brothers with bodily harm. At the same time in the minor leagues, players of the International League passed a resolution opposing playing with blacks. The resolution was specifically aimed at Buffalo second baseman Frank Grant and pitcher George Stovey of Newark.

Baseball in the Gilded Age, particularly the development of professional baseball, mirrored the events of society at large. Adopting the methods of business entrepreneurs, the baseball owners of the National League became monopolists in their own right. The owners solidified their franchises, made the players their legal chattels, and as an end product, solidified baseball's position as the "National Pastime." Even with these discouraging economic and legal developments, players performed with increasing levels of skill and dedication to the game; they made it truly a professional sport that required agility, specialized skills, and even intelligence. Baseball was ready to move into its "modern age" as immortals such as Ty Cobb, Honus Wagner, Cy Young, Nap Lajoie, and others became the first popular stars of the game.

The Development of College Sports

Prior to the Civil War there were little or no organized college sports. Students at Harvard, Princeton, Yale, and others participated in games and play, but school officials rarely involved themselves unless activities got out of hand such as at Yale in 1882 when students were subject to fines, suspension, or dismissal for playing ball games. Unofficial athletic contests between classes and among fraternities were prevalent at colleges in the antebellum period. The so-called muscular Christian movement, promoted by such advocates as Thomas Higginson whose article "Saints and Their Bodies" appeared in the *Atlantic Monthly* in 1858, also seemed to have a great deal of influence on promoting intercollegiate athletics. A *New York Tribune* reporter in 1860 credited Higginson for what seemed to be a striking revolution in college students' attitudes toward athletic competition.

For many years it was the "crew" man rather than the football hero who was the "big man on campus." Harvard and Yale participated in rowing as early as the 1840s. The first intercollegiate crew race took place in 1852 at Lake Winnipesaukee, New Hampshire. Some attribute the confrontation to a challenge sent by Yale to Harvard, while others credit a chance meeting of Yale crew members with the Superintendent of the Boston, Concord, and Montreal Railroad, who saw an opportunity for promoting his line. The Harvard crew outrowed several Yale crews for the victory. A *New York Tribune* reporter present at the race was skeptical and commented that "intercollegiate sport would make little stir in the busy world." Yet rowing would spread and become popular. On July 14, 1875, for example, thirteen six-man crews rowed in a collegiate regatta that included representatives from all the other Ivy League teams.

Other intercollegiate sports activities soon grew. On July 1, 1859, Amherst defeated Williams College 73-32, using Massachusetts' baseball rules and thirteen men to a side. Baseball became the most popular collegiate sport on college campuses in the first two decades after the Civil War.

Track and field began when students formed the Columbia College Athletic Association and issued challenges to other groups. In 1873 James Gordon Bennett, Jr., of the *New York Herald* offered a cup for the victor of a two-mile race to be held in conjunction with the Saratoga regatta. Three men competed, and the winner was a Canadian, a student from McGill University. The following year the competition was expanded to five events, and in 1875 a whole day was devoted to competition. The interest in the sport eventually led to the founding of the Intercollegiate Association of Amateur Athletes of America, which initiated its first competition in 1876.

The sport that would play the most important role in the development of college athletics was football. The beginning of collegiate sports was founded in student organizations. Students developed teams, coached them, and made the provisions for travel. The captain was generally the man who provided the leadership. Football would begin as a club sport, but by the turn of the century, as the game became popular and proved to be a money maker, the control would be taken away from the students. Criticism was leveled at the sport because violence was associated with it and because it appeared to cause students, both the participants and the rest of the student body, to neglect their studies.

Football of various types had been played in America for many years. The American college game of the twentieth century would reflect the influence of both rugby and soccer mixed with "old-fashioned" American innovation, much of it provided by Walter Camp, who, because of his contributions to the game's development, became known as the "Father of American Football." On November 6, 1869, Rutgers and Princeton played what was known as the first football game. It was not, however, football as we know it today. It was played with twenty-five players to a side on a field that was 120 yards by 75 yards. Players were not allowed to run with or throw the ball, but they could hit it with their hands to move it forward and received a free kick for catching it. Rutgers defeated Princeton 6-4. It would be sixty-nine years before Rutgers could make a similar boast.

Two sidelights to the affair are worth noting. Two players crashed into flimsy bleachers, "throwing a 'seething mass' of screaming spectators to the ground." According to a description of the scene in *College Football U.S.A.* (1973), edited by John McCallum and Charles H. Pearson, "a jerky little train," as one newspaper called it, was "crowded to the aisles and platforms with a freight of eager students." From football's inception, then, technology played a part in making the event possible, and the event itself was a popular undertaking.

In the spring of 1874 Harvard met McGill of Canada and was introduced to rugby. The two schools had a return match the next year, and from then on, Harvard abandoned what was known as the "Boston Game." Harvard, Yale, and Princeton accepted rugby rules, and in 1876 the Intercollegiate Football Association was founded.

Walter Camp, who played football at Yale for six years (team captain for three years and a member of the Intercollegiate Football Rules Committee for forty-eight years), was undoubtedly the most influential person in the development of the game.

In 1880 Camp introduced the starting of play by the "snapper back" or center passing the ball back to the "quarterback," thus changing the game completely from rugby, which initiated action with the scrum. The playing field in 1880 was 110 yards long and 53 yards wide.

To prevent stalling, Camp introduced in 1882 the method of downs to advance the ball and retain possession. According to Camp, if a team could advance the ball 5 yards in 3 plays or downs, it would retain possession of the ball. If it did not, it would have to relinquish the ball to the opposition. One dubious fellow asked Camp how would they know when 5 yards had been gained. Camp replied that the field would have to be ruled off with horizontal chalk lines every 5 yards. The fellow replied, "The field will look like a gridiron." From then on football would be known as the gridiron game and its players as "gridders."

Until 1882 games were decided by goals and not by points. Four touchdowns made one goal, and a goal kicked after a touchdown counted more than four touchdowns. After the 1882 Harvard-Princeton game ended in a deadlock, the referee declared Harvard the winner because Princeton had made two safeties. To prevent such controversy, Camp introduced the point-scoring method in 1883. In 1883 a field goal was worth 5 points; a touchdown was worth 2 points; a try after touchdown scored 2 points and a safety, 1. Evidence quickly showed that it was the touchdown that was the key score of the game, so in 1884 the scoring was changed—the safety earned 2 points, the touchdown 4 points, and the goal after touchdown 2 points. By 1898 a touchdown was changed to count even more, 5 points, and a try after touchdown, 1 point.

In 1881 the field's dimensions were changed to 100 yards by 53. Prior to 1888, all tackling was above the waist. Tackling below the waist was then allowed and often led to "flying tackles," which were later outlawed. In 1879 the practice of running interference or blocking was introduced.

The game of collegiate football spread in popularity. In 1878 in the Midwest, Michigan and Racine were doing battle. By 1882 Minnesota, Purdue, Indiana, and Notre Dame were also playing. In 1873 the president of Cornell University, Andrew White, had made a name for himself by refusing to allow the Cornell team to respond to a University of Michigan team challenge to play a game. He telegraphed: "I will not permit thirty men to travel four hundred miles merely to agitate a bag of wind." In 1875, rejoicing in Cornell's crew victory in the regatta at Saratoga, President White telegraphed the team that "the University chimes are ringing, flags flying and cannons firing. Present hearty congratulations to both the victorious crews." He also paid the debt of the crew's expenses and labeled the expenditures as "advertising."

Players on the gridiron had to be a hardy lot. Attired in moleskin breeches, canvas jackets, and sturdy shoes, the player had little additional protection other than a heavy head of hair and perhaps some primitive nose, mouth, and ear guards. With the development of such tactics as the flying wedge, the turtle back, and the tackle tandem, whereby the ball carrier was protected by a mass of humanity, the game was predicated upon power. Attempts were made to combat this style. Columbia devised a hurdle play whereby a player would leap on his center and jump off him like a diver. This stunt was combated by having an opposing man do the same, whereby the two would meet in midair, usually with catastrophic results.

Colgate was known for its "dust formation." The quarterback would call dust formation, whereby his linemen would pick up a handful of dust and throw it in their opponents' eyes. One old-timer could recall that "it was good for a lot of touchdowns, and the only defense against it was to pray for rain."

Carlisle, home of Jim Thorpe, featured a number of trick plays, including the hidden ball trick. Here the player receiving the ball would tuck it under his sweater and all eleven members would scamper toward the goal (sometimes they had football-shaped pads underneath to add to the deception), making it difficult for the opposition to decide whom to tackle.

Football was a tough sport, and no one came tougher than the legendary Pudge Heffelfinger, who played for Yale (1889, 1890, 1891) and was one of the roughest linemen around. He devised a tactic for stopping the flying wedge by flinging himself feet first at the lead man in the formation. He could still play football at the age of sixty-five.

With the violence of the game and substitution allowed only for injuries, criticism began to mount to abolish or change college football. In 1885 Harvard argued that giving three warnings for slugging was insufficient. In 1886 a rule change dictated that those who slugged would be immediately expelled from the game.

According to Robert Leckie in his *The Story of Football* (1965), the game got so rough that in 1893 at the site of the Purdue-Chicago game, the district attorney of Tippecanoe County in Indiana walked on the field and "threatened to indict all the players for assault and battery." In that same year, the commandant of West Point had his bugler blow recall during a game in which Army was playing Yale in order to break up fisticuffs between Frank Hinkey of Yale and Butler Ames of Army. In 1894 the casualties from the Harvard-Yale game played before 23,000 persons prompted the *Boston Globe* to publish a "hospital score," which listed all those with broken bones and other severe injuries. As a result of such mayhem, newspapers like the *New York Post* stated, "No father or mother worthy of the name would permit a son to associate with the set of Yale brutes on Hinkey's football team."

Further criticism was generated by the popular magazines of the day. The *Nation* perceived a relation between business practices and college football and declared "the spirit of the American youth, as of the American man, is to win, to 'get there' by fair means or foul, and the lack of moral scruple which pervades the business world meets with temptations equally irresistible in the miniature contests of the football field." Professor Eugene Richards of Yale, writing in *Popular Science Monthly* (1888), declared that sports like "football, baseball, lacrosse and polo" had as their purpose "not in excellence of achievement, but in defeating rival organizations." N. S. Shaler, writing in *Atlantic Monthly* in 1889, declared that "one of the most serious evils connected with athletic sports arises from the wild celebrations with which victory in important contests is received. All our larger colleges suffer from this evil."

Yet another writer in *Popular Science Monthly* in 1880, while acknowledging the "positive and serious evil of athleticism . . . in the schools" believed that an "athlete is better off and less likely to turn out vicious than a wholly idle university man or school boy." Even Professor Richards at Yale would make this declaration: "Anything that will help to counteract the disintegrating forces of city life, that will help to strengthen our city young men against the insidious forces of ill-health, against the forces of low-living that will tend to keep young men out of disorders, out of crimes against self and society, is to be welcomed as an ally of the best education. I maintain that the system of athletics existing at our colleges and our athletic clubs in all the cities of the land does this. It does more. Its work is not only to save but to form men. It helps our schools and colleges to send out into the world not merely scholarly ascetics, but men full of force and energy, men of strong fiber, physical and moral."

If moral reasons were not sufficient for maintaining athletics or restraining them, there was another important factor to consider—the financial side of the ledger. In 1873 the Yale-Rutgers football game only brought in $90. Twenty years later, the Yale-Princeton game brought $13,000 each to the participating teams. By 1903 Yale's football team was bringing in $106,000. The popularity of the sports, particularly football, and the money that they brought in, and the reluctance to part with that added income, would be a continued source of problems to university authorities to our present day.

Professional Football and Its Origins

Pro football was in its infancy during the 1890s. Traditionally 1895 has been given as the first year of professional football when John Brallier received $10 to quarterback Latrobe, Pennsylvania in a game against Jeanette, which Latrobe won 12-0. Recent research has revealed that Pudge Heffelfinger received $500 to come from Chicago on November 12, 1892, to play for the Allegheny Athletic Association against the Pittsburgh Athletic Club. (The document is displayed in the Pro Football Hall of Fame in Canton, Ohio.) Heffelfinger smashed the ball carrier for the P.A.C., grabbed the football from him, and went 25 yards for the only score of the game.

The 1895 game in which Brallier, the first "open professional," played was during the first season that Latrobe played a formal schedule, and it was done at the instigation of the YMCA. Brallier had demonstrated his versatility by playing both high-school football and college football for Indiana Normal at the same time. Brallier lived in Indiana, Pennsylvania. He was contacted by David J. Berry, the editor-publisher of the *Latrobe Clipper* who was also the team's manager. Although Brallier was reluctant to play for Latrobe, since he was entering Washington and Jefferson College in the fall, ten dollars enticed him to come. Brallier's first comment on arriving at Latrobe was, "It's a thrill seeing my first paved street."

Brallier's kicking was instrumental in the 12-0 win, both his punting and his two-point after touchdown kicks. According to the newspaper account, when Latrobe took a 12-0 lead "the crowd was now wild, and maroon and orange was waving everywhere, men, women, and children were yelling frantically, and football was surely endeared into the hearts of the people of Latrobe."

By 1897 Latrobe was featuring an all-professional team. Even prior to that Greensburg was fielding an all-paid team. When the Latrobe team beat the Duquesne Country and Athletic Club in Pittsburgh in 1900, a special train carrying three hundred spectators accompanied the Latrobe team to the big city. One newspaper account stated that there was "bitter woe" in the Duquesne camp at "the sting of defeat at the hands of the coke-eaters from the wilds of far off Latrobe." To be beaten by mill hands from out yonder was obviously not a pleasant prospect.

Although Pittsburgh would be represented by several football teams such as the Duquesne club and the Allegheny Athletic Club, the strongest team was the Homestead Steel team supported by the Carnegie Steel works. Here was a case where success was too much. Formed in 1900, the team was so powerful that it won all its games decisively and it had a difficult time finding opponents. It broke up after two seasons, having lost some $8,000 in its second season of operation. One writer has commented that one of the problems with lack of support was not just the matter of being too successful—the fact of the matter was—"Pittsburgh was a baseball town."

It would not be until the twenties that pro football found some semblance of real organization and not until the thirties that it would begin to prosper. But in the hills and valleys of the tough iron and steel country, pro football had its roots. When the industrial corridor moved into Ohio, the scene of pro football shifted as towns such as Canton, Cleveland, and Massillon took it over as their own.

Basketball

The development of basketball is certainly a familiar story. James Naismith, an instructor at the YMCA training school at Springfield, Massachusetts (later to become Springfield College), was asked by Dr. Luther Halsey Gulick, the head of the school, to devise a game which would keep a troublesome physical education class occupied, a task at which two previous instructors had failed. After a great deal of experimentation, Naismith came up with the idea of basketball—a game in which there would be "no running with the ball, no pushing, shoving, tripping, or striking of an opponent." Naismith asked the school's janitor, Mr. Stebbins, to nail up a couple of boxes to the balcony of the gym. He could find no boxes, so nailed up a couple of peach baskets. A ladder had to be used to retrieve the ball. Then metal baskets with a hole in the bottom to insert a pole and knock the ball out were used. Then a net bag was utilized, and the "official pulled a cord attached to the net to pop the ball out." The open bottom net was introduced in 1912.

The first teams played nine to a side since eighteen was the number that Naismith had in his class. Various experiments were made with different numbers of players—sometimes even fifty to a side. Finally in 1897 five-man teams were made mandatory.

Soccer and rugby balls were utilized until 1894, when the Overman Wheel Company began manufacturing basketballs. Spalding became the official basketball-maker in the late 1890s, but by 1905 the teams could choose the brand of ball they wanted. The ball has been altered in size a number of times. Currently, balls have to conform to a circumference of no less than 29½ inches and not more than 30 inches, and its weight must be between 20 and 22 ounces.

Several colleges played intercollegiate games prior to 1897; however, these were not with five-man squads. Chicago played Iowa on January 16, 1896, but the Iowa team was not an official university team. Yale's victory over Penn 32-10 on March 20, 1897, is considered to be the first five-man college basketball game.

The YMCA did much to promote basketball. It originated the game and it was a national organization that helped stimulate interest in the game. However, some Y's by the turn of the century (as in Philadelphia) had abandoned the game because of the "rough play." In order to have games, teams had to rent a place to play, and it wasn't hard to figure out that teams would have to charge admission to defray the costs.

Professional basketball began in 1896 when Trenton players were paid fifteen dollars and their captain sixteen dollars for playing at the Trenton, New Jersey, Masonic Hall. The first professional basketball league began in 1908 with six teams: Trenton and Camden in New Jersey, and Millville, the Pennsylvania Bicycle Club of Philadelphia, the Hancock Athletic Club, and the Germantown Club of Pennsylvania. The league lasted only three years and went out of existence after the 1902–1903 season.

Women's Sports

As noted earlier in this chapter, the popular writer Anne O'Hagan had been enthused by the "revolutionary" impact of sports on women. Early in the period, walking and croquet were the only two sporting activities for a "proper lady." Croquet proved to be popular, and for the "purists" who detested the garden variety, a national tournament was begun in 1882 at Norwich, Connecticut.

Roller-skating became a rage in the 1880s, and almost every town and city came to have its own rink. Once again technology had made a sport popular since it was the introduction of metal wheels with pin bearings which made for smooth skating. The activity was popular with girls and women, and at its peak in 1885, over $20 million worth of roller-skating equipment was sold.

Anne O'Hagan had also felt that the invention of the "safety" frame had done as much as anything to liberate women. With women now able to ride bicycles, clothing styles had to change. Looser and lighter clothing and divided skirts altered women's fashions and gave the lie to those who had perceived women as "frail and delicate" creatures.

Although most women did not attend college, even in the post-Civil War period, those schools that did provide education for women often offered a program of sports and athletic activities. Sophia Richardson, writing in *Popular Science Monthly* in 1897, could recall playing baseball at Vassar. She also mentioned the current enthusiasm for tennis and particularly basketball, noting that each class had its team and substitute. Other popular women's sports included archery, bowling, horseback-riding, skating, golf, and tennis.

O'Hagan noted that of 1,200 golf clubs in the United States only one prohibited women. (She did admit that women could not play on Sundays and holidays, however.) She also noted that with the spread of YWCA's and private athletic clubs for women (New York had six, and one of the clubs in Chicago had a swim tank) athletic opportunity was not unavailable for a girl out of college. A woman could continue to pursue recreation and exercise habits established in school.

Yet the athletic participation of women was not widespread. It would be a long time before there would be a total acceptance of the "athletic female" as being a "normal woman," and even then women athletes had to be "ladylike" and "womanly" first. The dominant "cult of true womanhood" emphasized passivity, controlled and restrained movement, and secondary, supportive roles as wife and mother.

Cycling

Bike-racing was a sport of the 1890s until the advent of the auto in the early twentieth century ended the bicycle boom. On June 30, 1889, Charles Murphy rode a bike on a specially built track of the

Long Island Railroad and was able to clock 57⁴/₅ seconds for a mile. He followed a locomotive that had a specially designed hood to protect him from the airstream created by the moving train.

Professional bicycle-racing was popular, but both the League of American Wheelmen and the National Racing Association had rules against black membership. Marshall "Major" Taylor, a black who disdained racing in the Negro races, was allowed to compete with whites because of his exceptional talent. Taylor claimed three national championships beginning in 1898 and then in 1901 defeated a number of outstanding European cyclists as well.

Boxing

Boxing was a shadowy affair in the post-Civil War period since it was outlawed in most states. The prowess of John L. Sullivan, nicknamed "the Boston Strong Boy," reinvigorated the sport, and he became one of America's most popular heroes of the time. His reputation was made by knocking out Jake Kilrain in a seventy-five-round battle at Richburg, Mississippi on July 9, 1889, in the last bare knuckle fight of all time. The temperature soared to 106 degrees and there were 3,000 fans present. After the seventy-fifth round, a doctor advised Kilrain's second not to let his boxer come out another round, as he was already bleeding from the mouth and ears.

Although Sullivan was a great fighter, there were several black fighters who might have wrested the crown away from him. George Godfrey was an outstanding black fighter of the 1880s, but Sullivan refused to accept his challenge. In 1892 Sullivan declared his intention to fight "all fighters—first come, first served—who are white. I will not fight a negro. I never have and never shall." This left out Peter Jackson, a tough black fighter who had previously fought a sixty-one-round draw in 1891 with Jim Corbett. However, after Corbett's victory over Sullivan, his manager declared that "Corbett will never meet Jackson again. We are against fighting negroes anymore." Obviously in boxing in the late nineteenth century Jim Crow was alive and kicking. In 1895 Charles Dana of the *New York Sun* reacted to the successes of black fighters by stating that the nation was in "the midst of a growing menace." He was referring to the development of black athletic prowess, particularly in the sport of boxing, and he warned that although a "narrow escape" had been made "from the humiliation of having a black man world's champion . . . the menace is still with us."

The bout between Gentleman Jim Corbett and John L. Sullivan on September 7, 1892 was noteworthy for several reasons. It was the first championship fight using the Marquis of Queensbury rules and padded gloves. It would be the advent of boxers who relied on speed and mobility rather than brute strength and power.

Sullivan had not fought in three years and was 20 pounds overweight. Corbett, at 6 feet 1 inch and 184 pounds, was swift on his feet, had a quick left jab, and was a good athlete. In twenty-one rounds Corbett dispatched with Sullivan, who never managed to land a solid punch.

Corbett held the crown for five years when he was conquered at Carson City, Nevada, by Bob Fitzsimmons' famous "solar plexus" punch. Two years later, Corbett's former sparring partner, James J. Jeffries, defeated Fitzsimmons. Jeffries was a man who often looked awkward in the ring, but he went undefeated until he was lured out of retirement only to be humiliated by Jack Johnson in 1910.

Sports of the Upper Classes —
Tennis and Golf

Sports such as tennis, golf, and yachting—as well as others like polo, fox-hunting, squash, and rackets—were generally sports of the upper class during the late nineteenth century. Tennis was introduced at a Christmas party in Wales, when Major Walter C. Wingfield introduced a game he called "Sphairstike" or lawn tennis, which proved popular. The Major patented the game but it was not successful. The game caught on in Bermuda, where an American tourist, Mrs. Mary Outbridge of Staten Island, New York, saw it and brought it to New York. She introduced it to the Staten Island Cricket and Baseball Club. The game spread quickly among the upper classes, particularly the women, who preferred playing doubles. Until appropriate clothing could be devised, women found the game of singles too energetic to play attired in cumbersome dresses.

As early as 1881, the United States Lawn Tennis Association was formed to standardize the rules. Those rules that were utilized by the all-England and the Marylebone clubs in Britain were accepted as regulations for U.S. tennis. Also in 1881, a national championship was held at Newport, Rhode Island. Prior to that time, there had been a number of club tournaments, all of which had declared themselves as determining the national champion. Now there would be an official champion. One writer, Will Grimsley, in his article "Tennis" in A

Century of Sports (1971), has said that Newport was a "natural" for the tournament since the "city was the shrine of the white flannel set. It was there that industrial tycoons built multimillion-dollar mansions, [and] presidents and princes rubbed elbows with the rich and ultra-rich."

Richard Sears was the first champion of the Newport National Championship and remained so for seven straight years. He had grown up watching his brother play. He had also gone to England, where he learned from English stars like William Renshaw. From Lawford's instruction Sears developed the Lawford stroke, which produced a disconcerting topspin.

Early tennis was looked upon as a polite game for ladies. Players served underhand with much of the play limited to the baseline. During Sears' title days, the game was evolving and becoming more dynamic. The overhand serve was becoming common, and lobbing and volleying strokes were being added as more net rushing took place.

Until the end of the century the game was dominated by eastern players. Robert Wrenn, F. H. Hovey, and Malcolm D. Whitman, all former Harvard players, captured the national title between 1893 and 1900.

Golf

In the early 1890s a Scotsman, John Reid, introduced golf on a permanent basis by playing a three-hole game on land belonging to a local butcher in Yonkers, New York. By 1892 Reid and his golf-playing pals had moved down the course a bit and named it St. Andrews. Soon after, Thomas Havemeyer, a member of Newport, Rhode Island, society, built a nine-hole course and developed the Newport Golf Club.

Chicago was the home of the first eighteen-hole course. Charles Blair Macdonald was the major player, having learned the game in Scotland. In 1895 both the Newport Golf Club and the St. Andrews Club of Yonkers announced that they would hold tournaments. The Newport was thirty-six-hole medal play while St. Andrews' tournament was match play.

Macdonald finished second to a Newport player, W. G. Lawrence of Newport. Macdonald protested that it should have been match play. At the St. Andrews tournament, he again finished second, losing to Lawrence Stoddard in an extra hole playoff.

In December, 1894, delegates from five golf clubs met in New York City and formed the United States Golf Association. Theodore Havemeyer was elected president. Plans were made for both U.S. Open and Amateur titles. Macdonald won the first amateur golf title.

Golf became quite popular within the last few years of the century, but it largely appealed to an older, wealthier group. The number of golf clubs increased from about 50 in 1895 to 1,040 in 1900. Women were playing golf as early as 1891. An unsanctioned women's tournament was held in 1894, and by 1895 women had their own USGA sanctioned tournament.

Track and Field, Pedestrianism, and the Olympics

Pedestrianism was a sport which saw its heyday during the 1870s. It consisted of long-distance races, generally held indoors, and the contestants attempted to outdistance each other. So popular was the sport that women professional pedestrians on the East coast in the early 1870s contested for prizes that ranged from $500 to $10,000. Women raced in ten states and Ada Anderson won the biggest prize when she walked a quarter mile every 15 minutes for a month.

In 1879 a black runner, Frank Hart of Boston, entered the competition in the last of the meets for the Sir Astley belt, an award offered by Sir John Astley, a member of Parliament and an avid sports fan. Hart took fourth place at Madison Square Garden and received $2,730. The next year Hart set a record of 566 miles for a six-day event.

America's greatest star pedestrian was Edward Payson Weston. In 1861 he attempted at the age of twenty-two to walk from Boston to Washington in ten days. He missed his goal by a half day. He won a purse of $10,000 for walking from Portland to Chicago within thirty consecutive days. Sportswriter Henry Chadwick pointed out that Weston had awakened Americans to the benefits of "healthful exercise."

Weston was a dandy. He usually averaged 5 miles per hour and was always nattily dressed. He carried a little whip with which he used to exhort himself to greater effort. In 1879 he walked 550 miles in 142 hours and won the Astley belt. The favorite, "Blower" Brown, had finished nearly 100 miles behind him. Weston continued walking almost to the end of his life. When he was eighty-eight, he was struck by a taxi and his walking days were over. He died two years later in 1929.

As mentioned previously, track and field had its origins in the Caledonian games of the Scots immigrants. The New York Athletic Club was the pioneer in amateur track and field. Formed in 1868, it constructed the first cinder track and was soon inviting competitors. Colleges, of course, had been competing since the first race at Saratoga in 1874.

As interest in pedestrianism fell away, American interest in long-distance running, which had always been great, declined as well. As official track-and-field contests began to develop a more formal structure in the latter years of the nineteenth century, Americans developed superiority in the field events and in running events of a mile or less.

Innovative procedures were developed during this period which decreased time in the sprints. In 1868 William Curtis was the first American sprinter to use spiked shoes, and Charlie Sherrill introduced the crouched start in 1888. Using both spiked shoes and a crouching start, John Owen of the Detroit Athletic Club in the 1890 AAU championships was the first American amateur to break the 10 second 100-yard dash, running it in 9⁴/₅ seconds. However, America's greatest and most versatile runner during the period was Laurence Eugene "Lon" Meyers, who held a variety of national and world records in a ten year span from 1878 to 1888. He captured fifteen American titles as well as several foreign titles. In addition, he was able to set American records for all distances from 50 yards to a mile during his competitive career. In 1879 Meyers set a world record of 45¹/₅ seconds for the 440-yard dash, having to sprint the last 120 yards minus one of his shoes. In 1880 he won national titles in the 100, 220, 440, and 880. Later in his career he would continually face charges of professionalism. Although he turned professional just before his final retirement, Meyers' greatest feats were as an amateur. He was certainly the "unquestioned king of track and field" in the ten years he competed.

In the first Olympic games held in Athens in 1896, American track-and-field athletes dominated. Of twelve events contested, the United States won nine of them, with Thomas Burke a double winner in the 100- and 400-meter races. The only race run beyond 1,500 meters was the marathon, won by a Greek runner, Spiridon Loues.

The Gilded Age saw industry and technology transform every aspect of people's lives. With greater free time and with many people needing a respite from dreary factory work, sports and athletics became a way of relieving the tensions and frustrations of modern day life, whether one was involved as an active participant or as a spectator.

2

The Origins and Evolution of Modern Sports, 1900 to 1920

The period between 1900 and 1920 witnessed the economic and social transformation of the United States into a powerful industrial nation. The same period saw the country assume the role of a world power. After the Spanish-American War the country was flexing its muscle and expanding its sphere of influence.

In 1907 Theodore Roosevelt decided to send an entire battleship fleet around the world in order to show Japan and other world powers that the United States had arrived as a naval power and had the capacity to execute such an unthinkable naval maneuver. The sixteen battleships of the "Great White Fleet" were enthusiastically received and celebrated wherever they stopped, and the two-year spectacular voyage showed that the "big stick" diplomacy could convince foreign nations that American interests, whether related to the protection of the Monroe Doctrine or the expansion of trade, would be secured by military preparedness and bold action.

Theodore Roosevelt was the symbol of American ambitions and cocky self-confidence. An impetuous and impatient man, he bullied his way around and managed to convince many that T.R.'s way was the only way. He firmly believed that the president should actively and fearlessly lead and that all other branches of government should follow. Although he was something of a demagogue and definitely a colossal egotist, Roosevelt developed a loyal and even idolatrous following among the common people. To them he was a fiery champion of the "little guy." He wanted to make things happen, to move the country forward, and he believed in a "square deal" that would insure, as he said, "no crookedness in the dealing."

Roosevelt helped to create a climate conducive to reform and the correction or amelioration of the worst political, social, and economic evils that had gone unchecked or unchallenged. Often supporting and encouraging progressive reformers and the journalistic muckrakers, he denounced the excesses of their zealous attacks while realizing the need for their exposés and revelations, as long as these led to constructive reforms. Roosevelt was not the reformer that his following believed him to be, but he was shrewd enough as a politician to realize that he could steal some of the thunder of the reformers and claim some credit for himself. In actuality, he was a middle-of-the-roader who more often than not settled for compromise and failed to push reforms to their logical and necessary ends. Many of his alleged victories over the trusts and monopolies were cosmetic and short-lived, as the monopolists and corporations outlasted the government in the courts or regrouped to learn how to circumvent new regulatory legislation.

The image that people had of Roosevelt was that of an active, robust man who symbolized the virtues of determined individualism. He had strengthened his slight-framed, asthmatic body by a regimen of exercise, and the transformation produced an imposing figure of robust health and unlimited energy. He could ride, shoot, wrestle, box, and play sports with the hardiest. In his self-confident physical health he denounced those who were flabby, pampered, and out-of-shape. Gathering around him a group of tennis-playing cronies who were called the "tennis cabinet," Roosevelt projected an image of the cowboy rough rider who continued the nineteenth-century tradition of rugged individualism and toughness gained by experience.

For Roosevelt, the sporting life of the big-game hunter, the rider, and the hiker and camper was an antidote to the sedentary business of government. More than anything, Roosevelt convinced people that self-determined individualism could survive and flourish in an age where big business, industrialization, and big government dominated their lives and economic realities. He fought battles and won; he went against entrenched interests and managed to have his way. He proved that middle age could be a time of enthusiasm and youthfulness, and his energy became a symbol of direct action and progress. The strenuous life was one worth living. Noise, bluster, and cockiness could be seen as virtues that produce excitement and color.

The period from 1900 to 1920 witnessed the rise of American imperialism and military might as the nation acquired new territories and possessions, expanding its empire beyond the continent. Along with imperialist advances went business and investment interests. Under presidents McKinley and Roosevelt, Elihu Root, as secretary of war, created a new military system that enlarged the regular army, put the

National Guard under federal supervision, created new officer-training colleges, and established a General Staff headed by a chief of staff. Root's reforms and changes upgraded the professionalism of the army and integrated all its functions with central planning and coordination. If America was going to claim her place in the world and protect her far-flung holdings, she must be ready to defend her interests and anticipate the possibility of war. This meant that the physical health and conditioning of young men would assume paramount importance, for military training could only build on the strength, reflexes, stamina, and physical training that were already being developed. Manly sports that involved tests of strength, stamina, coordination, and reflexes were to be valued for their indirect contributions both physically and mentally. Even if a youth did not serve in the armed forces, he could respect and honor those who did because of their superior physical conditioning.

Thus the restraint and propriety of the Victorian period were cast aside in favor of a new activism and manly directness. America had finally discovered its true identity as a nation that works, sweats, plays hard, and leads. The Victorian temper had restrained and curtailed those physical resources by emphasizing manners, culture, politeness, gentlemanly sports, and passive participation. An emerging urban and industrial society needed vigorous, athletic workers whose bodies were toned and strengthened by work and by sports. If properly controlled and directed, sports could provide the needed antidote to hours worked in factories or lives lived in tenements.

Along with scientific management and its emphasis on efficiency and productivity, came precision manufacturing. People had to learn to work in repetitive and efficient ways in order to meet the demands of the newly created assembly line. Electricity and its application to industry meant increasing potential for output. In 1899 electricity ran only 5 percent of the nation's machinery; by 1925, 73 percent of the machines were electrically powered. With the increase in use of electric power, the development of scientific management, and the increasing specialization of work, American manufacturers were producing 76 percent more goods in 1914 than in 1899.

Mass production brought dramatic changes in the lives of workers as they struggled to find their place and role in the new industrial system. Work became more regimented, more segmented from the total process of production, more redundant, and more carefully scrutinized and analyzed. By and large, the middle class benefited from these changes in terms of better wages and lower prices. The new immigrant labor took less desirable jobs where unskilled workers could be exploited. About 72 percent of the immigration from 1900 to 1910 was from southern and eastern Europe, bringing large numbers of Italians, Slavs, Jews, and Russians into the already teeming cities. Early efforts to stop the flood of immigration were at first aimed at the Japanese flooding the Pacific Coast but soon were aimed at southern and eastern Europeans who were seen as "undesirables."

Within the context of this social and economic confusion and rapid industrialization, sports began to assume a wider role than just activity, diversion, and exertion. Young people, especially males, needed outlets for their exuberance and energies. Within the crowded cities few spaces could be found for unorganized activities, and players on a neighborhood baseball team could be easily diverted from the game to get into trouble.

Thus organized sports were more desirable, and public organizations filled this need with the supervision and structure provided by the YMCA, the Boy Scouts, the public playground, union-sponsored sports activities, and athletic play sponsored by religious groups or ethnic organizations. Boys could be taught desired social values through participation in a sport: respect for authority and appreciation for the opportunities it provided, fair play by the rules, a code of manly conduct in open competition, the love of physical conditioning with its implied prohibitions (alcohol, tobacco, sex, gambling), and even a democratic respect for one's equal on the field of play even if he was a newly arrived immigrant. Indeed, access to organized sports and activities was important to ethnic groups seeking acceptance and identification with mainstream society. Many an immigrant's son lost the stigma of a foreign name or accent by demonstrating an equality or superiority of physical talent.

Ethnic teams also provided a focus for neighborhood identification and pride. Street gang toughs could fight it out for control of territory, but teams could just as easily win symbolic victories to prove that the "micks" or "wops" were American youths who could compete and win cleanly and fairly. Sports often provided a testing ground for equality. With the development of public school sports, the tryout for the varsity team and participation as a team member furthered this democratic element of sports. The fairness of coaches in evaluating talent and being unprejudiced about the tryouts were to many people the real test of democracy and local justice. To many an immigrant family their son's making the high-school team or playing in a public league was as important as the teacher telling them that their child had learned to speak and use standard, acceptable English.

In urban environments sports provided valuable outlets for youths who needed their energies channeled in constructive, socially approved ways. Parks, playgrounds, and sports facilities came to be seen as valuable community assets that could prepare youths for citizenship, adulthood, and work. Sports were also associated with improved health and physical robustness, a special concern during a reformist period when improved health standards were championed and promoted. To many, the American Dream meant better health, infant survival, improved diet, freedom from dreaded diseases, and longer life expectancy. The growth of sports in the period from 1900–1920 signaled an improvement in the general public health, especially in combatting childhood diseases or debilitating conditions, such as hookworm in the South. This condition affected almost 60 percent of southern school children before a campaign was undertaken to eradicate it. Sports, then, were the expression of new energies and better health as the nation belatedly realized the key to the future was in the healthy physical condition of its children.

Illustrations of this new sporting emphasis can be noted in the formation of the New York Public School Athletic League in 1903 under the impetus of Luther Halsey Gulick. The league sponsored team competition in track, baseball, basketball, football, soccer, cross-country, swimming, ice and roller skating, and rifle marksmanship. In 1907, 106 baseball teams competed, and the final game attracted 15,000 spectators. Within a few years several cities imitated the structure and activities of the New York Public School Athletic League. Additionally the Playground and Recreation Association of America began in 1913 to promote the Athletic Badge Tests to measure and promote the physical condition of boys and girls.

It should be noted that these programs and activities were only available to a small portion of the population who wanted and needed them. Progress was at first slow largely because of funding problems and because of negative attitudes about the value of organized competition. Many viewed sports as a waste of time, and parents often were afraid that their children's coaches or physical education teachers would have an undue influence in shaping values and attitudes. Other parents worried that sports would make their children excessively competitive and desirous of winning or introduce them to bad habits like smoking, drinking, or gambling—vices associated with professional athletes. However, parents also realized the youths' needs for physical conditioning, peer group companionship, and supervised leisure time. Recognition of these needs, combined with the development of capable and dedicated organizations that provided sports activities, helped make organized sports increasingly respectable and accepted. Parents came to believe that sports could compensate for their diminished control and influence over their children. Coaches, instructors, supervisors, and even game officials took the parents' place by insisting on fair play by the rules, physical and mental discipline, hard work, and acceptance of others' decisions and judgments, however arbitrary or seemingly unfair. Sports were in the process of becoming a social institution as well as a democratizing force.

The European gymnasium tradition with its emphasis on gymnastics and routine calisthenics was rejected in favor of a diversity of sports, more open-air sports, and games of spirited physical competition that produced winners and losers. In this sense sporting activity could be seen as a reaction to the increasing dominance of machinery and routinized labor in American life. With the rapid spread of the automobile (5 million cars by 1917) and the acceptance of automated assembly lines, people wanted to show that they could still run, throw, and use the body in fluid, coordinated ways. Sports were a release for impulses and physical needs that were becoming increasingly regimented and directed in work. Sports were a celebration of physicality, alertness, and spontaneity—all dominant nineteenth-century characteristics that had opened up the continent and tamed the land. In a society increasingly controlled by economic forces beyond the grasp of the individual, sports were an area where the individual could dominate and control factors and conditions, directing them to personal success and victory. Sporting activity provided an edge to life as well as a free area of individual physical expression. Sports were no longer considered trivial or wasteful; they were becoming, in fact, a central part of the American creed.

College Football

By 1900 college football became a national sport as the game was quickly adopted by midwestern schools that now could claim parity and even superiority with such Eastern powers as Yale and Princeton. Midwestern teams such as Michigan, coached by Fielding Yost, and the University of Chicago, coached by Amos Alonzo Stagg, fielded powerful squads that captured national attention. Michigan's 1902 team was dubbed the "Point-a-Minute" team, outscoring its opponents 550 to 0 in eleven games, including the first Rose Bowl game in which Michigan blasted Stanford 49-0. During the period from 1901 to 1919 there were ten different teams that were undefeated, untied, and unscored on (teams that played at least six season games), and only one of these, the 1909 Yale team, was from the East. From 1901 to 1905 Michigan won 57 games, lost 1, and tied 1 while rolling up 2,821 points and yielding only 42 points.

The game was rough and vicious, where players asked and gave no favors or quarter. The players wore no protective padding or helmets, and long hair to protect the head and scalp was the only head protection acceptable. Games were often no more than loosely organized mayhem, with wild, mass tackling (often around the neck), mass formations to protect the ball carrier, wild jumping on opponents, and exhibitions of brawn rather than agility. It was a game of plodding giants with loose officiating and almost constant arguments and quarrels over rules.

The mass momentum plays and the wild mayhem of tackling produced serious injuries and an alarming number of fatalities. In 1905, eighteen collegiate players were killed, and when President Theodore Roosevelt saw a newspaper photo of Swarthmore's tackle Bob Maxwell battered to a bloody wreck by the entire Penn team that had ganged up on him, the president issued an ultimatum that the rough play had to be controlled and minimized or he would outlaw football.

Late in 1905, sixty-two colleges and universities sent representatives to New York, and they formed the Intercollegiate Athletic Association in order to make uniform rule changes. Major rule changes in 1906 were aimed at opening up the game and discouraging the brutal power plays and massive formations around the ball carrier. These changes included: creation of a neutral zone between the offensive and defensive lines; a requirement that the offense have at least six men on the line of scrimmage for the snap; the increase of needed yardage for a first down from 5 to 10 yards; and legalization of the forward pass (with a 20-yard limit). Later changes in 1910 required seven men on the scrimmage line and the outlawing of interlocked interference, the flying tackle, and the pushing and pulling of the ball carrier to advance the ball. In 1912 the rule changes added a fourth down, reduced the length of the field from 110 to 100 yards, and removed the 20-yard limit on the forward pass. The gradual rule changes also increased the point value of the touchdown to six points in 1912 and reduced the value of the field goal to three points in 1909.

The new rules had the desired effect of making the sport less dangerous, although casualties continued to mount until 1909. However, the real impact of rule changes had to do with the changing style of the game. Prior to 1912 the game was a kicking game with the two teams bulling at each other in a slow, methodical way in order to get into a position to kick. The new game emphasized the scoring of touchdowns by crossing the goal line, and a score could be made by a completed pass or run from any point on the field. New skills were required of players, and each player would have to block on his own or run on his own. The line of scrimmage was now the beginning point of the play, and with 10 yards to go teams would need to rely on speed, deception, and movement rather than bullish charges into a brawling, dangerous mass.

The 1913 Army-Notre Dame game signaled the beginning of the new era of mobility and wide-open action that utilized the entire field. Notre Dame had been put on Army's schedule as an easy tuneup, but the then little-known South Bend school proved that its fifteen-member squad could master the eastern giant. The Irish had built a passing attack on the arm of Gus Dorais, and during the contest he alternated his passes between Knute Rockne and Joe Pliska, bewildering the Army team and sending it down to a 35-13 defeat. Dorais completed 13 of 17 passes for 243 yards through the air. He proved that one could throw over the bulky linemen, and his elusive receivers showed that even the lightest of backs could survive when only one man was fast enough to tackle them. The Notre Dame defense proved that even light linemen and backs could tackle larger men, especially when they were schooled and drilled in hard-hitting leg tackles that utilized the shoulder and conditioned body force.

Virtual unknowns quickly became football powers by emphasizing offense via the forward pass. Glenn Pop Warner's 1916 Pittsburgh team rode to the national championship on the pass and deceptive, innovative formations. In 1917 George Tank McLaren of Pittsburgh ran 91 yards from scrimmage and scored 13 touchdowns. In 1913 Washington and Jefferson finished 9-0, led by John E. Spiegel, a halfback who led the nation in scoring 127 points. Clarence E. Bacon of Wesleyan was the pioneer of the forward pass as he led his team to a 16-9-2 record from 1909 to 1912. Guy Chamberlain of Nebraska was a versatile back and end who scored 96 points in 1915. The 1920s would witness such great passing and running quarterbacks as Bo McMillin of Centre College, George Pfann of Cornell, William Spears of Vanderbilt, Frank Carideo of Notre Dame, and Morley Drury of Southern California.

In the period from 1900 to 1920 Harvard claimed four national championships, while Yale and Princeton each captured three. However, football powers were developing at Pittsburgh, Texas A & M, Georgia Tech, and Notre Dame as well as at out-of-the-way places such as Missouri Mines (undefeated, untied, and unscored on in 1914 while scoring 650 points in eight games) and Henry-Kendall in Tulsa (which was undefeated in 1916 and 1919 and 10-1-1 in 1920 while scoring 1,780 points and allowing only 81 points). The wide-open game produced such infamous routs as Georgia Tech's 222-0 win over Cumberland and St. Viator's (of Indiana) rout of 205-0 over Lane College of Chicago. In 1916 Ivan H. Grove of Henry-Kendall scored 196 points and led the nation, even though Leo Schlick of St. Viator had scored 100 points (12 touchdowns and 28 of 29 extra points) in the game against Lane College.

College football was ready to become a truly national sport with the beginning of the Southern Conference in 1915 (with Georgia Tech named national champion in 1917) and the development of such West Coast schools as California (national champion in 1920), under coach Andy Smith and Stanford under Glenn Pop Warner (co-national champions in 1926). Smith left Purdue in 1915, and Warner departed Pittsburgh in 1923 as the Golden West called for coaches that could provide an instant powerhouse.

World War I caused many major colleges to discontinue football during 1917 while others operated programs on a reduced level. Pittsburgh was named national champion in 1918 with a 4-1 final season record. In 1918 almost thirty major colleges eliminated football. The 1918 and 1919 Rose Bowl games featured service teams. In 1918 the Mare Island marines beat the Camp Lewis army team 19-7, and in 1919 Great Lakes navy blanked the Mare Island marines 17-0. Each major service camp had its football team, and the army and navy teams were especially strong. Elmer Oliphant, who played three seasons at Purdue and then four at Army, was a consensus All-American halfback in 1916 and 1917 and scored 45 points in a 1916 game and 125 points in the 1917 season. Coach Charles Daly's 1916 Army team was undefeated, and the Texas A & M teams of 1917 and 1919 were undefeated, untied, and unscored on.

Many college football players served in the war with distinction, and because of their previous physical conditioning they became company leaders and officers. The Selective Service Act of 1917 produced alarming medical statistics that revealed the deplorable physical condition of the youth of the nation. In the training camps football and boxing were used to toughen up draftees and to develop stamina. Soldiers chosen to play on the camp service teams received special privileges and were accorded honor and prestige. The war produced a concern for physical fitness as well as a new generation of male fans. For many men service sports were the first they had ever played, and they came to appreciate the conditioning and exercise the service sports programs offered.

Professional Football

Pro football in the period of 1900 to 1920 was in its infancy, largely confined to the Chicago area and to Pennsylvania and Ohio. The popularity of the game was strictly local or regional as the teams of athletic clubs challenged each other for city or state supremacy.

In 1902 the two Philadelphia baseball teams, the Athletics and the Nationals (Phillies), formed football teams and joined the Pittsburgh Pros in a league. The Athletics, coached by Connie Mack, claimed the pro championship because it had won 2 and lost 1 to the Phillies and was 1-1-1 against the Pittsburgh team. The eccentric and unpredictable Rube Waddell, who had come to the Athletics baseball team in 1902 from the Chicago Cubs, played for Mack's football team, and Christy Mathewson, a three-sport star (including football) at Bucknell, played fullback for the Pittsburgh Pros in one game.

The year 1902 also witnessed a ''World Series'' of professional football as five teams met in Madison Square Garden in December for a tournament. A doubleheader attracted some 3,500 enthusiasts who watched a game being played on a gridiron 35 yards wide and 70 yards long. The New York Athletic Club team was composed of former college stars and had a line that averaged 206 pounds, according to one reporter. Other teams that entered the tournament were the New York Knickerbockers, the Philadelphia Athletics, the Watertown (New York) Red and Blacks, and the Syracuse Athletic Club.

The Syracuse club was loaded with talent that included Glenn S. Warner, Bill Warner, the Pierce brothers of Carlisle, and Phil Draper from Williams College. Syracuse beat the New York Athletic Club squad 6-0 and went on to win its next two games to claim the tournament title.

In 1903 a second ''World Series'' tournament was held, and the Franklin, Pennsylvania, Athletic Club won easily over three other teams because it had loaded up with players from other teams by offering higher salaries. These first two tournaments were well-attended, but public sentiment was turning against football because of the high number of injuries and fatalities and because college coaches openly blasted the pros, implying that the game would make players dishonest and corrupt. Players had no loyalty to a team and were easily lured away by higher pay or other promised benefits. Often paid by the single game, players would be let go if they were injured or if other, more desirable players could be found to fill their positions.

After 1903 the pro football scene shifted to Ohio, and by 1904 at least eight pro teams had been organized. Interest ran high in 1905 and 1906 when the Canton Bulldogs and the Massillon team emerged as powers. Spirited rivalries developed between the Ohio towns, and teams tried desperately to secure the players who would insure success. The Canton team paid Willie Heston, a two-time All-American halfback from Michigan, $600 and expenses for one game, but his career was abruptly ended when he broke his leg on the first play. Heston had scored 72 touchdowns in four years for the ''Point-a-Minute'' team, but he would never score a professional point.

In 1906 arch rivals Canton and Massillon played twice, with Massillon prevailing in both contests. The games were overshadowed by a betting scandal that confirmed the critics' worst fears of the pro game.

Professional football received its greatest boost when Jim Thorpe turned pro in 1913, the year after he had won both the pentathlon and decathlon at the Stockholm Olympic games and had been proclaimed ''the greatest athlete in the world'' by King Gustav V. In 1915 Thorpe agreed to play for $250 a game with the Canton Bulldogs. Thorpe was the first great drawing card in the sport, and the two games between Canton and Massillon in 1915 drew 14,000 fans. During the 1916 season Thorpe led the Canton team to 10 straight wins as the Bulldogs claimed the title of pro champion of the world. Besides playing for the Canton team from 1915 to 1920, Thorpe played six seasons of professional baseball.

Pro football in the period from 1900–1920 suffered from internal problems such as the refusal of teams to organize and abide by uniform rules, the unscrupulous raiding of talent from other teams and even colleges, the turnover of players, betting and gambling scandals, and uneven competition. The increasing hostility of college coaches against the professional game also had its impact, and college football began to regain its popularity and respect after the number of deaths (113 fatalities between 1905 and 1910) declined. The Rose Bowl was revived in 1916, and the Ohio State team won the Western Conference in 1916, 1917, and 1920, turning many people's attention away from the Ohio professional teams. Pro football had a long way to go before it could escape the stigma of blatant commercialism, exploitation, and internal bickering. Only formal organization and some degree of respectability could bring stability and fan acceptance.

A number of black players played for professional football teams in the early period. ''Doc'' Baker played four seasons with the Akron Indians as halfback (1907, 1908, 1909, 1911); Henry McDonald played in the backfield for the Rochester Jeffersons from 1911 to 1917; and Fritz Pollard, who starred at Brown from 1914 to 1916, and was the first black to make Walter Camp's first-team All-American, played for four different professional teams from 1919 to 1926 and was the first black pro coach when he was player-coach at both Akron and Hammond.

College Basketball

Basketball was a growing but largely unheralded and unpublicized sport in this period. Conference play began as early as 1902 in the Eastern League, with the Western Conference beginning play in 1906, the Missouri Valley in 1908, the Southwest in 1915, and the Pacific Coast in 1916. The popularity of the sport was largely local because there was almost no intersectional play, and gyms were small, thus limiting crowd size.

Smaller colleges found that basketball could bring a degree of publicity to their schools and enable them to claim superiority in a major sport. Wabash College in Indiana was 66-3 in the period from 1908 to 1911, while the University of Chicago was 53-4 from 1907 to 1909.

The early game produced such remarkable players as Christian Steinmetz at Wisconsin, John J. Schoomer and Harlan O. Page at Chicago, and Barney Sedran of City College of New York. In 1905 Steinmetz averaged 25.7 points per game in Wisconsin's first varsity season, scoring 50 points in one game. Wisconsin quickly developed as a midwestern power, winning or sharing the Western Conference title from 1912 to 1914 (with undefeated 12-0 seasons) and taking the title outright in 1916 and 1918. John J. Schoomer led the Western Conference in scoring for three seasons from 1907 to 1909 as Chicago shared the title in 1907 and won it outright in 1908-1909. Harlan Page starred on the Chicago teams of 1909 and 1910. Barney Sedran, only 5-4 in height, led the City College of New York in scoring for three seasons and played fifteen years of professional ball after he graduated in 1911.

The period also saw great teams at Kansas (seven conference championships from 1908 to 1920), coached by Forrest C. "Phog" Allen, who led them to six consecutive league titles in the 1920s, as well as the beginning of notable coaching careers for Ward "Piggy" Lambert at Purdue (eleven Big Ten titles in a thirty-year career from 1916 through 1946), Harold G. Olsen (at Ohio State from 1922 through 1946 with five conference titles), and Walter Meanwell at Wisconsin (1911 to 1917, 1921 to 1934), and Missouri (1917 to 1920).

College basketball lacked a national tournament to showcase its talent and determine a real champion until 1938 (the year the National Invitational Tournament began) and 1939 (the year of the first National Collegiate Athletic Association tournament). However, the national Amateur Athletic Union did hold a national tournament that attracted YMCA, club, college, and military teams. The University of Utah at Salt Lake City won the 1916 AAU title; however, there were ten years in the period from 1900 to 1920 when no AAU tournament was held.

Pro Basketball

During the period 1900–1920, a number of professional basketball teams and leagues were organized in the East. The sport was loosely organized, and players often appeared with a number of different teams in various leagues. In 1898 the National Basketball League was formally organized with teams in Philadelphia, New York City, Brooklyn, and southern New Jersey. The New England League was also established, with its players being paid $150 to $225 per month.

Professional teams were often former YMCA clubs, such as the Buffalo Germans who became professionals in 1905, after winning the National AAU title as well as the demonstration basketball tournament held at the 1904 Olympic games in St. Louis. From 1895 to 1925 the Germans won 792 games and lost only 86, taking on all challengers. The New York Trojans won five championships in six years, and in 1908 went on a barnstorming tour and won 38 consecutive games.

Notable early professional players were: Max Friedman, who turned pro in 1909 and played in every pro league through 1927; Barney Sedran, who turned pro in 1911 and played for many teams in a fifteen-year career, including the New York Whirlwinds; and Nat Holman, who played for Germantown, the New York Whirlwinds, and the original Celtics. Holman and Sedran were the two premier little men of the game, making the Whirlwinds probably the best pro team of the early period until the original New York Celtics were reorganized in 1919. The Celtics lured players like Nat Holman and Chris Leonard away from the Whirlwinds and built a team around Dutch Dehnert, a talented pivot man who had never played high school or college ball, Joe Lapchick, one of the greatest big men of the game, and Johnny Beckman, the greatest foul-shooter of his time.

Pro basketball helped to popularize the game and expose more people to the developing skills of ball-handling, team play, and shooting as practiced by paid players. The pro teams introduced barnstorming—playing college, high school, AAU, and YMCA teams in towns all over the East and New England. The 1920s would see the formation of two great black barnstorming teams: the New York Renaissance Five team, organized by Robert L. Douglas, and the Harlem Globetrotters, who first hit the road in 1927 with Abe Saperstein as their manager and promoter.

Baseball

The turn of the century saw the rise of the American League, formerly the Western League, which gained its new name in 1899 and operated with seven teams, with Cleveland the easternmost team and Kansas City the team farthest west. Before the 1901 season the American League, under the direction of Ban Johnson as league president, declared itself a major league. The National League refused to recognize this new status and equality for the junior circuit, and the rival league began a bold plan of franchise relocation in the East and raiding of established players from National League teams. In 1902 the new league drew 300,000 more fans than the established circuit, and it drew away as many as seventy players as it ignored the claims of the reserve clause.

By 1903 the interleague competition and warfare had brought the National League to the grudging realization that it had to accept the fledgling league as an equal and negotiate a peace settlement. The truce involved the settling of contract claims, the mutual honoring of each other's contracts and reserve clauses, and allowing most of the players who had jumped to the new league to remain there. The National League agreement set up a three-member commission to govern organized baseball and decide its best interests. The minor leagues were assured of their integrity and were granted the same necessary protections that major league teams enjoyed.

In addition to the new business arrangements, agreements were reached regarding the conduct of players and the business of the game. Ban Johnson insisted that players and managers show respect for the umpires, that profanity be banned on the diamonds, that liquor be banned from ball parks, and that everyone connected with the game conduct himself as a professional. Up to this point, baseball had been thought of as a rowdy game played by swearing, quarrelsome roughnecks who were associated with alcohol, tobacco, Sabbath-breaking, and gambling. Johnson wanted the game to appeal to the whole family, in order to widen the basis of support. In 1910 President William Howard Taft could say: "The game of baseball is a clean, straight game, and it summons to its presence everybody who enjoys clean, straight athletics." This statement illustrates the increasing status of the game brought about by Johnson's efforts and by the nationalization of the sport.

The development of the World Series, played regularly after the agreement of 1905, added further to the positive status of the sport as the fall classic became the big event of the year in the sports world. The two leagues played parallel seasons, and people could only guess at which league was stronger or which team was dominant. The World Series decided these questions in a dramatic way that tested all the resources, talents, and strategies of the two teams. Now Christy Mathewson could face the best batters of the American League, and great managers could test each other in a series of wits and cunning.

The period of 1900 to 1920 saw great team dynasties and incredible levels of performance by hitters and pitchers. This was a period when the immortals of the game set records that would be difficult, if not impossible, for later players to better.

The Pittsburgh Pirates were the first dominant team of the period, winning three pennants from 1901 to 1903, and another in 1909 when the team won 110 games to break the Chicago Cubs' three-year pennant string (1906 to 1909). The Pirates were led by Honus Wagner, a versatile shortstop who had great range at his position and one of the strongest throwing arms ever seen. With the bat Wagner produced seventeen consecutive seasons in which he batted .300 or better, and he led the league in batting for eight seasons, claiming four straight titles from 1906 to 1909. He collected 3,430 career hits in his twenty-one professional seasons, with almost one-third of his hits for extra bases. He also had 722 stolen bases, copping 61 steals in 1907. Wagner was a mild-mannered player who was steady, dependable, and never involved in controversy. Other great hitters on the Pirates' team included Fred Clarke, the playing manager, who hit .351 in 1903, and Ginger Beaumont, who hit .357 to lead the league in 1902. The pitching staff included "Deacon" Phillippe, who won 67 games from 1901 to 1903, and Jack Chesbro, who was 28-6 in 1902.

The best National League team of the 1900 to 1920 period was undoubtedly the New York Giants, managed by John McGraw. The Giants claimed six pennants, winning in 1904 and 1905, taking three straight from 1911 to 1913, and winning in 1917 (five different teams claiming the pennant from 1914 to 1919).

The Giants had the most talented and durable pitchers of the period. With his famous "fadeaway" or screwball pitch and his incredible control (68 consecutive innings without a walk in 1913), Christy Mathewson was the master hurler who proved that a pitcher could be more than a thrower. Mathewson led the league in earned run average five times, with a 1.14 ERA in 1909, and he was tops in strikeouts five times, leading the league from 1903 to 1905. In 1908, his finest season, Mathewson was 37-11 and gave up only 285 hits in 390 $\frac{2}{3}$ innings pitched with 12 complete games. Matty was the workhorse of the Giants' teams, and his name became equated with control and smart pitching. In the 1905 World Series against the Philadelphia Athletics he pitched three shutouts in one week as the Giants claimed the Series in 5 games. Mathewson was one of the most loved and admired players of his day as he was known for his exemplary conduct, his discipline and moderation, and his modesty.

"Iron Man" Joe McGinnity teamed with Mathewson to give the Giants superior pitching. He pitched for New York from 1902 to 1908, with his great seasons coming in 1903 and 1904. He was 31-20 and 35-8 in those two seasons, appearing in over 400 innings both years. In 1903 he pitched and won doubleheaders on three occasions in the same month. After McGinnity left the Giants, Rube Marquard teamed with Mathewson to produce the three pennants from 1911 to 1913. Marquard won 19 straight games in 1912. However, the Giants teams lost all three World Series, losing in 1911 and 1913 to Connie Mack's Philadelphia Athletics.

The Chicago Cubs were the other outstanding National League team in the 1900 to 1920 period, winning consecutive pennants from 1906 to 1908 and repeating in 1910. The Cubs were ably managed by Frank Chance, the first baseman of the fabled Tinker-Evers-Chance double play combination, and the team relied heavily on Mordecai "Three Finger" Brown, who had six straight years of 20 wins or more (1906 to 1911) and led the league with a 27-9 record in 1909. In 1906 Brown recorded a 1.04 ERA with his 26 wins, and the Cubs won a record 116 games to run away with the pennant by 20 games over the Giants. That remarkable year the Cubs pitching staff had a combined ERA of 1.76 with 28 shutouts, while allowing only 381 runs as the Cubs scored 704.

In the 1906 World Series the Cubs faced the Chicago White Sox in the first crosstown series. The "Hitless Wonders" White Sox, who batted only .230 as a team during the season (almost 100 points below the Cubs), surprised the Cubs in six games as Nick Altrock, Ed Walsh, and Doc White combined to allow the Cubs only 15 runs. "Three Finger'' Brown was charged with two losses and was routed from the mound as the Sox won 8-3 in the last game.

In 1907 the Cubs' pitching staff redeemed itself, and the team swept the Detroit Tigers in four games. The Tigers could only score six runs, three of them in the first game that ended in a 3-3 tie. Ty Cobb, who had led the league with a .350 average and 116 RBI's, managed only a .200 batting average (4 for 20) and did not drive in a run. The Cubs embarrassed Tiger catchers by stealing 18 bases, but Cobb, who had 49 season steals, did not steal a base.

In 1908 the Cubs and Tigers met again in the World Series as both teams won pennants on the last day of the season. The Cubs won over the Giants in a playoff game because Fred Merkle's famous ''boner'' of not touching second base denied the Giants the winning run and resulted in a controversial tie game. In the World Series the Cubs took a commanding three games to one lead, winning handily and blasting Tiger pitching for 16 runs in the first two games. The final two Cub wins were shutouts by ''Three Finger'' Brown and Orval Overall. The Tigers had ten errors, four each in the first and third games. Overall and Brown won two games each, with Brown allowing no runs and Overall two. The fifth game in Detroit was witnessed by only 6,210, a record low turnout, but the defeat was mercifully short for the anemic batting Tigers, lasting only 1 hour 25 minutes.

After the Giants won their three consecutive pennants from 1911 to 1913, no National League team was dominant. Six different teams won pennants between 1914 and 1920. The American League would win five of the seven World Series during that time period.

In the American League the only team to win three consecutive pennants during the 1900 to 1920 period was the Detroit Tigers, who floundered badly in the World Series, coming close only against the Pittsburgh Pirates in the 1909 classic. Struggling back to tie the Series at 3 games, the Tigers were ripped 8-0 in the seventh game, and the Pirates had 18 stolen bases and were assisted by 19 Tiger errors, 5 in the second game, which the Tigers lost 8-6. Honus Wagner had 6 stolen bases, 6 RBI's, and hit .333 to lead Pittsburgh, while Ty Cobb had only 2 steals and hit .231 with 6 RBI's. Babe Adams pitched 3 complete games and recorded 3 wins while allowing only 18 hits and 5 runs.

The Tigers were led by Ty Cobb, a fierce, egotistical competitor who had the skills to back his brash arrogance. Cobb led the American League in hitting for nine consecutive seasons from 1907 through 1915, and then 1917 to 1919. Only Tris Speaker of Cleveland, who hit .386 in 1916, could break Cobb's remarkable string of batting titles.

Cobb also led the league in steals for six seasons, recording 96 in 1915. On the bases Cobb was anarchic, running wild and confusing the other team or surprising the opposing infield as he stole bases with impunity. He used his spikes and barrel-like slides to intimidate fielders and cause them to drop the ball or avoid him.

Cobb was a proud man who wanted the recognition, however grudgingly given, that he was the best in all phases of the game, and he seemed to thrive on being a loner and incurring the hatred of others. Few could deny the accomplishments of the man, but many preferred Tris Speaker as a better outfielder and an equally good hitter. Cobb competed against his teammates as well as the opposition, overshadowing such a fine hitter and fielder as Wahoo Sam Crawford, who batted after Cobb. Few knew or understood what demons drove Cobb to his level of fierce play, and he never revealed the complex dimensions of his personality. He was an old-time style of ballplayer who was a battler and roughhouse competitor, never enjoying the kind of praise and adulation that fans directed toward Christy Mathewson, Walter Johnson, Honus Wagner, and Napoleon (Larry) Lajoie. Cobb was subjected to heckling and jeers, which he answered with hits, steals, and fearless base running. He seemed to draw his energy from opposition, and he instigated much of it as a challenge to the dominant abilities that needed constant testing. Cobb hit over .300 in twenty-three consecutive seasons.

Connie Mack's Philadelphia Athletics were the winningest team of the period, taking six pennants and winning the World Series in 1910 and 1911, and again in 1913. They lost only four games in those three Series.

The 1910, 1911, and 1913 Athletics teams had strong pitching in Jack Coombs, Eddie Plank, and Chief Bender. The famous $100,000 infield of Stuffy McInnis at first, Eddie Collins at second, Frank "Home Run" Baker at third, and Jack Barry at shortstop consistently led the league in fielding average and fewest errors. Baker was a great World Series hitter, pounding out .409, .375, and .450 averages, while Eddie Collins hit .429, .286, and .421 in the 1910, 1911, and 1913 World Series wins.

The Boston Red Sox won pennants in 1903 and 1904 as well as 1912, 1915, and 1916, and the teams won the four World Series they appeared in. The 1912 and 1915 teams featured a talented outfield made up of Tris Speaker, Harry Hooper, and Duffy Lewis. The 1903–1904 Boston teams featured Cy Young, who came to the Red Sox in 1901 and then reeled off four spectacular seasons, leading the league in wins from 1901 to 1903 and giving the new league its first real star and box office attraction.

In 1918 baseball had to demonstrate its patriotism and commitment to the war effort by shortening the season to 125 games and beginning the World Series on September 5. The year before American League President Ban Johnson had offered $500 to the best drilled team, and some teams actually practiced the manual of arms with baseball bats for guns. However, because the war was of such short duration, baseball did not come under as close scrutiny as it would during World War II.

Earlier, in the 1914–15 season, the major leagues had to meet the threat and challenge of the Federal League, which lasted two full seasons with eight franchises each year. Although the rival league suffered heavy losses in 1914, the new teams were able to get such established stars as Joe Tinker, Eddie Plank, "Three Finger" Brown, Claude Hendrix, Chief Bender, and others to jump to Federal League teams. The Indianapolis team, which existed for one season, won the first title behind the .370 average of Benny Kauff, who also led the league in 1915 with a .342 average for the Brooklyn Feds. In 1915 the Chicago team, coached by Joe Tinker, won the second and last title, then challenged the major league's pennant winners. But they were coldly rejected.

In 1915 the league disbanded as owners were bought off by the $600,000 paid in compensation to them by the major leagues, and two of the Federal League owners were allowed to purchase existing major league franchises. The "outlaw" league had managed to attract some eighty established major leaguers, and it had survived two seasons of play. However, the most serious threat was a suit that Federal League owners had pending in court before Judge Kenesaw Mountain Landis regarding nullification of the reserve clause on the grounds that it constituted an illegal monopoly and restrained business. Landis, of course, was soon to become the powerful first Commissioner of organized baseball. The settlement was a gentleman's agreement, and players who had jumped contracts or who had left as free agents were accepted back on major league teams.

During the period from 1900 to 1920 baseball became a national sport that gained growing acceptance and integrity as it consolidated and strengthened its position as a pastime and business. Great talents like Mathewson, Johnson, Wagner, Young, Collins, and Speaker became national heroes as well as men who brought integrity and class to the game. The 1914 Giants and White Sox had taken baseball on a world barnstorming tour and played a game in ancient Egypt near the great pyramids.

In 1919 spitballs and trick pitches were banned, although seventeen pitchers were exempted and could legally continue their doctoring of the ball. The era of the "dead ball" was over, and 1920 would prove to be the most remarkable season on record, even though it was overshadowed by the ugly scandal and incredible betrayal of the game brought on by the Black Sox scandal. The game had become part of the national consciousness, and the season, with its spring training, regular schedule pennant races, fall World Series classic, and winter hot-stove league, became part of the rhythm of American life— a kind of secular liturgical year. The sport was praised by presidents, and Woodrow Wilson even traveled to Philadelphia in 1915 to see a World Series game between Boston and the Athletics. Baseball was ready for the Golden Age of Sport in the 1920s as new heroes like Ruth, Sisler, Hornsby, Heilmann, and others would replace the first immortal greats of the "national game."

Boxing

The period began with James J. Jeffries as heavyweight champion after his eleventh round knockout of Bob Fitzsimmons in June, 1899. Under the tutelage of Tommy Ryan, his manager, Jeffries, who was 6 feet 1½ inches tall and weighed 225 pounds, learned to fight out of a crouch and became an unbeatable champion. After holding the title for almost five years, Jeffries found it hard to find opponents, although Tom Sharkey had given Jeffries his toughest fight just a few months after he became champion. Jeffries defeated the tough, game Sharkey on points in a twenty-five round bout. In 1904 Jeffries agreed to retire and referee the fight that would produce the new champion. When Jeffries retired he went out as a fighting champion, defending his crown against the best contenders and beating Fitzsimmons and Jim Corbett twice in his career.

In the 1905 fight to claim the vacated title, Marvin Hart knocked out Jack Root in the twelfth round. However, Hart's reign was short-lived as he lost the title to Tommy Burns in a twenty-round bout.

The stage was set for the entry of the controversial Jack Johnson, the black boxer from Galveston, Texas, who was known for his knockouts and flamboyant personality. In 1908 at Sydney, Australia, Johnson met Tommy Burns and pounded him unmercifully until policemen entered the ring and stopped the fight in the fourteenth round. Johnson was a skilled boxer who had punishing fists and fast hands, and he had developed techniques of feinting that baffled his opponents.

The biggest moment in Jack Johnson's career, and the beginning of his troubles, was his defeat of Jim Jeffries, who had foolishly decided to return to the ring in 1910 to face Johnson. Jeffries had not fought for six years and had to shed almost 100 pounds to get down to 227 pounds. Johnson, who was in his prime, humiliated Jeffries after he discovered that the former champion was awkward and flatfooted. With his quick hands Johnson began to open up his attack and battered Jeffries at will as he verbally taunted his opponent. In the fifteenth round Johnson floored Jeffries with a left to the jaw. The ''great white hope'' could not dethrone the flashy, bald-headed Johnson, and the humiliating defeat for Jeffries set off white violence against blacks in cities across the nation.

In 1912 Johnson was charged with violation of the Mann Act. Despite highly questionable testimony and the belief by many that Johnson was being framed, he was found guilty of abduction and transportation of a woman across a state line for immoral purposes, drawing a sentence of a year and a day in federal prison. While free on bail and during an appeal of the sentence, Johnson fled to Canada and then went on to Europe. During the next few years he fought in Paris, South America, and Cuba.

In 1915 Jess Willard traveled to Havana, Cuba to meet Johnson, who had become rusty and fat as he enjoyed his international reputation and popularity. Willard, who came from Kansas, was called the ''Pottawatomie Giant,'' and with good reason. He was 6 feet 7 inches tall and weighed 270 pounds. In the twenty-sixth round of the Havana fight Johnson went down under Willard's clubbing blows. Later Johnson would claim that he had thrown the fight but few believed him.

Willard did not prove to be the fighting champion that Jeffries had been. He defended his title once in 1916 and did not fight again until July 4, 1919, when he met Jack Dempsey in Toledo, Ohio. Willard had never met the kind of fury and relentless attack that Dempsey displayed, and the champion was knocked down seven times in the first round. By the end of the third round Willard's cheek bone had been split, his nose smashed, and his body covered with welts that showed the power of Dempsey's unmerciful body attack. Willard's seconds threw in the towel, and the shortest heavyweight title fight up to that date was over.

Dempsey would hold the crown until he was defeated by Gene Tunney in 1926, and during his seven-year reign he became one of the popular sports heroes of the 1920s as he defended his title in million dollar fights against the Frenchman Georges Carpentier, with 90,000 in attendance, and the Argentinian Luis Firpo. Dempsey, the ''Manassa Mauler,'' started his career brawling in western saloons. His promoter, Tex Rickard, owned the Northern Saloon in Goldfield,

Nevada, where he staged championship fights for purses that were displayed in gold coins in the front window of the saloon.

The period saw significant changes in boxing. Prior to 1920 boxing was illegal in many states, and matches were permitted only in private clubs, but in 1920 New York legalized boxing under the control of a state commission. Politicians and legislators saw that boxing could provide revenues for state and city governments.

The age of the lumbering giants who fought flatfooted and relied on weight to pound their foes was over with Dempsey's quick humiliation of Willard. Jack Johnson, Jim Jeffries in his prime, and Dempsey brought movement, strategy, fast hands and combination punches to the sport. Like baseball, boxing was ready for the Golden Age. Both sports had to overcome negative attitudes and poor public images. Baseball would become the national sport, and boxing in the 1920s would become a national mania as Dempsey and Gene Tunney became popular heroes.

Golf

Golf spread rapidly in America from 1900 to 1920. By 1895 seventy-five golf clubs were established in the country and five clubs formed the Amateur Golf Association of the United States, which would become the USGA. The U.S. Open was first played in 1894; the PGA Championship was first contested in 1916.

Early competition was dominated by foreigners, notably Scotsmen and Englishmen who came to America to teach the increasingly popular sport. Soon, however, native talents began to develop. Walter J. Travis, the first master putter of the game, won the U.S. Amateur in 1900, 1901, and 1903, and in 1904 he claimed the British Amateur. Travis had taken up the game at the age of thirty-five, and he made up for his short drives with accurate approach shots and deadly putting. His success encouraged many a middle-aged businessman to take up the game. Jerome Travers claimed U.S. Amateur titles in 1907, 1908, 1912, and 1913, and in 1915 he won the U.S. Open as an amateur. Johnny McDermott, a 130-pound former caddy, was the first American to claim the U.S. Open as he won the 1911 and 1912 titles. McDermott was an egotist who believed that he could beat anyone and would play for any stakes.

In 1913 the two best golfers in the world toured the United States and gave exhibitions before enthusiastic crowds. Harry Vardon and

Ted Ray, both Englishmen, had numerous titles to their credit, Vardon having won four British Opens. Both golfers entered the American Open to be held at the Brookline, Massachusetts, Country Club.

Included in the field for the U.S. Open was Francis Ouimet, a twenty-year-old local amateur golfer who had once caddied on the course across the street from his home. Ouimet did the impossible and unexpected, tying Vardon and Ray by playing the last six holes of the final round in twenty-two strokes. The enthusiastic crowd carried Ouimet away from the eighteenth green on their shoulders, and the next day the partisan gallery cheered lustily as Ouimet finished the last two holes ahead, refusing to crack and besting the English greats by five and six strokes. Eight thousand people witnessed this great upset and victory for native American talent. In 1913 there were 350,000 golfers in the country; by 1923 more than 2 million could be found on the links.

Two other American golfers of note served their apprenticeships during this early period. Another golfer in the 1913 U.S. Open won by Ouimet was Walter Hagen, playing in his first national tournament. In 1914 he would claim that title and again in 1919 in a dramatic play-off over Michael J. Brady. In the 1920s Hagen would win five PGA championships (four consecutive from 1924–1927) and four British Opens. Chick Evans was the first midwestern golfer who gained a national reputation and loyal following. Overcoming his nervousness and often erratic putting, he won both the U.S. Open and National Amateur tournaments in 1916. Evans' 286 score in the 1916 U.S. Open would stand until 1932 when Gene Sarazen tied it.

American golfers quickly learned the mechanics and finesse of the game from their British and Scottish teachers, and the first native-born superstars of golf such as Walter Hagen, Gene Sarazen, John McDermott, and Bobby Jones, Jr., would become national stars, with Hagen and Jones becoming the first American international stars. Amateur golfers like Francis Ouimet, Jerome Travers, Chick Evans, and Bobby Jones, Jr., were celebrated more than the so-called "professionals," who competed not for purses but for percentages of bets placed by gentlemen backers or for side bets made by the golfers themselves. The first important tournament purse was the PGA tournament of 1916. Rodman Wanamaker donated a total prize of $2,580 with $500 going to the winner.

Golf developed in appeal and popularity in a nation that increasingly valued exercise and open-air sports. It was a sport that emphasized etiquette and polite manners, and appealed to businessmen and the upper-class elite who found the game challenging and diverting. It gained further popular acceptance when Presidents Roosevelt and

Taft accepted it. The sport especially appealed to those of English and Scottish background, those people who valued manners, polite and gentlemanly play, and controlled exercise. The middle and lower classes were, by and large, excluded from the prestige country clubs, not that they minded or protested.

Tennis

Tennis was largely confined to the East and New England before the turn of the century, with the U.S. Lawn Tennis Association national championship at the Newport Casino providing the showcase for early tennis stars. The Davis Cup competition begun in 1900 became the symbol of supremacy in international competition, and the United States won the 1900 and 1902 tournaments. Great Britain and Australia dominated Davis Cup play from 1903 until 1913, when the American team won after nine years of failure.

Like golf, tennis in the early years was a private or club sport played at courts in fashionable resorts or the enclaves created by the rich and prominent in the cities. As popular acceptance of the sport grew, more public courts on playgrounds were available to aspiring netters. These new courts had hard surfaces of cement, asphalt, or clay, rather than the grass courts of the lawn tennis popular with the upper class. In 1912 and 1913 Maurice McLoughlin would win men's singles championships, breaking the five-year domination of William A. Larned.

McLoughlin, dubbed the "California Comet," had learned the game on public courts in San Francisco, and he played with a dashing and aggressive style that changed the game. With his power serves, dashes to the net, strategic volleying, and daring shots down the sidelines, McLoughlin played an exciting and colorful game. Up to this time the game had been a cautious backline game of serve and lob with the forecourt almost unknown territory of play. McLoughlin was a great crowd pleaser, a non-Easterner who invaded the East and proved that the game was one that could require strength, court strategy, and dynamic energy.

By contrast, William A. Larned was unspectacular in his play, relying on careful placement and steady service. He rarely scored an ace on his serve, and he played in an unhurried, deliberate way.

McLoughlin led the American Davis Cup team to its 1913 win over Great Britain, the first U.S. win since 1902, and in 1914 the "California Comet'' bested Norman Brookes of Australia in what many have said was one of the greatest sets of Davis cup history. A marathon duel in their first set saw McLoughlin finally win 17-15 and then take the next two sets easily as his power game took over.

William M. Johnston, another Californian, succeeded McLoughlin as the premier player. Like McLoughlin, Johnston had a ready smile and genial disposition that won him loyal supporters. Johnston played a power game but was more deliberate and balanced. In 1915 and 1919 he claimed the men's singles championships, and he was a great doubles player, claiming a number of national championships when he teamed with Clarence Griffin.

McLoughlin and Johnston became the first heroes of tennis as they transformed the game into an energetic and exciting sport and conveyed an enthusiasm that was infectious. A staid, restrained game was in the process of becoming a dynamic sport.

Track and Field and the Olympics

American tracksters developed a reputation for speed and acceleration in the short sprints, for skill in hurdling, for jumping, and for the strength required in the weight events. Local athletic clubs and collegiate sports provided the facilities and the impetus for excellence. The famous Pennsylvania Relays, first held in 1895, grew so dramatically and became so popular that by 1925 it attracted 3,000 athletes from more than five hundred universities, colleges, and secondary schools. A crowd of 70,000 witnessed the finals at Franklin Field in Philadelphia. The Drake Relays soon became the midwestern showcase of track and field talent.

The development of American track and field shows the emphasis on specialization, especially in the sprints. Athletic club sprinters competed against the best collegiate talent, and in 1890 John Owen, Jr., broke the 10 second barrier in the 100-yard dash, pushed to his 9.8 record by Luther Cary, the fastest collegiate sprinter of the time. In 1895 Bernard J. Wefers, a student at Georgetown, equalled Owen's record and ran the 220 in 21.2 seconds to set a world's record that would stand until Charles Paddock would record a 20.8 clocking in 1926. Paddock also set a new record in the 100-yard dash when he blazed to a 9.6 clocking.

The Olympic games provided the ultimate test of American speedsters, and except for 1908, when a South African won, American sprinters won six of the first seven gold medals awarded in the 100-meter dash. American runners also dominated the 200-meter dash and the 400-meter, and they did remarkably well in the 800- and 1,500-meter runs. In the 1904 Olympics James Lightbody won both the 800- and 1,500-meter and repeated as champion in the 1,500-meter race in 1906. Archie Hahn claimed gold medals in both the 100- and 200-meter dashes in the 1904 Olympics, and Paul Pilgrim won the 400-meter dash and the 800-meter run in 1906 for an unusual double win. In 1912 Ralph Craig took both short dashes to join Hahn as one of the finest speedsters of the early Olympic games.

Craig's superb performances in the 1912 Stockholm Olympic Games were overshadowed by the remarkable efforts of Jim Thorpe, the American Indian athlete from the Carlisle Indian School in Pennsylvania. The 1912 Olympics captured the popular interest in America as the papers reported the triumphs of a team that won thirteen of a possible twenty-eight gold medals in track and field. The 400-meter dash medals were swept by the United States, with Charles Reidpath setting a new Olympic record and leading teammates Young and Davenport across the finish line, equipped for the first time with electric timing. In the 800-meter race, James E. Meredith broke the Olympic record by almost a full second, pressed to his new time by teammate M. W. Sheppard, who was one-tenth of a second behind.

But the story of the 1912 games was Thorpe, who won both the pentathlon and decathlon with ease. In the pentathlon Thorpe won all five events with scores that were twice as good as the second place finishers, and in the decathlon Thorpe won four first places and finished high up in the other six events. It was a remarkable performance of endurance, strength, and graceful agility for Thorpe, who abhorred rigid training and conditioning and relied on inexhaustible reserves of natural talent. To King Gustav V's praiseful accolade "You, sir, are the greatest athlete in the world," Thorpe replied "Thanks, King." Thorpe's two gold medals were later taken from him and his records stricken when the AAU discovered he had played semiprofessional baseball.

The first American Olympic teams were dominated by athletes from the Eastern colleges and athletic clubs, particularly the Ivy League (Eastern League) schools, the University of Pennsylvania, and the New York Athletic Club. However, the Midwest and West soon developed competitive athletes. In 1924 C. R. Brookins of the University of Iowa broke Alvin C. Kraenzlein's long-standing record in the low hurdles for the straightaway and curve. In 1925 DeHart Hubbard, a black athlete from Michigan, long jumped almost 26 feet and went more than a foot beyond the previous record. Earlier, H. P. Drew, a black athlete from the University of California, had tied the world's record for the 100-yard dash with a 9.6 clocking.

Almost 75 percent of the 1928 Olympic team was made up of individuals who listed their homes as in the Mississippi Valley and the West. Thus, in the period from 1900 to 1925 track and field became a truly national sport that was no longer dominated by the East. American methods of training were so envied and admired by foreign countries that after the 1912 Olympics many foreign countries hired American coaches to train their teams for the next Olympics. America developed an obsession with breaking records, and its athletes responded with major breakthroughs in performance such as those by DeHart Hubbard in the long jump, Harold Osborn in the high jump, Sabin Carr in the pole vault, and others who consistently set new marks. Americans took track and field seriously, and American members of Olympic teams had to learn to deal with the pressures of winning and dominating the Olympics.

3

The Heroic Age:
The Sports Explosion
of the 1920s

Flashy, flamboyant, fabulous—the age of Fitzgerald, flappers, speak-easies, the "It Girl," gangsters, rum running, Lindy's flight, a time of booming optimism and stunning feats of individual achievement—such is the popular image of the "Roaring Twenties." Recent scholarship has demonstrated that not all participated and shared in the economic prosperity or indulged in zany feats such as swallowing goldfish. Yet undeniably the decade was one of tremendous change, excitement, and accomplishment.

Sporting events and sport heroes provided much of the excitement and glamour of the age. A glittering galaxy of stars such as Babe Ruth, Red Grange, Bobby Jones, Helen Wills, and Jack Dempsey, by their splendid physical exploits and achievements, earned for the decade the title the "Golden Age of Sports." As John Betts has stated in his work *America's Sporting Heritage, 1850–1950* (1974), "more than in any previous era, entertainers, actors, musicians, aviators, and athletes were in the limelight. In a decade dedicated largely to escapism, and general levity, sports gained the publicity which made it one of America's foremost social institutions."

Not only did Americans swarm in huge throngs to arenas to cheer their heroes on, but they also became participants. Preston Slosson, writing on the twenties in his work *The Great Crusade and After* (1930), stated that "next to the sport of business, the Americans enjoyed most the business of sport." In 1928 it was estimated that almost one-fourth of the national income was spent for leisure activities and of that amount, about $200 million purchased sporting goods and equipment.

Golf was an especially popular pastime. By 1924 there were eighty-nine municipal golf courses in the nation for public play. By 1928 the investment in golf totaled over $2 billion, created jobs for 3,000 instructors, a half million caddies, and over 100,000 assorted workers.

Much important business was transacted in a foursome on the links or afterwards while players revived from strenuous play by sipping cool refreshments in the pleasant confines of the nineteenth hole. The country club became a social institution that reflected upper-class society's need for status and separation of the classes by means of recreational and social activities. So popular had golf and the spirit of play become that when President Harding was criticized for spending his leisure time on the golf links, the *Literary Digest* felt compelled to publish an article in its September 17, 1921, issue entitled, "Sports That Helped Our Presidents Make History." The article asserted the following: "When will we learn that we the people lose if the President gives all his time to the office of chief executive? He must get away from the Capitol and the White House and his official self and obtain a perspective of his job and the Nation's needs. He can't do this by sitting in any chair and hovering over any desk. So paradoxically it often happens that a President at play is really and truly a President at work. . . . He plays today that he may be a better executive tomorrow and on each tomorrow's morrow."

Sports attendance figures attested to the popularity of mass spectator sports in the twenties. The following examples aptly illustrate this popularity. On July 2, 1921, 81,000 fight fans jammed "Boyle's Thirty Acres" near Jersey City to witness the Dempsey-Carpentier fight and provided the first million dollar gate in ring history. In 1913 the World Series attracted 150,000 customers and gate receipts of $325,980. In the 1926 World Series between the St. Louis Cardinals and the New York Yankees, total attendance was 328,501, and the gate receipts were over $1.2 million, a record not surpassed until 1936. College football in the fall of 1927 saw 30 million rabid fans push their way through turnstiles, bringing in $50 million. Certainly the term "Golden Decade," as the figures indicate, reflected more than a description of record-breaking athletic feats.

Why did the twenties foster such an upsurge in sporting interest and produce so many great athletes? No single reason will suffice, but many factors contributed to bring about sports' "Golden Age."

First of all, the nation was weary of war and eager to return to normalcy. Yet the nation's optimism in the future was undaunted. The war for democracy had been won, the economy was booming, and there was chicken in every pot—or so it seemed. The *New York Times* in 1919 verified that America was war weary by commenting that "the nation, released from years of gloom and depression, is expressing the reaction by plunging into sport."

Secondly, the army experience of millions of Americans had introduced them to many sports. *Scientific American*, February 8, 1919, published an article entitled "How Uncle Sam Has Created an Army of Athletes." The article described how personal combat like wrestling helped to "develop the fighting instincts." While in the service, four million men and women were trained in such sports as football, baseball, basketball, soccer, boxing, track and field, and winter sports, as thousands of sports-proficient service personnel served as recreation directors and instructors. The army virtually transformed boxing from a "forbidden sport" to one of great popularity and undoubtedly created many future fans for the great Dempsey fights of the twenties. The army also promoted intercamp sports rivalries to keep up morale. In a football game between Camps Grant and Custer held in Chicago in the fall of 1918, the gate receipts totaled $40,000. With the promotion of football on such a large scale, future fans of Army-Navy football games—depending on the branch of their service—were virtually guaranteed.

Third, sports provided an outlet for the exaltation of the human spirit and individual achievement in a nation undergoing monumental changes. No longer was there a frontier to provide challenges and rewards for individual endeavors. America was fast becoming an urban rather than a rural society, its cities teeming with thousands of people crowded together in faceless, amorphous masses. But according to Roderick Nash, in his *The Nervous Generation: American Thought, 1917–1930* (1970), sports provided "living testimony of the power of courage, strength, and honor of the self-reliant individual, who seemed on the verge of becoming irrelevant as the covered wagon." Thus, for many Americans, sports in the twenties represented, as Roderick Nash has stated in his work, the following symbolism: "The American sports fan regarded the playing field as a surrogate frontier: the athletic hero was the twentieth-century equivalent of the pathfinder or pioneer. In athletic competition, as on the frontier, people believed, men confronted tangible obstacles and overcame them with talent and determination. The action in each case was clear and direct; the goals, whether clearing forests or cleaning the bases, easily perceived and immensely satisfying. Victory was the result of superior ability. The sports arena, like the frontier, was pregnant with opportunity for the individual."

Fourth, the technological revolution clearly influenced changing social patterns in the twenties. New machines increased productivity and reduced the work week from sixty to forty-eight hours. The automobile made Americans mobile and recreational opportunities and leisure pastimes more accessible. Under these influences, the work ethic had seemingly given way to the leisure ethic. So disgusted were the editors of the *Nation* with the emphasis on play and its potentially corrupting influences, particularly in regard to college sports, that they printed an editorial in the November 6, 1929, issue: "Destroy the stadiums. Yes, tear them down. . . . To a large extent the American college machine today serves no important educational purpose."

Fifth, sports received support from organized religion. In many cultures, from the times of the Greeks and the first Olympics to the present day, religion and sports have been closely associated. Many clerics, worried by the potential corruption of youth by the enticements offered by urban living, eagerly advocated youth involvement in sports as a good means of instilling Christian virtues as well as developing healthy bodies. In an article entitled "Sports as a Religious Factor," published in the *Literary Digest* in December 1921, the author, F. Townley Lord, found that it was "the religion of health mindedness that is going to save us from the perils of mere denominationalism and the futility of other-worldliness." He also declared that "if every Christian were a sportsman, we should have a healthier atmosphere in all our churches. We should be less parochial in our outlook and less given to that pettiness of mind which has so often hindered the work of God among the young." He concluded by noting the following: "To get our boys and girls out into the open spaces, to guide them along lines of noble comradeship, to fill them with respect for the body in its needs—this is surely to open up another channel along which the Gospel may flow into heart and mind."

Another article, published in the *Literary Digest* in 1924 and entitled "Muscular Christianity," by Rowland Thomas, extolled the athletic feats of ministers and ministerial students. The Scot parson, Eric Liddel, was depicted as one who "literally strives to run the straight race by God's good grace." Hal Cutbill, a ministerial student at Boston University and the 1920 Baxter Mile winner, was described as "the most prominent representative of the muscular school of Christianity in modern times." The *Literary Digest* article quoted Cutbill as having made the following observation with regard to religion and sport: "Athletics and religion are of mutual benefit. Clean athletics keep young men from crooked paths. And running is the cleanest of all sports. A man may cover up a yellow streak in football or baseball but it is bound to show up on a cinder path."

On the question of Sunday sports, some fundamentalist ministers such as the Reverend J. Frank Norris, known as the "Texas Cyclone," opposed sports participation on the Sabbath, declaring that "it is unthinkable and blasphemous that any form of sport should be as important as prayer. It is impossible to believe that Jesus would endorse sports on the holy day of his resurrection." More ministers, however, were of the opinion of Bishop W. T. Manning of New York, who believed that there was "nothing wrong with sport and recreation being indulged in on the Lord's Day" since "they have just as important a place in our lives as our prayers." Similarly, Dr. Albert C. Duffenbeck, editor of the *Christian Register*, declared that "if the Church will tell them to play and build up their bodies, I believe the people will, under proper instructions, come to the sanctuary to pray and build up their souls."

Finally, the expansion of sports publicity and technology greatly popularized sporting events and helped to immortalize sports heroes. Outstanding journalists such as Heywood Broun, Ring Lardner, Westbrook Pegler, and the incomparable Grantland Rice, who in one column managed to etch forever the nation's memory of the 1924 Notre Dame backfield—brilliantly chronicled the exploits of the stars of the playing fields and tactfully ignored their flaws.

The use of sports stars in advertising promotion provided a successful introduction of many new products to the consumers. Sports publicists and promoters utilized advertising techniques to promote similarly the reputations of athletic heroes. As one commentator, Preston Slosson, has stated in his work *The Great Crusade and After (1919–1928)* (1930), "The same arts of publicity which made bathtubs, face creams and vacuum cleaners universal were employed to sell sporting goods and the same press agenting which helped make the reputation of a grand opera star or a politician was also at the service of a pugilist."

The impact of newspapers was greater in the twenties because illiteracy had been reduced and newspaper circulation had increased. In 1899, 15 million copies were sold, but by 1919, 33 million were sold. As newspaper circulation increased, the newspapers expanded their sports coverage and the number of pages devoted to sporting news. For example, in 1890, sports totaled 4 percent of a Muncie, Indiana's newspaper's news content but by 1923, sports accounted for 16 percent of the news content.

So complete was the public's addiction to sporting news, that a *Dallas News* reporter covering the 1920 presidential election made the following observation: "Ohio has two contenders for the presidency of the United States and one contender for the baseball championship of the world. Ask anyone in the State today who's going to win and they'll answer 'Cleveland.' It would never occur to anyone to think that the questioner might be referring to Ohioan Cox or Ohioan Harding and the trifling matter of the country's presidency." Of course, the Cleveland Indians won the American League pennant in

1920 by two games over its Midwestern rival, the Chicago White Sox, and went on to defeat Brooklyn in the World Series, five games to two.

Another example of the growing importance of sports news and coverage was illustrated in 1928 when "the debarrment of the tennis champion William T. Tilden from the amateur ranks drove from the front pages a presidential campaign, the assassination of the Mexican president-elect, the mysterious death of a Belgian millionaire, and the search for lost aviators in the Arctic."

Perhaps the greatest communication development to popularize sports coverage was the radio. In 1930 over 12 million Americans responded affirmatively to a census question: "Do you own a radio set?" Ten years earlier that question need not have been asked.

As early as August 20, 1920, station WWJ of Detroit broadcasted the results of the World Series. In 1921 Pittsburgh's KDKA carried an account of the Johnny Ray-Johnny Dundee fight in April of that year and followed in July with the broadcast of the Jack Dempsey-Georges Carpentier fight. Five years later, on September 23, 1926, NBC carried the Jack Dempsey-George Tunney fight nationwide while WGY of Schenectady broadcasted the bout by short wave to England and South America. In 1925 WMAQ of Chicago was broadcasting home baseball games, and in 1926 the first World Series was broadcast. By the late 1920s most major athletic contests were being carried by radio. As one sport analyst noted: "Sportscasting had no crawling or creeping stages. It jumped down from the obstetrical table, kicked its heels in the air and started out to do a job" (quoted in *Sports in American Life* by Frederick W. Cozens and Florence S. Stumpf (1953).

Thus the popularity of sports in the twenties stemmed from many sources, and in a sense, provided a cultural unity to a diverse and variegated society which lacked many of the factors that contribute to a feeling of national identity. The three mass spectator sports of greatest importance in the twenties were baseball, college football, and boxing. Each sport will be examined individually in some detail to show their increasing popularity, mass appeal, and the changes within the sports that reflected broader cultural and social changes.

Baseball

Baseball developed as the nation's most popular sport because of the talent that developed in the twenties. The public needed heroes and celebrities who could be lionized and idolized, but the fans also wanted excitement. By its nature, baseball is a slow-moving, deliberate game—a lazy spring and summer ritual punctuated more by pauses and delays than by sustained action. But baseball changed dramatically in the twenties as it became more explosive and offensive in nature. Babe Ruth's patented towering home runs jumped off a bat that swung as mightily in a round tripper clout as it did in a glorious strikeout. Ruth hit balls out of parks that before had been seemingly home run proof, and the outfield fences took on a new meaning and symbolism. The fences were obstacles for Ruth and other power hitters to conquer, and the baseballs sent sailing into the bleachers were highly prized trophies. Baseball parks became places of explosive excitement as hitting became dominant. The National League saw only 138 home runs in 1918, but in 1929, 460 home runs were hit. In 1927 Babe Ruth hit 60 home runs, with Gehrig hitting 47, and in all 439 home runs were hit in the American League that year.

But home runs were not the only excitement. The twenties saw the development of great hitters like George Sisler of the St. Louis Browns, who in 1920 had a record 257 hits, with 122 runs batted in, and a .407 average which he upped to .420 in 1922. Rogers Hornsby led the National League in hitting for six consecutive years (1920 to 1925), hitting over .400 in three of those years. His average of .424 in 1924 established a record unsurpassed. In the American League three players hit over .400 in the 1920s: George Sisler in 1920 and 1922, Ty Cobb in 1922, and Harry Heilmann in 1923. In addition, the number of players with more than 100 RBI's jumped dramatically in the period from 1920 to 1929 as sixty-three players had over 100 RBI's in the National League, and seventy-nine in the American League surpassed the same figure. By contrast, only ten players in the National League had 100 or more RBI's in the period from 1910 to 1919 and seventeen in the American League for the same period.

The number of players with 200 or more hits in a season showed the same dramatic increase. In the National League from 1910 to 1919 only two players attained this figure and thirteen in the American League. In the period from 1920–1929 in the National League fifty players had 200 or more hits (twelve players in 1929) and fifty-two players in the American League. Between 1910 and 1919 there had been 32 no-hitters in the major leagues, with 7 pitched in 1917, but from 1919 to 1929 there were only 9 no-hitters pitched, with three years when no no-hitter was tossed.

Team batting averages also reflected the explosive increase in hitting. The 1921 Detroit Tigers averaged .316 as a team (including the pitchers) with Heilmann hitting .389. The Cleveland Indians averaged .308 the same year, and four other teams had team batting averages of over .300 during the twenties. This incredible increase in hitting added excitement and drama to baseball by putting men on base, providing for dramatic rallies, and scoring runs. Even the fans for the sixth place Cardinals, who were 65-89 in won-lost record in 1924, could rejoice in the hitting exploits of Rogers Hornsby's .424 average as he captured his fifth consecutive National League batting title with a league-leading 227 hits, with 82 extra base hits that season.

The hitting talent in the major leagues during the twenties was remarkably spread out, and a team like the Detroit Tigers, which did not even have a .500 won-lost record for the decade, had a remarkable hitter like Harry Heilmann, who won four American League batting titles and hit .403 in 1923.

While all this hitting inflated pitchers' earned run averages, the excitement which dominated baseball in the twenties was also generated by star pitchers. Although rule changes during the decade eliminated much of the doctoring of the ball to the pitcher's advantage, spitball pitchers continued to flourish. Urban Shocker of the St. Louis Browns had four straight 20 game seasons from 1920 to 1923, winning 27 games in 1921. Stanley Covelski, a spitballer pitching for Cleveland, had four straight seasons from 1918 to 1921 when he won 22 or more games. But the favorites of the fans were the fast-ball pitchers like Grover Cleveland Alexander, who won 15 or more games in seven years during the twenties and three times won 29 or more games; Walter Johnson, who won 23 games in 1924 and 20 in 1925; Carl Mays, who had three seasons of 20 games or better in the twenties; and later Lefty Grove, who after winning 20 games in 1927, had seven straight seasons of winning 20 games or more.

The fans wanted to see power pitching against power hitting, such as the famed Yankees' "Murderers' Row" of 1927 or the remarkable hitting team of the Detroit Tigers in the late twenties. Baseball provided the stuff of drama—exciting confrontations of talent, baseball savvy, power, and personalities. This conflict has always provided the universal, day-to-day appeal of baseball, and in the twenties pitchers had to learn to rely more on speed, variety of pitches, and knowledge of batters to curb the aggressive and explosive hitting of the period. The game became more sophisticated and skillful, and this was not lost on fans. The towering Ruth home runs which shot on a line up and out of the park were dramatic, but the game's excitement took diverse forms.

Take for example Walter Johnson's appearance in relief in the seventh game of the 1924 World Series. After failing in two previous games in the Series he pitched six shut-out innings to provide the Senators with the Series' win over the Giants, probably the most dramatic moment of baseball in the decade. Johnson was one of the most loved and respected pitchers of the period, and after seventeen seasons toiling with the Washington Senators (including eleven seasons when he won 20 or more games), Johnson experienced the joy of a World Series victory over a Giants team which had appeared in four straight Series and won world championships in 1921 and 1922.

The World Series in the 1920s provided the apex of baseball excitement. Two teams created dynasties for themselves in this period. The New York Giants won four straight National League pennants from 1921 to 1924 and experienced World Series victories over the Yankees in 1921 and 1922, losing to the Yanks in the Series in 1923 and to the Senators in 1925. The Yankees won three straight league championships twice in the decade, 1921 to 1923 and 1926 to 1928. They swept the World Series in 1927 and 1928.

Baseball became associated with New York City and with the Polo Grounds, as both the 1921 and 1922 Series were played there. Yankee Stadium, ''the house that Ruth built''—and filled—opened in 1923 at a cost of $2 million. Other National League cities shared the pennant after 1925 with the Pittsburgh Pirates winning in 1925 and 1927, the St. Louis Cardinals in 1926 and 1928, and the Chicago Cubs in 1929. The Pirates won the World Series in 1925, and the St. Louis Cardinals won it in 1926, so the teams in the hinterland proved that the Gothamites could be challenged. In 1924, 1925, and 1926 the World Series went seven games each time, with the seventh games being decided by scores of 4-3, 9-7, and 3-2. Each time the World Series was played it received more and more press coverage and radio coverage, especially since the Series was played in New York City seven out of the ten years of the period from 1920 to 1929.

Other reasons for baseball's popularity in the twenties were its dynamic qualities and its equally dynamic personalities on and off the field. Babe Ruth was known to be intemperate and lusty, although his positive popular image was carefully guarded by the press, but on the field he had the skills and power to overshadow his private excesses and indiscretions. He personified what people wanted for themselves in their own lives. They wanted public success, but they also wanted freedom to pursue their own private desires and pleasures. If they could do the job, then what did it matter how they conducted their private lives? Ruth also had that boastful pride and insouciance that the public admired. He was casual but confident, accessible yet aloof (a king or sultan), excessive in his pleasure yet hard working, earning his increasingly high salaries honestly.

Ruth also struggled with physical problems and injuries, overcoming them and even overcoming his own self-indulgence, which sometimes brought him fines and suspensions. Ruth even fought a battle with Commissioner Landis, asserting the freedom of the baseball player and banking on his star status and fan appeal to carry him through the confrontation with baseball's new czar. He also battled with his manager, Miller Huggins, yet Ruth's love of the game always brought him back to the role of the disciplined athlete. He dared pitchers to try to strike him out, and to Ruth a walk (he was walked 2,056 times in his career) was a triumph over an adversary pitcher. He was power personified, an orphanage youth who belonged with royalty and the rich, but Ruth never forgot his common origins or his popular appeal. He was the man who forged his own success on raw talent and remarkable reflexes. He made headlines and created stories, and he represented the spirit of a culture that sought excitement, hoopla, and even sensationalism. Even more, Ruth represented the struggle for individual freedom as he fought those who controlled his career or fought his own limitations in order to gain success.

Other baseball players also provided colorful images and reputations. Rogers Hornsby (called Rajah) fought the same battles against authority, first against Sam Bredon over Hornsby's salary as the Cardinals' manager and later with Judge Landis over divestiture of Hornsby's stock in the Cardinals team after Hornsby was traded to the Giants. Hornsby was also a cocky and self-confident individual who used profane language and was blunt in his comments. He answered his critics with his bat. Ruth and Hornsby both had a rawness to them that to their fans signified honesty, directness, and energy. They both deeply loved the game, swallowing their pride when necessary to remain part of the sport. They were men who played a boy's game, but in the twenties they made baseball a truly professional sport and big business.

Baseball became an increasingly urbanized sport with the minor leagues providing the connection to the rural parts of America. In New York City there were three professional teams, and together they attracted almost 26 million people in attendance at baseball games in the period from 1920 to 1929. The Yankees drew over a million in attendance eight out of ten years in that period, falling below that mark only in 1925 and 1929 (years they finished second). The Dodgers averaged 664,861 attendance a year during the twenties, and the Giants' average attendance was 863,550.

The only other city that could begin to match New York City's influence on baseball was Chicago (with two clubs), where about 14.5 million people attended baseball games from 1920 to 1929, with the Cubs drawing over a million three years in a row from 1927 to 1929. The Pittsburgh Pirates, who figured in two World Series (1925 and 1927), drew almost 6.5 million fans from 1920 to 1929, while the Detroit Tigers (who finished second only once in the decade) drew over 7.5 million in attendance. Baseball, then, became big business, but it also provided a "green space" in urban areas which connected city people with the forsaken rural origins.

Baseball stars were newsworthy celebrities to adults, and children looked on them as scions of character and virtue. Many of the players were rural country boys who had come to the big city to play, and many were sorely tested by the temptations and corruptions of big city life (alcohol, sex, gambling, and other forms of dissolution), which threatened character and endangered careers that depended upon physical conditioning. Thus, baseball players were a source of moral drama. People could vicariously enjoy their sports heroes' success, for in many ways the careers of the baseball players were the collective lives of society in the twenties written large. Fans sided with the ballplayers in their struggles against ownership, the management, the commissioner. The ballplayers' struggle for success and stability within the system symbolized the increasing complexity of modern life. Baseball players were local and national heroes, reflecting urban and even regional pride.

During the decade baseball became increasingly more professional as great hitters and great teams became a central focus of the game. Statistics grew in significance as the ball parks became places of excitement and drama. Baseball games provided both competition and contemplation. As baseball was a game in transition to a big business sport with high salaried stars, so was American society with its orientation to production, consumption, and business corporations with concentrations of talent and capital. Afternoons of baseball provided a break in the workaday world. People of all social and economic levels sought out the confines of a stadium to enjoy one of the most democratic sports in a society becoming increasingly stratified.

The Negro Leagues in the 1920s

Black baseball became successfully organized in 1920 when the National Negro Baseball League was formed under the guidance and control of Andrew "Rube" Foster, manager of the Chicago American Giants. Foster envisioned one national association with a Midwest and East division, and he strove to establish some degree of solvency and continuity to the NNBL. However, the league was faced with massive problems: the scheduling of games, the arrangements for home ball parks, the raiding of the better players by eastern teams, and equitable season schedules.

The black teams leased stadiums from major or minor league clubs or they were "road" clubs that had homes in a number of different cities. Franchises shifted or folded constantly, and the Chicago American Giants were the only team that was a continuous member of the league from 1920 to 1933. The Giants won the first three pennants in the league, but between 1923 and 1926 the Kansas City Monarchs were dominant. Because of scheduling problems, teams never played the same number of games, and one team might play only half as many games as another team. The league survived as a low-budget operation carefully directed by Rube Foster, who ruled with an iron will and strong self-interest to protect his 5 percent profits from all gate receipts.

In 1923 a rival league, controlled by Nat C. Strong, who was guaranteed 10 percent of all gate receipts, was formed with six teams. A war between the Eastern Colored League and the National Negro Baseball League soon developed, as players from the midwestern clubs defected to eastern teams because of the better money offered them. One NNBL team, the Indianapolis ABC's, lost ten players in 1924, causing them to withdraw from the league that year after the season had started and to be replaced by the Memphis Red Sox. The Indianapolis team came back in 1925 but had a miserable 17–57 record for the year.

The Eastern Colored League soon negotiated to play a World Series against the established league, and in 1924 the Kansas City Monarchs and the Hilldale team squared off, with Kansas City winning the Series 5 games to 4. Games were played in four different cities: at Shibe Park in Philadelphia, in Baltimore, in Kansas City, and in Chicago (the last three games). Between 1924 and 1928 (the year the Eastern Colored League folded during the season) the two rival black leagues played four World Series, with the National (western) league taking three of them, two by the Chicago American Giants in 1926 and 1927.

Negro league baseball in the twenties was undoubtedly stimulated by the general prosperity of the times, which gave blacks in the service industries more income and a desire for more social visibility in the black community. Black baseball met social needs within the black community as well as provided a focus for pride in black achievements both in business and physical ability. In cities like Chicago, Kansas City, Baltimore, and St. Louis blacks had developed their own society and culture around jazz music, black nightclubs, black business enterprises, and even ball parks that could be taken over, if only while the white team was away.

During a period of ugly racism, race riots, and the frightening rebirth of the Ku Klux Klan, blacks managed to build a viable and meaningful culture within their segregated communities. Black baseball teams provided entertainment and diversion, and baseball games allowed large numbers of blacks to gather together without any suspicion of rioting or rebellion. Black baseball players became local heroes, and their on- and off-the-field exploits became legends as well as exciting sources of gossip. The players were dandies, dressing in the latest fashions and becoming the trend setters. They were men who traveled and found immediate acceptance by blacks who wanted to see members of their race doing what white major leaguers were doing.

The black ballplayers' skills and records could be compared with those of the major leaguers, and even the names of the teams (Monarchs, Giants, Stars, Barons) suggested black pride and the high status of the players within the culture and society. Baseball was in its golden era, and the Negro leagues benefited from its widespread popularity and enthusiasm.

Black baseball in the twenties required the leadership of strong men who could resolve continual money problems, deal with unexpected contingencies, discipline players, and work out arrangements with white management. Rube Foster and Nat C. Strong provided this needed leadership for a period of time, but with Foster's illness in 1927 the Negro National League began to decline. Without central control and authority, problems related to player discipline and fan rowdyism became rampant. Cooperation between clubowners decreased, and the degree of professionalism among the players lessened, causing fans to stay away from ball parks. The Eastern Colored League folded in 1928, and no black World Series were held until 1942.

The thirties would see the emergence of barnstorming baseball, the Negro American League (which lasted from 1933 to 1948), and the practice of many black American players going south of the border to play in Cuba, Mexico, the Dominican Republic, and other Latin American countries. Thus, the situation in black baseball was constantly changing as blacks sought to display their skills and considerable talents wherever they found appreciation and acceptance. Players like Cannonball Dick Redding, Wilbur Bullet Rogan, Smoky Joe Williams, Nip Winters, Newt Allen, John Henry Lloyd, Cool Papa Bell, Martin Dihigo, and, of course, Josh Gibson had remarkable careers and starred during the decade. Satchel Paige was just beginning what would be a phenomenal career.

The black leagues in the 1920s provided an outlet and showcase for talents that few white fans would see. The major leagues grudgingly allowed the Negro leagues their existence as long as they paid their stadium rents and did not offer direct competition. When pitted against white teams in exhibition or barnstorming games, the black clubs more than held their own, and black fans often viewed these as "unofficial" World Series. Black players were known for their colorful chatter and banter, their penchant for the unusual and unexpected, their individual trademarks, and their sense of the style of play that was popular and crowd pleasing. Organized professional baseball, which has always been conservative, missed a great deal of talent and entertainment that black players would have provided. But the black fans loved and cherished their heroes' exploits and personalities in ways that more than compensated the athletes for their toils and lack of wider recognition.

College Football

If baseball reminded people of the past, then certainly college football was the contemporary game during the twenties. A violent clash of teams playing under tension and time limitations, football reflected the conflicts of the new urban society as well as the exhuberant spirit of the times with its hoopla and boosterism.

From about 100 players in 1889, the number of players involved grew to over 200,000 by 1926. During the earlier period, Walter Camp could select his All-American list from players at Yale, Harvard, and Princeton, but during the twenties the center of football power had shifted to the Midwest and West. California built a stadium which held 80,000 spectators, while Ohio State, Illinois, and Michigan erected stands accommodating at least 70,000. On Saturdays the stadiums teemed with boisterous spectators, many who had never been to college but who were caught up with the pageantry, color, and spectacle of the bands, the crowds, and the exploits conducted on the field.

College football in the twenties also reflected the democratic spirit, both in terms of teams and individuals. For example, as Robert Leckie notes in his *The Story of Football* (1965): "Again and again the teams from the little Indiana school came from behind to beat bigger and wealthier teams. For Notre Dame was then a 'poor boy's school,' where almost all of the student body worked to pay their way. With its never-say-die spirit, its dramatic and daring football, its habit of consistently drubbing bigger schools, Notre Dame was naturally a college for the American public to take to its heart.'' Also, college football proved that the small could still smite the mighty. Tiny Centre College of Kentucky—nicknamed the ''Praying Colonels''—beat mighty Harvard 6-0 on October 29, 1921, under the leadership of their outstanding quarterback ''Bo'' McMillin, who raced 23 yards on a reverse. Harvard had not suffered a defeat in football since 1916 and had gone unbeaten in seven of its previous seasons.

The most outstanding football player of the decade was undoubtedly Red Grange, halfback for the University of Illinois from 1923 to 1925. In his total career Grange played in 237 games, carried the ball 4,013 times for an average of slightly over 8 yards per carry, and produced 531 touchdowns. Son of the police chief of Wheaton, Illinois, and without a mother since he was five, Grange earned such titles as the ''Wheaton Iceman'' and the ''Galloping Ghost'' for his backfield heroics.

His greatest day on the gridiron came at home in 1924 against Michigan, the Big Ten conference favorite. Grange took the opening kickoff and raced 95 yards for a touchdown. The next three times he was given the ball, he streaked for touchdowns of 67, 56, and 44 yards. Removed by his coach, Bob Zuppke, after the first 12 minutes, he went back into the game in the third quarter. Grange responded with a 12-yard touchdown run and passed for another. The final score was 39-14 in favor of Illinois. Grange had rambled for 402 yards and had 5 touchdowns.

Grange somewhat tarnished his reputation by signing a professional contract with George Halas and the Chicago Bears twenty-four hours after his last collegiate game. Unfortunately, Grange never received his ''sheepskin'' from Illinois.

For millions, however, football during the twenties meant following the exploits of the ''Fighting Irish'' of Notre Dame. From 1920 to 1930, Notre Dame sported a fantastic record of 96 wins, 12 losses, and 3 ties. The architect of this football dynasty was Knute Rockne, a football player himself at Notre Dame from 1911 to 1913, who had helped popularize the use of the forward pass.

Notre Dame teams caught the public's attention because they represented a national team. Its players came from all areas of the country and were of many ethnic origins, thus giving millions of ''subway alumni'' a chance to identify with a college team. Of course, Notre Dame's ''razzle dazzle'' tactics and the emotional and colorful personality of Rockne, whose impassioned half-time exhortations such as his "win one for the Gipper" speech became legendary, provided much of the "mass appeal."

Perhaps no better example of the impact of the written word upon sport and college football could be given than the immortalizing of the Notre Dame backfield of 1922, 1923, and 1924 by the outstanding sports journalist of the twenties, Grantland Rice, when he labeled them the Four Horsemen. These players established outstanding records, climaxing their careers with an unbeaten record their senior year and a 27-10 win over Stanford in the 1925 Rose Bowl. Other teams perhaps have been more powerful—as it was, the backfield averaged only about 163 pounds—and it was probably not even the best Notre Dame team ever, but it became the best known. Grantland Rice, after witnessing Notre Dame's 13-7 victory over Army in 1924, stamped immortality upon them with these words in the October 19, 1924, *New York Herald Tribune* (quoted from Dave Camera, ed., *The Best of Grantland Rice*, 1963): "Outlined against a blue-grey October sky, the Four Horsemen rode again. In dramatic lore they are known as Famine, Pestilence, Destruction and Death. These are only aliases. Their real names are Stuhldreher, Miller, Crowley, and Layden. They formed the crest of the South Bend Cyclone before which another fighting Army football team was swept over the precipice at the Polo Grounds yesterday afternoon as 55,000 spectators peered down on the bewildering panorama spread on the green plain below."

A publicist from South Bend quickly published photographs of the now legendary backfield attired in football gear and mounted on horses. The public loved it, and as time passed their exploits and deeds became even more heroic. Notre Dame teams symbolized the collective team effort, and even their being a "Catholic power" was overlooked by a nation looking for invincible and memorable sports heroes.

The new emphasis on college football may have pleased alumni and fans, but many academics rebelled against the presence of poorly qualified student athletes and against the funds allocated to athletic facilities when many academic departments were sorely underfunded. According to one story prevalent in the twenties, the following incident was all too common on college campuses. The college dean, seeking to establish the eligibility of an All-American tackle asked him what was the sum of eight and six. The All-American pondered awhile and then replied, "thirteen." Instantly the head coach commented, "Aw Dean, give him another chance. He only missed by two."

Heywood Broun, one of the outstanding sports writers of the day, in a column in *Forum* in 1928 thought all the "petty bickering and suspicious pointing" could be ended by making football "frankly professional." He concluded by stating: "Think of the sentiment which might grow up around some veteran who held the post of full back at Yale for twenty years and when the inevitable diminution of his powers set in, he could be full back emeritus."

College football in the twenties had indeed become big-time, and with it came the problems of maintaining both academic and athletic excellence. These considerations still plague universities today.

The Not So Golden Era of Pro Football

In the 1920s professional football struggled to find a formula for success, fan acceptance, and organizational stability. Prior to 1920 professional football, which had been restricted to Pennsylvania and Ohio, had suffered from cutthroat bidding for players and betting scandals, and had resisted organizational efforts that would have imposed uniform rules and consistency. Only the name of Jim Thorpe, the hero of the 1912 Olympics, gave any real interest to the game. Competition was uneven, and players shifted from team to team as money was waved in front of them to lure them away to another club needing them for the big game. Football players were thought of as roughnecks and toughs, little better than barroom brawlers.

In September 1920 the American Professional Football Association was formed in Canton, Ohio, with twelve charter teams from five states (with five teams from Ohio and five from Illinois). Teams were required to pay a membership fee of $100, but no team ever paid the entry fee. In its first year of operation the league schedule was chaotic. Two of the charter franchises did not field teams, and four other teams joined the league later. Teams played both league members and non-members, and because no standings were kept, three teams claimed the season championship. Even with some hastily arranged playoffs between the three claimants the issue of a champion was never finally settled.

In 1921 the league was reorganized and Joseph F. Carr, founder and first owner of the Columbus Panhandlers team, was named league president. Carr served as president from 1921 to 1939 and played a key role in the slow developing success of pro football and its internal organization. In 1921 Carr faced his first test when he had to rule that the Chicago Staleys (with a 10-1-1 record) were the league's champion, although the Buffalo All-Americans (9-1-2) claimed the Chicago team included nonleague games in its final record. At the beginning of the 1921 season the league had eighteen teams operating, but five teams dropped out. Carr ordered these teams' records stricken from the final league standings.

In 1922 the league changed its name to the National Football League. The Canton Bulldogs were undisputably the league champions with a 10-0-2 record. The Marion, Ohio, Oorang Indians team, which finished 2-6, was sponsored by dog kennels and featured Jim Thorpe, Joe Guyon, and other American Indian players. The team folded the next year after a miserable 1-10 record, and Thorpe moved to the fourth of seven teams that he played for in the 1920s. He never played on a championship team, but he was a drawing card wherever he played.

In 1923 the Canton Bulldogs were again undefeated and claimed the league championship. The Chicago Bears, directed by player-coach George Halas, finished second, as "Papa Bear" began a remarkable reign of forty years of coaching.

In 1924 the Canton franchise was shifted to Cleveland so as to play before larger crowds, and the Bulldogs repeated as league champions for the third consecutive year. The team had two of the most talented tackles of the era: Wilbur (Pete) Henry and William Roy (Link) Lyman. Henry was a six-footer who weighed 250 pounds, while Lyman was 6 feet 2 inches and weighed 252. A sixty-minute performer, Henry punted (setting a record with a 94-yard boot) and kicked field goals (dropkicking one for 50 yards). Agile and elusive, Lyman introduced a shifting, sliding style of defensive tackle play. The player-coach of the Bulldogs was Guy Chamberlain, the most talented end in the NFL during the twenties.

The turning point for pro football was in 1925 when Red Grange was signed to play for the Chicago Bears. On Saturday, November 21, Grange had helped Illinois defeat Ohio State before 90,000 fans. The next day he was on the Bears' bench, watching his new team defeat Green Bay. On Thanksgiving Day 38,000 people crammed Wrigley Field to watch Grange in action against the Chicago Cardinals. Grange's punt-returning prowess was stalemated by Paddy Driscoll, who punted the ball away from Grange twenty-three times, and by the Cardinals' defensive line. Grange and his agent, C. C. (Cash and Carry) Pyle, took $9,300 of the $14,000 in gate receipts under the terms of a shrewd short-term contract negotiated by Pyle with George Halas.

After a game three days later that drew 28,000, the Bears played eight games in the next twelve days (seven of the games on the road), and with Grange as the star attraction drew in record crowds, including 65,000 against the New York Giants. Grange scored seven touchdowns and kicked two field goals in the first five road games but was hurt in Pittsburgh and did not play in Detroit. After Grange returned to action, the Bears began a tour to the South and Far West, playing in seven different cities against makeshift and quickly forgettable teams. The whole nation, it seemed, wanted to see the legendary "Galloping Ghost" rip off one of his patented open field runs where he eluded tacklers and sprinted for the goal line.

The tour was a tremendous financial success to the Bears and to Grange, even though the Bears finished 9-5-3 in the league in seventh place as their crosstown rivals the Chicago Cardinals were clearly the better team. The 1920s was an era of hoopla, publicity hypes, and star mania. Grange cashed in on his college fame and newspaper-created legend, bringing the big crowds to the professional game.

The 1925 season was marked with dispute as the Pottsville Maroons thought they had won the championship in their first year in the league. However, Pottsville made the mistake of playing the "Notre Dame All-Stars," featuring the Four Horsemen, at Shibe Park in Philadelphia, the home field of the Frankford Yellowjackets. The Frankford owners protested to the league office and to league president Joe Carr, claiming that its territory had been impinged upon, and demanded retribution.

Carr took the league title away from Pottsville and had the Chicago Cardinals add two games to its schedule, one against Hammond (which was 1-2) and one against Milwaukee (which was 0-5). The Cardinals won both games easily, playing the two games in a four-day period. The Milwaukee team used several high school players in the game and as a result was fined $500 and had its franchise pulled (although a Milwaukee team competed in the 1926 season). The Pottsville supporters were outraged but could only drown their sorrows and drunkenly claim that their coal town team was the "true" champion based on their convincing 21-7 win over the Chicago Cardinals during the season that Carr had so arbitrarily extended. Carr had now ruled twice in favor of Chicago teams to give them championships.

In 1926 C. C. Pyle tried to negotiate with the Bears to give Grange a five-figure salary and one-third ownership of the team. This time Halas drew the line and refused. Pyle tried to obtain a NFL franchise in New York but was refused. He then formed a rival league, the American Football League, which had nine teams. Grange had a rather unspectacular year for the New York Yankees team owned by Pyle, and the league folded after only one season. The new league's champion, the Philadelphia Quakers, played a postseason game against the seventh place team from the NFL and lost 31-0, so any notion of parity between the leagues was quickly dispelled.

The NFL had twenty-two teams compete during the 1926 season, with the Frankford Yellowjackets edging out the Chicago Bears for the title. New teams had been established in Kansas City and Los Angeles, but the most unusual team was the Duluth, Minnesota, Eskimos. This thirteen-player team, led by Ernie Nevers, played twenty-eight league and exhibition games, twenty-six of them on the road. After the regular season and an eighth place league finish, the Eskimos took to the road and played sixteen games during a four-month period. Nevers played in all but 7 out of 1,740 minutes. An All-American at Stanford and hero of the 1925 Rose Bowl, Nevers was a threat as a runner and passer who led the "Iron Men of the North" on their marathon schedule.

Nevers commanded the kind of money that Red Grange had demanded and received. In December 1925 he signed for $25,000 and 10 percent of the gate receipts for two all-star games against the New York Giants in Florida. He was paid $20,000 for the 1926 season.

A turning point for professional football came in 1927. After two years of relative prosperity, circumstances conspired to bring about a decline of popularity and interest. The rival American Football League folded, although one team survived when Grange's New York Yankees team joined the NFL. The NFL shrank to twelve teams from the twenty-two that operated in 1926.

Red Grange suffered a severe knee injury playing against the Bears, and even though he returned to action he was only a ghost of his former greatness, now only running instead of galloping. In 1928 he was out of football as he pursued a brief career in vaudeville and the movies. When the Duluth Eskimos franchise folded in 1927, Ernie Nevers quit football and played professional baseball for the St. Louis Browns, and coached at Stanford.

Both Nevers and Grange returned to football in 1929, Nevers playing for the Chicago Cardinals and Grange playing for the Chicago Bears. In November 1929 Nevers scored 40 points against the Bears to establish a single-game scoring record. Grange played six seasons with the Bears and became a skilled defensive back as well as a fine blocker, passer, and straight-ahead runner. In 1932 and 1933 Grange's persistence was rewarded as he played on championship teams, and he was an All-Pro selection in 1931. Nevers' career ended in 1931, and in his five years as a pro he never played on a championship team, although he was an all-league selection in each of the seasons.

The end of the decade saw the rise of the Green Bay Packer dynasty, just as the era began with the Canton-Cleveland Bulldogs dynasty. The Packers signed such talented players as Johnny (Blood) McNally, Cal Hubbard, Mike Michalske, and Arnie Herber to build a team that would claim three consecutive championships from 1929 to 1931. The era of the big-name player was over, as was the period of barnstorming and twenty-eight-game seasons. Pro football only briefly captured the imagination of a sports-hungry public. It pulled players like Grange, Nevers, Joe Guyon, and George Trafton away from campuses before they could finish college degrees. In 1926 George Halas helped push through a league rule that prohibited a team from signing a player whose college class had not graduated. The rapid expansion in 1925 and 1926 created uneven competition and weak franchises. But the twenties game did produce players who would later become coaches: Walt Kiesling, Johnny (Blood) McNally, and most importantly, Steve Owen and George Halas.

The Ring

Perhaps no hero gained more print during the twenties and more clearly reflected the tensions of that decade than did Jack Dempsey. In eight years of fighting, from 1919 to 1926, he garnered over $10 million for his efforts. Expertly managed by Tex Rickard, a master of public relations, Dempsey drew national attention to himself on July 2, 1919, when he literally pulverized the gigantic but aging champion, Jess Willard, whose corner threw in the towel at the end of the third round.

In his article "Jack Dempsey: An American Hero in the 1920's, in the *Journal of Popular Culture* (Fall, 1974), Randy Roberts comments that "a popular hero, helps to perpetuate certain collective values and to nourish and maintain certain socially necessary sentiments. Thus the popular hero serves a dual function: he both reflects the psychology of a society at a given time and acts to reinforce necessary social values." Roberts contends that the press perceived in Dempsey's victory over Willard a reverification of old American virtues and saw him as a "stable force" in times of race riots and the big Red Scare. Furthermore, Roberts argues that Dempsey's subsequent fights continued to mirror the tensions that plagued American society in the twenties. For example, Dempsey's victory over Georges Carpentier in 1921, which was the first title bout to be broadcast by radio, reflected lingering war tensions. Carpentier was a French war hero and a foreigner, while Dempsey, who had a deferment during the war, was regarded by many as a draft dodger. However, Dempsey flattened Carpentier in four rounds and the enthusiastic press reported that they were "weeping in the cottages of France." The fact of the matter was that most Frenchmen were not aware of the existence of either fighter.

In Dempsey's fight against the Argentine Luis Angel Firpo ("the Wild Bull of the Pampas") held on September 14, 1923, the press ballyhooed the phrase, "Nordic race against the Latin." Before 82,000 fans, Dempsey flattened Firpo seven times in the first round but was awkwardly knocked out of the ring by Firpo in the same round before vanquishing him for the count in the next round. Dempsey's victory was touted in the press as a "Dempsey corollary to the Monroe Doctrine," and "bold reaffirmation of Americanism." Dempsey was popular because he provided wildly dramatic fights in which his hammerlike punching and vicious attacks on his opponents created wild mass excitement. Out of the ring Dempsey was known as a dedicated family man, and he made international news when he made a tour of Europe in 1925 with his wife, motion picture star Estelle Taylor.

Dempsey lost his title defense to a clean-cut "All-American type," Gene Tunney. In his rematch with Tunney in 1927, which brought $2,658,000 in gate receipts and almost 105,000 spectators, Dempsey was victimized by a long count. He stood over Tunney for several precious seconds after having floored him before retreating to a neutral corner. Tunney was able to recover and defeat Dempsey.

Tunney never captured the attention or appealed to the popular imagination of the American public. Early in his career he had been caught by the press with a book by Shakespeare—and in an age which reflected a conflict between "high brows" and "low brows," and a distrust of the educated by the general public, Tunney did not represent the popular image of an American hero. The public liked humbleness in its heroes, and when Dempsey departed, the popularity of boxing declined significantly. But in the twenties Dempsey bouts provided big events which captured the popular imagination as the matches took on national significance, even if this significance was created by the imaginative press.

Tennis

Golf, tennis, and polo had remained games for the rich until the twenties. Because of its expense polo remained limited to the wealthy, but the other two sports became widely popularized during the twenties. Tennis owed its popularity to the efforts of William Tilden III and Helen Wills.

Tilden was a Californian whose smashing serve, all-around court brilliance, and sense of theatrics brought million dollar gates. From 1920 to 1929, Tilden was the number one ranked player in the nation. During that time he won the American National Title seven times, Wimbledon three times, and seventeen of twenty U.S. Davis Cup singles matches. Tilden's chief rival was "little" Bill Johnston, whom Tilden defeated seven times at Forest Hills in bitter and furious matches. Not only was he a competent player, but Tilden also possessed a sense of drama and artistry that thrilled the crowds.

Helen Wills, known as "Little Miss Poker Face" and "O Helen," was the premier American female tennis player of the decade. She was national champion seven times between 1923 and 1931. She also won at Wimbledon eight times beginning in 1927. According to Foster R. Dulles in his *America Learns to Play* (1940), Wills, along with Suzanne Lenglen, set new standards for American women because they "developed a game which compared favorably with that of all but the greatest men players" and "continued to play far past that age at which the ideal of 'female delicacy' had once decreed embroidery and china-painting as the only approved pursuits of women."

Golf

Golf was popularized in the twenties by two men with contrasting personalities—Robert "Bobby" Tyne Jones and Walter Hagen. At fourteen, Jones was playing in major tournaments. Between 1923 and 1930 he won thirteen national championships. In 1930 he accomplished the Grand Slam by winning the British Open, the British Amateur, the U.S. Open, and the U.S. Amateur. He then retired. To the end, Jones remained a rarity who was a "genuine amateur" and who "loved golf for the fun of it."

Just the opposite was Walter Hagen, a free spirit and a supremely confident golfer who won eleven national and international titles. Among his championships were the U.S. Open (two times), the British Open (four times), and the Professional Golfers Association tournament (five times).

Hagen was brash, outspoken, and colorful. Grantland Rice characterized him as "golf's super salesman" who "basked in the roar of the crowd." In match play against Bobby Jones in 1926 in two thirty-six hole matches, Hagen won 12 and 11. According to his friends Hagen lived by the following philosophy: "Don't worry. Don't hurry. You're here on a short visit. Be sure to smell the flowers." Undoubtedly such words struck a familiar chord in the hearts of those who became his fans.

Swimming

Swimming's two major stars during the twenties were Gertrude Ederle and Johnny Weismuller. Ederle was the eighteen-year-old daughter of an "Amsterdam Avenue liverwurst purveyor." On August 16, 1926, she became the first woman to swim the English Channel. Only five males had previously accomplished her feat, and the fastest time had been 16 hours and 33 minutes. Gertrude had covered the distance in 14 hours and 31 minutes, breaking the record by 2 hours. On her return home she was treated to a ticker-tape parade through New York City. Although she was never able to capitalize commercially on her fame, Ederle's performance certainly was an outstanding example of women's ability to achieve stellar athletic performances.

Johnny Weismuller was the Babe Ruth of swimming. By 1929 Weismuller held every freestyle world record from 100 yards to a half mile. He possessed five Olympic gold medals, and as a professional he won every freestyle race he participated in. At 6 feet 3 inches, Weismuller was dark and handsome and a star who remained unspoiled by his accomplishments. He was later able to parlay his athletic feats into an acting career, portraying Tarzan in the movies and swimming across set lagoons rather than swimming pools.

Basketball

The original Celtics, formed in 1918, brought basketball into the limelight during the twenties. Led by Nat Holman, the Red Grange of basketball, the Celtics' exciting play so captured the public that they drew 23,000 for a game in 1922 in Cleveland. Playing 150 games a year, in an eleven-year span the Celtics posted 1,320 victories and 66 losses. In 1926 the Celtics joined the American Basketball League,

founded by George P. Marshall. The Celtics proved to be too successful and, in 1928, for the good of the league, they were disbanded. Despite this, the league folded in 1929.

America at the Olympics in the 1920s

The American team sent to the 1920 Antwerp games was made up
largely of servicemen. The 351 athletes were sent to Belgium on a military transport ship, the *Princess Matoika*, which had been used in
World War I as a funeral ship to send dead bodies home from France
and Germany. Dismal conditions on the ship during the Atlantic passage and inadequate quarters in Antwerp caused a mood of rebellion
and discontent among the athletes. When an American athlete, Dan
Ahearn, was suspended because he missed a 10:00 P.M. curfew and
had moved his quarters to a hotel, two hundred men signed a petition
demanding Ahearn's reinstatement and pledging they would not
compete if the matter was not resolved. The U.S. Olympic Committee
grudgingly agreed, but the bitterness of the athletes continued
through the competition.

Despite the miserable and trying living conditions forced on them,
the American track and field team performed remarkably well. They
claimed nine gold medals and took the top two medals in the dashes.
Charley Paddock won the 100-meter dash, flashing his famous 12-
foot flying leap at the tape and earning the title "World's Fastest Human." Allan Woodring claimed the gold medal in the 200-meter
event as Paddock, who had celebrated a premature victory in the
longer sprint, ran out of energy, couldn't produce his explosive finish, and finished second.

Three Americans set Olympic records: Frank Foss in the pole vault,
Frank Loomis in the 400-meter hurdles, and Dick Langdon in the high
jump. In the 400-meter hurdles the Americans swept the top three
places with Loomis breaking the existing world record by one second.
Harold Barron and Fred Murray claimed the silver and bronze in the
110-meter hurdles. The U.S. relay team won the 400-meter relay, setting new world records, and Paddock collected his third medal. Earl
Eby finished second to thirty-six-year-old Albert Hill of Great Britain
in the 800-meter race, one of the most exciting and closest races of the
games. In the field events Patrick Ryan won the hammer throw event
with teammate Basil Bennett finishing third.

The American swimming team, led by Duke Kahanamoku and Norman Ross, won eleven gold medals, with the talented swimmers sweeping the 100-meter freestyle event and copping the top two places in the 400-meter freestyle. The diving team won five of the six medals, and a thirteen-year-old American girl, Aileen Riggin, won the gold in the springboard event, with two American women taking medals as well. The American women swimmers swept the 100-meter freestyle event with Ethelda Bleibtrey claiming the gold. She also won the 300-meter freestyle.

In other events American shooters claimed thirteen gold medals, and American rowers were dominant. The American rugby team also took a surprising first.

The 1924 Paris Olympics produced a star and hero of the magnitude of Jim Thorpe in the 1912 Stockholm games. Faced with strong opposition, Johnny Weismuller, then nineteen years old, won the 100- and 400-meter freestyle events, anchored the 800-meter relay team, and played on the bronze medal winning water polo team. Driven by his coach, Bill Bachrach, who told Weismuller that he would be a "slave" and "hate his [coach's] guts," the young swimmer shattered Olympic records, even knocking 20 full seconds off the existing 400-meter freestyle record. Weismuller swam equally well in sprints or distance races, and his spectacular wins at Paris made swimming a popular sport in America. Swimmers were now viewed as genuine athletes, the equal of track and field competitors.

In track and field the American team won twelve gold medals, with the Finns again providing close competition. Harold Osborn set a world record in the high jump (6 feet 6 inches) that would stand until 1936, and he prevailed in the decathlon with teammate Emerson Norton finishing second. Clarence "Bud" Houser captured the shot put and discus golds, outdistancing two teammates in the shot put.

The American team also claimed gold medals in the hammer throw, the 100- and 400-meter high hurdles, the broad jump, the pole vault (with a sweep of the event), the relays, and the 200-meter race with Jackson Scholz and Charley Paddock finishing 1-2. Scholz finished second in the 100-meter dash to Harold Abrahams of Great Britain. Paddock's reputation as the "World's Fastest Human" was short-lived.

Other notable American performances in the 1924 games included a world record-breaking broad jump by Bob LeGendre, competing in the pentathlon. LeGendre jumped 25 feet 6 inches, which was a foot farther than William DeHart Hubbard's gold medal jump, but LeGendre had to settle for a bronze in the pentathlon. Clarence DeMar claimed a third in the marathon, an event Americans dominated in 1908 with three medals but had slipped in badly in the 1912 and 1920 games. An American would not again win a marathon gold medal until Frank Shorter claimed one in 1972.

The 1928 Olympic performance of the American track and field team was dismal, to say the least. American sprinters and runners won only three gold medals, being shut out completely in the dashes and claiming only two medals in the 400- and 800-meter races. Ray Barbuti won the 400-meter event and anchored the winning 1,600-meter relay team to claim two medals. The U.S. 400-meter relay team also won, and American hurdlers took second and third in both hurdle events. Five gold medals were won in field events as Clarence Houser repeated as discus champion (the second American to do that) and the pole vaulters claimed three medals (repeating the feat of the 1924 team). In swimming Johnny Weismuller claimed two more gold medals. The American men's and women's teams dominated the rest of the competition.

Although the United States easily won the most gold medals (twenty-four) in the 1928 Olympics, the failure of the track and field team, notably the sprinters and the 1924 veterans sent to defend their titles, was unexpected. Major Douglas MacArthur, the president of the U.S. Olympic Committee, wrote in his official report after the games: "Nothing is more synonymous of our national success than is our national success in athletics." Sports reporters blamed the proliferation of coaches, managers, and trainers, the scheduling of the Olympic trials only three weeks before the games opened, and the overabundance of rich foods fed the athletes on board the S. S. *President Roosevelt*.

The 1920 team was angry, lean, and hungry, overcoming adversity and unified as a team in their grievances and discontent. They were representing a nation that had turned the tide of war in 1917–18, and they were participating in the games that had suffered an eight-year lapse during Europe's war madness. Many were servicemen, and all were newcomers to the Olympic competition.

The 1928 team was pampered and self-confident, sending a number of 1924 gold medal winners and a track and field squad of eighty-four members. Compared with the trials of the 1920 team on board the *Princess Matoika*, the 1928 team had luxury accommodations, and it is reported that the 300 member team ate 580 steaks at a single meal, as well as consuming prodigious amounts of ice cream on the voyage.

Perhaps the contrasts of these two teams reflect what was happening to America during the Roaring Twenties. With prosperity, consumerism, and affluence, the society had lost the edge that World War I had brought when it tested American idealism and determination. Nonproducing business managers, middlemen, advertising executives, and salesmen proliferated as service and luxury industries became more important. Uneasy feelings and signs of economic weakness were glossed over by an expanding stock market, burgeoning consumer goods, and self-confident boosterism. The "American way" was best and would continue to prevail as the "seize the day" philosophy and mood prevailed. The United States would always run faster and try harder.

The 1928 team was a product of the late twenties atmosphere, and its athletes were reported to have been overly conceited and cocky, disdaining necessary training and breaking rules. In retrospect, it's hard to pinpoint the real reasons for the disappointing performance of the athletes, but their problems seemed symptomatic of an America that had come to believe its own myths. The Great Depression would sorely test the nation's spirit and make it reexamine its values and image. The 1932 Olympics in Los Angeles would produce heroes like Babe Didrikson, Eddie Tolan, Bill Carr, and Buster Crabbe—all lean and hungry athletes who represented a new generation of dedicated Olympians.

1924 Winter Olympics

The year 1924 saw the inauguration of the first winter Olympics. In 1920 ice hockey (Canada first, United States second) and figure skating had been contested as part of the summer games. These had been transferred to the winter games with an expanded program of events that included bobsledding and various types of skiing, both Alpine and Nordic.

The first city to host the winter games was Chamonix, a famous French resort. Only sixteen nations took part and there was a total of only 293 athletes, of whom 13 were women.

Norway, Sweden, and Finland were the pacemakers for the inaugural games. The Finns and Norwegians divided all the medals for the speed skating contests except the 500 meter, which saw Charles Jewtraw of the United States surprisingly capture the gold. The only other medals won by the United States were a silver by the ice hockey team and a silver by Beatrix Loughran in women's figure skating.

1928 Winter Olympics

The 1928 Olympic winter games were held at St. Moritz, Switzerland, because the Dutch were unable to provide proper facilities and conditions for the winter sports. The 1928 games are possibly best known because they marked the debut of Sonja Henie, who won her first of three Olympic figure skating titles and whose skating brilliance revolutionized women's figure skating. She abandoned the bulky clothing of her predecessors and appeared in relatively short and colorful costumes. This new look, combined with her elegance and virtuosity on the ice, made her beloved by fans throughout the world.

The Norwegians dominated with five firsts and a tie for a speed skating title. The Swedes followed with two firsts, two seconds, and one third.

The United States did not compete in hockey so Canada took first place and Sweden took second place. This time Great Britain could do no better than fourth. American strength was concentrated in the bobsled event, where brothers J. and J. R. Heaton took first and second in the one-man bobsled event, while the United States took first and second in the four-man bobsled event. The only other medals won by the United States were Beatrix Loughran's bronze in women's figure skating, and O'Neill Farrell's bronze tie with a Norwegian and a Finn in the 500-meter speed skating event. The U.S. winter sports teams proved that they had a long way to go before they could compete with the squads from Scandinavia. Winter sports facilities in the United States were limited, and most athletes who competed were not trained for international competition.

Conclusion

Americans participated in many sports and cheered for many heroes during the twenties; those discussed represent the sports with the greatest spectator appeal and the heroes who appealed to the public the most. In an era when the nation was seeking escape from the memory of a disillusioning war and expressing a nostalgic longing for the past, athletics provided entertainment and a reaffirmation that the strenuous qualities which made America great could still be witnessed vicariously on the playing fields of the nation. Sports fans showered adulation on record breakers and identified with winners who prevailed through individualism, raw talent, and opportunism. Sports provided a focus for the energies of the period as millions of fans sought to share in the excitement generated by sporting events.

A Flame in the Dark:
Depression Era Sports

The Great Depression rocked the United States to its economic foundations as capitalist enterprise and big business failed to continue the prosperity, high standard of living, and limitless expectations that had been stimulated by the twenties. Of course the depression was worldwide, but Americans, who had been in an isolationist mood and who failed to see the international economic dimensions of the problem, wondered if the vaunted American system was bankrupt and in need of change. Because the crisis on this scale was unprecedented, no one knew whom to blame. Ordinary consumers were made to feel responsible because of their overconsumption and demand for easy credit and a share of the booming stock market. Radicals, socialists, and newly awakened critics of the competitive system railed at industry for greed, overproduction, profit gouging, and manipulation of the markets. Under the conservative Republican leadership of Herbert Hoover, the government took a hands off the economy attitude, whistled while the wolf was at the door, and preached about the importance of work incentive and "natural" adjustments to the shaken economy. The Hoover government believed that the situation was only temporary, and while Hoover and his economic advisors waited, the country slipped into massive unemployment, severe social dislocation, and unprecedented levels of deprivation, suffering, and starvation.

To many, the Depression called for extreme measures, even an overhauling of the economic system or the introduction of socialism or communism. The desperation of the bread and soup lines, and the unemployment lines in the city was matched by the desperation of rural farmers who were urged to kill new livestock or to plow under crops so that the surplus problem would be eased. Tenant farmers, sharecroppers, and land renters were squeezed off the land in the South and Southwest and left to their uncertain fate as they migrated to northern industrial cities or took to the road in search of work and sunshine in the promised land of California. Workers in plants risked jobs and even life and limb by unionizing and striking, discovering solidarity, brotherhood, and sisterhood in new social organizations that were previously unfamiliar and unacceptable to them. Finally, with Franklin D. Roosevelt's assumption of the presidency in 1933, the government was ready to take unprecedented and radical measures to provide relief, employment, and reconstruction of a nation devastated by economic as well as natural disasters such as floods and drought.

To call the early 1930s "hard times" is an understatement. They were harder than most people remember them as being, and the conditions profoundly affected a generation's outlook, social values, and expectations. Lives were not only disoriented and disrupted, but many were suspended and stalemated as inactivity, worry, delayed hopes, and family problems that could only be alleviated by employment came to dominate people's routines. People felt guilty and ashamed about their unemployment, poverty. or declining family circumstances as they bore the private burden of the depression. For some, antisocial behavior and criminal activity were the only responses that produced a reaction; the period's fascination with gangsters and outlaws shows how the populace could find release, even if it was only vicarious and temporary, for their own suppressed anger and frustrations.

The road back from economic collapse was a long and hard one, as the depression lingered far beyond anyone's expectations. Many of the New Deal programs were badly conceived and inadequately administered, but a number of them produced tangible results that improved people's circumstances and brought a measure of self-respect and decency to shattered lives. Even at the point that the Depression seemed over and the future showed promise, the country slipped back into another economic slide that was only headed off by the coming of the war and its stimulus to employment.

Sports were forced to adjust to new circumstances during the Depression as the "Golden Age of Sport" quickly became the "Lean Age of Survival." Athletes were assured of work, and because they did not undergo such drastic cuts in income or work time as the ordinary worker, there was no movement to organize against their employers. In the professional ranks competition for positions was fierce as a new kind of player emerged in pro football and baseball—tough, feisty, and aggressive. Sports provided the basis for the ongoing American myth of individual success and competition during a period of stagnation and paralysis. Athletes like Bronko Nagurski, Pepper Martin, and Joe Louis symbolized the individual who determined his own fate by sheer willpower and effort. During the dark days of the Depression sports provided an important diversion and interest that could be followed cheaply. Athletic activity, with its emphasis on exertion and its production of winners, stood in sharp contrast to the helplessness and impotence that many people felt. The athlete symbolized the social ideal of the aggressive and active person who succeeded on the basis of native talents.

Baseball

The Great Depression did not adversely affect the fortunes of major league baseball immediately after the stock market crash of October 1929. Indeed, the 1930 season was a remarkable one for hitting feats and team performances. Attendance in the National League in 1930 was almost 5.5 million, which bettered the 1927 season record for the twenties. The American League attendance was 4.7 million, which was down from the record attendance figures of over five million in 1924 and 1925. Curiously enough, the best attendance years in the twenties were the two consecutive years that the Washington Senators won the pennant and engaged in a World Series that went seven games. The National League surpassed 5 million (5.3) only in 1927, the year Pittsburgh battled against St. Louis, New York, and Chicago with only two games separating the first three clubs at the end of the season.

Attendance in the National League was up in the 1930 season because it was undoubtedly the most exciting season in the history of the league. Six of the eight National League teams hit over .300 as a team batting average, with the league averaging .303 overall for all teams. The New York Giants hit .319 as a team, with a remarkable .401 hitting performance from Bill Terry, who would average .341 as a lifetime batting average in fourteen seasons, all with the Giants. Fred Lindstrom hit .379 with 196 RBI's and 231 hits, while Terry had 254 hits in the 1930 season.

The Philadelphia Phillies, who finished dead last and lost 102 games in 1930, hit .315 as a team with Chuck Klein hitting .386 and driving in 170 runs and Frank O'Doul hitting .383 with 202 hits and 97 RBI's.

The Chicago Cubs hit .309 as a team, and Lewis Robert "Hack" Wilson had one of the most remarkable seasons enjoyed by a major leaguer. He hit .356, powered 56 home runs, and had 190 RBI's. His teammate Kiki Cuyler had 228 hits and compiled a .355 batting average. The St. Louis Cardinals hit .314 as a team in 1930 and scored 1,004 runs. Four National League teams had over 1,700 hits for the season with the Phillies amassing 1,783 hits, with three players (Chuck Klein, Art Whitney, and Frank O'Doul) collecting over 200 hits each and accounting for 659 hits. The number of batters above the .360 mark was phenomenal, and a number of players were close to the coveted .400 mark, notably Babe Herman of the Dodgers at .393, Chuck Klein at .386, and Lefty O'Doul at .383.

The National League had never seen such an outpouring of hits (twelve players with over 200 hits) and runs as the 1930 season. Only two league pitchers won more than 20 games, and Perce Malone of the Cubs and Remy Kremer of Pittsburgh both won just 20, with Kremer having a 5.02 earned run average. 1930 was a season of amazing individual and team performances in the National League. After 1930 no National League team would hit .300 as a team, with the Phillies coming closest in 1932 with a .292 team average. Perhaps in 1930 the players felt the pressure of the Depression and felt they needed to justify their salaries and wanted to solidify their position on the team.

National League ball parks were exciting and explosive places in 1930, but after this record-breaking year batting averages and run production would drop off dramatically. In 1931 only five players would have over 200 hits, with the league-leading Lloyd Waner of Pittsburgh (214 hits) coming in with 40 hits below Bill Terry, who had 254 hits in 1930. Only four players in 1931 had 100 or more RBI's, whereas in 1930 seventeen players had over 100 runs batted in. Chick Hafey of St. Louis won the batting title in 1931 with a .349 average, a mark which would not have even placed him in the top twenty batters of 1930, and Chuck Klein won the 1931 RBI title with 121, whereas seven players had exceeded that mark in 1930. Klein also hit 31 home runs in 1931 to lead the league, 25 fewer than Hack Wilson's record mark of 56 in 1930.

During the 1930 season in the American League three teams (New York, Washington, and Cleveland) hit over .300, the Yankees leading the league with a .309 average behind Lou Gehrig's .379 average and 174 RBI's and Ruth's .359 average and 153 RBI's. Fifteen players in the league had over 100 runs batted in, and eight players had over 200 hits. Al Simmons of the Philadelphia Athletics hit .381, had 211 hits, and batted in 165 runs while scoring 152 runs. But the league average was only .288 compared to the National League batting average of .303. The 1930 Yankees had exactly 100 fewer hits than the remarkable Phillies team that hit .315 and finished eighth.

Five American League pitchers won 20 games or more, with Robert Lefty Grove of the Philadelphia Athletics and Boston Braves winning 28 and losing only 5 with a 2.54 league-leading earned run average. Grove would lead the American League in ERA in 1930, 1931, 1932, 1935, 1936, 1938, and 1939. Grove won 175 games from 1930 to 1939 along with Vernon Lefty Gomez of the Yankees, who won 165 games during the same period. Grove was by far the best pitcher in the American League.

The American League was better balanced in terms of pitching and hitting, and the 1930 World Series, won by the Philadelphia Athletics 4 games to 2, bears out this fact. The Athletics outscored the Cardinals 20 runs to 11 runs, even though the Cardinals had 38 hits to 35 for the A's. The combined ERA for the Cardinals' pitchers was 5.40, while the Athletics' pitchers compiled a 1.73 combined ERA. During the regular season the Cardinal pitchers had a combined ERA of 4.28, and Wild Bill Hallahan was the top Cardinal pitcher with a 15-9 mark.

The amazing hitting barrage of 1930, especially in the National League, caused league officials to change the baseball to make it less lively. In 1931 the National League used a ball with a heavier cover and raised stitching in order to slow up the home run and extra base hits epidemic. The American League altered the ball less drastically, using a coarser and heavier thread for stitching to produce greater wind resistance. The changes produced the desired effect. Home runs were reduced, indeed in the National League more than cut in half, but hitting and run scoring were also diminished. A New York Times article for July 31, 1931, documented the drastic decline in overall hitting and concluded that the new ball "has just about shoved the game in the majors back to the hitless wonder days."

The issue of the ball and its composition and features became a prominent concern in 1931–32. By 1933 both leagues adopted a uniform ball, and the National League adopted the livelier ball used by the other league. League administrators, owners, and players realized that baseball was entertainment and that sluggers were greater heroes and box office draws than pitchers. Fans wanted colorful action and drama at ball parks during the Depression. Pitchers would have to develop new pitches and build stronger arms or more unusual deliveries in order to stay ahead of hitters.

After the hitting pyrotechnics of the 1930 season, what followed was destined to be less exciting and dramatic on all counts. As the country slipped more deeply into economic paralysis and crisis, baseball players seemed to suffer in the same way as did other workers from the uncertainty, malaise, and frustrations of the hard times. The Philadelphia Athletics, now at the end of the Connie Mack dynasty, won the 1931 pennant for a third straight season with a 13½-game bulge over the Yankees. The St. Louis Cardinals won by 13 games over the Giants.

As indicated earlier, run production and hitting fell off sharply in both leagues. Home runs in the National League dropped from 892 in 1930 to 492 in 1931, and no player better illustrates this decrease than Hack Wilson of the Cubs, who slipped from 56 home runs to 13, from 190 RBI's to 61, and from a .356 to .261 batting average. The American League was buoyed by Al Simmons' .390 batting average and by the home run output of Gehrig and Ruth, who both hit 46 in the 1931 season. Home run production in the American League dropped from 673 to 576 from 1930 to 1931, quite a contrast to the 400 drop in home runs in the National League. And in the 1932 season Jimmy Foxx would threaten Ruth's 1927 mark when Foxx powered 58 home runs.

Attendance in the National League dropped almost a million people, and by 1933 would plummet to 3.2 million. The American League also dropped almost a million in attendance, and in 1933 went down to 2.9 million. The cumulative batting average for the National League teams dropped to .277, and the runs scored dropped from 7,025 to 5,537, and league pitchers breathed a sigh of relief as the league ERA went down from 4.97 in 1930 to 3.86 in 1931. By contrast, the cumulative American League batting average went from .288 down to .278, with only a modest decrease in runs scored. The cumulative team average of the National League teams fell to low points in 1933 at .266 and .267 in 1938, while the low point for the American League was .273 in 1933.

The decline in attendance and the tailing off of player performances, notably in the National League, did not signal a precipitous cut in players' salaries. Many players took salary cuts, but these were relatively modest compared with the shrinking income and massive unemployment the general population faced (almost 12 million unemployed in 1933).

The Great Depression brought about significant changes in the salaries of major league players. The managers and stars saw their salaries cut substantially. In 1931 Ruth was paid $80,000, John McGraw earned $50,000, as did Connie Mack, and Rogers Hornsby pulled down $40,000. Top sluggers like Hack Wilson, Al Simmons, Bill Terry, and Lou Gehrig made $25,000 or more. But by 1936 the top manager, Joe McCarthy of the Yankees, made $35,000, and sluggers like Jimmy Foxx and Lou Gehrig suffered modest cuts in salary.

In 1931 more than two dozen players and managers received more than $20,000 per year, but by 1936 less than a dozen were in this group. The average player's salary was on the upgrade, and during the Depression stars could not be as individualistic, temperamental, and defiant as they had in the past. In the 1932 season the major league salary lists were cut by over $1 million, but by 1936 the total payroll was back to nearly $3 million. The payroll for the 1937 season was estimated to exceed $3.2 million, with the Yankees paying out about $368,000 in payroll. A total of thirty-six players in the 1937 season earned $15,000 or more, with twenty-four of these in the American League. Gehrig was paid $36,000 (tops for the majors). The Depression period brought an end to the excessively high salaries for stars, although salaries were decidedly inequitable because of the range of financial resources and attendance among the sixteen clubs.

Baseball perhaps recovered more easily and quickly from the Depression for five key reasons: (1) fan loyalty and the continuing high popularity of the game; (2) strong executive leadership among the owners; (3) the quick rectification of league mistakes such as the return to the livelier ball and the rescinding of an absurd rule that prohibited players from talking with fans; (4) the shrewd use of promotional devices such as the All-Star game, the Baseball Hall of Fame at Cooperstown, New York, with yearly inductions, and the use of films to promote interest in the sport; and (5) the careful and decisive handling of the Boston Braves franchise when economic disaster seemed imminent.

The well-established tradition of an inner-city series also added money to a baseball player's yearly salary. The clubs usually played four games during the season, and in 1936 the Chicago White Sox team split $48,752.22, having won the series four games to none, with the Cubs players splitting $44,389.65. Occasionally, city teams played each other in a charity game to aid local unemployment relief funds. In September 1933 the Boston Braves beat the Red Sox with 15,000 fans watching, and the gate receipts went to aid the Boston Unemployment Relief Fund.

Baseball clubs tried to lure fans to the parks with the same kinds of promotional gimmicks that the movie theatres used: lotteries, musical entertainment, special prizes or giveaways, low-priced concessions, and even the policy of letting fans keep balls hit into the stands. Despite all these efforts, gate receipts in the major leagues dropped from the record level of $17 million in 1929 to $10.8 million in 1933. In the 1933 season the St. Louis Browns team drew only 88,113 fans to

Sportsman's Park, while the Cardinals drew only 256,171 to the same ball park. Hard times were also felt in the Philadelphia Phillies ball park and at Crosley Field in Cincinnati.

Some club owners were reduced to desperate measures to try to salvage their financial interests. In 1934 Judge Emil Fuchs, owner of the Boston Braves, wanted to convert his ball park into a greyhound racing track and to transplant the Braves to Fenway Park, home of the Red Sox. His proposal created a furor among the administrators and owners. A League rule specifically prohibited gambling on ball park premises, and league officials quickly decided that dogs and gambling do not mix with professional baseball. Fuchs' proposal threatened to turn Braves Field into a circus and to reintroduce gamblers and bettors into the sanctuary that Commissioner Landis had created.

The financial situation of the Braves was serious. Club debts were estimated at $325,000, but League officials were aware of the dangerous precedent of a club folding. The Boston club had been in continuous operation since 1876. After Babe Ruth's presence failed to solve the team's problems at the gate, Judge Fuchs was forced out as the owner, and the League itself took over the administration of the franchise until a new owner could be found and the stockholders' situation resolved. The Boston situation was a complicated one, and by contrast the other city ball club, under the management of Tom Yawkey, spent $3.5 million dollars to try to build a winner.

The club owners considered other measures to try to cover their real and potential losses. At their winter meeting in 1931 the owners favored a ban on local broadcasting of games. This decision was eventually left up to individual clubs, and in the 1934 season both the Cardinals' and Browns' management banned radio broadcasting of their home games in St. Louis. Owners could not decide whether radio broadcasts were detrimental or beneficial to attendance, but eventually they decided that radio sustained and spurred fan interest. In 1937 the Chicago White Sox and Chicago Cubs received $21,000 each after granting local broadcasting rights to four Chicago radio stations. The $100,000 franchise charge paid by the Ford Motor Company for the 1934, 1935, 1936, and 1937 World Series benefited baseball players on all teams.

After the repeal of Prohibition in 1933, club owners had to decide whether they wanted the revenues from beer sold in their parks. Chicago and New York fans had quick access to beer, but those cities had never been bothered much by Prohibition anyway. Other clubs were dead set against beer in the parks, and others had the issue decided for them by local ordinances and court rulings.

Even with the decrease in attendance at major league parks, the owners and administrators announced in January 1932 that they would not cut ticket prices. Separate statements were issued by William Harridge, president of the American League, and John A. Heydler, president of the National League. Both pointed out that admission prices had not increased in twenty years, and Harridge noted that even ''during the boom period baseball made no attempt to take advantage of easy money.'' Heydler stated that ''baseball for years has prided itself as always remaining a great American game within the means of all classes.''

The National League announced in June 1932 that a new 10 percent federal tax that would apply to baseball would be added to the price of tickets, thus bringing about a rise in the price of tickets at almost mid-season. While most of the teams held the line on ticket prices or even increased them, two teams announced cuts in ticket prices. In February 1933 the Cleveland Indians reduced admission prices $.15 on two kinds of box seats, cut grandstand seats in the right-field area to $.85, created more bleacher seats for $.55, but kept the grandstand general admission price fixed at $1.10. In April 1933 the Cincinnati club announced ticket price reductions of $.05 to $.55 cents with weekday prices ranging from $.60 to $1.50. The club owners badly needed the revenues from ticket sales in order to meet expenses and salaries.

Some owners, for example, Phillip K. Wrigley, could absorb a reported loss of $600,000 in three years from 1932 to 1934 with the hopes of producing a winner. However, the Cincinnati Reds lost $46,451 in 1934 and had to take stringent measures in order to finish in the black the next year with only a small profit. By contrast, Wrigley reportedly lost $250,000 in 1933, the year he purchased Chuck Klein for $75,000 and Bill Lee for $30,000. What was one man's sport was another man's business.

The Depression brought about a few internal adjustments that changed the course of players' careers. Branch Rickey, vice president of the St. Louis Cardinals during the Depression, traded Taylor Lee Douthit to the Cincinnati team in June 1931. Douthit had been with the Cards since 1923 and had hit .336 in 1929 and .303 in 1930 (with over 200 hits in both seasons). But Douthit was now thirty years old and his salary was about $14,000. Rickey decided to trade Douthit and bring up Pepper Martin, who played the 1931 season for $4,500. Rickey's instincts were right, and Martin hit .300 for the season and performed brilliantly in the 1931 World Series with a .500 batting average (12 for 24), 5 runs scored and 5 batted in, and 5 stolen bases. Douthit was crushed by the trade and remained in baseball only two more seasons.

In the 1933 season (when the Cardinals dropped to fifth place),

Rickey sold Paul Derringer, a pitcher who had won 18 and 11 games in two previous seasons for the Cardinals, to Cincinnati for Leo Durocher. Derringer toiled for a team that never finished better than fourth place from 1930 to 1938 and had finished last four straight seasons. Losing over 20 games in 1933 and 1934, Derringer came back with 22 wins in 1935 and a 19-19 record in 1936. Derringer represents the player who survived the changes forced on his career by the Depression, and he developed into one of the National League's finest pitchers with 21, 25, and 20 wins from 1930 to 1940. The Reds won the pennant in 1939 and 1940, and were world champions in 1940 when Paul Derringer came back to win the fourth and seventh games against Detroit after being knocked out in the second inning of the opening game.

The fates of Douthit and Derringer were similar to those of many businessmen during the Depression. Many middle-aged executives were replaced by younger, hungrier men who would work for one-third or less of the previous man's salary. If the established executive showed any self-doubts or decrease in performance, then he was let go. Many men were demoralized and dispirited by their terminations, feeling their loyalty to the company had been violated, and could not adjust to new employment conditions. Many, like Derringer, survived temporary lapses of fortune and worked hard to prove themselves again.

Theories of baseball management during the Depression differed greatly. The Yankees continued to spend big money for salaries in the 1930s with their payroll of $275,000 in 1937 and their gross operating expenses of more than $600,000 the same year. The Yankees averaged about 909,000 per season in attendance from 1930 to 1939 with a team that won five pennants and finished second in 1931 and 1933 to 1935. By contrast, the Philadelphia Athletics, winners of three consecutive pennants from 1929 to 1931 and World Series winners in 1929 and 1930, began to sell off their star players in 1933 after attendance dropped to 297,138, half the attendance of the 1931 season.

In 1932 Connie Mack sold Al Simmons, winner of the 1930 and 1931 American League batting championships, to the White Sox for $100,000. At the end of the 1933 season Mack sold Lefty Grove with two other players for $125,000 and Mickey Cochrane to Detroit for $100,000. Jimmy Foxx, the league's leading home run producer for 1932, 1933, and 1935, was sold in 1935 with three other players for $300,000. Although by 1937 Mack made the A's financially solvent once again, the team became an almost perennial cellar dweller, finishing eighth in nine seasons in the period from 1934 to 1947. The always more than half empty Shibe Park was a grim contrast to the box office success of Yankee Stadium.

Other teams saw the Depression period as one of opportunity, foregoing caution and retrenchment by actively building solid baseball franchises. The Detroit Tigers put together a solid combination of talent, winning pennants in 1934 and 1935 under the managerial direction of Mickey Cochrane, who also hit .322 and .320 those two years. The Tiger hitting led by Hank Greenberg, Charley Gehringer, Goose Goslin, Marv Owen, and Billy Rogell produced a team batting average of .300 in both 1934 and 1936. The Tigers drew over a million fans in the 1935 and 1937 seasons, and the 1934 Tigers had the best attendance mark in the major leagues. Tom Yawkey of the Boston Red Sox also tried to emulate Frank Navin's success in Detroit by paying $250,000 to Washington for Joe Cronin and $125,000 for Robert "Lefty" Grove and two other players.

Yawkey even offered Cronin a five-year contract at $50,000 per year. Cronin managed the Red Sox from 1935 on, hitting over .300 from 1937 to 1939. Grove slumped to an 8-8 won-lost record in 1934, but won 20 games the next season and 17 games the next two seasons. But the Tigers were the darlings of the American League in 1934–35. Hank Greenberg, Charley Gehringer, and Marv Owen were products of the Tiger farm system. Billy Rogell, Goose Goslin, and Mickey Cochrane all came to the Tigers by way of shrewd trades. The Tiger infield of Greenberg, Gehringer, Rogell, and Owen combined for 462 RBI's in the 1934 season and 420 the following season. This was undoubtedly one of the hardest hitting infields in major league history. The Gehringer-Rogell combination at second base and shortstop presented the smoothest and most consistent fielding team of the period.

The Tigers provided a great lift to the spirits and hopes of Detroiters, for Detroit was an industrial city that was hard hit by the Depression. The determination, competitive aggressiveness, and consistency of this team brought hope to countless numbers who saw the value of teamwork and united effort. The fans supported the team at the gate and made Detroit one of the most financially solid teams in baseball.

The St. Louis Cardinals had two personalities who reflected the impact of the Depression on baseball talents. Pepper Martin was a wild and spectacular player who played the game with reckless abandon. He captured the imagination of baseball fans with his lower-class lifestyle, his unkept appearance, his "Wild Horse of Osage" base running, and his legendary 1931 World Series performance. He was an untamed spirit who disdained adulation in favor of a kind of hobo life of hunting and riding the rails. Martin symbolized the raw life of the Depression—the life of deprivation, lower-class or cheap enjoyments, the disdain for culture and manners, and the belief in unrestrained individualism. He overcame adversity, after slumping to a .238 batting average in 1932. But he came back strong in 1933 with a .316 average, scoring a league leading 122 runs and also leading the league in stolen bases from 1934 to 1936. In the 1934 World Series win over the Tigers Martin hit .355, scored 8 runs, and stole 2 bases.

Another free spirit of the Cardinals' "Gas House Gang" team was pitcher Jay Hanna "Dizzy" Dean. Dean, son of an Arkansas sharecropper, quickly earned notoriety for his loquaciousness and unpredictable behavior. Although he was destined only to have six good seasons with the Cardinals, Dizzy became a household word as fans all over America followed his exploits, his press statements and blunders with English language, and his expanding ego.

In the 1934 season Dizzy and Paul Dean went on strike because of Paul's low salary of $3,000. In a show of brotherly unity, Dizzy even tore to shreds his Cardinal uniform, and the brothers were suspended. During their absence, Pepper Martin pitched for the team, and surprisingly, the Cardinals won without their ace pitchers. Eventually the Deans ended their protest strike and rejoined the club, Dizzy winning 30 games and Paul winning 19. Dizzy won 109 games in six full seasons with the Cardinals, but Paul never won more than 5 games in a season after winning 19 games in both 1934 and 1935. Dizzy and Daffy combined in the 1934 World Series to handcuff the Tigers, each winning 2 games with Paul compiling a 1.00 ERA for eighteen innings and Dizzy a 1.73 ERA in twenty-six innings. In the seventh game, won by the Cardinals 11-0, Dean struck out five, allowed 6 hits, 5 of which were singles, and virtually taunted the Tigers to hit his pitches.

The frustrated Detroit fans eventually exploded into a garbage and foul language barrage in left field against Joe "Ducky Wucky" Medwick, who had not only collided with Marv Owen in a hard slide at third after Medwick tripled in the sixth inning, but who also blasted Detroit pitching for a .379 average in the Series. Commissioner Landis had to order Medwick removed from the game in order to quell the unsavory disturbance. Dizzy Dean livened up the Series when he appeared as a pinch-runner in the fourth game. Going into second base without sliding, Dean was hit in the head by Billy Rogell's throw to first and Dean was carried off unconscious. Dean amused everyone the next day when he told reporters that his head had been X-rayed and the doctors found "nothing."

Dizzy Dean was diverting news during the hardest years of the Depression. His cockiness was admired by many, and like Pepper Martin, Dean represented the uncultivated vigor of a simple country boy whose raw talent, enthusiasm for the game, and unforgettable antics endeared him to fans everywhere. He was a flamboyant and colorful personality in a period of desperation and despair. Like Ruth, Dean was a skillful athlete who never lost the enthusiasm and unbridled spirits or energy of a kid. Ruth could point his famous "called-shot" home run in the 1932 World Series before a hostile Chicago crowd and thumb his nose against the hecklers on the Chicago bench, while Dean, laughing merrily as he danced off second base after hitting a triple in the first game of the 1934 World Series, would call out to Detroit pitcher Firpo Marberry, "What was that you throwed me?"

The St. Louis and Detroit teams provided color and excitement in the mid-1930s, as did the Chicago Cubs. The Cubs won pennants in 1932, 1935, and 1938, but lost in the World Series all three times, being swept by the Yankees in 1932 and 1938 and losing four games to two to the Detroit Tigers in 1935. The 1935 Cubs team put on a spectacular pennant drive and won 21 games in a row, behind the hitting of Billy Herman (a league-leading 227 hits and a .351 average), Augie Galan (203 hits and a .314 average), Stan Hack (.311), Gabby Hartnett (.344 with 91 RBI's), and Frank Demaree (.325). Bill Lee won 20 and lost 6, and Lonnie Warneke won 20 and lost 13. With the exception of Warneke, who pitched brilliantly against Detroit in the 1935 Series and won 2 games with a 0.54 ERA in 3 games, the Cubs' pitching failed miserably under the pressure of the Series in 1932 (37 runs given up in 4 games) and in 1938 (22 runs given up in 4 games).

In 1935 the Cubs' fans could only remember the distant glory of the decisive sweeps over Detroit in the 1907 and 1908 World Series. Diehard Cub supporters would have to be long on memory for decades to come, and the 1945 World Series would only deepen the despair as the Cubs lost again to Detroit in the seventh game 9-3 at Wrigley Field.

The brief but brilliant career of Hack Wilson seems to personify the frustrations of the Cubs. Wilson drove in over a hundred runs and hit over .300 for five straight seasons (1926 to 1930) with the Cubs, and his record-setting season of 1930 has already been noted. Wilson was done in by heavy drinking and late nights, his body unable to take the kind of abuse that Ruth had rendered his. By age thirty-four, Wilson was forced out of baseball as the awesome power he displayed with 56 home runs in 1930 was sapped by the alcoholic binges.

The New York Yankees prospered throughout the Depression period, winning the pennant in 1932 and sweeping the World Series from the hapless Cubs. They finished second from 1933 to 1935, but then won four straight world championships. Under manager Joseph

McCarthy the Yankees established their second dynasty. "Iron Man" Lou Gehrig anchored the Yankee team, playing steadily at first base and driving in well over a hundred runs each season. In 1936 Gehrig hit .354, drove in 152 runs, and hit 49 home runs (leading the league). In 1934 he won the Triple Crown. The Yankee infield of Red Rolfe, Frank Crosetti, Tony Lazzeri, and Gehrig had 409 RBI's, while Joe DiMaggio hit .323 and drove in 125 runs in his rookie season. Bill Dickey hit .362 with 107 runs batted in during the 1936 season, and Dickey handled the talented Yankee pitching staff with consistency. He became an "Iron Man" behind the plate, catching in 100 or more games for thirteen consecutive seasons. He hit well over .300 in ten seasons, compiling a lifetime average of .313. He played in 38 World Series games, and the Yankees won seven of the eight World Series that Dickey played in.

With a sharp eye for developing talent and shrewd trades, the Yankees added such players as Tommy Henrich (in 1937), Joe Gordon (in 1938), and Charley Keller (in 1939). The pitching staff of Lefty Gomez and Red Ruffing was always supported by a cast of pitchers who managed to win their share of games and to pitch well in the Series. John Joseph Murphy became a brilliant relief pitcher for the Yankees, saving 107 games and winning 93 games from 1932 to 1946. In sixteen and one-third innings of World Series relief pitching, Murphy had a 1.10 ERA with 2 wins and 4 saves.

The Yankees produced a second dynasty because of three central factors: shrewd management and business operations, a brilliant on-the-field manager, Joe McCarthy, and the incentive of money. Players on Yankee teams were paid on the average almost three times the salaries of other teams' players. The Yankee players shared in the World Series money, which for the winners averaged about $5,600 even during the Depression. Even the losers in the Series could look forward to doubling their average annual salary.

Other economic developments in the 1930s helped to strengthen the financial situation of baseball during a difficult period. The All-Star game was introduced in 1933, and proceeds from this game helped to support the "Association of Professional Baseball Players of America," which helped ex-ballplayers and umpires who had fallen on hard times and needed financial assistance. The 1934 All-Star game fans at the Polo Grounds saw Carl Hubbell, ace screwball pitcher for the Giants, strike out Babe Ruth, Lou Gehrig, Jimmy Foxx, Al Simmons, and Joe Cronin in succession in the first two innings. This set the tradition of dramatic confrontations between the stars of the two leagues, and the midsummer classic added to interest in baseball as well as helped build legends.

The 1934 World Series between St. Louis and Detroit was broadcast on the radio for the first time, adding $100,000 to gate receipts, and baseball clubs began to profit from local broadcasts of games. In 1939 NBC telecast the first major league baseball game, featuring the first game of a doubleheader between Brooklyn and Cincinnati at Ebbets Field. This telecast featured after-the-game interviews, done by Red Barber, of the winning Cincinnati pitcher, both managers, and several Dodger players. Although broadcast over an experimental channel and seen only by a few hundred people, the telecast was the promise of the future when television would come to influence and to a large extent control the fortunes and futures of sports.

Night baseball was introduced in Cincinnati in May 1935, when President Franklin D. Roosevelt threw a remote control switch that lighted Crosley Field. The Reds badly needed to bolster a sagging attendance, and night baseball provided an opportunity for working people to see the games. In 1938 Johnny VanderMeer pitched a no-hit, no-run game against the Boston Braves in Cincinnati, and then pitched another no-hitter in Brooklyn at the first night game in history at Ebbets Field. Although VanderMeer eventually lost more career games than he won (119-121) and never won 20 games in a season, he won a place in baseball history with his after-dark performances in 1938.

The introduction of night baseball coincided with a decided upturn in attendance, and by 1940 almost all parks had lights. The Boston Braves held out until 1946. The Chicago Cubs have never had home games at night as William Wrigley opposed the lights on the grounds that the poles were ugly and unaesthetic and the belief that night games would interrupt the life of the neighborhood where Wrigley Field was located. Thus, Wrigley Field has become a kind of historical monument to the environment of baseball in the past, as well as the location of marathon games and astronomical scores.

Another significant development in the early thirties was the building of Cleveland's Municipal Stadium (1930–1932), which opened July 31, 1932. The stadium cost $2.5 million and had a capacity of 78,129. The 1935 All-Star game had an attendance of 69,831 in this stadium, but the Cleveland baseball club did not play regularly here until after World War II because of haggling over the terms of rental. But the Cleveland Municipal Stadium would eventually be the wave of the future, as few owners could afford to build new facilities. Most clubs got by with inadequate or aging ball parks, a situation that eventually caught up with both the Dodgers and the Giants and helped to force their moves to the West Coast in 1957.

The Depression era saw many changes and advances in baseball.

Many franchises experienced hard times and survived the Depression only by radical cost-cutting, player sales and trades, low budget salaries and expenses, and the grim endurance of low attendance. The St. Louis Browns attracted fewer than 100,000 fans in 1933, 1935, and 1936. The Cardinals, winners of the pennant in 1935, drew only 325,056 fans that year. But baseball endured the Depression, and indeed certain teams actually prospered during the difficult times because they sought new talent, spent money for star players, and invested money in minor leagues and scouting systems. Player performances seemed to be adversely affected by the low spirits, bad news, hardships, and failing attendance, especially from 1931 to 1933.

However, the early thirties also saw the introduction of a new breed of ballplayer into the game: the scrappy, hard-playing, and gamey spirits who livened up the game with enthusiasm, boastful pride, and superior athletic skill. Baseball provided an important release and escape from the unemployment and breadlines. Those who could not afford to go to the ball park could at least listen to games on the radio and read the sports columns. The fans found heroes in ballplayers who either made it straight to the big leagues as brash and cocky success stories, or who held on despite advancing age and triumphed when their careers seemed threatened. The 1932, 1933, 1934, and 1935 World Series were filled with bitter contention, spirited animosity, rivalry, vulgar language, and emotional outbursts, thus reflecting the repressed tensions of the period and the gritty toughness of ballplayers as they contested for the big prize of the winner's share.

The fortunes of baseball teams enlivened cities that were hit hard by the Depression, especially Detroit, Chicago, and St. Louis, thus bolstering local pride and creating drama and excitement in a grim period. In the third game of the 1933 World Series between the Giants and the Senators, President Franklin D. Roosevelt was rolled into the Senators' ball park in his wheelchair, and he threw out the first ball. His appearance at the ball park caused a thunderous ovation and then wild excitement as the players scrambled for the prize of the ball he had thrown.

Although he had been in office less than a year, Roosevelt had gained the confidence of the American people as a decisive and fearless leader. He brought back the smile, high spirits, optimism, and undaunted hope. He would later push for more night baseball games so that wartime workers would be able to see games, and he would give the famous "green light" for baseball to continue during the war years. This incident from 1933 shows how baseball parks provided a focus for national life. The game and the parks have always served as an oasis of pastoral greenery and contemplative repose, as well as a place of dramatic confrontation and excitement. During the Depression baseball kept alive dreams and hopes that were otherwise crushed or delayed.

The Depression era was not without an element of zaniness and stuntsmanship, but the period was also filled with personal tragedy for past ballplayers. In May 1933, Al Simmons, Jimmy Dykes, and Red Kress planned to try for a world's record catch with Ted Lyons throwing three balls to each player from the 628 foot Sky Ride Tower at the World's Fair. When White Sox owner Louis A. Comiskey learned that the ball would reach a velocity of over 145 miles per hour with an impact of 60.7 foot-pounds, he called the stunt off to prevent injury.

Later, in August 1939, Joe Sprinz, a catcher for the San Francisco minor league club, tried to catch a ball dropped from a blimp 800 feet above the ground. The force of the ball driving into his outstretched glove smashed the glove into his face, fracturing his jaw, damaging his nose, and knocking him unconscious. The *New York Times* newspaper account also noted that "he dropped the ball." Perhaps Sprinz was trying to make baseball history in the only way he could because he had never made news in the big leagues. He had a .170 lifetime average in three major league seasons with only 53 at bats.

Even the great ones tried to hang on and to cash in on previous reputations. Grover Cleveland Alexander, a Hall of Famer in 1938, was working in early 1939 in a flea circus museum on West Forty-Second Street in New York City. He demonstrated his famous pitches and the slider that he used to strike out Tony Lazzeri with the bases loaded in the seventh game of the 1926 World Series. Alexander was plagued by epilepsy and alcoholism, but he was one of the game's greatest players and a proud man who spurned charity as many people did during the hard times.

College Football

The Depression presented economic challenges to many college football programs. Yet in 1931 seventy thousand fans crammed their way into the Rose Bowl to see Alabama down Washington State 24-0. However, rising costs and violence in the game threatened college football programs. The president of Butler University announced in 1932 that its athletic program had put the school $1 million in debt and that athletic expenditures were "millstones about the neck of the school which bid fair to bankrupt and close it within five years." President Henry Smith of the Carnegie Foundation for the Advancement of Teaching suggested, perhaps tongue in cheek, that the colleges turn to horseracing as a revenue-producing sport.

At the twenty-fifth annual National Collegiate Athletic Association convention in 1931, several college presidents, notably from the Ivy League, commented strongly against football's role in university life. Dr. James R. Angell of Yale stated: "I believe that any system which by its very nature encourages proselytizing among boy athletes in the secondary schools is pernicious. I do not believe there is any obligation on the part of the college to furnish the general public nor even the alumni with substitutes for the circus, the prize fight, and the gladiatorial combat."

In a similar vein, Dr. Charles W. Kennedy of Princeton declared: "I earnestly hope that the colleges of our country . . . will deflate intercollegiate football and restore it to its natural place in the life of the undergraduates. Should they fail to do so, I predict that it will be done for them by the forces of undergraduate and public opinion."

Other critics portrayed the sport as too brutal and violent. Statistics on fatalities seemed to substantiate the critics' contentions. In 1930 there were only thirteen fatalities attributed to football. In 1931 this figure soared to forty. To combat these charges of brutality, and to eliminate potentially hazardous situations, the most sweeping rule changes in the college game were instituted in 1932. The most important of these were the following:

1. The ball was dead when any portion of the player, except his hands or feet, touched the ground.
2. The use of the flying block and flying tackle was prohibited.
3. Equipment needed to be covered with padding at least three-eights of an inch thick.
4. Players on defense were forbidden to strike an opponent on the head, neck, or face.

Yet despite these changes twenty-five fatalities were recorded in 1934 and thirty in 1935. Further statistics compiled for the 1935 football season revealed 55,444 injuries for 66,000 high school teams, and 9,900 injuries to 829 college teams. The end results were an estimated 1 million days of education lost.

By October 1932, *Time* magazine could report that college football attendance on the Pacific Coast was unchanged, while football attendance declined by 15 percent in the Midwest and 20 percent in the

East. However, by 1935 Time could report that college football attracted 20 million spectators, an increase of 12 percent in the numbers viewing college gridiron battles, bringing attendance totals to the level of 1929.

Yet Time commented that this increase in attendance was not to be construed as a sign of prosperity returning but attributed it to the policy of colleges strengthening their schedules, avoiding "set-ups" or "patsies" so that the confrontations were as attractive as possible. As proof, Time noted that ten years earlier, only a few late season games drew 50,000 spectators, while it pointed out that two late season games in 1935 had drawn 161,000.

Spectator behavior also caused concern. At the University of Wisconsin, four alumni who were former athletes served as a football day enforcer squad to discourage overly rowdy behavior. And in Montgomery, Alabama, Sheriff Haygood Patterson offered his solution for crowd rowdyism by suggesting that a pillory be located outside the stadium where "caged drunks" could be exhibited after the games.

Although economic prospects might have been bleak and dismal during the decade, college football did not suffer a lack of successful elevens. The unbeaten Alabama team that whipped Washington State in the 1931 Rose Bowl and the unbeaten 1934 team, led by the passing wizardry of Dixie Howell and ends Paul Bryant and Don Hutson, were regarded by experts as two of the strongest teams to come out of the South. In 1931, in one of the big games of the decade, Southern California opposed Notre Dame before 52,000 fans at South Bend. The crowd included such Notre Dame subway alumni as New York Mayor Jimmy Walker, Chicago Mayor Anton Cermak, and industrialist Edsel Ford. Southern Cal stopped a three-year unbeaten Notre Dame victory skein by eking out a 16-14 victory with a last-minute field goal.

Meanwhile on the West Coast, Stanford enjoyed banner years in the early thirties as they appeared in three successive Rose Bowls—1933, 1934, and 1935. The Stanford team was led by the "Vow Boys"—so called because they vowed that they would never be beaten by USC. (They kept their vow.)

In the Big Ten, Michigan shared the title with Northwestern in 1930, with Purdue and Northwestern in 1931, and held outright championships in 1932 and 1933. Although Michigan fielded an inferior eleven in 1934, it did feature an All-American center named Gerald Ford, who went on to become president of the United States when Richard M. Nixon, a former football player at Whittier College, resigned over the Watergate scandal.

The middle years of the decade were dominated by the coaching of Bernie Bierman of Minnesota and Jock Sutherland of Pittsburgh. Bierman's Minnesota teams captured the Big Ten title in 1934, 1935, 1937, and 1938, with his 1934 and 1936 teams being honored with national championship trophies. Highlights of Bierman's tenure at Minnesota included a dramatic 1934 victory over Sutherland's Pitt team and the appearance of Bud Wilkinson (later to become one of the game's great coaches) as quarterback of the 1936 national championship team after having toiled two years as a lineman. An oddity that year was that Minnesota did not win the Big Ten title, having lost to Northwestern 6-0. Notre Dame later beat Northwestern, however, and the wire service awarded the mythical national championship to the Gophers.

The Michigan team featured the great running of Tom Harmon, although he never played on a championship team and the Maize and Blue never beat Minnesota in his career from 1938–1940. Harmon was a talented halfback who could run, pass, and kick with equal skill. In his career he rushed for 2,134 yards, passed for 17 touchdowns, and scored 33 touchdowns. He passed for over 1,000 yards, averaging 13 yards per pass. Harmon led his team to wins over Ivy League powers Yale and Penn in the 1939 season, and in the 1940 opener he ran for 4 touchdowns and passed for 1 against California. Harmon ended the season with 33 career touchdowns, breaking Red Grange's scoring record and winning the national scoring title two times.

Harmon gave up a certain career in pro football to pursue a sportscasting career in Detroit, but he did eventually play two years of pro ball (1946–47) for the Los Angeles Rams. Wartime injuries slowed him down, and he quit to return to his promising sportscasting career. He became the first of many players to turn to the microphone in order to stay with the game.

Some of the greatest individuals to ever set foot on the gridiron performed during the thirties. Three of the most outstanding stars included Jay Berwanger of the University of Chicago (first Heisman Trophy winner in 1935), Colorado's Byron ''Whizzer'' White (All-American, 1937 and later to become a Supreme Court justice), and Iowa's Nile Kinnick (winner of the Heisman, Maxwell, and Walter Camp trophies in 1939).

By the end of the decade such teams as national championship Texas Christian University in 1938, Texas A&M in 1939, and the strong teams of General Bob Neyland of Tennessee in 1938 and 1939 indicated that the old guard of college football was changing. Also, in the West, UCLA fielded its first undefeated team in its history, featuring a halfback tandem of Kenny Washington and Jackie Robinson, both young black Americans who would be pioneers in the professional sports world.

To many athletes college football was a godsend during the Depression, offering the security of an education and usually an on-campus job. College football provided excitement during dull and grim times, and fans were even willing to pay scalper's prices for tickets to the "big game." The 1935 showdown between unbeaten Ohio State and Notre Dame caused such excitement that last-minute ticket seekers paid $50 for ducats.

Bernie Bierman built his dynasty at Minnesota by finding first-generation college students who wanted a degree and wanted to play football—a strong offer during a period of economic crisis and widespread unemployment. Bierman built a team around loyalty to him and the school, and he established the winning tradition that forms the cornerstone of a successful college athletic program. The Big Ten schools discovered Notre Dame's success formula, and during the Depression the "alma mater" was more than just a phrase in a school song. It was a home, a place where one could still find fun, companionship, security, and meaning in one's work (football or studies) with hope for the future when one graduated.

Professional Football

In the thirties, professional football became truly "professional," eventually rivaling baseball for the sports fans' dollar. The Green Bay Packers, New York Giants, and Chicago Bears emerged as the top teams. Yet in the early thirties, pro football's prospects for survival seemed about as good as President Hoover's prospects for reelection. On November 8, 1931, the New York Giants emulated baseball and held pro football's first ladies' day for their game against Portsmouth, Ohio. In 1932 the league was reduced to eight members, and the Chicago Bears played the Portsmouth Spartans in the Chicago Stadium for the NFL championship.

Because of December blizzard conditions in the Windy City the game was played indoors on a makeshift field that was only 80 yards long. The goalposts were moved from the end zone line to the goal line for the purposes of safety, and the in-bounds hashmarks were set 10 yards from the sidelines. The only touchdown, a pass from Bronko Nagurski to Red Grange, was disputed by the Portsmouth team, which claimed that the jump pass was thrown less than 5 yards behind the line of scrimmage. The pass came on a fourth down and goal to go. Nagurski faked a plunge and threw a short toss to Grange, a play that Nagurski had perfected.

The dispute over this touchdown was to change the game as the line of scrimmage became the legal firing line for passes the next season. The jump pass would soon give way to the quarterback who set up to pass and thrust forward, not fall backward.

New offensive territory was opened up by the rule change. Some 11,000 plus spectators watched the Bears triumph 9-0. Total receipts at the gate were $15,000, the amount that a modern day player in a Super Bowl contest receives for a losing effort.

In 1936 a rival league, the American Football League, sprang up with six teams. However, this league, which included the Los Angeles Bulldogs, folded in 1937. Another rival league was revived in 1940–41, but folded unceremoniously.

The next year, following suggestions of George Preston Marshall, owner of the Boston franchise, the teams were divided into two divisions and a playoff was established between division winners. In addition, to add scoring punch to the game, goal posts were placed at the goal line to make field goals easier. Also a rule change allowed a forward pass to be thrown anywhere behind the line of scrimmage instead of five yards back of it.

Professional football during the early thirties reflected the philosophy that football was a man's game played between the tackle positions. It was a rough, tough game, dominated by the single wing, which emphasized overwhelming defense combined with blocking manpower. Such an offense required durable, powerful runners such as the legendary Bronko Nagurski of the Chicago Bears. But even this 230-pound battering ram was affected by the rule changes. In the 1933 championship game, utilizing the new rule on passing, Nagurski on a crucial play began his usual charge toward the line but then rose up abruptly and passed to a receiver. The Bears won the game 23-21 when Nagurski passed to Bill Hewitt, who lateraled it to Bill Karr for the score. Further innovation in the pro game came in 1934 when the New York Giants, trailing 10-3 at the half, were supplied with basketball sneakers to ensure better footing over the frozen Polo Grounds field. The end result was that the Giants scored 27 points in the second half and won 30-13.

In 1934 Beattie Feathers of the Bears rushed for 1,004 yards on only 101 attempts to become the NFL's first 1,000 yard rusher. It would be 1947 before another player (Steve Van Buren of Philadelphia) reached that plateau. Feathers followed the devastating blocking of Bronko Nagurski, and Feathers' record was set in eleven games as he missed the last two games of the season due to a shoulder injury. Feathers' 9.94 average gain still stands as the record in that category.

In 1936 the pros instituted the football draft with initially dismal results. Its first choice, Jay Berwanger of the University of Chicago, the first Heisman Trophy winner, declined to join the pros. Eventually, the collegiate draft would become the mainstay of the restocking of the National Football League and of ensuring a competitive distribution of talent, since the team finishing last in the standings would have first choice in each round of the next player draft.

Two players in the thirties would be harbingers of pro football play in the post-World War II period. The first of these was Don Hutson, premier pass receiver of the Green Bay Packers. He was the first pass receiver to utilize the advantage of faking on pass routes, and this ability, combined with his brilliant speed, allowed him to lead the league in pass receptions in eight of his eleven seasons in the league. Hutson led the league five consecutive years from 1941 to 1945, catching 14 passes in a game against the Giants in 1942. Hutson's name is long remembered, but the quarterback who threw him the passes has been largely forgotten. However, Arnie Herber led the league in pass completions and touchdown passes in 1932, 1934, and 1936, throwing for 1,239 yards in 1936, when the Packers won the NFL championship.

"Slinging" Sammy Baugh was the other revolutionary player of the thirties. Master of the spot pass, Baugh could utilize his passing in both long and short situations. Baugh had been an outstanding passer at TCU—some say the best ever in collegiate football.

George Marshall, who had moved his Redskin team to Washington from Boston, had the presence of mind to see that the future of pro football was a game that would appeal to families. He introduced marching bands, parades, and Indian medicine. He also saw the value of the forward pass, selecting the rookie quarterback Baugh in 1937 to lead his team. Baugh's passing propelled the Redskins into the 1937 championship game against the "monsters of the Midway," the powerful Chicago Bears. Baugh proved too much even for the Bears. Hitting for touchdown passes of 55, 77, and 35 yards, Baugh's aerial attack doomed the Bears to defeat—a foreshadowing of the importance to the pro game of the passing attack and a quarterback who could execute it.

Baugh led the league in passing for six seasons, never twice in a row, and in his remarkable season of 1945 completed 128 of 182 passes (70.33 percent) and had only four interceptions. He also led the league in punting from 1940 to 1943, averaging over 45 yards per punt in his career.

By 1938 *Time* magazine could report that the NFL was so proud of its product that it played a game in Paris before 25,000 bemused Parisians who thought the game was "too much like an autobus collision." *Time* did report that the Parisians cheered the most when the teams huddled—although it gave no reason for the crowd's unusual response.

The pro football game saw important innovations and developments in the thirties. The first pro-college All-Star game was played at Soldier Field in August 1934 with almost 80,000 in attendance. The Pro Bowl game between the NFL champion and a team of all-stars was first played in Los Angeles in January 1939. The first pro football game was televised in New York City in 1939, but television would not become a reality in pro football until the 1950 season.

The Depression era also saw pro football go through a period of retrenchment and instability. From twenty-two teams in 1926 during the Golden Age of Sports, the NFL shrank to ten teams in 1931 and to eight franchises in 1932, the bottom of the Depression. A number of franchises moved, and others were forfeited or collapsed. By 1936 the franchise situation stabilized, and by 1937 there were ten teams, all playing eleven games each. Franchises were held together by determined business-promoters like George Marshall, George Halas, Earl "Curly" Lambeau, Timothy J. Mara, and others. The league strengthened its image with the popular College All-Star game, which showcased college talent in their first true test against the pros. The league began keeping official statistics in 1932, thus giving football a basis for comparison of performances that it definitely needed as well as a means of publicity. The Spaulding Sporting Goods Company published the annual football guides from 1935 to 1941, when the league began publishing its *Official Record Manual*.

Pro football in the thirties was played by tough, hardened veterans. The game was violent, and required a determination to play with injuries. Red Grange had seriously injured his right knee in 1927, and he had to become a defensive specialist when he lost his speed and ability to make cuts. He retired from football in 1934. It took courage to try to stop the 6 foot 2 inch, 230-pound Bronko Nagurski, and on one afternoon two tacklers who tried to corral Bronko went off with broken collarbones after attempting to tackle him in the open field on the same run. This grim character of the game appealed to people hardened by the Depression conditions. Pro football players were individualists, such as George Musso who shunned wearing protective pads. As franchises became stabilized and team traditions were being built, fan interest increased. The 1940 championship game was carried by the Mutual Broadcasting System to 120 radio stations, an indication of expanding national interest. By the end of the thirties, with the development of a new style of play and with an emphasis on entertainment, pro football had established itself as one of the premier sporting attractions.

Basketball

Basketball remained defense oriented as the center jump after each basket dictated a style that demanded a kangaroo-like center, clever ball-handling guards, and swift, fast-moving forwards who would be constantly in motion. The most clever exponents of this shifty, pass-oriented ball playing were to be found in the depths of Gotham City. City College of New York, Fordham, Columbia, Long Island University, and Manhattan all fielded strong teams, but the best of the lot was the so-called "Wonder Five" of St. John's University.

Composed of Matty Begovich, a 6 foot 5 inch center from Hoboken, and four Jewish players from Brooklyn—Mac Kinsbrunner, Max Posnak, Rip Geyson, and Allie Schuckmann—and coached by Buck Freeman, the St. John's five reflected the defensive orientation of the decade. During their four years together, only one opponent managed to amass over 40 points against St. John's. In the 1929–30 season they held their opponents to under 21 points a game. Employing speedy passing and close-knit teamwork, the Wonder Five were able to reel off a victory total of 86 wins in 94 games in four years together. The Wonder Five toured as an independent team for two years after graduation and then spent five years playing together as the Jewels in the American League. In 1938 they disbanded, having played together as a unit for eleven years.

Basketball had never proven to be a major box office attraction, but this was to change in the thirties. In 1931 Mayor Jimmy Walker of New York City sought to procure unemployment relief funds through the sponsorship of benefit basketball games at Madison Square Garden. On January 19, 1931, a triple header, featuring New York college teams, attracted over 15,000 people with hundreds more turned away. Later, on February 22, 1933, over 20,000 attended a seven-game extravaganza at the Garden.

The profit potential of good college basketball was exemplified by these charity exhibitions, which attracted many sharp-eyed promoters who sought to encourage the Garden to stage college games and to act as promoters. The Garden management turned down many of the more spurious offers, waiting for a more solid, stable program to be offered. To the forefront stepped a clever, twenty-five-year-old sportswriter for the New York *World Telegram*, Ned Irish. Backed by the financing of the New York Giants organization, for whom he worked part time in public relations, he obtained an agreement whereby he would promote college basketball in Madison Square Garden. According to the terms, Irish would guarantee the Garden $4,000 plus a percentage of the profits over $4,000. His strategy was to feature local schools against strong teams from all over the country. In his initial doubleheader, held on December 29, 1934, Notre Dame played NYU in the featured game and the matchup attracted over 16,000 fans. Irish had proven that college basketball could sell, and by the end of the decade, the aim of any big time college program was to play at the Garden in the "Big Apple."

Not everyone was happy with college ball in Madison Square Garden. In its January 6, 1936, issue the *Nation* commented, somewhat prophetically, that "it's obvious that a college basketball team has no more place in a professional sports arena like Madison Square Garden than a Jew in Hitler's bath tub." And another commentator solemnly declared with equal insight that the "game will not be long immune to professionalism and overemphasis."

Prior to World War II collegiate basketball reflected a geographical dimension. The East possessed the most adept passers and ball handlers, West the most accurate shooters, and the Midwest and West the most aggressive rebounders. Yet despite its reputation for shooting accuracy, western basketball was held largely in contempt by eastern exponents of the game. Difficulty in transcontinental travel prevented an accurate estimation of western collegiate basketball proficiency. In 1931 UCLA traveled to the Midwest and lost 6 of 7 games. In 1935 California visited the East Coast and worked its way back west, losing seven in a row after an initial victory. These few instances of intersectional rivalry seemed to provide credence to eastern claims of basketball superiority.

In 1936, however, a Stanford team, featuring the one-handed shooting of its star Hank Luisetti traveled to the East. Stanford first beat Temple 45-38 in Philadelphia and then on December 30, 1936, played Coach Claire Bee's Long Island University team. The proud possessors of a 43-game winning streak, they were the foremost exponents of the eastern game—intricate passing and use of the two-hand set shot. The LIU win streak was stopped at 43 as Stanford stifled the Blackbirds behind Luisetti's 15 points and superb passing. The press and the public were captivated by the unorthodox tactics of Stanford's so-called "laughing boys."

Besides superior field goal accuracy, Luisetti was capable of dribbling and passing behind his back and passing while faking in midair while on a drive to the hoop. Today this action is part of the repertoire of every alley ball player but at that time was a feat of unparalleled proportions. In his senior year, Luisetti scored 50 points against Duquesne, set a single season scoring record in the Pacific Coast Conference that stood for twelve years, and established a national four-year college scoring record with 1,533 points. Luisetti's greatest impact was that he was a star in a game that had featured teamwork and coaching strategy. Though he did not originate the one hander, he was properly credited for popularizing it. He had proven that with new techniques a single player could dynamically alter years of basketball concepts and theories.

A revolution overtook college basketball in 1938. There were several reasons for this. First, the center jump was eliminated, and second, the first national basketball tournament was established. Coach Sam Barry of USC had long campaigned for the elimination of the center jump, contending that it gave an automatic advantage to a team with a much taller center as well as slowed down the flow and rhythm of the game. According to research that Barry and others had done, the elimination of the jump except at the start of each half resulted in an additional four minutes of playing time and had an increase in scoring of about 10 points a game.

In 1938 the Metropolitan Basketball Writers Convention sponsored an intercollegiate basketball tournament for the purpose of determining a national champion. The six teams in the tournament included New York University, Long Island University, Bradley, Temple, Colorado, and Oklahoma A&M. Left out of the tournament were such outstanding teams as Purdue, the Big Ten champ, Dartmouth, the kingpin of the Eastern Intercollegiate Conference, and Stanford, the Pacific Coast Conference leader. In the finale, Temple's Owls coasted by Colorado to the tune of 60-36. In 1939, undoubtedly stung by the success of the National Invitation Tournament and angered by the number of outstanding teams that had not been invited to the NIT, the NCAA began its own tournament. The tournament finals were held at Northwestern University's gym, and Oregon emerged as the first NCAA champ with a 46-33 victory over Ohio State in the finals. Nicknamed the "Tall Firs," the Oregon team featured a 6 foot 8 inch center and a pair of 6 foot 4 inch forwards, a fairly short front line by today's standards. The team had stamina as well as disciplined play. The five regulars played 39 minutes of the game, and scored all the 46 points, and the Ducks did not call a time out while Ohio State called five. Oregon had a controlled fast-break attack, and they shifted from a zone to a man-to-man easily and quickly. To demonstrate their staying power, they had, in December 1938, played 10 games in twenty-two days from Portland to Philadelphia and San Francisco. The team was made up almost entirely of native Oregonians, and the two guards, Bobby Arnet and Wally Johansen, had played together since junior high.

The fast-moving, aggressive Oregon team signaled a new open style of play combined with conditioning, instinctive teamwork, and businesslike determination. As the game opened up, accurate outside shooting with two-hand set shots was replaced by fast break drive-ins, patterned breaks whenever rebounds permitted them, and plays that worked the ball inside to the big men.

The institution of the NCAA tournament initiated great discussion each year as to whether the NIT or the NCAA crowned the true national champion.

Chicago was also host in 1939 to the world's first professional basketball tournament. Pro basketball during the decade was definitely a third-class, haphazard organization. Teams played in the equivalent of today's semipro leagues, as "amateurs" in industrial leagues, or in barnstorming outfits.

The most successful "pro" outfit of the thirties was a team of black touring pros, the New York Rens. Organized in 1922 in Harlem by Bob Douglas, the Rens hit their high point in the years 1932 to 1936 when they won 473 and lost 49—many of their losses coming on controversial calls by obviously biased officials. In fact, the entire 1932 to 1936 teams were inducted into basketball's Hall of Fame.

The Rens' team reflected the results of racial discrimination in the other pro sports. Fat Jenkins, the Rens' captain, for example, belied his name by being the fastest baseball player in the Negro National League. Bill Yancey starred for twenty years as a hard-hitting shortstop. Bruiser Saitch won numerous Negro national tennis team titles but was never asked to play on the Davis Cup teams or against the established white stars of the era.

The 1933–34 season provided the Rens with their greatest success. That year they ran up a string of eighty-eight consecutive wins and finished the season with a 127-7 record. Although the Rens claimed the crown of world champions during the 1932–1936 seasons, there was no official champion.

Basketball during the thirties initially reflected a regional approach in terms of styles and appeal. New York, the Midwest, and West were the hotbeds of the hoop game. In 1936 *Time* magazine estimated that 100 of the top 500 basketball players in America came from Indiana. It commented that "to the state as flat as a gym floor, basketball has an overwhelming universal appeal like hockey in Norway." The Hoosier "madness" produced a climate of small-town pride in the high school basketball team, and made local heroes of home town boys who carried the honor and reputation of their town. The famous Indiana state championship tournament became a ritual providing excitement that broke the routine and dullness of rural and small-town life near the end of the winter.

Basketball in the thirties provided excitement to a Depression

America that found regions of the country isolated from each other and locked in the grip of economic paralysis and insulation. Basketball games connected towns, and teams reflected community pride and spirit, bringing people together in an era that was notably lacking in fun and the shared excitement of competition. Appropriately enough, the first NCAA national tournament lost money—$2,531 to be exact. The finals of the tournament were moved to Madison Square Garden in 1943. The late thirties saw more teams traveling and playing games in other parts of the country, and this had the long-range effect of standardizing the rules of interpretation and officiating. Indeed, basketball helped to bring the country out of its regional and local isolation as college basketball became more financially secure and profitable. The competition now became truly national.

Although college basketball was still dominated by whites during the decade, this did not mean that ethnic animosities had been eliminated. In its February 24, 1936, issue, *Time* reported that after NYU's team of one Swede, one Irishman, and eight Jews lost to Georgetown 36-34, NYU's campus newspapers claimed that the health and safety of the players were endangered by "Georgetown's insane . . . Jew hating following." Obviously basketball, the "City Game" as it is known in today's vernacular, was already serving as a social steppingstone for an ethnic minority.

In summary, college basketball during the early years of the decade was dominated by defense and passing. With the elimination of the center jump, the popularization of new shooting techniques, and the introduction of college contests to the Madison Square Garden, basketball became modernized and was ready for a new era as well as a new decade by 1940.

Boxing

Joe Louis was the story of boxing during the thirties. He was the son of an Alabama sharecropper, Munroe Barrow, who became mentally imbalanced while struggling to support his family on worn-out land. Louis's mother remarried a widower named Pat Brooks, who moved his family to Detroit in 1924 because of better job opportunities.

In Detroit, Joe attended Brewster Trade School, where he learned woodworking and boxing. However, boxing lost its priority for Joe once he gained a job at a Ford plant. His stepfather had been laid off at Ford, and Joe became the breadwinner of the family. Although lacking time and energy, Joe kept up his interest in boxing. Even after he lost his first amateur bout, Joe found his appetite for the ring had been whetted.

His stepfather, well aware that black Americans were faring even worse than their white counterparts in the Depression, persuaded Joe that he should abandon boxing and be content with having a job. His mother, however, gave her moral support and, more importantly, financial aid to underwrite her son's boxing career.

As an amateur, Louis won 50 bouts, forty-three by knockouts, and lost only 4. His amateur record so impressed veteran sportswriters that Nat Fleisher of the New York *Amsterdam News* warned his readers to "watch Joe Louis," while Walter Stewart of the *New York World Telegram and Sun* eloquently described Louis's ring qualities in the following words: "He is a pugilistic symphony with a tempo geared to bring him across the ring with all the grace of a gazelle and the cold fury of an enraged mountain lion. He is a new type fighter who shows a style combining exquisite harmony of movement with crushing power stored in each hand."

On July 4, 1934, Louis fought his first bout as a professional and recorded his first win when he decked Jack Kracken at Chicago in the first round. Almost three years later on June 22, 1937, he would capture the world heavyweight championship with an eighth round knockout of James Braddock. America's love affair with the "Brown Bomber" had begun.

Louis's backers—John Roxborough, a prominent black Detroiter, and Julian Black, a Chicago promoter—carefully brought Louis along, knowing full well the difficulties of promoting a black professional athlete in economically distressed times. Boxing was a suspect sport that still reeked of the racism directed at its last black heavyweight champion, the controversial Jack Johnson. Yet Joe Louis's appearance came at a fortuitous and opportune time. Boxing needed a "savior," and the American people needed a hero. Louis proved to be both.

Louis battled his way to 27 straight wins, including a fourth round victory over the recently deposed champion Max Baer at Yankee Stadium, a fight that brought the million-dollar gate back to boxing. Then he ran into the German champion, Max Schmeling. Schmeling knocked Louis out in the twelfth round of their bout, exploiting Louis's propensity to lower his guard while jabbing, which left him vulnerable to the right cross.

Undaunted, Louis continued a new victory skein and through the unscrupulousness of Joe Gould, the manager of the current champion, James Braddock, was able to secure a title bout. Braddock previously had been contracted to fight Schmeling in Madison Square Garden. But Gould, in return for a percentage of the profits to be derived from the Twentieth Century Sporting Club's bouts for ten years, signed a contract for a bout with Louis. A Newark, New Jersey, judge later declared the first contract invalid. Thus on June 22, 1937, Louis became World Heavyweight Champion, knocking out Jim Braddock in eight rounds in Comiskey Park in Chicago before 45,000 deliriously happy fans.

The fight of the thirties was the second Louis-Schmeling battle. The long-awaited confrontation contained large doses of irony. By 1938 affairs in Nazi Germany had aroused the ire of many Americans. The Nazi press and propaganda machine, trying to recoup their pride after the embarrassment of the 1936 Olympics, promoted the fight as a contest that would demonstrate Aryan supremacy. To combat this German wunderkind and representative of the master race was a black American whose people had suffered from the results of racial bias and prejudice.

Americans all over the country united as one to support their champion. On June 22, 1938, 70,000 excited ring fans crowded into Yankee Stadium to produce a total gate of $940,096.17. They were not disappointed. At 3:04 of the first round, the referee stopped the count at 5 after Louis had knocked Schmeling down three times and administered one of the most thorough beatings ever witnessed in a championship bout. Meanwhile, German fans had to be content with a delayed account of the fight. Mysteriously, the German radio network's master switchboard had been thrown immediately following Schmeling's first knockdown.

After the fight, Michigan's governor, Frank Murphy, personally congratulated Louis, telling him that "Michigan is proud of you." Louis's victory meant so much more. He certainly had proven to be a superior master in the ring—a deadly fighting machine who had vanquished the champion of the hated Nazis. More importantly, he served as a positive inspiration to millions of impoverished black youths who could now identify with an authentic American hero who was of their race.

Louis's victory set off spontaneous street demonstrations in Harlem, and in other places whites and blacks united in celebrations. As Anthony O. Edmonds has pointed out in his "The Second Louis-Schmeling Fight—Sport, Symbol, and Culture" in the *Journal of Popular Culture* (summer, 1973), Americans felt helpless to stem the tide of Nazi aggression in Europe, and this bout symbolized American abhorrence of Nazi doctrines of supremacy and nationalism. Louis himself was aware of the political implications of the fight, and his determination was steeled by the talk of master race and Nazi supremacy. Louis appealed to whites and blacks, and during his twelve years as champion he held the title with dignity and pride. His life symbolized the hopes of many blacks who had been transplanted into northern cities during the Depression when tenant farmers and sharecroppers were squeezed out of the southern landholding system. Louis was the product of the city, representing what hard work, family support, discipline, and raw skill honed into professional talent could accomplish. He was the man of the hour in 1938, and he was a symbol of the new black man who could assert himself and find a place in a society where acceptance was always qualified and grudging. With one event he truly became a national figure and proved himself equal to the task and superior to his foe.

Track and Field

Track in the thirties hailed the emergence of numerous black stars, particularly in the sprints and jumping events. In 1932 Los Angeles hosted the Olympics, and black trackmen played a starring role. In a stirring 100-meter final Eddie Tolan was given the electric clock's decision over Ralph Metcalfe in what appeared to be a dead heat. He won in 10.3 seconds, an Olympic record, and returned the 100-meter crown to the United States after a twelve-year absence. In the 220-yard dash event Tolan also flashed to victory in a record 21.2 seconds, again edging out Metcalfe. The 400-meter race, featuring two white American stars, was an equally dramatic affair. Ben Eastman, the world-record holder at 46.4 seconds, was edged out by Bill Carr, who set a world record of 46.2.

The 1936 Olympics held in Berlin were really a mockery of the Olympic ideal, for Hitler had sought to make the games a demonstration of German athletic superiority. Playing an instrumental role in demolishing the myth of Aryan supremacy were the so-called black auxiliaries—the small band of American black track and field athletes who helped gain twelve gold medals for the team.

The chief thorn in Hitler's side was the incomparable Jesse Owens. A year earlier on May 25, 1935, on a memorable afternoon in Ann Arbor, Owens, representing Ohio State at the Big Ten championships, had demonstrated that he was one of the greatest track stars of all time. Within the span of 70 minutes, he established three world records and tied another. He ran the 100-yard dash in 9.4 seconds and tied the world record, long jumped 26 feet 8¹/₄ inches (a distance only broken by Ralph Boston twenty-five years later), won the 220-yard dash in 20.3, a world record, and ran the 220-yard low hurdles in a record 22.6 clocking.

At Berlin, Owens swept the 100-meter dash in 10.3, closely followed by Ralph Metcalfe. He then raced to an Olympic record of 20.07 in the 200-meter with Mack Robinson taking second place. He then beat the German long jumper, Luz Long, leaping 26 feet 5¹/₄ inches, a record that stood until 1960. Jesse also ran a leg on the 400-meter relay team, helping them to establish a world record for the event.

Owens was a gifted and disciplined athlete with an immense dedication to his sport and a concentration on performance. His victories in Berlin were personal triumphs over racial theories and prejudice that blacks had struggled against for generations. He was a quiet and unassuming man who took his victories with pride and restraint, letting the bursts of speed and controlled, powerful acceleration speak of his personal pride and skills.

The black athlete has often competed against the sport and the records, rarely finding full social acceptance after the performance. But the 1936 American team had several black athletes who wore their country's banner with pride and dignity. These men signaled the fact that black athletes could dominate a sport that was open to them. However, it would take a war to change the climate that would lead to the end of the "color line" in professional sports.

Other outstanding black sprint athletes who starred at the Berlin Olympics included Archie Williams, who captured the 400-meter race with Jimmy LuValle of UCLA (the only Phi Beta Kappa on the Olympic squad) coming in third; Johnny Woodruff, who outlasted Italy's Mario Lanzi in the 800 meter; and Cornelius Johnson, who leaped 6 feet 7⁷/₈ inches to win the high jump with Dave Albritton taking second. America's black track athletes had truly demonstrated that the German contention of Aryan superiority was unfounded.

In addition to the outstanding performances of the black athletes on the 1936 Olympic team, white athletes also performed well. World record holder in the mile, Glenn Cunningham, finished second in the 1,500-meter run, yet he ran under the world record as did the three runners who finished behind him. Unfortunately for Cunningham and the others in the 1,500-meter field, Jack Lovelock of New Zealand sprinted the last lap in 57.8 seconds, shattering the world record by a full second.

Other medal winners for the U.S. in track and field included Glenn Hardin in the 400-meter hurdles; Forrest Towns in the 110-meter hurdles; Earle Meadows in the pole vault; and Glenn Morris, the decathlon winner, who led a U.S. sweep of the medals, with Robert Clark finishing second and Jack Parker third.

One of the most dramatic American victories came in the discus throw. Germany's Willie Schroeder, holder of the world record in the event, was the favorite to capture the event. German spectators chanted "Take the discus in your hand and throw it for the Fatherland." Schroeder finished fifth while American Kenneth Carpenter finished first and Gordon G. Dunn finished second. An American had not won this event since 1924.

The Germans swept the rest of the weight events, while the Finns went 1-2 in the 5,000-meter, 1-2-3 in the 10,000-meter, and 1-2 in the 3,000-meter steeplechase.

Japan's Kitei Son was a surprise victor in the marathon and Shoryu Nan of Japan was an even more surprising third. Finns finished fourth and fifth.

In women's track Helen Stephens, a slender farm girl from Missouri, established a world record in the 100-meter in 11.5 and then anchored the gold medal 400-meter relay team in 46.9. One member of the relay team, Annette Rogers, had been a member of the gold medal team in 1932.

The Berlin Olympics were the last for twelve years. Despite the $30 million lavished on the games and the technical and mechanical efficiency demonstrated by the German authorities, the politicization of the games made many wary that the Olympic spirit could be maintained. Hitler's subsequent militaristic actions after 1936 demonstrated that the games in Berlin were merely a showcase for fascism and, for the Germans, not a true demonstration of the Olympic spirit.

1932 Winter Olympics

The 1932 Winter Olympics were held in Lake Placid, New York, and provided many Americans with firsthand views of sports that they had perhaps only read about or had seen in pictures or in films. Prior to this time there were no ski tows in operation in the United States. In 1933 the first ski tow went into operation at Woodstock, Vermont, and skiing would become a major winter sport for Americans. Today the sport attracts over 3 million participants annually.

Speed skating and bobsledding were the events dominated by Americans. The speed skating domination was explained by the fact that the event was held under American rules. Europeans skated in pairs against the clock, while Americans raced in a pack in heats to get to the finals, much like the competition in track and field. Despite the European protests, the events were held in that manner. The American experience in pack racing, where sharp elbows and the ability to avoid getting boxed in sometimes counted for as much as sheer speed and endurance, gave them the edge.

The United States was led by the duo of Jack Shea, who captured the 500- and 1,500-meter events, and Irving Jaffee, who swept the 5,000- and 10,000-meter contests. Ivar Ballangrud, the great Norwegian star of the 1928 Olympics, could only manage a silver medal in the 10,000-meter event. Meanwhile, in the bobsled competition, Americans took the gold and bronze in the two-man event and the gold and silver in the four-man event.

In ice hockey the United States again competed and took their familiar second place finish. Canada once again captured the gold.

Sonja Henie of Norway captured her second Olympic crown in women's figure skating. Americans gained a bronze in the women's figure skating and a silver in the pairs skating. Once again Finns, Swedes, and Norwegians dominated the skiing events.

The number of teams attending the winter Olympics at Lake Placid was only seventeen. Japan entered a team for the first time. And, as noted previously, the exposure given to winter sports helped stimulate American interest in them, particularly figure skating and skiing.

1936 Winter Olympics

The winter games of the 1936 Olympics were held at Garmisch-Partenkirchen in southern Germany. Adolf Hitler was present, and a capacity crowd of 15,000 filled the stadium while thousands of others waited outside, hoping to obtain tickets.

The 1936 Winter Olympics were not a successful venture for the United States from a medal standpoint. The United States took first and third in two-man bobsledding, a third in the 500-meter speed skating, and a third in ice hockey. Great Britain finished first and Canada second. (Canada had protested, to no avail, the number of naturalized Canadians who played for the British team.) Otherwise the games belonged to the Scandinavians and the Germans.

Sonja Henie captured her third straight Olympic title and parlayed it into a movie career. Norwegians also dominated the speed skating event, with Ivar Ballangrud of Norway taking the 500-, 5,000-, and 10,000-meter events.

The downhill and slalom runs were computed together for one title, and Germans captured the gold and silver in both the men's and women's competition. Sweden and Norway dominated the rest of the skiing competition.

Tennis

Tennis during the thirties was still basically an amateur game. This simply meant that amateurs were given expense money under the table. Even during the depths of the Depression, tennis remained an upper-class game supported by society's elite, not only in the United States but in other parts of the world. In its July 13, 1936, issue, *Time* magazine made the following comment: "[Tennis] is played where golf, polo, jai alai, jujitsu and baseball are unknown. Tennis amounts to the sort of outdoor Esperanto perfected by that spry, cosmopolitan bunch of young men and women who in white clothes and becoming suntans buzz around the world to play it."

Of course *Time* was not including the great number of black Americans who played the game and were not allowed on the tennis circuit. By 1939 *Time* could report that 150 black tennis clubs existed with 28,000 players and that blacks promoted their own national championship tournament which was the climax of thirty-five sectional and state tournaments.

The two outstanding male tennis stars of the thirties were Ellsworth Vines and Don Budge. Vines, however, had a very brief reign. In 1931 at the age of nineteen he beat George Lott 7-9, 6-3, 9-7, 7-5 at Forest Hills. In 1933 he swept both Wimbledon and Forest Hills. After the 1933 season, Vines signed to play a professional tour. Playing against the legendary Bill Tilden, he and Tilden toured seventy-two cities, and grossed $243,000, of which Vines earned $52,000. In 1937 and 1938 Vines and Fred Perry toured together. The first year Vines outdueled Perry 32-29, and the tour grossed $412,181. Again in 1938 Vines held the edge 49-35, but the gross was only $175,000.

In the mid-thirties amateur tennis was dominated by Fred Perry, the English champion, and a host of other European stars. In the late thirties one of the greatest American stars ever to set foot on a tennis court emerged from California. His name was Don Budge. Previously enamored with such sports as baseball and basketball, Budge did not take a major interest in tennis until he was fifteen. Budge played an awesome full court game. He possessed an explosive serve and a strong forehand, but most importantly, he had a devastating topspin backhand which he could unleash with deadly accuracy, either down the line or cross court.

In 1937 he won a dramatic match against Baron Von Cramm of Germany in the Davis Cup semifinals. Von Cramm had received a call from Hitler just prior to the game, which added tension to the proceedings. Von Cramm, in his defense, was no supporter of Hitler and was later imprisoned by the Nazi regime. Down 1-4 in the decisive fifth set, Budge rallied to win the final set by the score of 8-6. An ironic sidelight to the match was that America's greatest tennis player in the twentieth century up to that time, Bill Tilden, was the German tennis team's coach.

In the final round of Davis Cup competition against Great Britain, Budge swept both his singles matches and partnered with his close friend Gene Mako for a doubles victory. The triumph brought the cup to the United States for the first time in ten years. That year Budge also won the singles, doubles, and mixed doubles at Wimbledon and also captured the national crown at Forest Hills, once again beating the unfortunate Von Cramm.

In 1937, Budge earned tennis immortality by winning the Grand Slam—the singles championships of Australia, France, Great Britain, and the United States. This accomplishment was no accident but the result of careful planning. Budge had first traveled to Australia, where he played in a number of local tournaments as a warmup for the Australian Nationals. The strategy worked as he swept easily past a promising newcomer, John Bromwich, by scores of 6-4, 6-2, 6-1 and then went on to capture the other three events of the Grand Slam. That year he also led a successful defense of the Davis Cup. At the age of twenty-three he turned professional and toured the country with Ellsworth Vines, winning 21 matches and losing 18. In the meantime his heir apparent Bobby Riggs, also from California and a crafty, sleight-of-hand court artist in contrast to Budge's free swinging power game, won the national title at the age of twenty-one in 1939.

Women's tennis during the period was dominated by Helen Wills Moody, Helen Hull Jacobs, and Alice Marble. Helen Wills Moody had begun her career in the twenties, when she won six U.S. women's championships and four Wimbledons. She won another national crown in 1931 and then gained four more Wimbledon titles in 1932, 1933, 1935, and 1938.

Her chief rival was Helen Hull Jacobs, a chunky, speedy and athletic youngster, who like Wills hailed from California. Jacobs won her first national championship in 1932, a year Moody did not enter the tournament. The following year the final match in the U.S. nationals created a controversy that has intrigued tennis fans for years. In the finals of Forest Hills, Moody was dueling Jacobs. Down 8-6 in the first set and trailing 3-0 in the second, Moody defaulted, saying that she could no longer continue. Years later Moody would explain that her back pained her so that she was forced to withdraw. A back operation in 1934 seemed to corroborate her explanation and she resumed her tennis career, defeating Jacobs in the 1935 and 1938 Wimbledons.

Alice Marble was another Californian to emerge as a tennis star. In 1936 she triumphed at Forest Hills and won at both Wimbledon and Forest Hills in 1939. That same year she was named outstanding woman athlete of the year.

U.S. tennis during the thirties remained largely a regional affair, dominated by players from California. Relatively untouched by the Depression, the "amateurs" carried on a lifestyle that few could afford but many would envy.

Golf

The Depression severely curtailed the development of golf. Many tournaments were simply abandoned, and many others drastically slashed their prize money. Miniature golf, a cheaper and simpler version of the original, proliferated. In 1931 a so-called balloon ball that weighed no more than 1.55 ounces and whose diameter was not to be less than 1.68 inches was introduced but quickly abandoned for one whose weight was to be 1.62 ounces with 1.68 inches minimum diameter.

On top of the economic effects of the Depression, golf during the thirties suffered another devastating blow when its greatest star, Bobby Jones, retired at the ripe old age of twenty-eight. He was at the height of his career. After his retirement, however, Jones designed and developed the Augusta National Course on 365 acres of a former indigo plantation. Its first tournament was inaugurated in 1934 and called the Augusta National Invitation. From 1935 on it became known as the Masters and has remained one of the most prestigious and important tournaments on the professional golfers' tour.

Gene Sarazen and Harry Cooper were golf's luminaries during the early thirties. In the mid and late thirties such names as Jimmy Demaret, Horton Smith, Ralph Guldahl, Denny Shute, and Byron Nelson (1937 Masters, 1939 U.S. Open) began to dominate the tournament trail. But it would not be until the fifties that television and popular stars like Ben Hogan, Sam Snead, and Arnold Palmer would create a mass appeal for golf.

In the thirties golf was still thought of as the gentleman's game played by businessmen who wheeled and dealed as they stroked and putted. It was played in a country club setting, which made middle-class people feel uneasy and out of place, especially during a time when the business of the country was no longer business but basic survival. No one golfer dominated the game as Walter Hagen had in the twenties when he won four straight PGA tournaments and four British Opens to become the first international golf star. In the twenties golf had been expanded by the swelling ranks of businessmen, lawyers, and financiers. With the Depression these men often suffered a reversal of fortunes and career. Country club memberships were one of the first things to go in hard times. Golf clubs were set aside and seemed expensive dust collectors when bread, meat, and milk were on almost everybody's mind.

The keynote of sports in the thirties was the adjustments and exigencies forced on them during a period of uncertainty, retrenchment, and financial reorganization. Sports played the role of morale booster, diversion, and the continuation of cherished American myths during trying and often desperate times. The businessmen owners and promoters of professional sports survived the Depression through innovation, experimentation, and tight economics. Athletes rose to the spirit and challenge of competition to perpetuate the games that meant so much to the American outlook on life.

BASEBALL
The Making of the National Game

New York state was, of course, the home of baseball in its infancy with Cooperstown shrewdly and convincingly claiming to be the cradle of the game. The first professional team was from Cincinnati; the Red Stockings became a nationally known team in 1869–70. With their 56 victories and 1 tie, they were an unbeatable team until the Atlantics took them 8–7 in Brooklyn, June 1870. The three 1865 Cazenovia, New York, players shown here are Will Chappel, pitcher, John A. Curtis, batter, and Will Cruttenden, catcher. Although obviously a staged studio shot with an inappropriate backdrop, the photograph is interesting for its documentation of team uniforms and lack of equipment. Pictures such as this were the forerunners of baseball cards and were frequently sent through the mail. Baseball teams reflected local civic pride and competitive spirit, and rivalries between towns were intense. Although not formally paid to play, the early ball players enjoyed other benefits such as local notoriety and popularity, gifts and other favors bestowed locally, and opportunities for travel.

The Cincinnati team of the American Association of 1882 had a 55–25 record and featured Will White, who won 40 and lost 12 with 480 innings pitched in 54 games. White was 43–22 in 1883 and 34–18 in 1884. While pitching for Cincinnati of the National League in 1879, White pitched in 680 innings, had 75 complete games, and allowed only 676 hits. 1882 was the first year of operation for the American Association, which continued until 1892. In competing with the established National League, the American Association raided players, cut ticket prices in half to 25 cents, and scheduled games on Sunday. A temporary truce between the warring leagues was reached in 1883 and a postseason series between the league champions was played in 1884. The 1880s were a decade of turmoil, change, and conflict in professional baseball with the challenging of the reserve clause, the competition of the Union Association and the Players' League, and the formation of the Brotherhood of Professional Ball Players in 1885. Team rosters were in upheaval as the monopoly of the National Leagues was challenged, but certain reforms and improvements were introduced, notably Sunday baseball and league control of umpires. Each position on the team had a different kind of uniform, as the photograph of the 1882 Cincinnati team indicates.

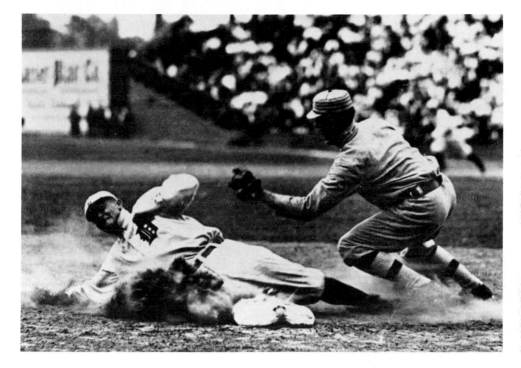

In a twenty-four-year legendary career Ty Cobb compiled a .367 lifetime batting average, a mark that will undoubtedly stand forever. Cobb led the American League in hitting nine consecutive seasons (1907–1915) before this remarkable string was broken by Tris Speaker's .386 average in 1916. Cobb then went on to win three more straight batting titles. As a baserunner he had no peer, leading the league in pilfers six times and setting a long-standing record of 96 steals in 1915, a record that stood until Maury Wills stole 104 bases in 1962. A fierce and often vicious competitor, Cobb studied and practiced every phase of the game to gain a greater edge. On the bases Cobb's menacing spikes and his patented hook slide made him feared, envied, and hated. Cobb's desire to win and to excel drove him to play that bordered on the compulsive and neurotic and made him a loner and isolate. After twenty-two years with the Detroit Tigers, the last six as a player-manager, Cobb was dropped by his club because of a scandal involving alleged game fixing and betting. Cobb was cleared by Judge Landis and played his final two seasons with Connie Mack's Philadelphia A's. Cobb never played on a World Series championship team as the Tigers lost three consecutive Series in 1907, 1908, and 1909. Cobb was enigmatic and unknowable, and his reputation as a brawler and tough has clouded his legend and records.

Christy Mathewson (Big Six) was one of the best-loved and most admired American athletes of all times. College educated, temperate, well-disciplined, and modest, Matty developed his famous "fadeaway" or reverse curve pitch, winning 20 games in his first full season with the New York Giants. After slipping to 14–17 in 1902, he came back with brilliant seasons for twelve consecutive years. In 1908 he was 37–11, and he won 373 games in 17 seasons. He was a control pitcher, allowing only 846 walks in 4,783 innings pitched. In the 1905 World Series, Mathewson pitched 3 complete game shutouts against the Philadelphia Athletics as the Giants took the Series in 5 games. Mathewson died at the age of forty-five of tuberculosis.

Walter Johnson was known for his fast ball and for strikeouts, 3,508 victims in his twenty-one-year career, all with the Washington Senators. Johnson led the American League in strikeouts twelve times, eight seasons in a row from 1912 through 1919, and in 1913 he had a 1.09 ERA while compiling a 36–7 record. Johnson toiled for twenty-one years for a second-division club, although in 1924 and 1925 the Senators won pennants, and in 1912 and 1913 the team finished second. Johnson's most dramatic moment was in the seventh game of the 1924 World Series when he came in to relieve Firpo Marberry and pitched four innings of shutout ball to win the Series for Washington. Johnson had lost games one and five, but at the age of thirty-six with eighteen years of toil he was rewarded before his hometown fans with the prize that had eluded him and his team. Johnson, who joined the American League in 1907 (six years after its beginning), helped establish that league and became a star of the caliber of Christy Mathewson and Grover Cleveland Alexander, Johnson's counterparts in the National League.

Front row: Lynn, Risberg, Leibold, Kerr, McClellan, Williams, Cicotte.
Middle row: Schalk, Jenkins, Felsch, Gleason, E. Collins, J. Collins, Faber, Weaver.
Back row: Jackson, Gandil, McMullin, Lowdermilk, Mayer, Murphy, Sullivan, Wilkinson.

The 1919 Chicago White Sox team included eight players who would forever wear the infamous label of the "Black Sox" and would be barred from professional baseball for their lifetimes. Led by the greedy and conniving Chick Gandil, the team's first-baseman, and ably abetted by star pitchers Eddie Cicotte and Claude "Lefty" Williams (who combined for the five losses to Cincinnati), the eight players managed to throw the series for the promise of a few thousand dollars each, with the exception of Gandil, who maneuvered the gamblers and his teammates to gain big rewards. The whole episode was one of stupidity, greed, betrayals, sinister threats, and duplicity. It is generally agreed that the desperate act of the Chicago players was caused by several factors: low team salaries and a pay cut in the 1919 season; the post World War I atmosphere of corruption and declining moral values; Charles Comiskey's stingy and parsimonious policies regarding per diem food allowance and cleaning of uniforms as well as his arrogant and hard-hearted negotiations with players; the rancor and divisive factionalism among the Chicago players; the guile and treachery of Gandil and the economic desperation of Cicotte. The White Sox would be a long time recovering from the scandal of 1919–20 and did not appear in the World Series again until 1959, forty years later.

Judge Kenesaw Mountain Landis rescued baseball from scandal and corruption in 1920, when as the first commissioner he banned for life eight of the Chicago White Sox players who had participated in the fix of the 1919 World Series. In his authoritarian and decisive actions Landis restored integrity and public confidence in the game, although the problems of gambling and game fixing were not fully solved by the stern judge. Emotionless and untalkative, Landis oversaw baseball's ''best interests'' with decisions that were often unpopular or resisted, but his almost twenty-five years as the ruling czar of the game were marked by confidence, a quiet use of his wide ranging powers, and genuine concern for the long-range welfare of the national game. Landis diligently protected the legal status of players' contracts, ordered the freedom of numerous minor league players, suspended players, had a running battle with Babe Ruth, and avoided publicity that might weaken his authority. To many, Judge Landis seemed a tyrant, but his contributions to the growth and popularity of baseball far overshadowed any of his numerous edicts and judgments.

Rogers Hornsby (the ''Rajah'') was probably the greatest righthanded hitter of all time, hitting over .400 three times, with a .424 average recorded in 1924. He had a stormy personal life and was brash and outspoken as a player, often profane and blunt in his comments. His greatest seasons were with the Cardinals (1915-1926), and he won six consecutive league batting titles from 1920 to 1925 while leading the league in hits four of those seasons. The cocky Texan demanded and received big salaries but squandered his money and ended up broke and in debt when his career as a regular was finished in the early 1930s. Hornsby was a self-disciplined athlete who avoided tobacco, alcohol, movies, and books—anything that would weaken his sharp batting eye. Of his 2,930 career hits 1,011 were for extra bases, and his lifetime .358 average is second only to Ty Cobb's .367 mark.

Front row: Ruether (p), Dugan (3b), Paschal (of), Bengough (c), Thomas (p), Gazella (inf), Bennett (mascot).

Middle row: Shawkey (p), Giard (p), Grabowski (c), O'Leary (coach), Huggins (manager), Fletcher (coach), Pennock (p), Wera (inf), Collins (c).

Back row: Gehrig (1b), Meusel (lf), Ruth (rf), Moore (p), Pipgras (p), Combs (cf), Miller (p), Hoyt (p), Lazzeri (2b), Koenig (ss), Shocker (p), Durst (of), Woods (trainer).

The 1927 World Champion New York Yankee team, which won 110 games and finished 19 games ahead of the second place American League team, has been called the greatest team ever assembled. The Yankees swept the World Series from Pittsburgh as three Yankee pitchers had complete games. The team's batting average during the season was .307 with Gehrig hitting .373 with 175 RBIs, Ruth recording a .356 average with 164 RBIs and 60 home runs, Earle Combs matching Ruth's batting average, and Lazzeri and Meusel hitting well over .300 and driving in over 100 runs each. Six Yankee pitchers won 10 or more games with four hurlers winning 18 or more. Gehrig had his greatest season, leading the league in RBIs, doubles, and total bases. Earle Combs had 231 hits, and Ruth, Gehrig, and Combs scored a combined 444 runs out of the 975 team runs scored. Of the team's 1,552 total hits 552 were for extra bases.

Pepper Martin (shown here in a 1936 photograph) was known for his head-first slides and brash, daring baserunning during the Depression thirties. Known as the ''Wild Horse of Osage,'' Martin brought intensity and enthusiasm to the game, capturing the baseball public's attention and fascination. Martin's up and down career, his setbacks, and his dramatic comeback in 1933 after a disastrous season in 1932 seemed to personify the fortunes of a nation. Martin led the league in stolen bases three times. A dedicated and unselfish team player, he played where he was needed. His 1930 World Series performance against the Philadelphia Athletics became legendary as he hit .500, stole 5 bases, and personally accounted for the Cardinal victories in games two and five. During WW II Martin came back to play in 40 games for the Cardinals and hit .279. Martin brought color and excitement to the game in a period when baseball needed these qualities, and he was a symbol of the simple, little man (he was 5 feet 8 inches in height) who could overcome adversity and prove that a $4,500 salary man could excite fans and play with color and flair. Martin's dirty uniform was the symbol of his competitive intensity and hard work.

Front row: Marion (lf), O'Dea (c), Martin (of), Gonzales (coach), Southworth (manager), Wares (coach), Garms (of), Jurisich (p), Verban (lf).

Second row: Byerly (p), Schmidt (p), Keely (c), Fallon (lf), Hopp (of), Bergamo (of), Kurowski (lf), Leo Ward (traveling secretary).

Third row: Butch Yatkeman (clubhouse boy), Donnelly (p), Wilks (p), Litwhiler (of), Sanders (lf), Dr. Weaver (trainer), M. Cooper (p), Lanier (p), Musial (of), Brechzen (p), W. Cooper (c).

Front: Sam Cooper (batboy), Bob Scanlon (batboy).

The 1944 St. Louis Cardinals, managed by Billy Southworth, won 105 games and beat the St. Louis Browns in the wartime World Series 4 games to 2 with all games played at Sportsman's Park, the home of both ball clubs. The Cardinals were involved in the 1942 and 1943 Series, defeating the Yankees 4 games in 1 in 1942, but the tables were turned in 1943. The 1944 Cardinals were led by Stan Musial (.347 average), Johnny Hopp (.336), and Walker Cooper (.317). The infield of Ray Sanders, Emil Verban, Marty Marion, and Walt Kurowski was efficient, committing only 112 errors and turning 162 double plays. The team's record .982 fielding average was broken by Cleveland in 1947. The Cardinals were the best baseball team during the war years due to the brilliant managing of Billy Southworth, a well-organized and effective farm system, shrewd trades, and a core of veteran players.

Jackie Robinson broke the "color line" in professional baseball in 1947, hitting .297, scoring 125 runs, and leading the National League with 29 steals. Overcoming racist abuse, death threats, and isolation, Robinson quickly proved himself as a player of diverse talents who would play wherever he was needed. He was a proud, competitive individual who answered his tormenters with daring base running, timely hitting, and steady field play. He hit over .300 in six consecutive seasons with a league-leading .342 average in 1949 and compiled a lifetime .311 average in ten seasons. After finding his position at second base, he became a favorite with the fans, appearing in six consecutive All-Star games. He was joined by Roy Campanella, Don Newcombe, Joe Black, Jim Gilliam, and Sandy Amoros as the Dodgers pioneered the way in bringing talented black players to the majors. Many teams were reluctant to integrate their teams, but the Dodgers became known as the "colored folks" team. They had a national following of proud blacks who in 1955 followed a team that had four black starters and featured Don Newcombe, who was 20-5 and hit .359 as a pinch hitter. This 1955 team defeated the Yankees in a 7-game World Series with Roy Campanella and Sandy Amoros playing key roles in the Series victory.

Satchel Paige made his long-delayed debut in major league baseball with Cleveland in July of 1948, the year after Larry Doby broke the color line with that team. Paige was 6-1 in his first season, helping to clinch the pennant for the Indians. Before coming to the majors in his forties, Paige pitched for eight different teams in the Negro leagues, starred on black barnstorming teams, and played winter ball in the Caribbean. After two seasons with Cleveland, Paige was released and returned to the Kansas City Monarchs for the 1950 season. Bill Veeck, who had brought Paige to Cleveland, signed him to a contract with the St. Louis Browns in 1951, and Paige pitched brilliantly in the 1952 season, winning 12 and losing 10 for a team that was 64-90. After his last season with the Browns in 1953 Paige played minor league ball. The ageless veteran delighted crowds and continued to display an amazing variety of pitches with his unique pitching style. Laconic and easy going, Paige made contributions to baseball at all levels in a career that lasted over forty-three years. In 1971 Paige was honored with full and equal induction into the Baseball Hall of Fame. A commonsense philosopher, Paige was always a delightful raconteur and advocate of an easygoing way of life that conveyed his deep love of the game and his pride in pitching skills.

Joe DiMaggio hit .323 his first season (1936) with the Yankees, and in his thirteen seasons he won only two batting crowns, back-to-back titles in 1939–40 with .381 and .352 marks. At the peak of his career he spent three years in military service during WW II, and in 1941 he hit in 56 consecutive games. During his remarkable career the ''Yankee Clipper'' led a team that became a dynasty as the Yankees won nine World Series of the ten that DiMaggio played in. In the field DiMaggio was graceful, moving with the ease and sureness that are the result of great fielding instincts. A proud and self-disciplined athlete, DiMaggio overcame injuries to play with consistency and grace for his 6-foot 2-inch, 193-pound build. ''Jolting Joe'' was immortalized in song, and his brief marriage to Marilyn Monroe along with his lifetime devotion to her added to his legendary status. Like Stan Musial, DiMaggio was the son of immigrant parents, and baseball was for them an avenue to success, fame, and personal greatness. Both have returned to the game far more than they have gained from it financially.

Stan Musial, shown here swinging for his three thousandth hit in 1958 during his sixteenth full season with the St. Louis Cardinals, became, along with Ted Williams, one of the greatest scientific hitters of the modern-day game. He led the National League in hitting seven times with three consecutive batting titles (1950-52) and recorded a .331 lifetime average. An All-Star game performer twenty-four times in his twenty-two-year career, Musial hit well over .300 in his first full sixteen seasons in the majors. Musial was one of the most respected men in the game, always a gentleman and one of the foremost ambassadors of the game. He later became a successful banker, restaurant owner, and executive of the St. Louis Cardinals team.

Willie ''Say-Hey Kid'' Mays began his major league career with the New York Giants in 1951 by going hitless in twenty-two times at bat, but by the end of his first season hit .274. After his career was interrupted by military service in 1952 Mays came back and won the league batting crown with a .345 mark and 110 RBIs. This was his only batting title in a twenty-two-year career, but he led the league in stolen bases four consecutive seasons (1956-1959) and home runs four different seasons with 52 round trippers in 1965. He hit .300 or better ten times and had 30 or more homers in eleven seasons. Mays was one of the greatest multifaceted players, excelling in hitting for average and power, base-running and stealing, and spectacular fielding. Mays was among the first of the genuine black superstars. *Sporting News* named him as the Baseball Player of the 1960s Decade. His home runs and total bases statistics make him one of the greatest power hitters and baserunners the game will ever be blessed with.

Front row: Don Wert, John Wyatt, Tony Cuccinello, Wally Moses, Mayo Smith, Hal Naragon, John Sain, Wayne Comer, Willie Horton, Mickey Lolich.

Second row: John Hand (equipment), Bill Behm (trainer), Julio Moreno (batting practice pitcher), Jim Northrup, Ray Oyler, Earl Wilson, Fred Lasher, Don McMahon, Al Kaline, Charles C. Creedon (traveling secretary).

Third row: Dick Tracewski, Norm Cash, Ed Mathews, Jim Price, Jon Warden, Denny McLain, Gates Brown, John Hiller, Dick McAuliffe.

Back row: Roy Face, Bob Christian, Mickey Stanley, Joe Sparma, Daryl Patterson, Pat Dobson, Tom Matchick, Bill Freehan.

The 1968 Detroit Tigers hit only .235 as a team and had no .300 hitters, with Al Kaline's .287 the highest individual average. However, the team scored a league leading 671 runs and allowed only 492 runs, committed only 105 errors, and led the league in fielding average with center fielder Mickey Stanley fielding 1.000. Denny McLain won 31 and lost only 6 with a 1.96 ERA and 280 strikeouts in 336 innings pitched. In the World Series Mickey Lolich recorded 3 wins in 3 complete games, and Denny McLain, after being bombed in game four, came back to win in game six, backed by 13 runs. The 1968 Tigers, which included four black players (Willie Horton, Gates Brown, Earl Wilson, and John Wyatt) helped to reunify a city that had been torn apart by the 1967 Detroit racial riots.

Front row: Gus Mauch (trainer), Joe Pignatano (coach), Rube Walker (coach), Yogi Berra (coach), Eddie Yost (coach), Joe Deer (assistant trainer).

Second row: Tug McGraw, Gary Gentry, Al Weis, Cleon Jones, Gil Hodges (manager), Jerry Grote, Bud Harrelson, Ed Charles, Rod Gaspar, Duffy Dyer.

Third row: Jim McAndrew, Tommie Agee, Cal Koonce, Ken Boswell, Tom Seaver, Jerry Koosman, Ron Swoboda, Wayne Garrett, Bobby Pfeil, Lou Niss (traveling secretary).

Back row: Nick Torman (equipment manager), J. C. Martin, Ron Taylor, Ed Kranepool, Don Cardwell, Conn Clendenon, Nolan Ryan, Art Shamsky, Jack DiLauro, Roy Neuer (clubhouse attendant).

The 1969 "Miracle Mets" hit only .242 as a team and were led by Cleon Jones (.340 average with 75 runs batted in) and Tommy Agee (.271 average with 76 RBIs). Utilizing limited talent to the fullest, manager Gil Hodges brilliantly platooned his players, and Tom Seaver posted a 25-7 record with 18 complete games. After blasting the Atlanta Braves in 3 straight games, scoring 27 runs, and hitting .327, the Mets beat Baltimore in 5 games, sweeping 4 in a row after losing the opening game of the World Series 4-1. In the last 4 games the Orioles could score only 5 runs. The team that had entered the National League in 1962 and lost over 100 games its first four years had performed a "miracle" and had temporarily diverted the nation's attention from Vietnam and the furor of the antiwar demonstrations at home. The Mets also brought back a world championship to New York City for the first time since 1962.

Front row: Rose, Morgan, Kluszewski (coach), Grammas (coach), Anderson (manager), Flynn, Rettenmund.

Second row: Stowe (equipment manager), Campbell (traveling secretary), Bench, Plummer, Kirby, Foster, Billingham, T. Carroll, Darcy, Eastwick, Perez, Borbon, Starr (trainer).

Third row: Driessen, Chaney, Griffey, Nolan, Concepcion, Armbrister, C. Caroll, McEnaney, Crowley, Geronimo, Gullett.

Front: McGinn (batboy).

The 1975 Cincinnati Reds, known as the "Big Red Machine," won 108 games and finished 20 games ahead of the Los Angeles Dodgers in the National League's west division. They crushed Pittsburgh in the playoffs in three games and then defeated the Boston Red Sox in a thrilling 7-game World Series in which 5 games were decided by 1 run. In the seventh game the Reds overcame a 3-0 deficit to win 4-3, giving Cincinnati its first world championship since 1940. During the regular season the Reds scored 840 runs and had 168 stolen bases. The starting team featured four .300 hitters: Joe Morgan, Pete Rose, Ken Griffey, and George Foster. However, the secret of the team's success was the bullpen duo of Will McEnaney and Rawley Eastwick, who combined for 37 saves while relievers accounted for 50 saves. The starting pitching staff had only 22 complete games as "Captain Hook" Sparky Anderson brilliantly managed a ten-man pitching staff.

Pete Rose, popularly known as "Charlie Hustle," has become one of the greatest hitters of the modern-day game as he has turned his singles into extra bases or scored runs with base running skills that excite fans. In his first sixteen years, Rose had over 200 hits in ten seasons. He led the National League in hits six times with a career high of 230 hits in 1973 when he led the league with a .338 average. An intense and aggressive player, Rose personifies the hustling, hard-working player who has joined the elite group of 3,000 hits and moved into the class of Ty Cobb, Hank Aaron, Stan Musial, Tris Speaker, Honus Wagner, Eddie Collins, Willie Mays, and Nap Lajoie. Blessed with a relatively injury free career, Rose has moved into a position to challenge Cobb's 4,191 career hits. He will undoubtedly join the immortals in the Hall of Fame.

Reggie Jackson symbolizes the modern-day superstar with all his benefits and problems. Blessed with amazing talents and skills, Jackson has become controversial, highly publicized, temperamental, and always quotable, sometimes to his own detriment. After eight seasons with the Oakland A's and after numerous battles with Charley O. Finley, Jackson went to Baltimore for the 1976 season and then to the Yankees in 1977. With Oakland, Jackson led the league in strikeouts four consecutive seasons, but has steadily reduced his propensity for wild swinging and has become a more consistent hitter. Jackson has become known for his World Series exploits, powering 5 home runs in the 1977 Series against Los Angeles with 3 successive homers (each on the first pitch) in game six. Jackson hit .450 in this Series to lead all players.

All photographs in this photographic essay on American baseball are courtesy of the National Baseball Hall of Fame and Museum, Inc., Cooperstown, New York. The authors would like to thank Jack Redding of the Museum's Reference Library for his invaluable help and many courtesies.

5

Sports under the Gun: The Impact of the Second World War on Sports During the 1940s

By the end of 1940 the world had witnessed the triumphant march of the totalitarian war machines of the Axis alliance. In 1935 Benito Mussolini's forces invaded Ethiopia. In 1937 aggressive Japanese military might embarked on the Second Sino-Japanese War. Most frightening of all, the rejuvenated German military legions under the fanatical leadership of Adolf Hitler had demonstrated an insatiable appetite for conquest. Beginning in 1936 with the occupation of the Rhineland and in 1938 with the invasion and annexation of Austria, the Panzer forces rolled inexorably onward.

In 1939, Czechoslovakia and Poland fell to the German blitzkrieg. After a brief respite, German forces with lightning quickness swept aside the defenses of Denmark, Norway, Luxembourg, Holland, and Belgium. Undeterred by French and British resistance, Hitler's forces claimed France on June 22, 1940. With his hegemony over Western Europe secured, Hitler unleashed his Luftwaffe against England as a preparation for invasion.

In the United States the events in Europe dominated the headlines. The United States became increasingly involved in Britain's defense efforts. The gift of fifty overage destroyers to England in exchange for naval bases and the passage of a Selective Service Act in August gave clear indication of the imminence of direct American participation in the European conflagration.

In this atmosphere of uncertainty, American sports attempted to carry on with "business as usual." Yet normalcy in the sports world lasted only two years. From December 7, 1941, to VJ Day in 1945, the American sports world would set aside its priorities for the war effort. From August 1945 to the end of 1949, sports benefited from the pent-up consumer demands. Thus, because of the uniqueness of the decade, American sports in the forties must be discussed within the context of three separate periods.

Baseball 1940 to 1942

The forties were a period of constant change as well as a period of unexpected events and precedents. Before the 1940 baseball season even began, a group of wealthy sportsmen from the West Coast offered $5 million to the St. Louis Browns, Philadelphia Phillies, and Boston Reds to transfer a franchise to Los Angeles. Their spokesmen noted that the problems of transportation had been reduced by the development of the airplane. It would be 1958 before the Dodgers and Giants moved to the West Coast and brought baseball to its continental destiny, but the idea had been planted and the investment money was clearly there.

Fortunately for baseball, the move did not come about in 1940, for the war would surely have meant that the West Coast franchise would have had to be moved or operations suspended during the war, and one of the leagues would have been seriously disrupted. It was not until the 1947 season that the Yankees did all their season traveling by plane, the first major league franchise to do so.

The 1940 season in the American League was a three-team race among Detroit, Cleveland, and New York. The Tigers won by a game over Cleveland and two over the Yankees. Detroit was led by Hank Greenberg, who hit .340 and had a league-leading 41 home runs and 150 RBI's. Rudy York had 134 RBI's with 33 home runs, and Charlie Gehringer, in his seventeenth season with Detroit, hit .313 with 81 RBI's. As a team the Tigers hit .286 and scored 171 more runs than their opponents. The pitching staff was led by Bobo Newsom with a 21-5 record and Schoolboy Rowe, who was 16-3. Al Benton had a league-leading 17 saves in relief, and Tiger pitchers struck out 752 batters, 66 more than the Cleveland staff.

In addition, the 1940 season saw a spectacular performance by Bob Feller, who won 27 games with 261 strikeouts in 320 innings and a league-leading ERA of 2.61. Feller had 31 complete games in the 43 games that he pitched. Joe DiMaggio led the league with a .352 average and 133 RBI's, while baseball's other premier hitter, Ted Williams, hit .344 with 133 RBI's. It was a season of home runs, with 883 hit in the American League, a record that would not be broken until the new plateau of 973 in 1950. The American League teams scored 726 more runs than the National League in 1940.

The 1940 season for the National League saw significantly lower batting averages and little of the power hitting that excited American League fans. No player in the National League had over 200 hits (with three in the other league), and after Debs Garms of Pittsburgh, who hit .355 in 358 at bats, Ernie Lombardi of Cincinnati had the next highest average at .317. The overall earned run average for league pitchers was 3.84 (compared with 4.38 for the American League), and the Cincinnati pitchers had an earned run average of 3.05 with 91 complete games. Bucky Walters, who led the league in wins and innings pitched, had an earned run average of 2.48. Paul Derringer won 20 games, and together Walters and Derringer had 55 complete games with 602 innings pitched. Joe Beggs won 12 games in relief with 7 saves, and Junior Thompson won 16 out of 17 complete games while Jim Turner won 14. The Reds hit .266 as a team (about the league average), but led the league with brilliant and steady fielding, committing only 117 errors (a mark broken by the St. Louis Cardinals in 1944 when they committed only 112 errors). Cincinnati won going away with a 12-game bulge over Brooklyn. Four of the Reds' players led the league in fielding at their respective positions.

The 1940 World Series saw the Reds triumph over Detroit in seven games. Bucky Walters was the pitching star of the Series with 2 complete games, giving up only 8 hits and 3 runs in those games. After being knocked out in the second inning of the first game, Paul Derringer came back to win games four and seven for Cincinnati, with complete games in both wins. Catching these two pitching aces in the Series was Jimmy Wilson, a forty-year-old coach, who was pressed into service after Ernie Lombardi was injured in the second game. Wilson hit .353 in the Series, but Bill Werber led the Reds with a .370 average on 10 hits. The games were well played, and the last game was not decided until the bottom of the seventh when Cincinnati scored twice.

Bobo Newsom pitched brilliantly for the Tigers, winning the first and fifth games easily and losing the heartbreaking seventh game. Newsom's father died after seeing his son win the opening game, and Newsom's performance afterward was one of the grittiest in World Series history; he pitched the final game of the Series with only one day off. Newsom only allowed 4 runs in twenty-six innings of pitching, and he struck out seventeen Redlegs. During spring training with the Tigers in 1942 Bobo showed up with a car that had a ''Bobo'' neon sign on it and a horn that played ''Hold That Tiger!'' He was one of the most colorful figures in baseball, and in his twenty seasons in baseball he played for nine different teams, appearing on the Washington Senators' roster five different times. The big disappointment for the Tigers in the 1940 Series was the ineffective pitching of Schoolboy Rowe, who was 16-3 during the regular season but who was knocked out of the box in the fourth inning of game two and pulled in the first inning of game six.

The 1941 season saw the New York Yankees come back after a one-year absence as league champions. They dominated the league and won easily by seventeen games over Boston. They would repeat as American League champions in 1942 and 1943.

The 1941 Yankees were a powerful slugging team, hitting 151 home runs. Charlie Keller had 33 round trippers with 122 RBI's, DiMaggio had 30 circuit clouts with 125 RBI's, and Tommy Henrich had 31 homers with 85 RBI's. Joe Gordon chipped in 24 home runs and combined with Phil Rizzuto to execute 109 double plays. Bill Dickey, in his fourteenth season with the Yankees, was the best catcher in the league, committing only 3 errors. Of course, Joe DiMaggio put on one of the greatest hitting exhibitions in baseball as he hit safely in 56 consecutive games from May 15 to July 17.

The Yankee pitching staff was lead by Red Ruffing, who had been pitching in the American League for eighteen years and was nearing the end of a brilliant career, and Lefty Gomez, coming back from a sore-arm year in 1940 to win 15 and lose only 5 games in 1941. The Yankees had eight pitchers who won 8 games or more, and Johnny Murphy had fifteen saves with a 1.98 earned run average. Red Ruffing hit .303 and was 6 for 15 as a pinch hitter.

The most dramatic story of the 1941 season was the .406 average compiled by Ted Williams of Boston. Williams led the league with 37 home runs, 145 walks, and 135 runs scored. He struck out only 27 times during this remarkable season, and his .406 mark was the first time any player in the American League had batted over .400 since Harry Heilmann hit .403 for Detroit in 1923.

The 1941 season in the National League saw Brooklyn win in a close race over St. Louis. Again, this was a season for pitchers rather than hitters. The league earned run average was 3.63, even lower than the 1940 season. The Dodger pitching staff compiled a 3.14 ERA, as Whitlow Wyatt and Kirby Higbe each won 22 games and combined for 42 complete games.

Pete Reiser led the league with a .343 batting average, and Dolf

Camilli powered 34 home runs and had 120 RBI's to lead the league in these departments. The Dodgers scored 800 runs and scored 219 runs more than their opponents.

The 1941 World Series was the first appearance for the Dodgers in twenty years, and hopes ran high in Flatbush that the Bums could prevail. It was the first subway Series since the Yankees easily prevailed over the Giants in 1937. All games of the 1941 Series were close except for the fourth game, which the Yankees won 7-4. Dodger fans pointed to the bad luck suffered by their team. In the third game Fat Freddy Fitzsimmons was forced to leave the game when he was hit in the knee by a vicious line drive in the seventh inning. Up to this point Fitzsimmons had pitched a four-hit shutout and was ahead 1-0. In game four the Dodgers led 4-3 in the top of the ninth with two outs. Mickey Owen let Hugh Casey's third strike get away, and Tommy Henrich reached first. The Yankees then scored 4 runs in the inning, and Johnny Murphy held the Dodgers in the bottom of the ninth. Peewee Reese committed 3 errors in the Series in two key games. The Yankees were led by the hitting of Joe Gordon and Charley Keller, who together knocked in 10 of the 16 runs scored by the Yankees. The Dodger bats were notably silent, with Pete Reiser hitting only .200 for the Series.

In 1942 the Yankees won big again in what was to be the last normal season before the chaotic war years. The Yankee pitching was magnificent, with a team earned run average of 2.91. Ernie Bonham, Spud Chandler, Red Ruffing, and Hank Borowy combined for a 66-21 won-lost record. Bonham, Chandler, and Borowy had earned run averages of 2.27, 2.38, and 2.52, respectively. Gordon and Rizzuto again led the league in double plays, and the team scored almost 300 more runs than their opponents for the season. Yankee batting power decreased in terms of home runs (43 fewer than 1940) and hitting (17 points in team batting average from 1940). DiMaggio slipped to a .305 average, by far the lowest of his career up to that point. Only two Yankee regulars hit over .300—DiMaggio and Joe Gordon, who hit .322.

Ted Williams won the Triple Crown in 1942 with a .356 batting average, 36 home runs, and 137 RBI's. Again he led the league in walks (145) and runs scored (141). It was his last season until 1946, as he would spend the next three years in the service. However, Williams did not win the Most Valuable Player Award in 1941 or 1942. The 1942 season saw George Case of the Washington Senators win the stolen base title for the fourth consecutive year, and in 1943 Case would steal 61 bases.

In the National League the St. Louis Cardinals under the brilliant leadership of Billy Southworth won the first of three consecutive pennants. The Cards were 10½ games behind Brooklyn in mid-August but closed the gap and won by two games.

The Cardinals' pitching staff compiled an amazing 2.55 earned run average, with the staff striking out 651 batters. Mort Cooper led the league in almost every category with a 22-7 record, 22 complete games, 10 shutouts, and a 1.78 earned run average. Johnny Beazley won 21 and lost 6 with a 2.13 ERA, and Max Lanier and Howie Krist won 13 games each. The hitting and fielding were not spectacular, but the RBI's were distributed throughout the team, and the team led the league in doubles and triples (hitting only 60 home runs). Southworth used thirteen men with great effectiveness, knowing when to rest players and brilliantly judging the effectiveness of his batters against certain pitchers. The earmarks of the Southworth team were consistency, team pride and a spirit of sacrifice, few mental errors, and strong fundamentals in executing defense. He also rotated his eight pitchers effectively.

The 1942 World Series surprised everyone except the Cardinals. After losing 7-4 in the opener to the Yankees and Red Ruffing, who won his seventh World Series game, the Cardinals stormed back to beat the Yankees in four exciting and close games. Johnny Beazley pitched complete games in the second and fifth contests, winning by scores of 4-3 and 4-2. Enos Slaughter hit, ran the bases, and scored key runs, and Whitey Kurowski hit a game-winning triple in the second game and a two-run homer in the top of the ninth in the fifth and deciding game. Ernie White, who was 7-5 in the regular season, shut out the Yankees in game three, giving up 6 singles and striking out six with no walks. It was White's only World Series appearance, and after a 5-5 record in 1943 and three years in military service, he never won another major league game. Amazingly, the Cards survived 10 errors in the Series, but the balance and timely hitting of the St. Louis team prevailed. Cardinal pitchers gave up only 8 walks and 13 earned runs, and Hal Lanier's relief pitching in game four was brilliant as he held the Yankees scoreless in the last three innings after the Yankees had erupted for 5 runs in the bottom of the sixth.

College Football

College football faced the forties burdened with renewed attacks by critics who assailed its very legitimacy and place in institutions of higher learning. The chief bombshell to be dropped came when President Robert Hutchins of the University of Chicago announced that the school was dropping its football program. Hutchins proclaimed that "there is no doubt that football has been a major handicap to education in the United States" and that it had "done much to . . . originate the popular misconceptions of what a university is." Citing the fact that 50 percent of Big Ten football players were physical education majors, Hutchins summed up his position by stating, "I think it is a good thing for this country to have one important university discontinue football." Hutchins' action did not set a trend. Football remained king in the Midwest. The 1940 Walter Camp All-American team had four Big Ten players on it, and the 1943 team had eight midwestern players on it, four from Notre Dame.

The elimination of football at Chicago proved to be a blessing in disguise for Stanford University. Clark D. Shaughnessy, the University of Chicago's coach, left unemployed by President Hutchins' decision, was hired by Stanford University to head its football program. Inheriting a team that had lost every conference game the year before, Shaughnessy was faced with a tremendous rebuilding program, or so it would seem. Shaughnessy, while in Chicago, had served as an advisor to the Chicago Bears and together with George Halas devised a new offensive concept. Utilizing the old T formation, Shaughnessy added a split end and a man in motion, which greatly enhanced the offensive capabilities of the formation.

The offense matched Shaughnessy's backfield personnel. Frankie Albert, a magician with the ball, was a left-handed passer who possessed the aplomb of a Western gunslinger. He was aided and abetted by Norman Standlee, a 6-foot 1-inch fullback, Pete Kmetovic, a slashing, shifty, broken-field runner, and Hugh Gallarneau, a brilliant all-around backfield man. In 1940, Stanford's "Cinderella squad" reversed its misfortunes of the previous year and streaked its way to a 10-game victory skein, capping the season with a 21-13 victory over Nebraska in the Rose Bowl. The New York Times declared it to be one of "the most amazing comebacks in football." So enthralled were Stanford students that they sang this ditty to the tune of "God Bless America."

> God Bless Clark Shaughnessy
> Frankie Albert too
> Stand beside them and guide them
> And they'll bring victories to you

In the Big Ten, Minnesota featured undefeated elevens in 1940 and again in 1941. However, these victory streaks did not come easy. In 1940, Michigan, led by the exploits of the fabulous triple-threat back Tom Harmon (33 TDs, 237 points, and an average of almost 6 yards per carry for three seasons) almost took the measure of the Gophers, losing only by the slimmest of margins, 7-6. In 1941, Minnesota trailed Northwestern 7-2 when the Gophers called a play without a signal, catching the Wildcats napping and resulting in a long touchdown run by Bird Higgins. The Associated Press ranked Minnesota as the number one team in the country in 1940 and 1941, and running backs George Franck and Bruce Smith were All-Americans from those mighty teams.

Yet the clouds of war hung menacingly over the gridiron. Events in the rest of the world could not be ignored by collegiate gridiron enthusiasts. This realization was poignantly demonstrated during the 1940 Army-Navy game. Over 102,000 people saw Navy defeat Army 14-0 in a rather lackluster affair. Preceding the game, the song "Army and Navy Forever" was played and a voice came over the public address system commenting that the "ceremonies symbolized the comradeship of the cadets and midshipmen not only in their fifty years of football rivalries but in the common cause of national defense." Between 1943 and 1944 about 350 colleges abandoned football for the remainder of the war. The game was deemed inappropriate for a time when the onrushing forces of totalitarianism and fascism threatened free traditions and institutions.

One major rule change in 1941 greatly altered the collegiate game for twelve years until it was rescinded in 1953. This change in the substitution rule allowed players to substitute for one another at any time except during the last two minutes of the first half, but the substitute could not be withdrawn nor the outgoing player returned to the game until one play had intervened. This virtually guaranteed the use of platoon football. *Time* observed that this would mean collegiate contests would feature "coach vs. coach rather than team vs. team."

Professional Football

The 1940 title game between the Chicago Bears (8-3) and the Washington Redskins (9-2) promised to be an even affair (particularly since the two teams had played in the last game of the season and the "Skins" won 7-3), featuring two of the league's premier passers, Sid Luckman of the Bears and Sammy Baugh of the Redskins. Hardly anyone was prepared for the end result—a shattering 73-0 victory by the Chicagoans. The Bears scored on their second play from scrimmage when Bill Osmanski swept around left end for a 68-yard scoring jaunt; and the rout was on.

George Halas, coach of the Bears, had carefully prepared for the game by bringing in his former advisor, Stanford coach Clark Shaughnessy. Shaughnessy helped refine the T formation the Bears had previously utilized, introducing a number of concepts that had aided his Stanford team to their perfect season. He also introduced a series of counter plays to take advantage of the Redskins' propensity to shift their linebackers in the direction of the man in motion. So effective and devastating was the resulting offensive display that ten different Bears scored 11 touchdowns. The impact of the Stanford season and the Bears' playoff victory revolutionized offensive football at all levels of the game, and as Robert Leckie has noted in *The Story of Football* (1965), "within five years, most teams in the country, high school, college, and pro, were using the T." The 1940 championship game was the first broadcast on network radio with the game carried on 120 stations of the Mutual Broadcasting System.

In 1941 the Chicago Bears continued their championship success, thrashing the New York Giants 37-9 in the title game on December 21, 1941. Coming two weeks after Pearl Harbor, the game attracted only 13,341 fans. Two players in the game, Young Bussey, quarterback for the Bears, and Jack Lumins of the Giants, would later be killed in the War. The NFL would see 638 of its players in military service in World War II, and 21 of that number would give their lives for their country.

The 1941 Chicago Bears team scored 396 points in eleven games, a record not broken until 1950 by Los Angeles, and gained 4,265 total yards. The premier player in 1940–41 was Don Hutson of Green Bay, who led the league in scoring and pass receiving, and Cecil Isbell, the Packers' quarterback, who led the league in passing in 1941 and 1942. Isbell became the first quarterback to throw for over 2,000 yards and over 20 touchdowns in a single season. The leading ball carrier in the league in 1940 was Byron "Whizzer" White, who had proved that college football and academics could go together. He had graduated Phi Beta Kappa from Colorado and received a Rhodes scholarship to Oxford. He became a U.S. Supreme Court justice, appointed by President John F. Kennedy.

Boxing

During the early forties, Joe Louis won the reputation of being the "fightingest" heavyweight champion of all time. In 1941 Louis defended his crown six times in six months. Hardbitten sportswriters derisively referred to Louis's opponents as "The Bum of the Month Club."

On June 18, 1941, Louis fought an extremely tough match against Billy Conn, a former light heavyweight champion from Pittsburgh. Conn was a quick, skillful ring tactician, capable of launching a bewildering assortment of punches. The fight drew a crowd of 54,487 and produced a gate of $450,743. Conn proved to be a crafty and clever opponent and after the first twelve rounds, appeared to be the eventual winner. Flushed with confidence of the impending victory, Conn attempted to slug it out with the Brown Bomber. With less than a minute to go in the round, a flurry of blows from the Detroit Dynamo sent Conn sprawling to the canvas. Conn was counted out and Louis declared the winner at 2:58 of the round. Louis would make no further defense of his crown before being inducted into the army. After Louis entered the armed forces, the heavyweight title was "frozen" during the war.

After Louis was mustered out of the service in 1946 he fought Billy Conn again, this time dispatching with him in the eighth round. Ringside seats cost a record price of $100, signaling the postwar boom that all sports would enjoy. Louis was paid $625,916 for the fight, the largest amount he ever received for a title fight purse.

College Basketball

The 1939–40 season was highlighted by the first telecast of college basketball. On February 28, 1940, WXBS, later to become WNBC, televised the Pitt-Fordham and NYU-Georgetown doubleheader from Madison Square Garden.

Time magazine reported in 1940 that basketball had a larger following than any other sport, with some 70,000 teams engaged in playing the game at all levels. The article further pointed out that professional basketball was staging a comeback after a decade of eclipse by brilliant college teams. It offered as proof the number of Chicago "addicts" who packed the Madison Street Armory to witness the battle to win the title "world champion" between the Harlem Globetrotters and the Chicago Bruins. The Globetrotters roared back from an 8-point deficit in the last five minutes to edge the Chicago team 31-29 to earn the crown and the $1,800 first prize money.

On the college level, Indiana finished second in the Big Ten to Purdue. However, Indiana had defeated the Boilermakers twice during the regular season and thus were chosen to participate in the NCAA tournament. The Hoosiers marched through their early round opponents, and then roared by an exhausted Kansas, who had ousted a tough South Carolina team in a grueling semifinal match. The final score was 60-42 in favor of Indiana.

In 1941, Wisconsin rebounded from a ninth place finish from the previous season and claimed the Big Ten title. Riding the crest of a 14 game winning streak, the Badgers swept into the finals. Opposing them in the finale was a tall and talented Washington State team, paced by 6-foot 8-inch center Paul Lindeman, and Dale Gentry, an All-American football end, Cougar coach Jack Friel, and Ray Sundquist, an All-American guard. The Washington State squad utilized a fast break attack, depending on a two-platoon system to exhaust opponents. Such strategy proved to be to no avail as Wisconsin controlled the boards and dictated the tempo of the game in eking out a 39-34 win. Wisconsin was led by All-American center Gene Englund, who scored 13 points, and Johnny Kotz with 12. Kotz was also named as the tournament's most valuable player.

The NCAA tournament final was broadcast nationally for the first time by the Mutual Broadcasting Network. A local station originated the broadcast, and the game was announced by a local broadcaster aided by a sportswriter from the Washington State student newspaper who earned a princely sum of $10 for his efforts.

Tennis

Bobby Riggs, who won the national title in 1939, lost in the 1940 finals to a tough twenty-two-year-old from Oklahoma city, Don McNeill. McNeill bounced back from losing the first two sets to edge Riggs in five sets. Riggs was a superb craftsman who, although lacking devastating power, possessed marvelous strokemanship and court savvy.

In the 1941 finals, Riggs didn't have to worry about McNeill's challenge since he was stopped in the semis by flamboyant Frank Kovacs, the son of an immigrant Hungarian upholsterer. Kovacs possessed a devastating power game but never seemed to live up to his potential. He was most noted for his amusing court antics, such as sitting down on the court or throwing three balls in the air and hitting the middle one for an ace. On a windy day, Riggs thwarted Kovacs' power and aggressively parlayed a varied attacking game into a three set triumph.

In the women's final, Sarah Palfrey Cooke, runner-up in 1934 and 1935, became the first woman's champion from the East since 1926 when she defeated Pauline Betz in two sets. Cooke teamed with Margaret E. Osborne to win the doubles title, and she was the doubles champion, teaming with Alice Marble for championships from 1937 through 1940. In 1941 Cooke won the mixed doubles with John A. Kramer, proving her one of the most durable women tennis players to ever take the courts.

Golf

The threat of war had not diminished golf's popularity, and there was a tremendous resurgence and interest in the game. This enthusiasm was generated by exciting and colorful personalities, many of whom hailed from the Lone Star state of Texas. Included among this group was the flashy Jimmy Demaret, who won half the tournaments on the winter-spring tour in 1940, and Ben Hogan, who earned prize money in 56 consecutive tournaments during the same year.

In the 1940 Open held on the windswept Canterbury Golf Club outside of Cleveland, Gene Sarazen, who had last won the Open in 1932, shot a 34 on the back nine to tie Lawson Little for the lead at the end of regulation play. Little triumphed in the playoff round.

In 1941 the Open was held at Fort Worth, Texas, and many partisan Texans came to the Colonial Club to support such state heroes as Byron Nelson, Jimmy Demaret, Ben Hogan, and others. The tournament began with rain-drenched fairways and ended in 95 degree temperatures. Aging Craig Wood, forty-six and wearing a corset because of chronic back pain, emerged victorious, carding a 284, trailed by Denny Shute of Chicago, 3 back at 287. Wood also captured the Masters that year, again recording a one stroke victory, this time at the expense of Byron Nelson. In 1941 Ben Hogan was the PGA moneywinning champion, with a total of $18,358; but by 1945 Byron Nelson would win over $63,000 in one season.

Minorities

The beginning of the decade also saw some movement in favor of greater participation in sports by black Americans. Jackie Robinson, a multisport star at UCLA, led the Pacific Coast Conference in scoring during the 1940 basketball season. John Woodruff's 1:47:7 time for the 880 and 1:47 flat for the 800-meter broke the records set in 1939 by another black track star, John Borican. Borican himself established a new record for the three-quarter mile run when he shattered a fifteen-year record by running the distance in 3:01:2. Also Jimmy Herbert ran the fastest quarter mile indoors, breaking Long Tom Halpins' mark of 49.6 that had stood since 1913. Yet it is interesting to note that in newspaper or magazine accounts of these athletes' exploits, the word "Negro" always preceded that athlete's name—whether out of journalistic astonishment or racial prejudice is difficult to determine.

In April 1940 the *New York Times* could report that sports' editors of New York's college newspapers had met to condemn the discrimination against Negro baseball players in the major leagues. This was to have been the first of a series of meetings and projects intended at mobilizing student opinion against discrimination in the major leagues. It's interesting to speculate how quickly improvement in civil rights guarantees or integration in sports would have developed without the war. World War II altered American lives profoundly, including the role of black athletes in the American sporting world. The war had a democratizing effect, as changes in military regulations regarding black soldiers signaled changes in society. The predominance of sports in the armed services served to expose many whites to black athletes and their skills, and many soldiers realized that sports after the war needed the talents of gifted black athletes if these sports were to be considered truly competitive. The changes came grudgingly and slowly, and tokenism seemed the order of the day. But black athletes had waited a long time, and the war created new hopes for opportunities.

The War Years

The rain of Japanese bombs upon Pearl Harbor on December 7, 1941, jolted the nation and sent shock tremors throughout the sports world. Would sports, particularly those at the professional level, survive during wartime? This question was never fully answered throughout the duration of the conflict. President Roosevelt would never firmly declare a clear policy on the status of professional sports. Beginning on January 17, 1942, and continuing throughout the war, Roosevelt would issue periodic statements for the continuation of major league baseball competition (but only if it did not interfere with the war effort), since it "provided relaxation for a hard working populace" and since "people needed to take their minds off things."

A basic premise or guideline laid down by Roosevelt, however, was that any player subject to the draft would not be deferred. Thus, baseball and football owners approached each wartime season apprehensively, watching in agony as more of their best players departed for combat training. Eventually, as the war dragged on, pro football and baseball managers found themselves suiting up teams composed of 4F's, inexperienced youths, and aging veterans, long gone in the tooth, never knowing whether the leagues would complete the season of competition. Fans complained about the lower quality of play and competition, but no one wanted to see sports suspended during the war.

Intercollegiate athletic programs suffered from manpower shortages and stringent travel restrictions. Many colleges simply abandoned intercollegiate competition altogether.

Golf and tennis suffered, since a combination of gas rationing and the military need for the rubber used in the respective balls made equipment scarce. Most of the golf and tennis balls subsequently manufactured during the war were composed of a combination of reclaimed and crude rubber or a synthetic variety which gave tennis balls a "soggy bounce." This meant that an average golf drive of 225 yards would be generally 15 yards short of that mark with the ersatz ball in use.

Civilian sports programs were not forgotten. In February 1941, a Division of Recreation was formed as a part of the Federal Security Agency. As a part of $150 million provided to fund the Community Facilities Bill, $17 million was appropriated for building recreation units.

In order to secure funds, a community had to initiate a report. All pertinent agencies were ordered to offer aid to the community when requested. A Federal Security Agency field representative acted as a conductor for various agencies and programs and as a conduit through which various aid programs were directed. Hundreds of recreation buildings were constructed under the program, and by the midpoint of the war, it was estimated that over 2,500 communities had participated in the recreational development program. Many of the programs operated twenty-four hours a day so that they could meet the needs of shift workers. As one director (quoted in Cozens and Stumpf's *Sports in American Life*, 1953) commented, "The swing-shift worker could swim, dance, play badminton, bowl, roller skate, often up to 4:00 A.M. or would play golf in the early afternoon."

Baseball in the War Years

The 1940 and 1941 sports seasons were played amid the threats of world war, which grew as Hitler's Nazi divisions swept across Poland and into Russia, as well as most of Western Europe. Although determined to stay out of the war if possible, the United States nevertheless had to prepare for its eventuality.

The Selective Service Act went into operation in the fall of 1940, and within two years over 31 million men would be registered with their draft boards. Over half of these men would serve in the armed forces during the war, and total United States casualties from the war would be just over a million.

The first regular major leaguer to be drafted was Hugh Mulcahy, a pitcher for the Philadelphia Phillies who had never had a winning season in three full seasons and who had twice been a twenty game loser. Mulcahy was drafted in March 1941 and missed almost five full seasons, coming back to pitch in five games late in the 1945 season. By 1941, 328 out of 607 major league players were active in the armed forces, and by 1945, 509 out of 565 active players were serving in the armed forces. By 1941, 5,800 players from the major and minor leagues had enlisted or been drafted, and by 1945, 5,400 were still in uniform.

The war had a tremendous impact on the careers of major leaguers. Some of the older players who were overage and ineligible for the draft enlisted even though they knew that the wartime conditions would prolong their careers. Charlie Gehringer, a nineteen-year major league veteran with the Detroit Tigers, enlisted at the age of thirty-nine in 1942 and served for three years in the U.S. Navy, directing a physical fitness program and rising to the rank of lieutenant commander. Ted Lyons, the workhorse pitcher of the Chicago White Sox from 1923–1942, enlisted in the Marines at the age of forty-two and served for three years. He did pitch during the 1946 season, but his career was over. He managed the White Sox for part of the 1946 season and all of the 1947 and 1948 seasons. Mickey Cochrane, whose skull had been fractured in three places in 1937 by a pitch that ended a short but brilliant career, enlisted in the navy. He managed the Great Lakes naval training service team, which won 63 and lost 14 in one season and beat the St. Louis Cardinals.

The war ended the careers of some baseball players, but it also enabled certain players to return to the major leagues after an absence of some years. Rip Radcliff never returned to baseball after a three-year hitch in the military, but in ten seasons he had compiled a lifetime

.311 batting average with 532 RBI's and 598 runs scored. He had hit .300 or better five times with a .342 average for the St. Louis Browns in 1940. Players like Babe Herman and Pepper Martin came back to the big leagues as the availability of players grew desperately short in 1944–45. Herman had not played since the 1937 season, but in 1945 the Dodgers brought him back as a pinch hitter. He hit .265 in 34 at bats and had 9 RBI's for his 9 hits. After a three-year absence, Pepper Martin returned to the Cardinals and played in 40 games during the 1944 season, hitting .279.

Others came back only for cameo appearances, with perhaps few fans remembering the name. Chief Elon Hogsett came back to the Tigers at the age of forty-one, to pitch in only 3 games during the 1944 season. Jimmy Foxx returned to the game in 1944 after being out of baseball for a year. For the Philadelphia Phillies in 1945 he hit .268, with 7 home runs and 38 RBI's. He also pitched in nine games, pitching one complete game and compiling a 1.59 ERA in twenty-two and two-thirds innings.

To those who remembered them, the return of these veterans was heartwarming. They still had enough of their old skills to display, and on the whole fans were kind to those who came back to help out during the player shortage of the war years. Joe Cronin continued to play wherever he was needed on the Boston Red Sox team, and in 1943 he was 18 for 42 as a pinch hitter. Perhaps the oldest returnee was Paul Schreiber, who had last appeared in 1923 for the Brooklyn Dodgers. Schreiber pitched in two games for the Yankees in 1945. Hod Lisenbee pitched in 31 games for the Cincinnati team in 1945, having last pitched for the Philadelphia A's in 1936.

The appearance of such players as these had led sports historians to characterize baseball during the war years (1942 to 1945) as a game played by old-timers, draft rejects, borrowed Cuban or Puerto Rican players, underage players, and inadequate minor leaguers who just filled the gap until the real professionals returned. To a certain extent this description is true, but it is an unfair and harsh characterization. Those who played during the war years deeply loved the game and endured difficult circumstances as far as travel and hotel accommodations. Many of them knew their role was only temporary and that they would be displaced within a few years or might even be drafted themselves as draft regulations changed with manpower needs.

Baseball provided an important morale booster on the home front as well as the war front. Wartime industry workers found important entertainment at ball parks, and those working in the plants listened to radio broadcasts of games. With severe wartime restrictions on automobile use for pleasure, ball parks became the center of neighborhoods and cities, and in 1945 both leagues drew well over 5 million fans, a promise of a new postwar boom for baseball.

On the war fronts American troops followed the major leagues' season daily, and the World Series was broadcast worldwide. Baseball's continuation during the war signified things as normal back home. The game continued exactly the way it had in the past. The teams were the same, and enough stars and established regulars continued their careers during the war years to provide stability and a measure of respectability. The Japanese recognized the importance of baseball news and broadcasts to American troop morale when they tried unsuccessfully to jam broadcasts of the World Series over the Armed Forces Radio Network and when they stormed Allied positions screaming "To hell with Babe Ruth."

Baseball owners and management, however, were not always certain about baseball's role in wartime. Several questions were raised, and the debate was extensive. First, there was the question of whether players should be draft exempt or whether they should be given special classifications or considerations. This question was clearly and unequivocally answered in President Franklin D. Roosevelt's famous "green light" letter of January 15, 1942, to Baseball Commissioner Kenesaw Mountain Landis. Roosevelt noted the importance of baseball as recreation for hard-working people who needed relatively inexpensive entertainment that would last for two hours or so, and thus would not impair working efficiency because of late hours. Roosevelt encouraged the adoption of more night games to accommodate workers on day shifts. However, Roosevelt also noted that "individual players who are of active military or naval age should go, without question, into the services" and that "if any individual has some particular aptitude in a trade or profession, he ought to serve the Government." In this famous letter Roosevelt indicated that this was a personal and unofficial point of view.

It was clear that the final decision rested with Judge Landis and the club owners. Roosevelt offered his private encouragement to continue, even with the loss of talent and the probable lowering of the quality of the teams and overall play. In writing this letter, Roosevelt recognized the value of baseball as a recreational and emotional outlet during a time of national crisis. Further, he indicated his absolute trust in Landis's ability to handle the matter of draft eligibility and government service "with complete justice." This was a kind of private agreement between two gentlemen, and Landis would never betray the trust that Roosevelt placed in him. In 1944, when J. G. Taylor Spink of *Sporting News* wrote to Roosevelt asking for special considerations for baseball players, Judge Landis emphatically wrote to

General Lewis B. Hershey, director of Selective Service, that baseball wanted no preferential treatment since this would violate his earlier gentleman's agreement with Roosevelt and since favored treatment would produce "bitter public resentment," thus damaging the reputation of the game and compromising its integrity.

Roosevelt's trust was well founded, and Landis, along with the owners, set out on a course that would insure continuation of the game even though the uncertainties were great. The discontinuation of the game might be seen as a sign of national weakness or uncertainty about a great democracy's future. From a business point of view the collapse of baseball franchises would disrupt the continuity of the game and create problems when veterans returned and could no longer rejoin their old teams. Thus, baseball's survival was symbolic of the survival of the nation, its cherished institutions, and its style of life. Soldiers sent to the far flung reaches of the world could be assured that spring training would start, that a full season would be played, and that the autumn excitement of the World Series would be experienced. Baseball provided an important emotional and psychological connection to the homeland, to sanity and order, and to innocent play and good times. As Arthur Daley so movingly wrote in the *New York Times* for April 14, 1946, when the season was about to begin with 90 percent of the veterans returned in the National League, "Dreams of baseball [during the war years] were dreams of sanity. To the dreamers the game was a symbol of the things-that-were, of the things-yet-to-be."

Commissioner Landis helped baseball to lead the way as a national symbol of the cooperation, patriotism, and sacrifice that were needed throughout the country in order to mobilize for war and to support the war effort. With few exceptions players willingly suspended their careers when drafted, or they volunteered for enlistment. Many served three and four years until the forces of totalitarianism and militarism were defeated. Landis made $25,000 available for an equipment fund to provide bats, balls, and athletic equipment for servicemen, and the proceeds from the 1942 All-Star game went into this fund. At ball parks baseballs were retrieved from stands and sent to war training camps for the soldiers' use.

Baseball demonstrated its patriotism in other ways. It showed its willingness to cooperate with the Office of Defense Transportation by reducing and economizing on travel. During the 1943, 1944, and 1945 spring training sessions the teams practiced in northern camps and made do with cold weather and makeshift arrangements. Games were scheduled for mornings, afternoons, twilight, and twilight-night doubleheaders to allow more workers to see them. The major leagues assumed greater importance as the minor leagues shrank from forty-four to twelve.

Thus, organized baseball set the tone and example for a nation that was undergoing serious wartime shortages and restrictions. Baseball players visited war industry factories to encourage greater production and efficiency and to promote war bond sales. The players pledged a percentage of their salaries to buy war bonds and clubs played special benefit games for war relief funds and sports equipment funds. Servicemen were admitted free to major and minor league games, and clubs sponsored salvage days, when fans were admitted free for bringing certain amounts of scrap metal, kitchen fat, or waste paper. By 1945, 4.5 million servicemen had been admitted free to games. In New York City a War Bond League was established in which players for the Yankees, Dodgers, and Giants were given performance votes and popularity votes by supporters who purchased bonds as votes. Over $1 billion was raised by this War Bond League as baseball parks became an important, if not key, center of the war bond drives.

The players of the war years also performed important services to the overall war effort. Many played with physical handicaps, or they were overage for a game that demanded stamina, quick reflexes, and agility. But their determination and dedication to the game should be recognized. Some unkind fans might question their loyalty or patriotism and label them as "draft dodgers" or "shirkers." They played to the best of their ability, trying to concentrate on the game during a period of wartime uncertainty. They faced unfavorable comparison with the professional regulars, and they must have wondered about the level of their skills and the quality of their performance. Many played for only a few games, as teams desperately sought new talent or winning combinations. The Boston Red Sox used ten different third basemen in one wartime season, and the personnel on teams was constantly changing.

This uncertainty and the shifting of players reflect the more widespread disruptions in American society brought on by the war. Over 27 million people moved during the war, and 1.6 million people left the South to migrate to northern industrial cities. Family life was disrupted or changed when women went to work and school attendance for those between the ages of fourteen and nineteen dropped.

As blacks became increasingly involved in wartime industry and military service, they sought to decrease racial discrimination in employment and military service. In June 1943, a serious riot erupted in Detroit, the "arsenal of democracy" where wartime industries were crucial. The June 23, 1943, doubleheader between Detroit and Cleveland was played with 350 armed troops stationed in small groups throughout Briggs Stadium. The next day's game was played before 2,000 armed troops and 6,617 paying customers. Thirty-four people (25 blacks and 9 whites) were killed in the riots, 700 injured, with 1,200 people jailed. Baseball was not immune from pressures and conflicts felt within society as a whole. It felt the disruption and uncertainty caused by the war, and the pressure exerted by blacks for fuller participation in society was felt in baseball as black groups challenged the unofficial but nevertheless solid "color line" that excluded talented black players.

Baseball was not in control of its own future in the turbulent war years. At times its role seemed uncertain and doubtful as the war continued. Wartime editorials written during the World Series excitement apologized to the troops on the battlefront for diverting the country's attention away from the more important soldiers' struggles. Baseball owners drew up contingency plans to continue on a reduced scale if necessary, and in 1944 one owner, Alva Bradley of the Cleveland Indians, had the audacity to suggest that owners suspend operations for the remainder of the war rather than present "a low form of comedy" during the upcoming 1944 season. Bradley was afraid that baseball would become a "farce" as players tried to play positions that they did not know or for which they did not have the skills. Bradley received stern and angry replies from other club owners and executives, notably Branch Rickey, then with the Dodgers. Rickey believed it was the "game's duty to carry on," and he believed that as long as baseball continued (including the minor leagues) there would be enough players to fill major league uniforms.

Baseball found a role for itself during the war, and it proved its vital role as morale booster, example of wartime cooperation, and exemplar of patriotism. The game did not suffer during the war years. It simply changed, assuming a symbolic role of normalcy and routine, and this emotional role far overshadowed any significant decline in the quality of play. With individual stars gone for an indefinite period, the emphasis was on team play, consistency, and endurance under difficult circumstances. These were the same values that society was learning and experiencing as the country pulled together with a common goal and learned the satisfactions of self-sacrifice and unified work effort.

The 1943 Yankees coasted to a 13½-game margin over the Senators, although this New York team was dramatically changed in personnel from the previous season. Only Joe Gordon, Frankie Crosetti, Charlie Keller, and Bill Dickey were left from the 1942 team. Gordon and Keller would be absent from baseball in 1944 and 1945 when they served in the military. At the age of thirty-six, Dickey hit .351 in 242 plate appearances. The highest average among Yankee regulars was Billy Johnson's .280 effort.

Five of the pitchers of the 1942 team were available in 1943. Spud Chandler was 20-4 with a league-leading 1.64 ERA. Ernie Bonham won 15, and Hank Borowy, one of the best pitchers in the war years, won 14. Johnny Murphy continued his brilliant relief pitching, winning 12.

Overall performance in the American League began to show the effects of the draft and enlistments. Only four regulars batted .300 or better, and runs scored dropped dramatically. Rudy York of Detroit and Yankee Charlie Keller demonstrated home run power, but after these two the number of players with power was small.

The Cardinals repeated as pennant winners in 1943. Ten different pitchers won games, with Mort Cooper winning 21 and losing 8. The top three pitchers in the league in the earned run category were all from St. Louis: Howie Pollet, Max Lanier, and Mort Cooper. The pitching staff registered 94 complete games with 21 shutouts and compiled a 2.57 ERA. Stan Musial hit .357 to win the batting title easily, and he collected 220 hits. A first-year outfielder fresh from a knee operation by the name of Danny Litwhiler fielded 1,000 as he was the first outfielder to have a perfect season. Again manager Billy Southworth managed and utilized his available talent with skill, and this time the Cards were ahead almost all the way, winning by 18 games over Cincinnati.

The Yankees turned the tables on the Cards in the 1943 World Series, winning 4 games to 1. The usually sound-fielding Cardinals committed ten errors, and the hitters left thirty-seven teammates stranded on the bases. Spud Chandler pitched two complete games and only gave up one earned run. Marius Russo, who was 5-10 during the season, pitched a complete game and scored the winning run when he doubled and came home on a long fly by Frankie Crosetti. St. Louis managed to score only nine times in the Series, although they had numerous opportunities.

The 1944 season was unusual for many reasons. To no one's surprise the Cardinals again won easily with consistent although unspectacular hitting and solid pitching. Their fielding was steady and smooth. The team committed only 112 errors with four players being the league's best in fielding at their positions. Musial hit .347, with Johnny Hopp not far behind at .336.

The real surprises of 1944 were the St. Louis Browns, who won their pennant on the last day of the season as they swept their four-game series with the Yankees. The Browns only hit .252 as a team, which was next to last in the league. Their top hitter was Mike

Kreevich, who hit .301. Vern Stephens led the league with 109 RBI's and had 20 of the team's 72 home runs. The team averaged almost thirty-two years of age, but they played inspired and competent baseball. The pitching staff of Nels Potter, Jack Kramer, Bob Muncrief, and Sig Jakucki combined for 62 wins, and George Caster saved 12 games in relief.

The Detroit team had spectacular pitching from Dizzy Trout and Hal Newhouser. Newhouser led the league in wins with a 29-9 record, and Trout was 27-14 with a 2.12 ERA. Newhouser finished second with a 2.22 ERA. Trout had 33 complete games and Newhouser had 25. Together they pitched in an astonishing 662 innings. But no other pitcher on the Detroit staff had a winning record. This combined effort of Trout and Newhouser shows the sacrifice that pitchers made during the war years when the pitching staff was short.

In the 1944 World Series the Cardinals defeated a stubborn, yet clearly inferior Browns team. The Browns committed 10 errors, and the Cardinals had only 1 error. Cardinal pitchers fanned forty-nine Browns' batters, and forty-three Cardinals struck out. The Cardinals had brilliant relief pitching from Blix Donnelly in the first and second games. In the second game he pitched four scoreless innings in relief and struck out seven. Ted Wilks came in as a relief pitcher in the sixth inning of the sixth game and snuffed out a Browns' rally that had men on second and third with only one out. Wilks, who had been knocked out in the fourth inning of game three, won by the Browns 6-2, retired the last eleven batters in a row to preserve Hal Lanier's victory. Harry Brecheen and Mort Cooper pitched complete games to win the fourth and fifth games after the underdog Browns had surprised everyone by winning two of the first three games in the Series.

The World Series created a great deal of excitement and national interest. All games were played at Sportsman's Park, and the fans were evenly divided. The Browns were sentimental favorites as underdogs, and they personified the gritty determination of a patchwork team that had managed to win a pennant against great odds. They made the Series exciting and interesting, and the Cardinals had to play their best to win. The Series was carried on Armed Forces Network Radio all over the globe and received extensive coverage in armed forces newspapers.

The two opposing managers, Billy Southworth and Luke Sewell, even shared the same apartment due to a wartime housing shortage. The only thing missing from the Series was the presence of Commissioner Landis. He was seriously ill and would die in November 1944. His absence from the games took some of the color and meaning away from the 1944 fall classic. The highlights of the Series were seen by millions of troops on film, and after the win a contingent of Cardinal players visited American troops in the Aleutian Islands and Alaska. The 1944 Series showed that baseball in wartime, despite the absence of many stars and regulars, could be exciting. The drama was still there, and the quality of the game had not been affected adversely.

The 1945 season saw the greatest shortage of experienced players as many of those players who were draft exempt during the 1942, 1943, and 1944 seasons were reclassified and sent into the military service. The scarcity of players called for resourceful and, some might say, even desperate measures. Pete Gray, a one-armed outfielder, was purchased by the St. Louis Browns, and he appeared in 77 games, hitting .218 and striking out only 11 times in 234 at bats. In the field he was charged with 7 errors and made 162 putouts. Gray's burning determination to play baseball was appreciated by many major league fans, just as they would take to their hearts the efforts of Lou Brissie, who made it to the majors in 1948 despite a reconstructed left leg and braces on the other as a result of enemy shellfire in Italy. The paucity of talent in 1944 and 1945 was partially answered by the use of Mexican, Cuban, Puerto Rican, and South American players.

Hitting in the American League during the 1945 season dropped off sharply, as the league batting average was .255 and home runs became rare events. Snuffy Stirnweiss of the Yankees won the batting title with a .309 average, and only three league regulars hit over .300. A number of players did hit over .300, but they did not have the required number of at bats.

The Detroit Tigers won the 1945 pennant in a close race with the Washington Senators. Hank Greenberg, who had returned from the service on July 1, 1945, hit 13 homers, had 60 RBI's, and batted .311 in 78 games. In the final game of the season Greenberg hit a grand slam home run against the St. Louis Browns in the top of the ninth after the Browns had led 3-2. Another veteran, Al Benton, had returned to the team for the 1945 season after a two-year absence. Benton came on in relief against the Browns in the bottom of the ninth and sealed the dramatic Tiger win.

The 1945 Tigers were jokingly referred to as the "Nine Old Men." The centerfielder, Doc Cramer, was forty years old and hit .275 with 58 RBI's and 36 extra base hits. He also led the league in fielding average, committing only 2 errors. The team fielded by the Tigers averaged almost thirty-five years old, and the youngest regulars were thirty years old. The pitching staff was again led by Hal Newhouser, who was 25-9 and who led the league with a 1.81 ERA and 212 strikeouts. Dizzy Trout won 18, and Al Benton won 13 with a 2.02 ERA. Virgil Trucks would rejoin the team late in the season and would pitch in two games of the World Series.

The Tigers led the major leagues in attendance, drawing almost 1.3 million fans. In the National League Brooklyn, Chicago, and New York all drew over a million in attendance. In 1946 attendance in the National League would jump from 5.2 million to almost 9 million, and in the American League the gate jumped from 5.6 million to 9.6 million. The postwar baseball boom was underway, and in the 1948 season both Cleveland and the Yankees would draw well over 2 million, and eight other clubs would attract over a million. This postwar boom led to fierce competition for new talent, and the "bonus baby" became part of baseball lingo. Bobby Brown was paid a $50,000 bonus in 1946, while Alvin Dark was paid $40,000.

The Chicago Cubs won the 1945 National League race by three games over the Cardinals. The Cubs were led by Phil Cavarretta, who hit .355 and led the league. The Cubs had solid hitting with Stan Hack, Andy Pafko, Don Johnson, and Peanuts Lowery. Hank Borowy and Claude Passeau led the league's pitchers in ERA, and the pitching staff was stingy with walks (only 385) and long on complete games (86). The fielding was steady with only 121 errors. Hank Wyse won 22 games, and Paul Derringer won 16 at the age of thirty-nine in his last major league season.

The 1945 World Series had been described as a comedy of errors, mistakes, inept play, mental lapses, and mindless base running. The Tigers managed to win in 7 games as the oldsters were put to the supreme physical test of endurance. Although his troubles in the field were legion, Doc Cramer led the Tigers with 11 hits, all singles. Hank Greenberg had 7 hits, 5 of them for extra bases, and drove home 7 runs. Hal Newhouser pitched two complete games and won the fifth and seventh contests after he had been bombed in the first game and only lasted three innings. Newhouser struck out twenty-two Cubs in the Series. Recently returned from the service, Virgil Trucks pitched a complete game in the 4-1 Tigers' win in the second game, and Dizzy Trout did the same in game five. Claude Passeau pitched a masterful one-hitter in the third game for the Cubs with only Rudy York able to reach him for a hit.

The Cubs depended too heavily on Hank Borowy, using him in four games. He pitched brilliantly in relief in game six when he held the Tigers hitless for the last four innings and preserved a 8-7 Cub win in twelve innings. But manager Charlie Grimm decided to start Borowy in the seventh game, and he did not survive the first inning as Detroit scored five times off Borowy and Derringer.

The 1945 World Series set records for gate receipts (almost $1.6 million) and attendance (333,457). The Series had more than its share of lax and loose play as players forgot to make throws, failed to catch fly balls, or threw the ball wildly over a teammate's head. Runners fell down or were picked off. However, no one could deny that the games were not exciting or unpredictable. This was to be the last of the wartime Series, as the fall classic was played just one month after the articles of surrender were signed by Japan on the battleship *Missouri* in Tokyo Bay and six months after V-E Day. In such a joyous mood the fans overlooked the foibles of the older players who had kept the game alive and made the war years interesting in their own way.

College Football

The abrupt removal of the Rose Bowl from California in 1941 at the loss of $20 million out of fear of Japanese attack cast a dim light on the future of wartime collegiate football. In January of 1942, *Newsweek* reported college football coaches opposed to curbs on college sports. Many of them were reportedly reacting to a statement by Ellwood A. Geiger, executive assistant to John B. Kelley, OCD director of physical fitness, who called for an increased need in intramural athletics and compulsory physical education. Despite the coaches' support, by 1943 over 300 colleges had given up the sport including such gridiron heavyweights as Stanford, Fordham, Alabama, and Georgetown. Those who maintained programs did so only with such rule changes as lifting the ban against freshmen participating in college sports.

Reacting to the wholesale abandonment of football by so many colleges, veteran Columbia football coach Lou Little claimed in the January 17, 1943, edition of the *New York Times* that physical education directors were seeking to eliminate coaches. He further asserted that football must be preserved in colleges because the game developed a desire for competition. He stated that World War I veterans came back men and brought back the "spirit of fight" with them, making post World War I football the most aggressive in football history. He further stated: "When I take part in a sport, I want to win and kick the brains out of the other fellow. I'm not content to play with someone. I want to play against them."

Dan Ferris, secretary-treasurer of the AAU, echoed Little's remarks concerning the desirable relationship of competitive sports to warfare. According to the January 17, 1943, *New York Times*, Ferris said,

"No nation can be successful in war while its functions are frustrated by a people not physically fit at home and on the home front. This was amply displayed in the last war and history is repeating itself. The U.S. is far from being a physically fit nation but the men who make up the armed forces abroad are the pick of the nation's physically fit citizens. Competitive sports have played and are playing a most important part in improving the physical condition of our people and while sports are not considered essential to the war effort at the moment, I predict before we win this war every government official from the President on down will regard competitive sports as a necessary element if not an absolute requisite for victory."

In an article written for the Oct. 27, 1945 *Michigan Alumnus Quarterly Review* ("Football and the Battlefield," pp.66–75), Colonel John R. Lovell and Clinton B. Conger perceived that "battle plans and football plays showed striking similarities in fundamentals of strategy." Colonel Lovell, a former assistant U.S. military attache, and Conger, a former United Press staff correspondent in Berlin, had been interned for five months at the beginning of the war. While incarcerated, they had "bull sessions" on football and warfare which "resulted in this article." The authors found that football was at least twenty-five years ahead of warfare strategy. According to their study, the flying wedge, introduced in 1884 by Princeton and Lehigh, was still being used by the British Army at Cambrai in 1916. The forward pass, legalized in 1910 in football, meant that gridiron victory could be achieved through the air as well as on the ground. However, air power as a means to military victory was not fully exploited until 1935 when the German Luftwaffe amply demonstrated its potency.

Furthermore, the co-authors concluded that many famous battles of World War I and II have been merely versions of popular football plays. For example, Rommel's sweep around left end at Bir Hacheim was simply another version of football's sleeper play and Fielding Yost's football textbook could well be a modern military manual. They came to the following conclusion: "Our fighting forces of today are made up of tens of thousands of men who know football as they know their right hand, who can grasp the principles of modern warfare on that basis with an advantage given to no other nation in the world. Before we played any big games against Germany, we had a mighty good squad. It is more than probable that some American tank officer, reaching fortified German positions after driving back the German panzers, thought back to an autumn day when he was a quarterback. 'These guys,' he probably muttered, 'are no tougher than State College—and if the coach's pet back cut over tackle and scored against State, it ought to land us right in Berlin this time.' And it will.''

How effective and persuasive this eloquence was in defining and in evaluating football's contribution to the war effort cannot be quantitatively determined. What is known is that the navy and marines, under the leadership of Commander Tom Hamilton, the head of physical education for naval aviation cadets, clearly advocated football as superb training for combat. Thus, naval personnel at 191 colleges and universities with V-12 and other naval training programs were allowed to play football. Preflight programs such as those at Iowa and North Carolina fielded teams as well as the universities that hosted them. As in World War I, the premier military team was that of the Great Lakes eleven. The Iowa preflight team was ranked second in the country in 1943, and sixth in 1944. The 1944 top ten teams included six service-related football teams.

The army, with 100,000 students at 209 colleges in various programs, was not allowed to participate in intercollegiate athletics. As a result, most universities with army programs were forced to drop football for the duration of the war.

In 1942, the full impact of the war had not yet struck. That year Boston College and Georgia Tech were ranked one and two for most of the season, but both were decisively whipped to ruin their unblemished records. Holy Cross beat Boston College 55-22 and Georgia smashed Georgia Tech 34-0. Ohio State, paced by Les Horvath, the 1944 Heisman Trophy winner, was voted national champs. Its only loss, 17-7, was to a fine Wisconsin team, led by Elroy ''Crazy Legs'' Hirsch. The fact that twenty-one Ohio State players became ill on the Wisconsin trip and were not at full strength for the Badger game may have influenced *Collier's* to consider the Wisconsin loss a ''fluke.''

In 1943, Notre Dame had an outstanding team. Its quarterback was a sensational passer, ''Accurate'' Angelo Bertelli, against such unbeaten powerhouses as Navy, Army, Michigan, and the Iowa Seahawks. Unfortunately for Notre Dame, after having completed 25 of 36 passes for 512 yards and 10 touchdowns in 6 games, Bertelli was drafted in the middle of the season and spent the rest of his Saturday afternoons during the football season listening to Notre Dame play on the radio from marine boot camp at Parris Island.

Johnny Lujack capably filled in for Bertelli, directing the Irish to a 26-0 victory over a powerful Army team. In the last game of the season, Great Lakes Naval Training Station, whose team was composed of numerous former All-Americans, eked out a 19-14 victory over the Irish on the desperation pass in the last thirty seconds. Four Notre

Dame players, including Bertelli, were named to the *Collier's* All-American team.

Also in 1943, the Army-Navy game was played at West Point instead of a stadium in a large metropolis, with tickets limited to residents within a ten-mile radius and to army personnel on duty. Despite the protests of various Congressmen, Under Secretary of War Robert P. Patterson rejected all pleas to move the game, stating that the usual circumstances for the game were "incongruous with the war effort" and that restrictions were necessary "because of transportation and fuel shortages."

During the 1944 and 1945 football seasons, college football was dominated by the Black Knights of Army. The 1945 All-American team included four Army players. With other college elevens decimated by the draft and manned by 4F's and seventeen-year-olds and wounded veterans, the army squads boasted more than abundant manpower. Key players were the backfield tandem, known as "Mr. Outside" and "Mr. Inside"—Glenn Davis and Felix "Doc" Blanchard, respectively.

Davis, at 5 feet 9 inches and 172 pounds, ran the 100-yard dash in 9.8 and in 1944 scored 20 touchdowns with most of them coming on jaunts of more than 30 yards. Doc Blanchard was a 6-foot, 210-pound fullback and was able, according to one authority, to "run 100 yards in ten flat, punt a football 50 to 60 yards, sweep the flats and rip apart the middle of opposing lines, week after week."

In 1944 the Army team scored a total of 504 points, averaging 56 points a game, and became the first West Point eleven to go undefeated. Highlighting the season was Army's 59-0 walloping of Notre Dame, avenging thirteen straight years of losses to their rival.

The following years the Cadets again went undefeated, paced by the touchdown twins and again shellacked Notre Dame, this time by a 48-0 score. The Army teams of 1944 and 1945 certainly were in a class by themselves during those war years.

Pro Football

In 1942 pro football teams, eager to do their part for the war effort, played a series of games against two army all-star units—an eastern unit headed by Colonel Robert Neyland and a western unit led by Major Wallace Wade. According to an Army spokesman, these games had a twofold purpose: (1) to raise funds, and (2) to make the "public better acquainted with the army as a winning organization."

A total of eight games were played, with Major Wallace Wade's team winning two of five games, while Neyland's team won two out of eight in a nine-day period, losing only to the powerful Chicago Bears 14-7 after having whipped the New York Giants and the Brooklyn Dodgers. Over $400,000 was raised for the Army Relief Fund.

The NFL player rosters were drastically decimated by the war's requirements for manpower. A total of 638 NFL players served in uniform. Of this number, 355 were commissioned officers, 66 received battle decorations, and 21 died in combat.

In 1942 the Washington Redskins beat the Chicago Bears 14-7 for the NFL title. In 1943, 1944, and 1945, the Bears, the Packers, and the Rams won titles respectively.

The real wartime story was the struggle of the NFL to simply survive. Rosters were reduced from thirty-three to twenty-eight men. The Cleveland Rams halted operations in 1943 only to resume the following year. Also in 1943 Philadelphia and Pittsburgh played as the Phil-Pitt Eagles while in 1944 a Card-Pitt team was formed. Many players worked in essential industries but were allowed time off for practice and games, and veterans were lured out of retirement. The Chicago Bears, for example, in 1943 brought Bronko Nagurski out of a six-year retirement to lead them to the title.

Despite the reduction of teams to only eight in number and the obvious dilution in the quality of play, the NFL remained quite popular. The *New York Times* reported in 1943 that attendance averaged 23,644 per game, an increase of 39 percent over the 1942 season.

By the 1945 season with the war having ended in August, NFL rosters were flooded with returning service personnel, and total season attendance soared to over a million. In the season's finale, the Cleveland Rams beat the Washington Redskins on a fluke play, 15-14. Sammy Baugh attempted to pass out of his end zone, but the pass hit the goal post, which was an automatic safety. The rule was changed the following year.

Basketball

Basketball enjoyed the largest rise in popularity in its history during the war years. By June of 1945, *Time* magazine could report that basketball was America's number one sport, with over 75 million in attendance.

College basketball in particular would boom during World War II. With rosters composed of only a dozen or so players, the sport was less affected by the wartime manpower requirements. Also the trend toward tall teams—West Texas State, for example, boasted a 6 foot, 10 inch tall center and a front line that averaged 6 feet, 6 inches—meant that a greater number of basketball players received deferments. Yet like football, some colleges dropped the sport or were forced to field teams composed primarily of freshmen.

In 1942 Stanford trounced Dartmouth 53-38 to take the NCAA title while West Virginia topped Western Kentucky to capture the National Invitational Tournament.

In 1943 Ken Sailors, a remarkably skilled athlete possessing a talent for both offense and defense, led the Wyoming Cowboys (with a 31-2 record) to triumph in the NCAA championships over Georgetown. Starting in that year, and continuing for the next two years, the NCAA and NIT champions played a benefit game at Madison Square Garden for the Red Cross Benefit Fund. In that first year, Wyoming beat St. John's 52-47. However, some experts maintained that the best team that year was the Illinois squad, which featured the so-called Whiz Kids, but which did not play in either of the two major postseason tournaments. The Illinois team went 12-0 in the Big Ten that year.

In 1943–44, the team that caught the public's fancy was the Utah "Blitz Kids," who averaged six feet in height and slightly over eighteen years in age. Because their conference had dissolved for the war's duration and the army was utilizing its gymnasium, the Utes played mostly service teams and practiced in church gyms. Turning down an NCAA bid, the Utah squad accepted an invitation to play in a strong NIT field, which included such "toughies" as Kentucky, St. John's, Bowling Green, DePaul, and Oklahoma A&M. But the western squad did not fare well and was beaten by Kentucky 46-38.

This was not the end of the Utah season, however. A late withdrawal by Arkansas caused Utah to be invited once again to participate in the NCAA tournament. This time they accepted and rolled their way to the finals, edging Dartmouth 42-40 in the championship game. Then in a real irony, they were matched in the Red Cross Benefit game against the NIT champs, St. John's of New York. The "Running Redskins," paced by 6 foot 3 inch freshman All-American Arnie Ferrin's 17 points, raced by the Redmen from St. John's 43-36. Ferrin made All-American in 1944, and came back in 1947 and 1948 to repeat the honors, leading his team to a 1947 NIT championship.

The year 1945 may well be marked as the beginning of modern basketball with the development of the good, big man. As early as 1943, Oklahoma A&M, under the coaching leadership of Hank Iba, featured a 7 foot freshman center, Bob "Foothills" Kurland, and billed itself as the "tallest team on earth." In 1944, Harry "Big Boy" Boykoff at 6 feet

9 inches was described by *Time* magazine as looking "like a Heron in full flight" and was cited by one self-styled expert as a "major reason why goaltending became part of the game." But in 1945 everyone was interested in the possibility of the gargantuan Kurland playing against another phenomenon, 6-foot, 10-inch George Mikan of De-Paul. Both men were chosen as All-Americans from 1944 through 1946.

Mikan had been carefully tutored by Coach Ray Meyer through a program which featured rope skipping, shadow-boxing and running to increase his agility. The dream game became a reality in that last year of the war. DePaul triumphed in the NIT tournament, and Oklahoma A & M captured the NCAA postseason laurels.

The so-called battle of the goons packed 18,148 into the old Madison Square Garden in New York. The confrontation itself did not live up to its early billing and was something of a disappointment. Mikan fouled out with 14 minutes gone in the contest, and the Aggies from Oklahoma secured a 52-44 victory. Kurland also was less than spectacular, scoring only 14 points despite Mikan's premature departure. No matter, big-time college basketball had demonstrated that through the showcasing of giants, who moved with an agility heretofore considered impossible, it could become such an attractive spectacle that even the exigencies of war could not dim the public's enthusiasm for it.

Boxing, Golf, Tennis

Many boxing champions, including Joe Louis, were inducted into the service. Often they were used as physical education and combat instructors and gave exhibitions to aid morale. Louis gave unstintingly of his service. In 1943 he led a boxing troop that entertained troops in Scotland, North Africa, Italy, and Alaska. In order to raise money for service charities, a rematch was planned between the Brown Bomber and Billy Conn. The bout, however, was cancelled when it was discovered that portions of the proceeds would be used to pay off personal debts of the fighters.

While in the army, Louis was instrumental in helping to promote desegregation. For example, while at Fort Riley, Kansas, he met Jackie Robinson, who complained that he and eighteen other blacks had applied for officer training but were being denied entrance to the officers' candidate program. Louis complained to Truman Gibson, a special advisor on black affairs to the secretary of war. He also threatened Brigadier General Donald A. Robinson, the commanding officer of the Cavalry Training Center at Fort Riley, by withholding his boxing exhibitions unless Jim Crow regulations were abolished. Within a week Robinson and the other black officer candidates were admitted to officer candidate schools and all became officers.

Louis also was refused admission to a movie theater in England in 1943. The cashier explained that the American commanding officer had ordered that blacks were to be prohibited from attending movies which admitted white soldiers. Louis complained, the order was revoked, and the offending officer was removed from his command.

By 1942 the golf tour was reduced to about two dozen tournaments. The U.S. Open was canceled and instead in 1942, the Hale America Open was played at Ridgemoor Country Club in Chicago. A portion of the prize money was paid off in war defense bonds, and the tournament profits were split equally between the U.S.O. and Navy Relief. The PGA tournament was played in 1944 and 1945, the only major tournament to survive the war. Byron Nelson lost the 1944 PGA to Bob Hamilton but Nelson won the 1945 tournament.

By 1943 many of the outstanding golfers such as Sammy Snead, Lawson Little, Jimmy Demaret, and Lloyd Mangrum were in the service. Mangrum later was wounded twice in the Battle of the Bulge.

Tennis suffered primarily the same fate as golf. In 1939, 90,000 tons of rubber—enough to equip 5,500 army trucks—had been used for tennis ball manufacturing. This supply was cut off immediately with the onset of wartime conditions. For four years tennis aficionados had to play with balls manufactured of synthetic rubber or, more commonly, soggy, rubber "victory balls."

The war effectively ended the amateur tennis circuit. Ted Schroeder, defending national singles champion, and Gardnar Mulloy, ranked number three, were lieutenants in the navy while Fran Parker, ranked number two, served in the army. Other noteworthy and nationally known players such as Don McNeill, Bitsy Grant, and Frank Kovacs were also in the service.

Pauline Betz dominated women's tennis during the war years, winning the national singles title in 1942, 1943, and 1944. Her reign came to an end in 1945 when Sarah Palfrey Cooke defeated her, although Betz came back to win in 1946.

Ted Schroeder won the national singles crown in 1942. Joe Hunt, another Californian, beat a youthful Jack Kramer in the 1943 Forest Hills Final. Hunt was killed in 1945 in an airplane accident. In 1944 and 1945 Frank Parker, a player of limited natural ability but with a capacity for hard work and a burning desire to succeed, defeated William F. (Billy) Talber of Cincinnati in both finals.

The impact of the war could be plainly ascertained by the makeup of the 1944 draw at Forest Hills, which was reduced to only forty-four players. So disappointed in the type of play in the 1944 tournament was *Time* magazine, that it described Pauline Betz and Frank Parker, the men's and women's champions respectively, as the "two most colorless tennis champions in two decades." Enthusiasm for the game was no doubt affected by the fact that Wimbledon, the prestige tournament, was not played from 1940 through 1945. However, tennis made a comeback after the war. The Jack Kramer-Bobby Riggs national and international tour in late 1947 attracted gate receipts of $383,000.

Armed Services Sports in World War II

As indicated earlier, navy personnel in programs conducted at colleges and universities could participate in sports programs that were offered at the schools they attended. As to the extent of the sports programs, they varied with the physical equipment available and the attitudes of individual commanding officers.

The navy's four preflight training centers—St. Mary's, and the Universities of Iowa, Georgia, and North Carolina—provided athletic competition in accordance with the so-called Hamilton Plan. Hamilton, ex-Naval Academy coach, had devised a program which would "contribute to the war effort in general and to flying cadets in particular." The sports curriculum of the cadets included the following mandatory sports: football, basketball, soccer, wrestling, boxing, tumbling, swimming, track, hand-to-hand, engineering (ditch digging, wood chopping and other manual labor). As reported in *Time*, July 27, 1942, the navy selected these sports for the following reasons: "Each sport has its relevance to war: the body contact of boxing and football, the sustained muscular strain of wrestling, the teamwork of basketball and soccer, the know-how of tumbling, the muscle building of labor. But the sports considered most valuable for Navy fledglings are swimming, track and hand-to-hand."

Soldiers serving overseas began to have access to abundant athletic equipment. In January 1943 the *New York Times* could report that 75 percent of the athletic equipment currently manufactured was being procured for armed forces personnel. By August 1944 the *New York Times* could report that 90 percent of all sporting equipment, $20 million worth, was being purchased by the army and navy. Such games as soccer, speedball, touch football, volleyball, basketball, and baseball were most popular. According to a 1944 *Time* magazine report, the most popular sport overseas with servicemen was volleyball. An army spokesman indicated that it had many advantages such as "simple equipment, small court, easy to camouflage and had plenty of action." In August 1944, the War Department drew up additional plans to promote competitive athletics because it felt that combat required physical and mental conditioning.

Boxing played a prominent role in the army's plan for physical development and moral improvement. In December 1944, in one army competition, 3,000 men fought each other in a tournament that whittled their numbers down to 186 in six days. At Camp Butner, near Durham, North Carolina, every soldier boxed as "a regular part of his physical training," according to *Time* (May 24, 1943). Under the direction of Major General Edwin P. Parker, fights were conducted nightly except Sundays to determine contenders for division championships. In addition, the camp featured the "Battle Royal," in which two platoons armed with gloves and watched by instructors went at each other en masse. In another version of mass boxing, called reconnaissance fighting, a squad armed only with boxing gloves would be sent out in the bush. There they would be ambushed by two other squads also armed with boxing gloves. The rationale for such procedures was given by Lieutenant Colonel James L. Grier, a one-time boxer at West Point, and a battalion commander at Camp Butner. According to Grier such activities accomplished the following: "The mission of combat soldier is to close with the enemy. Every man has a fear of the unknown and if he does not know what physical combat is, he will fear it. Mass boxing overcame this natural reluctance."

By 1945, as the war was winding down, organized tournaments and games between various units and theaters of operations were being provided by the armed forces, circumstances permitting. For example, soon after the liberation of Rome, a so-called Spaghetti Bowl football game was played. The following year it was played in Florence before 25,000 spectators. In the September 2, 1945, edition of the *New York Times* it was announced that the winner of the Mediterranean Theater baseball championship would soon meet the winner of the European Theater in a three out of five championship series. Also in October of that same year, a football game between the 508th Parachute Regiment and a U.S. Air Force team was held in Frankfort on the Main, Germany, with some 20,000 GI's in attendance.

Certainly the exigencies of war had not caused GI Joe and GI Jane to lose their enthusiasm for sports viewing or participating. During the war sports enlivened the boredom of war and broke the regimen imposed out of hard necessity. Sports teams provided a means of unit identification and pride, and competition was a morale booster, as men who would never go to college could participate on camp or regiment teams and feel a proud identification and sense of belonging. Sports also symbolized the normal, peaceful world that all hoped to return to after interrupted lives. Their value on the home front and in the war theaters was recognized by those who directed the war effort.

Postwar Sports

In *The Crucial Decade and After* (1960), an incisive, witty, and entertaining analysis of the period 1945–1960, Eric Goldman made the following observation: "Americans of late 1945 and 1946, their zest for luxuries pent up by four long years of war, their victory turned into endless nagging problems, were hardly averse to the inconsequential. The big football weekend roared back; television sets sold like red meat; women snapped up lamé skirts, sequin-trimmed aprons, cartwheel hats with pastel-blooms waving in billowing nets. Any night was likely to burst into New Year's Eve."

Not only did the football weekend resume its popularity—witness Michigan's record attendance of eighty-six thousand—but other sporting attractions were drawing unprecedented crowds. In 1946 the Indianapolis Speedway counted 175,000 in attendance, baseball turnstiles produced 18.5 million paid attendance while basketball saw 75 million pay to see the sport on all levels of competition.

Many observers had predicted that another sports boom such as that which followed World War I would occur. One sports sage solemnly declared that judo and bayonet fighting (with padded armor) would become two of the more popular sports in postwar America, due, of course, to the number of service personnel who had been trained in such combat skills.

As early as 1944 American businessmen, seeking to cash in on the anticipated sports boom, inaugurated plans to establish two new major pro football leagues—the All-American Football Conference and the Trans American League. Although not all new sporting ventures proved to be successful, the prognosticators proved to be accurate crystal ball gazers as a "sports boom" did indeed sweep America in the years immediately following World War II. The war years on the home front had produced a cultural need for shared public events and social contacts beyond the home and job.

Baseball from 1946 to 1949

The 1946 season saw the Boston Red Sox at long last win a pennant, as Joe Cronin, who had been purchased as a player-manager by Tom Yawkey in 1935, lead the Red Sox to a twelve-game margin over Detroit. The Boston club was bolstered by the return of Ted Williams, Johnny Pesky, Dom DiMaggio, and Bobby Doerr. Williams resumed his phenomenal hitting with a .342 average, 38 home runs, and 123 RBI's. Pesky led the league with 208 hits and compiled a .335 average. Rudy York came to Boston from Detroit and played a solid first base along with driving in 119 runs. Bobby Doerr was the slickest and most consistent second baseman in the league, leading all others in putouts, assists, double plays, and fielding average. The pitching staff was led by Boo Ferriss' 25 wins and Tex Hughson's 22 wins and 22 complete games.

Bob Feller returned from four years in the navy to establish his unquestionable supremacy as the best American League pitcher. He won 26, had 10 shutouts, struck out 458 in 371 innings pitched with a 2.18 ERA. He had a remarkable 36 complete games.

The St. Louis Cardinals bested Brooklyn in a dead heat for the National League pennant in 1946. Tied after the regulation season with ninety-six wins each, the two teams played the first pennant playoff in major league history. The Cardinals won two games from the Dodgers in the playoff series. The St. Louis club was led by the hitting of Stan Musial (.365 with 228 hits), the run-producing hits of Enos Slaughter (130 RBI's), and the steady hitting of Whitey Kurowski. Howie Pollet came back after three years in the service to fashion a 21-10 record with a league-leading 2.10 ERA.

In the World Series the Cardinals beat Boston in seven games. The last game was decided in the bottom of the eighth as Enos Slaughter raced home from first base on a single while Johnny Pesky made a fatal hesitation in making the relay throw to the plate. Harry "The Cat"

Brecheen was clearly the star of the Series as he won three games, pitching complete games in the second and sixth, and appearing in relief in the final game. In the fourth game the Cardinals had 20 hits in a 12-3 romp. Harry Walker, a .237 hitter in the regular season, pounded out 7 hits and drove in 6 runs, in addition to driving in Slaughter to win the deciding game. The games were filled with excitement as baseball returned to its prewar quality. The two great hitters in the Series were disappointments: Ted Williams could muster only 5 singles, and Stan Musial had 6 hits, including 4 doubles and 1 a triple, for a .222 average.

The Yankees came back to prominence in 1947 after a three-year absence as American League champions. They won easily over the faltering Tigers. The Yanks' batting was unspectacular but consistent. Three players had close to 100 RBI's: Joe DiMaggio with 97, Tommy Henrich with 98, and Billy Johnson with 95. Allie Reynolds, whose pitching career was uninterrupted by the war, won 19 games, and Spud Chandler led the league with a 2.46 ERA, even though he was 9-5. Joe "Fireman" Page won 14 in relief with 17 saves and a 2.15 ERA as a reliever. Spec Shea won 14 games in his rookie year and allowed the fewest hits per nine innings.

Ted Williams won his second Triple Crown in 1947, hitting .343, slugging 32 homers, and knocking in 114 runs. He again lost the Most Valuable Player award, this time to DiMaggio, as he had in 1941. Williams bested the Yankee Clipper in all categories except fielding, where DiMaggio had a brilliant season with only 1 error.

In the National League Brooklyn won out over St. Louis, blasting the Cardinals' hopes of avenging their 1943 World Series loss. The Dodgers were a well-balanced hitting team that lacked high averages. Except for Ralph Branca (21-12), Joe Hatten (17-8), and Hugh Casey (10-4 with 18 saves), the pitching staff was unremarkable.

The nucleus of a Dodger dynasty was forming around Jackie Robinson, the first black player in the major leagues. With the aid of Branch Rickey, Robinson came to the Dodgers after a year with the Montreal farm team. Robinson's resolve to play professional baseball had been steeled as a result of his military service in the army, where he became a second lieutenant. His enthusiasm for the game and his steady, controlled play made him a favorite with fans and teammates at Montreal. He was confident of his abilities, and his multitalented career in college football, basketball, baseball, and track gave him considerable exposure to white athletes, fans, and the press. He was truly the product of a national experience, born in Georgia, raised and matured in California, seasoned in the army where he quickly became an officer, further experienced in Kansas City where he played for the Monarchs all-black team, and finally groomed for the major leagues by playing in Canada.

Robinson had learned the ways of whites. He knew the kind of bigotry and racism he would face, and he was prepared for it. But he also knew how to win over the friendship and admiration of whites with his easygoing, relaxed demeanor. He had come to the majors to play ball and would be judged on his talents. He knew that he carried the hopes of black people with him, and he knew that a flair for the dramatic and daring would inspire those who avidly followed him. He made the Dodgers a national team with a black following, and he rallied the pride of Flatbush behind a revived team. In answer to ugly taunts and racial slurs, he defied pitchers on the bases by doing the unexpected. He stole home nineteen times in his ten-year career, leading the Dodgers consistently in runs scored. He paved the way for other talented black players to join the Dodgers, and by 1954 four of the Dodger regulars were black. Robinson had a combination of personal pride, healthy defiance of white attitudes of racial superiority, natural insouciance of a gifted athlete, and gritty determination to prove himself. He played where he was needed, proving his versatility and team spirit. On the bases he was a black spirit, always moving or threatening to steal, ready to take the extra base. He relished all aspects of the game equally. Soon others like Larry Doby and Satchel Paige would follow, and Willie Mays would capture the imagination of the baseball world. The success of these black athletes demonstrated how wrong baseball was in unofficially barring blacks through the gentlemen's agreement of owners.

The 1947 World Series was by far the best of the decade. The Series was the first to be televised, and the receipts at the gate were over $2 million. After losing the first two, the Dodgers came back to tie the Series, and then fought back to win the sixth game 8-6 after losing the fifth 2-1. Spec Shea won two games for the Yankees, and Joe Page saved the first game with four innings of relief and won the deciding game with one-hit shutout pitching for the last five innings. Hugh Casey pitched brilliantly for the Dodgers, winning games three and four and saving game six. The Series featured two dramatic slugfests, 9-8 and 8-6, with both of these won by the Dodgers. In the fourth game Bill Bevens was one out from a no-hitter with a 2-1 lead, but he put two runners on and Cookie Lavagetto doubled home both runners to spoil the no-hitter and win the game for the Dodgers. Bobo Newsom had finally experienced the taste of a world championship, even though he had been knocked out of the box in the second game and appeared briefly in game six.

This was the right choice of a World Series for exposure on national television. The fan interest during the season had been high as a record 20 million people attended games. During the Series baseball had survived its first real threat to the reserve clause. Danny Gardella, a New York Giant outfielder, sued organized baseball for $350,000, challenging the sacred reserve clause as a violation of the Sherman and Clayton antitrust laws and challenging his suspension from play under the terms of the reserve clause. Gardella and seventeen other major league players had jumped to an "outlaw" Mexican league, seeking bigger salaries. Commissioner Happy Chandler suspended them all for five years, and some of the players filed suits when they wanted to return. Max Lanier and Fred Martin dropped their suits when they received $5,000 in cash, but Gardella took his case to the Supreme Court. Organized baseball came up with $60,000 in an out-of-court settlement, which Gardella accepted along with his unconditional release from the Giants. In June 1949, Commissioner Chandler gave the players a general amnesty. Gardella only appeared in one major league game after this, and by 1949 Branch Rickey defended the reserve clause by saying those who opposed it "lean to communism," thus bringing the cold war into baseball. The threat to the reserve clause disappeared and was forgotten, just as Rip Sewall's famous "blooper" pitch was blasted out of sight by Ted Williams in the 1946 All-Star game.

The 1948 season saw two surprises. The Cleveland Indians won their first pennant since 1920, and the Boston Braves prevailed for the first time since 1914. The Indians tied Boston during the regular season and won the one-game playoff. Billy Southworth displayed his usual talent for intelligent management, taking the Braves to a 6½-game spread over his old team, the Cardinals, and Lou Boudreau, the shortstop-manager for the Indians, hit 2 home runs and 2 singles in the playoff game against the Red Sox. Boudreau had hit .355 during the season with 106 RBI's and had led the league in fielding at his position.

The Indians were a solid ball club, leading the league in hitting and in home runs, as Joe Gordon hit 32 and Ken Keltner contributed 31. Gordon, Boudreau, Keltner, and Eddie Robinson combined for 432 RBI's and 97 homers to give Cleveland one of the hardest hitting infields since that fabled Tiger infield of 1934 and 1935 that featured Greenberg, Gehringer, Rogell, and Owen. Larry Doby, who broke the color line in the American League and had appeared in 29 games in 1947, hit .301 in 1948 and became a regular. The Cleveland pitching staff featured Gene Bearden (20-7 with a league low 2.43 ERA), Bob Lemon (20-14), and Bob Feller (19-15). Lemon and Feller led the leagues in innings pitched. Satchel Paige was 6-1 at the age of forty-two.

Paige, a veteran of the Negro leagues, brought with him an amazing array of pitches and motions that baffled hitters and created great fan interest. He had a laconic style that reflected a man who had waited a long time to arrive where he belonged and who along the way had learned the value of patience and endurance. Paige possessed a folk wisdom that made him ageless and quotable. His six rules for a healthy and easygoing life have become legend, especially his "and don't look back. Something might be gaining on you."

The Boston Braves of 1948 created their own legend around the pitching combination of Johnny Sain and Warren Spahn. Sain won 24 games, pitched in 315 innings, and had 28 complete games. Spahn won 15 and pitched in 257 innings, and the Braves' pitching rotation was described as "Spahn and Sain and pray for rain." However, Bill Voiselle (13-13 with 216 innings) and Vern Bickford (11-5) were an important part of the pitching staff as was Bobby Hogue, who was 8-2 in relief. Manager Southworth rotated his personnel brilliantly, using reserve players with skill and effectiveness, and the distribution of RBI's among the thirteen players Southworth used indicates his skillful use of talent.

The 1948 season in the National League was one of power hitting. Ralph Kiner and Johnny Mize both hit 40 home runs. Stan Musial had one of his finest seasons when he batted .376, hit 39 homers, batted in 131 runs, and had 230 hits. He also led the league in doubles and triples. Musial's 1948 season was one of the best overall performances of a hitter in all of baseball history. Almost half of his hits were for extra bases as Musial amassed 429 total bases.

The Indians won the 1948 World Series in six games. Gene Bearden, a navy veteran who had aluminum plates in his knee and head from war wounds, pitched a 5-hit shutout in the third game and pitched one and two-thirds innings of relief in the last game to give Bob Lemon his second win of the Series. The two teams scored the same total number of runs (only 17), but the pitching of Bob Lemon, Bearden, and Steve Gromek, who allowed only 2 runs in three games, was too much for the Braves. The fifth game was played before 86,288 spectators at Cleveland Stadium. Cleveland batted only .199 in the six games, but Boston scored 11 of its Series' 17 runs in one game.

The 1949 season saw the Yankees and Dodgers reassert their supremacy. The Casey Stengel era began as the Gotham terrors would win five straight pennants. The Yankees' batting was consistent but unspectacular. DiMaggio hit .346 but was hobbled with a foot injury much of the season. Tommy Henrich, a ten-year veteran, led the regulars with a .287 average and hit 24 homers. The Yankee pitching staff was exceptionally well balanced with four pitchers winning 15 games or more, and Joe Page saved 27 games and appeared in 60 games.

The Dodgers pitching staff had five pitchers with 10 or more wins, and the Brooklyn team edged out St. Louis by one game in the pennant race. Jackie Robinson led the league with a .342 average with 203 hits, drove in 124 runs, and had 37 stolen bases. The Dodgers were blessed with such gifted power hitters as Gil Hodges, Carl Furillo, Duke Snider, and Roy Campanella. During the season the Dodgers had scored 113 runs more than second-place St. Louis.

Although the Yankees won the 1949 Series in five games, the games were close and exciting. The first three games were decided by a single run. The first and third games were decided in the ninth innings, with Tommy Henrich homering to open the bottom of the ninth in the first game and Johnny Mize hitting a two-run pinch hit single in the top of the ninth in the third game and Olmo and Campanella hitting solo homers in the bottom of the ninth as Brooklyn fell one run short. Yankee relief pitching in the fourth and fifth games put down Dodger rallies in the late innings. The Dodgers lacked relief pitching, and Don Newcombe failed in game four after his heartbreaking loss in the opening game. Steady Joe Page pitched shutout ball in two and one-third innings in the fifth game as the Dodgers had erupted for four runs in the seventh. Page had been there before, having pitched five innings of one-hit relief in the seventh game of the 1947 Series between the same teams. Because three of the Series games were played at Ebbets Field, attendance was down as were gate receipts. The 1947 contests had drawn 389,763 spectators and had produced over $2 million in receipts, with television rights enriching the pot. The attendance record would stand until the 1957 Series between the Yankees and Milwaukee Braves.

The 1940s were a period of challenge and change for baseball. The war years brought new popularity to baseball as people sought new order and stability in their lives; baseball seemed to symbolize a successful readjustment and return to normalcy after a traumatic war. Over 20 million fans paid to see major league games in 1949, and the minor leagues had jumped back up to fifty-nine leagues.

Many soldiers had played baseball regularly in training camps and even in war zones. In 1946 there was a GI World Series for the championship of occupied Germany, as well as a regular league season of over forty games. The 60th Infantry Regiment of the 9th Division won the series 4 games to 2 over the 508th Parachute Infantry Regiment with Carl Schieb, a major league pitcher with the Philadelphia A's, winning two of the games.

In 1945 the *New York Times* carried a report that a baseball diamond had been cut in the turf of the Nuremberg Stadium, a Nazi shrine where giant parades had been held to honor Adolf Hitler. The war had taken baseball to the world, and the ritual and rules of the game symbolized sacred values of American life.

On the home front baseball had established a role for itself as a morale booster, patriotic example, and symbol of life as normal in deeply troubled and uncertain times. The war also helped push the entrance of black players into the major leagues as some racial barriers fell under wartime conditions and blacks experienced a new degree of freedom and wider participation in American society. Even the threat of the outlaw Mexican League in 1946 can be attributed to the pressures created by a large number of players coming back to the game and a certain number seeking greener pastures as a postwar baseball boom was beginning.

Other notable developments in the forties included Judge Landis's banning in 1943 of William Cox, the owner of the Philadelphia Phillies, for betting on baseball games. After Landis's death in 1944 his successor, Happy Chandler, suspended manager Leo Durocher for the entire 1947 season when Durocher was seen consorting with well-known gamblers on opening day. The player pension fund was established in February 1947, giving players some degree of future financial security. Certain teams such as the Dodgers, Indians, and Giants took definite steps to bring black players into their organizations, but most teams delayed integration as long as they could. But the late forties made it clear that black players were part of the future of the game and that black talents would in fact provide new measures of performance. The development of the careers of Willie Mays and Hank Aaron in the mid-1950s would bring new dimensions to the game and new records. Robinson and Mays would come to represent the total ballplayer who excelled because of speed, fielding skills, competitive spirit, and natural hitting ability.

The 1940s illustrate that baseball is sensitive to changes and shifts in American society. The war years forced changes or brought about conditions that created adjustments. Baseball emerged from the war years to move into a new era of prosperity and popularity. Once the threat to the reserve clause was met and dealt with, baseball management and ownership sought to solidify their increased profits as the game became more businesslike.

Players in the fifties would become more specialized and less colorful in terms of personalities, and they sought financial security in an age that saw increasing receipts from television but more competition from other sports. Baseball entered the world of the organization man, the quiet generation, and the pursuit of affluence and personal gratification. The fifties would be a microcosm of the three previous decades: a new age of leisure and affluence (the Golden Twenties), a return to war (the Korean Conflict), and severe economic recession (the Depression). But baseball became less of an index of national life and popular sentiments. The 1950s would see three franchises move (the Boston Braves to Milwaukee in 1953, the St. Louis Browns to Baltimore in 1954, and the Philadelphia A's to Kansas City in 1955) and two clubs (the Brooklyn Dodgers and the New York Giants) move to the West Coast. The stability of baseball would soon be a thing of the past.

College Football

From 1946 to 1955 Notre Dame and Army were the predominant college football elevens, for with the exception of 1948 both teams were among the top ranked teams in the country. In 1946 Army and Notre Dame clashed in a titanic battle of unbeatens, and much like the celebrated conflict between Michigan State and Notre Dame some twenty years later, the game ended in an unsatisfactory tie—a 0-0 deadlock.

Coach Frank Leahy's return to Notre Dame from the service began an unbeaten streak of 39 games which was not halted until the Purdue game of the 1950 season. Those Irish teams featured such outstanding linemen as Leon Hart, Jim Martin, George O'Connor, and Bill Fischer. Leahy's backfield included such stellar performers as Johnny Lujack, Terry Brennan, and Emil Sitko. Also an outstanding team in 1946 was UCLA, going undefeated in the regular season but being shellacked 45-14 by Illinois in the Rose Bowl.

Michigan had an outstanding team in 1947 under the excellent leadership of Fritz Crisler, who was one of the first coaches to exploit fully the new free substitution rule by utilizing separate platoons for offense and defense. Paced by Bob Chappuis and Chalmers (Bump) Elliott, Michigan swept through the Big Ten and smashed Southern California 49-0 in the Rose Bowl. The following year, Crisler retired and left the Wolverines in the hands of Bennie Oosterbaan, who promptly duplicated the 1947 team's efforts and captured the national championship title to boot.

Oklahoma and California were two new powerhouses that emerged in 1948 whose successors were carried over into the 1950s. Oklahoma, under the legendary Bud Wilkinson, captured Big Seven conference championships from 1948 to 1959.

The University of California, known as the "Graveyard of Coaches," rose to prominence in 1948 and 1949, winning conference championships in those years. It narrowly lost in the Rose Bowl both those seasons, first to Northwestern and then to Ohio State.

College football's success was once again tainted by scandal and accusation that it was simply a "business" during this postwar period. Critics reported in *Time* magazine in October 1946 that "traffic in talented footballers" was "greater than in 1929" and stated that "beefy tackles and flashy half-backs, fresh out of GI uniforms in three days would be on college elevens, often on different campuses from the ones that they trod before." An Oklahoma A&M official said Oklahoma had spent $200,000 to buy a football team and additionally claimed that some players were receiving $5,000 to $10,000 to play football.

President Paul F. Douglas of American University, which abolished football, echoed a familiar refrain in *Time* (October 14, 1946) when he declared: "Post war college football has no more relation to education than bullfighting or agriculture. . . . I see no reason why one corporation should hire a specialized group of employees to outrun, outbump and outthrust the specialized employees of another corporation. . . . A football player is nothing more than a human slave caught in the biggest black market operation in the history of higher education."

Whether the sport had reached the proportions that President Douglas asserted cannot be proven, but certainly in the postwar period, athletic recruiting again was a dilemma that college officials had not solved. Returning veterans offered glory-hungry schools a possible ticket to instant success. And the fans were there to fill the stadiums as attendance soared to over 15 million in 1947. College football had arrived as big business.

Professional Football

From 1946 to 1949 pro football fans were treated to a "war" between the National Football League and a new rival, the All-American Conference. The brainchild of Arch Ward, sports editor of the Chicago *Tribune*, the new conference was conceived in a hotel room in 1944 and began actual operation in 1946. Bankrolled by millionaires who enjoyed football and who had been denied entrance into the NFL, the league established franchises in such cities as Los Angeles, Chicago, San Francisco, New York, Buffalo, Baltimore, Cleveland, and briefly in Miami and Brooklyn. Such college stars as Frankie Albert, Lou Groza, Angelo Bertelli, Y. A. Tittle, Buddy Young, and Ben "Automatic" Agajanian signed up with the new league.

Players of both leagues benefited from the competition. Prior to World War II players received an average of about $150 per game. By 1949 the average minimum salary was $5,000 a year and not too many players were earning the minimum.

An attempt to reach an agreement with the NFL before competition started between the two leagues was rebuffed by NFL Commissioner Elmer Layden, who responded to his rival's overtures with the terse statement: "Let them get a football first."

The Cleveland Browns, named after Coach Paul Brown, won division and league titles in the first four years of the AAC, quarterbacked by Otto Graham. When thwarted by pass defenders, Graham would hand off to truck-like fullback Marion Motley, who would rumble off huge gains with all the impetus of an unleashed avalanche.

By 1949 the handwriting was on the wall for the AAC as it operated with only seven teams and its championship game between the Cleveland Browns and San Francisco Dons attracted only a meager crowd of 22,550. The winner's share amounted to only $266.11 per man. An agreement to join the two rival leagues was announced in 1949 but did not occur until 1950 when three of the AAFC teams joined the NFL. The NFL in 1946 attracted 1.7 million fans and signed its first black player, Kenny Washington, formerly of UCLA, to play for the Rams. Woody Strode would also play for the Rams. (Two other blacks, Marion Motley and Bill Willis, played for the Cleveland Browns in the rival league.)

The Chicago Bears beat the New York Giants in 1946 by a score of 24-14 to win the NFL championship, but the game was marred by the suspension of Merle Hapes of the Giants for not reporting a bribe attempt.

In 1947 the Chicago Cardinals, a perennial loser, captured their first NFL championship since 1925, powered by their "million dollar" backfield of Paul Christman, Pat Harder, Charlie Trippi, and Elmer Angsman. In the title game the Cardinals edged the Philadelphia Eagles 28-21.

The following year the same two teams were rematched, with the Eagles prevailing 7-0 in a blinding snowstorm. In 1949 rain dampened the passing attack of the Rams led by Bob Waterfield and the running of former Army All-American Glenn Davis, and the Eagles shut out the Rams 14-0.

Pro football in the postwar forties had proved popular but not popular enough to sustain two football conferences. The large-scale capital provided by television, which would sustain a rival conference some fourteen years later, was not there since television transmission was still in its relative infancy.

By 1949 the pro game was substantially different from the college game. Most teams utilized various forms of the T formation with the emphasis on passing. Offense and defense were played with separate "platoons" with the result that the two-way player was becoming as extinct as the dodo bird. With various rule changes aiding the offense, NFL teams averaged 5 touchdowns per game, which was about double the 2.7 average for 1936. Pro football had become more reputable and attracted more fans than in the past during the four years following the war but it had not yet reached its popularity peak.

College Basketball

As with college football, the war's end signaled a flood of GI's to the college campuses armed with the GI bill, eager to hit the books and the courts. Many coaches were fearful that the trend toward larger players would create havoc on the courts and eliminate the "little men" of the game. One commentator in *Newsweek* sardonically recommended that teams should post a "50 caliber machine gunner over the basket to keep big fellows at a distance." His conclusion was that "We have got to hold the line or send for oxygen."

Bob "Foothills" Kurland did lead Oklahoma A&M to its second consecutive NCAA title in 1946. It was the first college team to accomplish this feat. Yet by 1949 a small man, Bob Cousy, would be the toast of the collegiate basketball world. Also in 1949 the rules would be changed so that a coach could talk to his players during a time-out, and television would telecast a basketball game at the University of Utah in Salt Lake City.

The two dominant teams during the 1947–1949 period were Kentucky and Holy Cross. Holy Cross's rise to the pinnacle of college hoop stardom was an unbelievable rags-to-riches story. Boston fans lacked any basketball tradition, its fans preferring baseball, boxing, track, and hockey, not necessarily in that order. Not only did the Crusaders have the handicap of coming from an area lagging in basketball interest, but the team lacked even a gym. Coached by Doggie Julian and led by star shooter and All-American George Kafton (who usually was good for at least 25 points a game) and a bevy of fine ball handlers (whose spherical manipulations were so expert that opponents jealously labeled the Holy Cross "fancy pants"), Holy Cross captured the 1947 NCAA championship, winning 24 of 27 and then posting a 58-47 triumph over Oklahoma in the title game. A little-used reserve was a freshman named Bob Cousy.

Although Holy Cross would not win another NCAA title during the Cousy years, they would come close. What is more important is that Cousy revolutionized the game with his mastery of the behind-the-back dribble and his sleight-of-hand passes. His crowd-pleasing antics, which drew sell-out throngs even in Boston, made college basketball bigger than ever in attendance, and Cousy was the model that the kids on the playground sought to emulate.

Kentucky was the dominant team in college basketball team in the years 1945 to 1954. It produced three NCAA titles, one NIT title, and eight conference champions. The Kentucky successes were somewhat soured by revelations that several key players were involved in betting scandals which rocked the basketball world in the early 1950s.

The architect of the Kentucky triumph was the "man in the Brown Suit," Adolph Rupp. Paced by such outstanding players as Alex Groza, Ralph Beard, and "Wa Wa" Jones, the Wildcats won the NIT title in 1946 but were beaten in the 1947 finals by the Utah Redskins 49-45. The Wildcats again captured NCAA titles in 1948 and 1949, led by the 6-foot 7-inch, 220-pound Groza, who was labeled by the media as a "scoring machine."

Rupp's key to success was discipline, both on and off the court. He banned sloppy dress, card playing, and towel stealing, reasoning that he didn't want to be "packing around a bunch of tramps, gamblers, and thieves." Rupp's consistent record of success made him the idol of his coaching peers as much as Cousy was the idol of the kids on the playground. Rupp would bring four NCAA national championships to Kentucky.

Professional Basketball

In the immediate postwar period, professional basketball has been described by one follower of the game as a "small-time, penny ante sport, because it attracted so many small-time, penny ante operators.'' Basketball became known as a ''carnival sport'' and reputable big city promoters wanted no part of it, although its popularity had grown during World War II. As a result, the Basketball Association of America was formed, which included franchises in Washington, Philadelphia, New York, Boston, Chicago, St. Louis, Cleveland, Detroit, Pittsburgh, Toronto, and Providence.

Another pro basketball league also was formed and called itself the National Basketball League. Its most famous player was George Mikan, the bespectacled giant from DePaul who signed a five-year, $60,000 contract with the Chicago Gears in 1946. This was thought to be a fabulously wealthy contract for the day since no one else was making that kind of money. The Gears lasted only one year and then Mikan landed with the Lakers of Minneapolis. Once signed, Mikan moved to Minneapolis, thus setting a precedent for other pro athletes to move to the city that they played in.

Mikan led the Lakers to an NBL title in 1947–48, but the country could not support two basketball leagues and a merger took place. The new league called itself the National Basketball Association. Once again in the 1948–49 season, Mikan led the Lakers to a league championship. Slow afoot, he was a devastating player inside with a deft touch to his hook shot. Mikan was the pro league's first major superstar, and he attracted fans who had never witnessed a pro basketball game before.

By the end of the decade professional basketball finally had arrived. It still lacked a 24-second clock, black players, and TV exposure which would be necessary to give the NBA ''first class'' status.

Boxing

The boxing world eagerly awaited the return bout between Joe Louis and Billy Conn, and promoters were eager to give it to them. In 1949, 45,266 paid $100 per ticket to see the bout. Conn's ability, however, had been sapped by age and the war, and Louis was not in much better shape. Louis eventually decked Conn at 2:19 of the eighth round.

Worried about Louis's performance, his manager had the Brown Bomber checked by a physician, who advised Louis to give up boxing because he was losing his reflexes. However, Louis kept on fighting. Against a tough Jersey Joe Walcott, he barely eked out a close decision. In a return bout in June, Louis knocked Walcott out in the eleventh round. Louis retired then in order to bail himself out of some dire financial straits.

Louis's retirement left a huge void in the heavyweight title picture. The rather lackluster contenders for the title were short on ability and charisma. Two who emerged from the masses to become the leading contenders for the vacated crown were Ezzard Charles, a twenty-eight year-old black boxer from Cincinnati, and Joe Arnold Cream, alias Jersey Joe Walcott, a veteran of twenty years in the ring.

On June 22, 1949, the two contenders fought for the vacated title in Chicago. The bout was dull and boring, highlighted by the fainting of Charles's manager when the decision in favor of his fighter was announced. Charles triumphed in two more defenses of his title before the end of the decade.

Tennis

In the postwar years of the forties, a wave of hard-hitting Californians came out of the West bringing with them the power game of the California cement courts, the smashing service, and the put-away volley. In 1946, twenty-three-year-old Tom Brown from California, fresh out of the army, outlasted two-time defending national champion Frank Parker in the quarter finals at Forest Hills and ran over Gardnar Mulloy in the semis, but his aspirations for the throne were crushed by another Californian with an even bigger power game, Jack Kramer. Kramer, possessor of a hot serve and a superb backhand, polished off Brown in three sets.

In 1947 Kramer repeated his feat, repelling ex-champion Parker in a long five-set duel, 4-6, 2-6, 6-1, 6-0, 6-3. Kramer then turned professional to tour against Bobby Riggs.

It was assumed that with Kramer's departure, American tennis was without players of world championship caliber, but out of obscurity came Pancho Gonzales—a twenty-year-old Californian who achieved instant stardom. A 6-foot 8-inch, 185-pound tiger on the court who played with explosive abandon, Gonzales and his 110 mile per hour serve swept to the 1948 national singles championship. There was some doubt, however, to the legitimacy of Pancho's claim to the crown since Ted Schroeder, reputed to be America's best amateur, did not enter the competition.

Any doubts as to Gonzales's supremacy were cleared up the following year. Both Schroeder and Gonzales waltzed through preliminary opponents to find themselves facing each other in the finals. Gonzales dropped the first two sets, which included a bitter 16-18 first set loss, but stormed back to triumph.

Gonzales also joined the pro tour after his 1949 Forest Hills triumph. But Kramer and Gonzales had demonstrated that size, speed, and power were now trademarks of the modern tennis game and that finesse and shot placement would have to temporarily take a back seat. From 1947 through 1951 five different American men won the singles championship at Wimbledon, and American women won each year from 1946 through 1958.

Golf

Golf in the United States immediately rebounded from its wartime doldrums. The United States, as well as Great Britain, resumed their Opens in 1946. Lloyd Mangrum, another one of the Texas golfing contingent, captured the 1946 Open, winning after beating Byron Nelson and Vic Glizzi in a thirty-six-hole playoff. Lee Worship, Ben Hogan, and Cary Middlecoff captured the Open in 1947, 1948, and 1949. Middlecoff's triumph in 1949 was marred by the fact that odds-on favorite, Ben Hogan, did not play. He was recuperating from a head-on auto accident in which Hogan suffered a fractured pelvis, shattered rib, broken ankle, and collarbone while trying to shield his wife from the impact.

Conclusion

The forties were unique—amateurs still dominated the sports world. World War II had had a major impact on athletics. It was disruptive, but like World War I, had stimulated interest in sporting activity. Television was in its infancy, so that boom in professional sports bolstered by TV exposure and TV dollars had not yet arrived.

The sports world in the forties still had not solved racial problems. Blacks were playing in professional football, and Jackie Robinson had broken the color barrier in baseball. This was just a start.

Collegiate sports still had not abolished discriminatory practices. For example, in the November 20, 1947, *New York Times*, a report stated that the University of Nebraska student government wanted the university to withdraw from competition with the Missouri Valley Conference unless its clause prohibiting black athletes was eliminated. James Lee, the secretary of the AAU, demanded the abolition of the Sullivan Trophy because it was won by Olympic decathlon star Bob Mathias in 1949 rather than by black track star Harrison Dillard. Lee wanted either an abolition of the Sullivan Trophy or the elimination of southern writers' votes when a black athlete was involved in the voting. A spokesman for the Sullivan Trophy voters responded that Dillard was the number one pick of every southerner who voted in the poll. Whether this is true or not, the fact was that the civil rights process for black athletes, although making some inroads by 1949, had a long road to go before equality was achieved in the sports world. The racial changes brought by the war gave promise to black athletes, but the hard realities of day-to-day performance in white-dominated sports leagues would test the character and resolve of many a black athlete.

6

The Flashy Fifties: Sports in the Gray Flannel Suit Era

"Hula hoops, bunny hops, 3-D movies. Davy Crockett coonskins, chlorophyll toothpaste, 22 collegians stuffed into a phone booth. Edsels and tail finned Cadillacs. Greasy duck's-ass hairdos, leather jackets, souped-up hot rods, dragging, cruising, mooning. Like crazy, man, dig? Kefauver hearings, Howdy Doody, Kukla, Fran, and Ollie. Bridey Murphey, Charles Van Doren, Francis Gary Powers. *The Catcher in the Rye, The Power of Positive Thinking, Howl, On the Road.* Patti Page, Pat Boone, Vic Damone; Little Richard, Chuck Berry, Elvis Presley; The Platters, The Clovers, The Drifters; Bill Haley and the Comets, Danny and the Juniors. Mantle, Mays, Marciano. Pink shirts, gray flannels, white bucks. 'I Like Ike.' "

This is the nostalgic image authors Douglas T. Miller and Marion Nowak, coauthors of the definitive work on this decade entitled *The Fifties: The Way We Really Were,* (1977) contend that many Americans have of the period. Yet as the authors clearly point out in their work, to "paint the fifties picture in the soft pastels of that decade's tail-finned cars . . . is both wrongheaded and dangerous." Instead they would cogently argue that the decades that followed did not represent some abrupt change in direction from the "genial but apathetic" fifties. Further, they contend that many of the problems people were forced to grapple with in the sixties and seventies were present during the fifties but were ignored. As they have stated: "No, all the problems of recent years were present back then. Only the way we riveted our eyes on consensus made us not recognize them. Avoiding crucial issues, we aggravated them. Our own self-betrayals made the upheavals of later years inevitable."

Well, what were these changes that authors Nowak and Miller so strongly believe altered America during the fifties? In the first place, most of the decade was not made up of placid, pleasantly dull years. The years 1950 to 1953 witnessed the fighting of the Korean War and the Red Scare inspired by the witch hunts of Senator Joseph McCarthy. The year 1956 saw the potential for World War III break out when the Israelis, the French, and the British invaded Egypt and the Hungarians valiantly revolted against the Russians. In 1957 Sputnik went up and people wanted to know why Johnny couldn't read three foreign language journals and do Boolean algebra just like the smart Russian kids. Also in 1957 began a severe recession which had many recalling the dreadful economic climate of the "terrible thirties."

The American population grew tremendously in total numbers and became more homogeneous during the decade. In the thirties population had increased by only 9 million while in the fifties it skyrocketed by 28 million, as over 4 million children were born every year. By the fifties, 95 percent of the population was native born. The period saw phenomenal gains in population, particularly in the West. California added 5 million people during the decade and grew at a rate of 1,600 per day. Arizona and Nevada exceeded California's growth rate.

The National Defense Highway Act of 1956 authorized the building of 40,000 miles of interstate highways, a development which had disastrous impact on mass transit and made America more reliant on the auto than ever before. The car culture was fueled by cheap gas and made mobile by a restless population.

Further road-building programs, low cost home mortgage guarantees, and tax deductions provided by the federal government acted as a "federal subsidy to the middle classes." Increased mobility meant people could live in the suburbs. Home ownership in the fifties grew from 9 million to 32.8 million. As millions moved out of the cities to the suburbs, 20 million people—many of them blacks, Chicanos, and poor rural southerners—moved into the cities or remained there.

In the suburbs, with their housing developments containing identical looking houses, people tried to construct lives that would bring them happiness and security. These adults, raised during the thirties, would do almost anything to avoid the economic deprivation that they had known so vividly during their childhood. The security they sought meant that they had to conform to the wishes of the companies that employed them. They became "organization men," rootless managers of an industrial society who jumped when their company told them to in order to maintain a comfortable life-style. "The Man in the Gray Flannel Suit" was the image of businessmen of the day— bland, obliging, efficient—who didn't rock the boat. Yet sociologists wrote of executive unhappiness in the midst of the cornucopia of plenty on the part of those who did not achieve "group consensus." In 1947 only 5.7 million American families had annual incomes over $7,500 but by 1959 12.3 million families did. Works such as *The Lonely Crowd* (1950) by David Riesman detailed the new executives' need for group acceptance, as did William H. Whyte Jr.'s *The Organization Man* (1957).

Pampered, spoiled, trapped in a suburban sprawl environment, and forced by society into a prolonged adolescence heretofore not experienced in history, the suburban youth turned to new heroes— particularly in the rock and roll field. The new music of the fifties symbolized in its lyrics young people's need to be accepted, yet in its wild, syncopated beat and the wild dances it spawned, stood for the young people's rebellion against the mores and customs of a faceless, technocratic, and bureaucratic society—"the dehumanizing status quo."

The role of minorities was also brought into sharp focus. The *Brown v. Board of Education of Topeka* decisions of the Supreme Court in 1954 and 1955, which overturned the "separate but equal" doctrine, meant the beginning of a new militancy of purpose by minorities, particularly blacks, to make the American Dream a reality for themselves. Even with the favorable ruling from the Supreme Court, they could not obtain proper schooling for their children because of the defiance of public officials. For instance, Governor Orval Faubus of Arkansas called out the National Guard to prevent the integration of Central High School in Little Rock, Arkansas. President Eisenhower ordered that 10,000 National Guardsmen be nationalized, and he sent a thousand troops of the 101st Airborne Division to restore order and to insure that the Court's ruling would be enforced. Such incidents indicated that peaceful integration and equal civil rights for all would not be an easy task to accomplish.

What impact, then, did changing lifestyles have on the sporting world? In short, these cultural developments had a tremendous impact. Americans had more free time, more mobility, more money, and a TV set. In 1946 there were only 7,000 television sets, but by 1960 they numbered 50 million. By 1959 *Fortune* magazine estimated that Americans were spending $41 billion of their consumer income on the so-called fun market. Fessenden S. Blanchard, the father of platform tennis, wrote in an article entitled "The Revolution in Sports" in the May 1956 *Harpers Magazine* that Americans were going in for participatory sports. He pointed out that in 1936 there were only 1,000 boat trailers sold; in 1952 the number had grown to 39,200. Americans possessed in that same year 5.25 million recreational crafts, of which 4 million were power craft under 16 feet and 500,000 were sailboats. In 1954 the states received $76 million in revenue from the sales of hunting and fishing licenses. The sale of fishing tackle alone brought in $150 million annually.

Mr. Blanchard also found that 20 million people played table tennis, another 20 million bowled, and 2.5 million belonged to the American Bowling Congress. Over 4,000 roller rinks attracted another 17 million customers; 20 million participated in softball; and 3 million golfers played at least ten rounds apiece per year.

Those individual sports which showed a decline according to Blanchard's study included tennis, indoor badminton, and squash.

College basketball at Madison Square Garden showed a 50 percent decline in the first four years of the decade, but in 1956 there were 2 million basketballs sold while in 1936 only 500,000 had been purchased. Hockey attendance was down 20 percent, and baseball attendance also underwent a decline. Boxing had not had a $1 million gate since 1946. Professional basketball and professional football showed attendance increases, however.

What did this mean? Indeed, Mr. Blanchard quoted the *Wall Street Journal* as stating that, Americans were "on the greatest sports binge in history." But the emphasis was on participation sports. Television overexposure had almost killed off boxing attendance, and "the tube" had also put the baseball minor league system into a long period of contraction and consolidation. Baseball itself was not a game particularly suited for television, which could not show the whole field on the small screen. Baseball also seemed somewhat anachronistic, its slow pace somewhat out of step with the quickening pace of the decade. Professional basketball, however, with the 24-second clock forcing constant action, the quick surge of the teams as they flowed smoothly up and down the floor alternating from offense to defense, and the proliferation of scoring captured the interest of even the most casual observer who was remotely interested in sports.

Pro football, on the other hand—whose action depended in reality on those who were handling the ball, such as the quarterback, running backs, and receivers—could be quickly and intimately covered by the television camera. With the development of outstanding passers such as Johnny Unitas and others, and with its increased exposure on Sunday afternoons, professional football played other, more sociological roles. It became a safe topic at the office to talk about the scores of the Sunday games. For lower- and middle-range executives, it offered a chance to provide conversation and to offer equal opinions on a topic that would not put them in any direct confrontation with their superiors. In addition, for the upward bound executive, attachment in some manner to a pro football or basketball team gave him some kind of roots. While on a trip he could always consult the newspapers or attend a game, thus providing a sense of familiarity even in a new town or city. In addition, loyalty to a team gave him a sense of personal identity which he lacked in the technocratic world. The success of the Lions, Colts, Rams, or whatever team he followed, could be thought of as his successes. So were the defeats, but even they brought comfort, since it was nice to share the knowledge that even guys bigger, stronger, and quicker than he did not win all the time. Pro football provided an emotional release for pent-up energies and hostilities that had to be suppressed and controlled in a business world demanding urbane sophistication and calculated social exchanges.

Sports were also a democratizing element during the fifties. An article entitled "Spectator Sports Lose Out" in the October 15, 1955, issue of *Business Week*, noted that "more people in lower income brackets are spending their money on golf. The fellows that used to be caddying are out there playing now." Another commentator noted that "if you can tell a machinist from a VP on a golf course or fishing pier you have sharper eyes than I."

The *Business Week* article agreed with Mr. Blanchard's observations that participant sports were occupying more and more of Mr. and Mrs. Average American's time and money while spectator sports were, on the whole, "losing out." According to the article, television was partially responsible but "most of all, though, the loss seems to stem from the average fan's changed habits of living. He lives farther out of town, has a bigger family, has more time for travel and participant sports—besides owning a tv set."

The article noticed that both labor and management favored sports participation by workers. An assistant regional director for the CIO was quoted in the *Business Week* article as declaring: "Sports of any type bring the right kind of living, plus increased revenue, to any town that can support them." The article also noted that such major companies as Sylvania Electric, before selecting a new plant site, sent out questionnaires to several potential cities asking detailed questions about sport facilities for its employees.

Not only did sports provide a healthy outlet for plant employees but as the *Business Week* article pointed out, "sporting events mean money to stores, hotels, restaurants, bars, transit lines, and even local manufacturing companies." (*Business Week* discovered one company that found it more profitable to quit making bats for professional baseball players and to concentrate on the manufacture of Little League bats.) Thus, as Mr. Blanchard stated in his conclusion in his article in *Harpers*, "Sports, indeed, have become one of America's major industries, elaborately promoted and highly profitable for all sorts of people."

The sporting world also had to contend with the problems of the real world in terms of civil rights. Jackie Robinson had broken the color barrier in baseball in 1947, and blacks were playing football at the same time. The following decade would see by its end more black athletes playing both collegiate and professional sports. As sports franchises expanded to the South, the conflict of highly trained and intelligent athletes being forced to accept separate housing and eating facilities and to face the jeers and possible threats to life by prejudiced spectators was a problem that college administrators and professional team management had to deal with whether they liked it or not. Certainly in the fifties, the integration of sports, although not always proceeding smoothly, was a highly visible testimony that whites and blacks could work together for a common goal—a lesson that undoubtedly had some impact upon the masses who watched the athletic contests.

For one writer, sports was a preparation for war. Writing in the September 1952 issue of *Recreation* and with the Korean War as his reference point, S. L. A. Marshall noted that American young men "have held all too lightly what organized sport can do for a people and how mass physical fitness related to national survival. In team play, a man learns to play the game for its own sake, and not for personal vainglory. Finally, it is this same spirit which holds together an infantry company in the face of the enemy. Real contending power comes of each man's love for his comrades, and not of his hate for the other side." In addition, Marshall found that sports like football or baseball teach important tactics such as "hitting the dirt" and most importantly throwing. He noted that often in American companies the soldier with the strongest arm, usually a former baseball player or football quarterback, would throw the majority of the grenades for his company while the other men "acted as a bucket line, passing their grenades to him, and cheering while he heaved." He gave the example of Corporal Don Crawford and Pfc. James C. Curcio, Jr., of Baker Company, Ninth Infantry Regiment, in the battle of Chongchon, who with nine other men were surrounded by 200 Chinese. For two hours the Chinese grenaded the area. Curcio and Crawford "caught or fielded approximately forty of the 'hot' grenades and pitched them back into the Chinese lines."

Not everybody participated in sports during the fifties in order to become a better combat soldier. However, it would seem from the evidence offered that during the decade sports began to play an even more important role in society—not only in terms of the revenues produced but in terms of its value to society—as a healthy means of using one's increased leisure time and as a means of identification in a society where it was increasingly difficult to be recognized as an individual.

Baseball

Baseball faced an uncertain future in the early fifties as attendance began to decline from the postwar boom years of 1946–1948, when both leagues had from 9 to 10 million fans click through the turnstiles. The 1948 season in the American League saw slightly over 11 million paid attendance, with Cleveland and New York each drawing well over 2 million. Six of the eight National League teams drew well over a million in 1948. This resurgence of interest in baseball was not to last. By 1953 attendance in the American League had dropped to about 7 million, and in the 1952 season the National League had only 6.3 million in attendance.

This decline in baseball's fortunes can be attributed to a number of factors. A severe economic recession cut into money available for leisure activities. The nation was in an unsettled and uncertain mood with the McCarthy investigations, the prolonged and draining Korean War, and the escalating cold war with Russia as the United States sought to "contain" her ideological and military adversary. The era of the crisis had begun, and even a steady and calm President Eisenhower could not solve complex world problems or shape the direction of history. This national mood of uneasiness indirectly affected baseball, which is a game that prospers under settled, status quo conditions. Although baseball still served as an island of stability and continuity to many during the fifties, it no longer served as a national rallying point or a symbol of cherished American ways and traditions as it had during World War II.

American society underwent dramatic changes in the fifties, and these new patterns of life affected baseball. Americans became a nation of suburban dwellers with the automobile as the new symbol of affluence and independence. Cities lost their centers as populations spread out and underwent a homogenization that valued success, social contacts, organizational values, and conformity. Inner-city ball parks had relied heavily on neighborhood and local identification with the team, on easy access to the parks by walking or using mass transportation, and on the ritualistic passing on of baseball lore and fanship from father to son.

With the growth of suburbs and the diffusion of big city life these connecting patterns were broken. Commuting took time that could be devoted to watching an occasional baseball game. Suburbs lacked the ethnic and family identifications of inner-city neighborhoods or districts, and life on the fringe of the city could be impersonal and anonymous. The city was now a place of work, a place to get in and out of so that one could mow the lawn or do maintenance on suburban property. The older stadiums—notably Ebbets Field, the Polo Grounds, and the Boston Braves field—lacked adequate parking facilities and were declining in appearance. Fathers had less time to spend playing ball with their sons, talking sports, or going to games. Baseball became an occasional outing rather than a consistent pattern. The automobile enabled people to escape the city and seek the countryside or recreational areas. The "car culture," as it has been aptly described, significantly affected baseball in many ways, and youths' interests in the latest model cars replaced the collecting of baseball cards or the local following of a team's fortunes.

The growth of television also had its negative impact on baseball. In 1947 fewer than 10,000 people owned television sets, and programming was only a few hours a day with a few stations broadcasting. However, by 1957, there were over 40 million sets in homes, bars, hotels, and motels, and 467 stations offered programming. Although programs were initially of inferior and mediocre quality, the loyalty of watchers was surprising, and even minor program innovations were followed with avid interest. Television brought musical entertainment, new media personalities, a different news format, game shows, and even high-level theatre and drama to a mass audience. Its quality of being a "live happening" cut into the movie industry, which, like baseball, underwent a dramatic drop in attendance. To baseball, television was competition, especially with the advent of daytime programming that cut deeply into the attendance of women at ball games. Television provided the suburban home with its electronic connections to the city, and most watchers did not see it as the "vast wasteland."

Baseball would have to make its peace with television, as it did with radio in the twenties. But the relationship was always an uneasy one. Few baseball men were certain whether television exposure stimulated or hindered attendance, but television contracts could be lucrative and bring in needed additional revenues. Many argued that baseball as a game was definitely unsuited for television because the stationary camera could only focus on one segment of the play, and perception of the whole field of play and all interactions is crucial to the simultaneity of the game.

It should also be mentioned that technical innovations in radio also had an impact on baseball. The transistorized portable radio was a development of the fifties, enabling one to take the radio outside where other leisure pursuits were being enjoyed. Baseball broadcasts could now be followed at the beach, on the lakes, on the golf course, or in the backyard. It was now easier to follow baseball and do other things at the same time. Radio remained tremendously popular, especially with the advent of rock and roll music stations and top forty format stations with disc jockeys as new popular culture kings. Young people now had "their own" music and their own singers of youthful rebellion, suppressed teenage sex, adolescent longings, and new consumerism. Buying 45 rpm records and hanging out at record shops and local teenage hotspots became new patterns of life and new interests.

Baseball, a game of tradition and slow-moving precision, found itself in a culture explosion where pleasure seeking, novelty, and momentary excitement became the gauge of value. Mass advertising discovered the teenage market and glorified the teen culture for purposes of sales and expanding consumer markets. The teen stars were gyrating, pulsating rock and roll singers, disc jockeys, and film rebels like James Dean and Marlon Brando. Baseball players no longer were national heroes, and they underwent a significant identity change during the fifties.

It has been noted that baseball players in the fifties became organization men, seeking economic security and professional status much in the same way as did their counterparts in business, the "men in the gray flannel suits." Consciously rejecting star status, fan adulation, and overblown publicity and media hype, the players became team players who fit into a system and were concerned with their futures both in baseball and afterwards. To a large extent, this is true. Players were less flamboyant and controversial, largely because this behavior was not appreciated by conservative owners and because competition was intense and one had to concentrate on steady and consistent performance. Owners and managers sought team players who could find their individual role and play it within the group structure. Players had to be adaptable and adjustable, and Jackie Robinson's career with the Brooklyn Dodgers exemplifies this. He started out as a first baseman in 1947, switched to a second baseman from 1948 to 1951, played the outfield and third base in 1953 and 1954, and finished in 1955 and 1956 by playing four different positions. Yogi Berra also learned to play the outfield in the late fifties after Elston Howard assumed some of the Yankee catching duties, becoming the first black player for the Yanks in 1955.

The Yankees were the epitome of the team concept. Under Casey Stengel's leadership and tutelage the team won four consecutive pennants from 1950 to 1953 and again from 1955 to 1958. They won four straight World Series from 1950 to 1953, and won world championships in 1956 and 1958, defeating the teams (Brooklyn and Milwaukee) that denied them World Series wins in 1955 and 1957. Stengel was the consummate manager who rarely overmanaged, conveyed a solid knowledge of the game and strategy, brought out the best efforts of journeymen players and castoffs, and conveyed an unmistakable pride of the Yankee organization. Stengel utilized his players intelligently and effectively, knowing when to work rookies into the lineup and when to bring up hungry ballplayers from an excellent farm system. Stengel platooned his players brilliantly, and he used starting pitchers like Allie Reynolds, Johnny Sain, and others in relief along with such relief specialists as Tom Morgan and Bob Kuzava.

The Yankees combined steady, timely hitting with a rock-ribbed defense that never led the league in fielding average in the fifties but that specialized in seldom committing mental errors or beating itself. Other teams such as Boston, Cleveland, and Detroit were stronger hitting teams but lacked the balanced pitching, the consistency, and the businesslike concentration of the Yankees. The Yankee front office was a shrewd judge of talent and promise, building a dynasty around Yogi Berra, Gil McDougald, Hank Bauer, Mickey Mantle, and Bill Skowron and complementing them with new talents and timely acquisitions. Mantle proved to be a real superstar, winning the Triple Crown in 1956 and leading the league in home runs in 1955, 1956, and 1958. He was a disciplined and dedicated ballplayer who overcame injury, physical handicap, and great pain to become a great hitter and fine outfielder.

Two of the best hitters in baseball during the 1950s were National Leaguers. Stan "The Man" Musial won four batting titles (three consecutively from 1950 to 1952 and the fourth in 1957), having 200 or more hits in 1951 and 1953, and never finishing lower than fourth in batting from 1950 to 1958. He went over 3,000 hits in 1958 and finished his twenty-two seasons (in 1963) with a .331 lifetime average. Musial was a quiet, unassuming man who played with a concentration and discipline that distinguished him. Along with Ted Williams, he made hitting an exact science of bat contact, fluid, graceful swing, and perfect control of his strike zone.

Richie Ashburn of the Phillies was the other notable hitter of the period. He won batting crowns in 1955 and 1958, and three times he went well over 200 hits. Ashburn actually had 104 more hits than Musial (1,875 hits to 1,771) during the period from 1950 to 1959. Ashburn played in 731 consecutive games from 1950 to 1954, and during his fifteen years averaged 146 games per year. Both men were all-around players who toiled for teams that were rarely in contention, but both personified professionalism and self-discipline.

Ted Williams won consecutive batting titles in 1957 and 1958, pounding out a .388 average in 1957 and dropping sixty points to .328 in 1958, but still repeating. Mantle was the most consistent hitter in the fifties, hitting over .300 five times and hitting .365 (a career high) the year Williams hit .388. The best hitting team of the decade was the 1950 Boston Red Sox, who averaged .302 as a team and featured six .300 or better hitters, with Billy Goodman's league-leading .354 and two players (Walt Dropo and Vern Stephens) who led the league with 144 RBI's. The American League averaged .271 in hitting in 1950, with both Detroit and New York averaging .282. Eleven players had over 100 RBI's in both leagues; thus 1950 has to be considered one of the greatest hitting seasons in the history of baseball. The American League teams scored 6,253 runs, a figure that compares with the most productive years of the twenties, but by 1952 the run total dropped to 5,191. The Detroit Tigers featured some of the best American League hitters with Al Kaline and Harvey Kuenn winning batting titles in 1955 and 1959, and Kuenn twice collecting over 200 hits.

American League batting averages would never approach the remarkable .271 of 1950, falling to .253 by 1959. The National League far outdistanced the rival league in extra base hits and home runs. From 1950 to 1959 there were 456 more doubles, 197 more triples, and 1,828 more home runs in the National League. In 1955 the National League power hitters propelled 1,263 home runs with the Dodgers hitting 201, and in 1956 the league saw 1,219 home runs with the powerful Cincinnati Reds rapping out 221 round trippers. Ralph Kiner, Ted Kluzewski, Ernie Banks, Duke Snider, Eddie Matthews, Willie Mays, Henry Aaron, Wally Post, and others confirmed the reputation of the Senior Circuit as the power hitter's league.

The National League also had two of the premier pitchers of the decade: Warren Spahn and Robin Roberts. From 1950 to 1959 Spahn won 20 or more games in eight seasons and led the league in complete games four times with a personal high of 26 in 1951. Spahn led the league with a 2.10 ERA in 1953, won a key game in the 1957 Series against the Yankees, and won two games to keep Milwaukee in the 1958 summer classic, again against the Yankees.

The Spahn-Lew Burdette combination was perhaps the best left-right handed pitching duo of the decade, and Burdette's three victories in the 1957 World Series win over the Yankees, with two shutouts and three complete games, was the pitching accomplishment of the decade. Robin Roberts won more than twenty games per season from 1950 to 1955, led the league in wins from 1952 to 1955, led the league in complete games from 1952 to 1956, and toiled during more innings from 1951 to 1955 than any other National League hurler. Spahn and Roberts were control pitchers and the workhorses of their particular teams. Spahn struck out 2,583 and walked 1,434 in his twenty-one-year career, while Roberts struck out 2,357 and walked only 902 in a nineteen-year career.

The fifties saw the disappearance of the workhorses who pitched complete games and the advent of the relief specialists. Allie "Superchief" Reynolds saw his last season in 1954, finishing with a 13-4 record and 7 World Series winning games to his credit. Bob Feller retired in 1956 after eighteen seasons with the Indians, pitching in 570 games. Bob Lemon retired in 1958 after appearing in 460 games in fifteen seasons. Relief specialists like Don Mossi, Ray Narleski, Elroy Face, Jim Konstanty, and others came to be a consistent feature of the fifties game. Face had a remarkable 18-1 record for Pittsburgh in 1959, all his wins coming in relief. Face's elusive "forkball" was a pitch that he made famous as a relief specialist.

The game was becoming more specialized with short, middle, and long relievers; with pinch hitters like Smokey Burgess and Johnny Mize; and with the platooning of players. Superstars like Mantle, Mays, and Aaron were the exceptions. Managers sought winning systems and an organization that would build consistency, productivity, and disciplined team play. Players accepted this approach readily because it offered security and longevity. The burden of being a "personality" or "star" relied upon for the big season was relieved, and ballplayers became "organization men" who had designated tasks, clearly understood assignments, and team goals.

The Chicago White Sox pennant of 1959 illustrates perfectly the dominant team concept. The team had only one .300 hitter, Nellie Fox, who hit .306. Sherman Lollar led the team with 84 RBI's, but Luis Aparicio had 56 stolen bases with team members adding 57 more. The team topped the league in fielding average, and relief specialists Gerry Staley and Turk Lown had 29 saves and 17 wins between them to complement brilliant seasons by starters Early Wynn and Bob Shaw. Nellie Fox and Luis Aparicio won golden gloves for fielding percentage, proving the adage that winners are solid up the middle. Manager Al Lopez handled the pitchers effectively, utilizing a three-man pitching staff and two spot starters.

The decade saw other significant changes in baseball with the re-tirements of Joe DiMaggio in 1951 after playing in his tenth World Se-ries and reaching a salary of $100,000 a year, Jackie Robinson in 1956 after the World Series, and George Kell in 1957. These were three of the finest hitters in baseball and all three had better than .300 lifetime averages. They were class ballplayers and gentlemen whose deep love of the game, strong personal pride, and all-around play marked them for the Hall of Fame. Musial and Williams would soon end their careers and bring to an end an era of great hitting that provided proba-bly the greatest source of fan interest from the post World War II era to 1960. The next era would feature Hank Aaron's successful assault on Babe Ruth's home run record and Pete Rose's development as the greatest modern day hitter.

Franchise shifts showed the precarious situation of certain clubs during the fifties. The Boston Braves moved to Milwaukee in 1953, the first franchise shift in fifty years. The St. Louis Browns moved to Baltimore in 1954, and the next year saw the Philadelphia A's move to Kansas City. These baseball clubs escaped antiquated parks, indiffer-ent fans, and traditions of futility. They sought new population cen-ters that could draw fans from a surrounding metropolitan and inter-state region, and ball parks that would be accessible to the commuting fan. By 1958 the Dodgers and Giants had moved to the West Coast, making baseball a truly national game and tapping a California mar-ket that had supported quality minor league teams in the Pacific Coast League. Baseball moved out of the hands of businessmen owners to become municipal operations, as cities financed the building of parks in return for concessions, parking fees, and rental charges. California attracted two of the best teams in baseball, not franchises that had been marginal or lacked financing. The California weather promised fewer rainouts and better opening season weather.

Los Angeles quickly responded with a pennant and World Series wins in 1959 and 1963, and the Giants won the pennant in 1962, los-ing to the Yankees in seven games in what was one of the most excit-ing Series of the sixties.

The fifties were filled with memorable moments and achievements, some of which deserve brief mention. The New York Giants provided the "miracle finish" of the decade, coming from $13\frac{1}{2}$ games behind in 1951 to tie the Dodgers and defeat them in a dramatic three-game playoff. The winning play was Bobby Thompson's three-run "shot heard round the world" in the ninth inning with the Giants behind 4-2. In 1952 Walt Dropo, recently traded to the Tigers, hit safely in twelve consecutive times at bat in three games, equalling a record set by Mike Higgins in 1938. The Dodgers' win over the Yankees in the seven-game Series of 1955 provided perhaps the most emotional moment, as "them Bums" gained sweet revenge for all the losses to the Yankees and seven straight failures in World Series play. The Dodgers came back after losing the first two games, and Johnny Podres and Sandy Amoros became the darlings of Flatbush. After losing three games at Yankee Stadium, the Bums won the seventh game there 2-0 with Podres winning in his second complete game. Four of the Dodgers were black (Campanella, Gilliam, Robinson, and Newcombe), and one was a Cuban, Sandy Amoros. Don Larsen's perfect no-hit game in the fifth game of the 1956 Series had to be the stellar individual pitching performance of the decade, as the Yankees turned the tables on Brooklyn (after the Dodgers had romped in the first two games) and won the deciding game at Brooklyn.

The team success story of the fifties was the Milwaukee Braves, with pennants in 1957 and 1958 and a successful franchise shift. The 1952 Boston Braves drew only 281,278 fans or curiosity seekers, and the franchise lost a half million dollars. In 1952 the Milwaukee team drew 1.8 million and over 2 million from 1954 to 1957, although a definite decline set in after 1.9 million in 1958 went down to 773,018 in 1963. The Los Angeles Dodgers would soon go through the same kind of boom.

The New York City monopoly on baseball was not broken. Five of the ten Series in the fifties were all New York affairs, and the Yankees were involved in eight World Series during the period. Baseball was now played in three time zones, and the sport was ready to move into a period of expansion and a decade that saw the Yankees win World Series in 1961 and 1962 but lose in 1960, 1963, and 1964. After 1964 the dominance of the Yankees was over, and Baltimore emerged as the most successful team in the American League. The game was ready for dramatic changes in the team concept, the distribution of talent and salaries, and the styles of ballplayers' lives and careers. Owners and managers now had to deal with players as individuals and stars, and the player who was grateful to play in the big leagues, who was quiet and accepting of team rules, and who loved the game more than money was becoming a relic of the near distant past.

College Football

In his popular history of the fifteen-year period after the war entitled *The Crucial Decade* (1956), Eric Goldman commented that in

1946, "the big football weekend roared back." College play on the gridiron grew more sophisticated as many of the players were older than the usual undergraduate. Great numbers of them had played service ball and were going to college under the liberal benefits of the GI Bill. As Donald S. Andrews, author of a paper entitled "Into the 1950's: The Growing Popularity of American Collegiate Football," delivered before the 1979 convention of the North American Society for Sport History, explains it, with the departure of the service veterans, colleges found it necessary (in order to insure the high revenues that the gridiron games brought in) that the "heightened entertainment value had to be maintained and athletes from all over the country were actively solicited, thus turning recruiting into an active business. Consequently, American collegiate football underwent a profound and additive transformation of its commercial entertainment value during this period resulting in the game's reaching unforeseen popularity heights during the 1950s."

The emphasis on the entertainment side of college athletics prompted distinguished educator Harold W. Stoke, former president of the University of New Hampshire and of Louisiana State University, and the then dean of the Graduate School at the University of Washington, to write an article entitled "College Athletics: Education or Show Business?" which appeared in the March 1954 edition of the *Atlantic Monthly*. Stoke found that the increased leisure time of Americans "created social vacuums" and the "American system of education—and particularly higher education—is one of the most efficient devices ever invented. It is flexible, highly varied and in touch with virtually the entire population. It is manned by aggressive and accommodating people: it is suffused with a thoroughly practical philosophy. Hence, to its already great and growing array of services—its teaching, research, adult education, military training, and general public service—it has added another, public entertainment. Yet of all the instrumentalities which universities have for entertaining the public, the most effective is athletics."

Stoke suggested that athletes be relieved of the responsibility of academic requirements and that eligibility rules be turned over to athletic management, thus restoring "institutional and personal integrity." Arguing that "those who recruit players and the players who are recruited are too often corrupted not because of the bargains they strike, but because the bargains are in violation of pledges all have agreed to uphold," Stoke wanted to make "winning athletics" a "legitimate university operation" thus making "recruiting . . . not only legal but justifiable." Stoke argued further that "Educators now find that what was once the recreation of students in schools has been transformed into a responsibility of the educational system to supply the public with entertainment.''

Stoke provided statistics which supported his contention that college sports were entertainment and big money makers. In 1953 college football audiences numbered 40 million, and college basketball was attracting almost as many. A half million people saw the bowl games of 1954 in person, and almost 70 million listened to them on radio or watched them on television. Gate receipts for the bowl games amounted to over $2.5 million.

U.S. News and World Report in its August 24, 1951, issue, in an article entitled ''College Football: Big Business,'' also found college sports, particularly football, to be lucrative and part of the ''entertainment business.'' Citing gate receipts of $100 million for the 1950 season alone, the magazine stated that ''major league baseball by comparison is small time stuff with a 'gate' of about $20 million. Investment in football plant and equipment is estimated conservatively at $300 million and is growing year by year.''

The article also pointed out why prime athletic recruits were needed. It stated: ''A fleet foot, a pair of slippery hips, a good eye plus a superior throwing arm may be worth tens or hundreds of thousands of dollars to a college—the difference between profit and loss on the ledger limited to three years. The hero of today is the graduate of tomorrow. The search for heroes is intense and competition keen, the range of offers limited.''

The article gave financial analyses of football expenses at a number of Big Ten schools. For example, Purdue in 1950 took in $597,110 in athletic revenues and spent $208,758. Some $15,399 was spent for equipment while $191,586 was listed as ''competition expense.'' Similarly, Minnesota received $900,000 in sports revenues and listed $205,000 as expenses for ''repairs and alterations.'' Making big money meant one had to spend big money.

The problems associated with recruiting meant that in order to compete for the good athletes, someone was going to offer more or do more for them than the rules allowed. In football, the major scandal which shook collegiate football was the West Point cribbing scandal of 1951. In August 1951 West Point announced that ninety cheating cadets included ''Robert Blaik, son of the football coach and an All-American quarterback, other students on the Army first team, and members of the varsity squads in most other sports.'' In addition, it was revealed that a special six-week cram course and ''entertainment'' were given athletes about to enter West Point.

In an emotional press conference Colonel Blaik said the press and the public should "stop knocking football, God help this country if we didn't play football. . . . General Eisenhower came to West Point with his greatest desire to play football." Despite Blaik's impassioned plea, on August 9, President Truman ordered a thorough examination to determine if the military academy "was 'overemphasizing' football and other competitive sports."

The West Point scandal had far-reaching implication. *Life* came out in its September 17, 1951, issue with a scathing editorial that indicted the collegiate game, coaches, and college administrators alike. *Life* asked: "Just what entertainment value the show has is doubtful. The coaches in their greed to win games and keep earning better money than the philosophy professors have invented the rule of unlimited substitution." The article concluded that in light of the West Point cribbing scandal and the basketball fix scandals of 1951 that the "only real argument in academic circles is over the television rights."

Life then went on to address the crux of the problem as it saw it—the failure of college administrators to perceive the evil that they were fostering by allowing athletic programs to get out of hand. *Life* further editorialized in the following words: "We look to the college teachers—and especially the college presidents—for firm and impartial guidance along the road to culture and morality. . . . We put a lot of faith in our colleges and we deserve to have it justified. A college president who is sorting out his contracts for high school prospects with one hand and selling tickets to the stadium with the other, can never keep our faith. . . . Of course, the college president will say that he doesn't really sell the tickets—that in fact he has nothing whatever to do with football. Maybe not, Mr. President, but someone is certainly committing the crime in your name. In fact your football team is violating all the ethics you are trying to teach in your classrooms. Whether you are an active conniver in this fraud or just the victim of a crime under the tent you appear equally guilty to any casual bystander. Better forget about those stadium bonds and start worrying about your real franchise in American life."

Even the film industry entered the criticism against collegiate athletics. A 1951 film entitled *Saturday's Hero*, starring John Derek, examined "fictionally the exploitation of young men at one college because of their physical abilities." As one commentator assessed the movie: "*Saturday's Hero*, nurtured by a variety of sports scandals, became a successful movie, touching America's collective conscience, asking questions that needed to be asked."

Undoubtedly responding to the widespread criticism of the game, in January 1953 the return to a single-platoon football was approved by a vote of NCAA members. According to the rule change, a player withdrawn from a game during the first or third periods may not return during the period from which he was withdrawn.

Many coaches at big school powers were downcast at the rules change. Woody Hayes was reported in the January 26, 1953, issue of *Time* as stating that "we simply cannot train a boy to play offense and defense in that time." Biggie Munn, coach of new football power, Michigan State, "morbidly predicted that the new rule would throw the picture wide open next fall."

Newsweek of January 26, 1953, reported that small schools had been the leaders in seeking the abolishment of two-platoon football. Armed with statistics showing that in recent years fifty schools had abandoned football because of increasing costs, the small schools had won the day. College football would end the fifties with two-way players, and as the editors of *College Football U.S.A. 1869 . . . 1973* (1973) stated, "fans who had heretofore become disaffected, because of the dehumanizing effects of the automation that crept in under the pushbutton, two-platoon system, once again valued the entertainment return of weekend visits to the campus."

How did the average undergraduate take his football? The editor of the *Yale News* reported in the January 17, 1954, *New York Times Magazine* that an "undergraduate often doesn't even know the cheers." Some writers thought that the scrutiny of draft boards over grades was partially responsible for the lack of interest by students.

In 1957 *Life* published an article entitled "Sad News From the Campus: Nobody Loves the Football Hero Now." According to the article, "the football hero has long been not only a vital part of United States folklore but a national phenomenon as well. From the '20s through the '40s his room on campus was looked upon as a shrine by reverent freshmen." *Life* found that this was not the case in the fifties and no longer were the athletic stars' "sweat shirts treasured as momentos." There were few pep rallies, and even outright criticism of athletes was evident. Several Indiana football players said they were going to quit the team because of criticism from the student body. One Michigan faculty member interviewed said it was "unfashionable to glorify an athlete right now." *Life* concluded that a lack of recognizable stars and the rising commercialism of the game were the major reasons behind the "decline and fall of the football idol."

Commercialism and scandal were not the only problems that college football had to deal with during the decade. On January 8, 1951, Lieutenant John Trent, captain of the 1949 West Point football team, was named by the Football Writers Association of America as its 1950 Man of the Year. The award had to be made posthumously. Lieutenant Trent had been killed in bitter fighting in Korea during 1950. With 137,000 Americans killed or wounded in the "police action," and a need for more manpower evident, college coaches for the first four years of the decade had to fear the loss of a player not only because of bad grades, but also because of a draft notice.

On the field during the fifties, Oklahoma was the team of the decade. Already a powerhouse in the late forties when Bud Wilkinson succeeded Jim Tatum as coach, the Sooners strung together a winning string which began in 1948 and stretched to 31 consecutive victories until they were upset 13-7 by a fine Kentucky Wildcat team led by quarterback Babe Parelli in the 1951 Sugar Bowl. After a loss to Notre Dame in 1952, Oklahoma put together another winning streak, this time of 47 games, which was stopped by Notre Dame in 1957 by a score of 7-0.

Wilkinson compiled an enviable record at Oklahoma during the fifties. Oklahoma was the number one ranked team in 1950, 1955, and 1956. During an eight-year period they won 73 games, lost 5, and tied 2. In addition, they were 4 and 1 in bowl play for an overall 76-6-2 record.

Princeton saw a resurgence of football prowess in the fifties. The Tigers captured the Ivy League title in 1950, 1951, and 1955. Instrumental in the Princeton success was halfback Dick Kazmaier, Heisman trophy winner of 1951 and a member of the College Hall of Fame. Kazmaier, who was on the fifth string as a freshman, became an All-American. During his last two seasons Princeton was unbeaten, and he was number one in total offense leadership his senior year. Probably his most outstanding game was when he powered the Tigers to a 53-15 victory over title pretender Cornell in 1951. Kazmaier hit on 15 of 17 passes for 236 yards and 3 touchdowns and then rushed for 124 yards and 2 more TDs. Certainly he was one of the great halfbacks of the decade.

The 1950s also saw the emergence of Michigan State as a national football power. Led first by coach Biggie Munn and then succeeded by Hugh "Duffy" Daugherty, the Spartans went 8 and 1 in 1950; in 1951 they were 9-0 and ranked number two in the nation; and in 1952 they again went 9-0 and were ranked number one in the nation. During these seasons, Michigan State played as an independent. Beginning with the 1953 season, Michigan State entered Big Ten play and was 8-1 for the season and tied Illinois for the title. State was chosen to go to the Rose Bowl in 1954, since Illinois had gone two seasons previously in 1952. The Spartans edged the UCLA's 28-20. Two years later the Spartans finished second to Ohio State with an 8-1 record but went to the Rose Bowl because of the Big Ten's no-repeat rule. They once again met the UCLA Bruins, with the Spartans winning 17-10 on a dramatic field goal with 7 seconds to go. Certainly the Spartans were the surprise squad of the decade. Big Ten teams won nine of the Rose Bowl contests during the fifties.

The early fifties was a period of running quarterbacks—men who were expert at the option play such as Notre Dame stars Paul Hornung and Ralph Guglielmi. Outstanding passers included Purdue's Lenny Dawson, who in 1955 set a conference record when he completed a 95-yard touchdown pass, but as long as the split T was the dominant formation, the running quarterback prevailed.

The Big Ten Conference was not dominated by two teams as would be the case in the sixties and seventies. Seven different teams would win the title or share it during the decade with only Minnesota, Northwestern, and Indiana unable to claim a share of the title or outright possession.

The Big Ten Conference produced some outstanding players during the period: Minnesota's Paul Giel; Ohio State's Vic Janowicz (1950 Heisman Trophy Winner); Jim Parker, Ohio State's two-time All-American end; Ron Kramer of Michigan; Michigan State's Sonny Grandelius, Lynn Chandnois, Bill Wells, Don Coleman, Dave Kaiser, Al Dorrow, Tom Yewcic, and Earl Morral; Illinois' Ray Nitchske and J. C. Caroline; Iowa's Alex Karras, Kenny Ploen, and Randy Duncan; and Purdue's Lenny Dawson. Yet there were three players who stood out from all the rest in the conference. These were Alan Ameche of Wisconsin, Don Coleman at Michigan State, and Howard Cassidy of Ohio State. The Outland Trophy for the outstanding interior lineman was awarded to Big Ten players from 1955 through 1957 as Calvin Jones, Jim Parker, and Alex Karras won the award.

Ameche, a fullback at Wisconsin from 1951 to 1954, was the Heisman Trophy winner in 1954. During his career he rushed 3,345 yards, scored 25 touchdowns, and had six games in which he gained over 100 yards. He was three-time conference, two-time All-American, and 1953–54 All-American Academic Team. Ameche is a College Hall of Fame member.

Don Coleman played football at Michigan State during the 1949, 1950, and 1951 seasons. He was the lightest tackle in the Big Ten at 181 pounds but was one of the quickest and fiercest linemen ever to tread a gridiron. Don would often block two or three men on a play. In a game against Penn State in 1951 he made all the tackles on kickoffs and punts. Spartan coaches stated that Coleman threw 80 percent of the important blocks which resulted in big plays. He was All-Conference and All-American and was the first player at Michigan State to have his jersey retired. Coleman was one of the first black football players to be inducted into the College Hall of Fame.

Howard "Hopalong" Cassady was All-American in 1954 and 1955 and Heisman Trophy winner in 1955. During his senior year Cassady led Big Ten rushers with 711 yards, a 6-yard-per-carry average and was the top scorer with 66 points. In his four years at Ohio State Cassady scored a total of 222 points and 37 touchdowns to set a school record. Ameche, Coleman, and Cassady were indeed three of the premier players not only of the Big Ten and of the fifties, but of all time.

Other outstanding players during the period included Bill Vessels, Oklahoma's outstanding back and Heisman Trophy Winner of 1952; Dick Modzelewski, Maryland's outstanding tackle on Jim Tatum's great Maryland teams of the early fifties; Notre Dame's Heisman duo of Johnny Lattner (1953) and Paul Hornung (1956); Jim Brown, Syracuse's All-American running back; and Texas A&M's great running back, John David Crow.

Early in the decade other new teams cracked the top ten and had outstanding seasons. Jim Tatum's Maryland teams were powerful, going 9-0 in 1951, and then went unbeaten in 1953 to claim the number one spot and win Coach Tatum the coach of the year award. Georgia Tech put together a 31-game winning streak, which was ended by Notre Dame in 1953.

Generally USC and UCLA were the class of the West Coast. In 1951, however, Stanford went 9-1 and featured two time (1948 and 1952) Olympic decathlon champion Bob Mathias in its backfield.

In the East, Syracuse won the Lambert Trophy in 1953 and in 1956 ended up eighth in the polls behind the power running of Jimmy Brown and then was ranked number one in 1959 and received the first award of the MacArthur Bowl of the National Football Foundation.

Louisiana State under the leadership of Paul Dietzel was the only major team in 1958 to go undefeated, and they were ranked number one and coach Dietzel was named Coach of the Year. In 1959 LSU ended up ranked third, but its fabulous running back, Billy "Boom Boom" Cannon, won the Heisman Trophy.

Army also saw a brief resurgence behind such stars as the 1958 Heisman Trophy Winner Pete Dawkins and the strange strategy of using a lonesome end—Bill Carpenter—who never returned to the huddle and who confused the opposition, needless to say. Certainly these and other players who probably deserve mention thrilled thousands of fans, and many of them went on to careers in the National Football League.

Faced with declining attendance, the NCAA authorities believed that haphazard televising of college games had been responsible. In 1951 they set up a "television control plan, limiting the number of televised games both nationally and regionally." According to the NCAA it was "also designed to give college football wider television circulation than could be achieved independently, and assures the viewing public of a balanced diet of the best that college football has to offer." Of course, only a few teams could be on during the season, and as time would prove, they would be the ones who would primarily benefit in terms of recruiting and publicity from the television exposure.

As already mentioned, the NCAA was forced by scandals and costs to member schools to go to a one-platoon system in 1953. By 1959, however, liberalization of the rules meant that a lot of "platooning" was going on. As the professional game became more appealing, the colleges found that they were in competition for the entertainment dollar and that they would have to keep pace with the pros in this matter.

In order to spice up the college game and make it more attractive, the rules committee at their winter meeting in 1957–58 altered the method of scoring (rules which had not been changed in forty-six years). Two points were awarded for the conversion after the touchdown if it was run or passed and the three-yard line was made the line for the conversion attempt.

College football at the end of the decade was a sport beginning to make a comeback from scandals and claims of overemphasis during the early years of the decade. Attempts to return to "cheaper" football had proven to be "uncompetitive" with the pros, and it was only a matter of time until full platooning was allowed. Football made too much money and was deemed to be the financial keystone of most college athletic programs. Thus it had to keep the turnstiles turning and the television audience watching.

Although the fifties had seen black stars such as Don Coleman at Michigan State and Jimmy Brown of Syracuse, most of the major football squads were white. In the South the teams were all white. It would take the Civil Rights movement of the sixties to jog the consciences of college athletic administrators before more black ball players would appear on the football playing fields.

Professional Football

Pro football during the 1950s was definitely a growth sport. In 1950, 1,977,556 fans watched league games with each game averaging 25,353. By 1960 spectator attendance had risen by almost 300 percent to 3,128,296, with an average attendance of 40,106. The opening year of the decade saw the first games in the NFL after the merger with the All-American Conference. Ironically, the decade would end with another league being formed to challenge the NFL.

There were a number of reasons why pro football became popular. First, the free substitution rule had an enormous impact upon the game. Instituted in 1950, it was in direct opposition to the move that the colleges would make in 1953 when they returned to one-platoon football. With two-platoon football, the pro teams could utilize specialists better and could concentrate in training on various facets of execution. The result was a better, more polished game. Finesse on offense could now be met with finesse on defense. In addition, the platoon system extended the longevity of players' careers and allowed football to develop perennial stars, as in baseball. Fans could now talk about pro football players' feats year round, too.

Television also played an important role in the development of pro football during the fifties. In 1950 the Los Angeles Rams became the first NFL team to televise all of its games. The result was a 50 percent drop in attendance from the previous year. The Rams immediately blacked out home game telecasts. Taking a cue from the NCAA, which restricted television programming of games, the NFL, under Commissioner Bert Bell's direction, declared that there would be no televising of an NFL game within seventy-five miles of a stadium where an NFL game was being played. In 1952 the U.S. government filed an antitrust suit against the NFL, but after fighting the suit in court, the NFL emerged victorious. On November 12, 1953, Judge Alan K. Grim of the Federal District Court for Eastern Pennsylvania ruled in favor of the NFL. This meant that hometown fans, whose appetites had been whetted by watching their team perform in away games, and anxious to view them in person, could not view them at all.

Another factor in the NFL's popularity was that there were exciting stars such as Otto Graham, Ollie Matson, Jimmy Brown, and Bobby Layne. Many of these players had been stars in college, and the increasing number of college graduate fans wanted to follow the careers of the players they had seen perform on the college gridiron. Also, the games often provided "high drama." Many believe that the 1958 playoff game between the Baltimore Colts and the New York Giants, which was won by the Colts 23-17 at the 8 minute, 15 second mark of overtime, gave professional football "the last kick in the pants" it needed, as it was witnessed by millions on television.

Pro football also became popular with blacks, as many of the offensive stars of the decade, such as Joe "the Jet" Perry, Ollie Matson, and of course, the incomparable Jimmy Brown, were black.

The fifties were also the era of the passing quarterback. Included among this select company were Cleveland's Otto Graham, Los Angeles's Norm Van Brocklin and Bob Waterfield, Detroit's Bobby Layne, New York's Charlie Conerly, and Baltimore's Johnny Unitas. These men could not only pass the ball with precision and accuracy, but were real field generals and could inspire their fellow players. Thus in crucial portions of the game when coolness under fire was needed, these men excelled—and that's why they were champions.

For fully half the decade, from 1950 to 1954, the NFL was dominated by three teams: the Cleveland Browns, the Los Angeles Rams, and the Detroit Lions. These were the only teams that competed in the NFL championship playoff games for those years.

In the 1950 playoff game between the Cleveland Browns and the Los Angeles Rams there were a lot of bad feelings. Many old NFL die-hards had regarded the All-American League as a "bush" league operation and were somewhat chagrined to see one of the three teams that had been brought into the NFL from that conference. Also, the Los Angeles Rams had been known as the Cleveland Rams before the competition from the Browns drove them out of Cleveland and to the Coast.

The Browns, however, were not patsies. Coached by offensive genius Paul Brown, quarterbacked by astute field general Otto Graham, who had under his command such receivers as Mac Speedie, Dante Lavelli, and Dub Jones, and powered by the bull-like rushes of Marion Motley, the Browns of 1950 were a formidable crew.

Under the leadership of Jumbo Joe Stydahar as coach, the Rams had excellent quarterbacks in Bob Waterfield and Norman Van Brocklin, and excellent receivers in Glenn Davis (Mr. Outside of the West Point attack in the forties), Bob Boyd, and Elroy (Crazylegs) Hirsh. Tank Younger was only one of many powerful Rams running backs who could be called on to deliver the mail.

The 1950 NFL championship game was a seesaw affair with both teams trading touchdowns. With only 27 seconds gone, Waterfield hit the fleet Davis, who scampered 82 yards for a touchdown. The Browns quickly retaliated when Graham tossed a 27-yard scoring pass to Dub Jones, and on it went. With a minute to go in the game and trailing 28-27, the Browns intercepted a pass and with 28 seconds to go, Lou Groza kicked a field goal to win the game. However, in 1951 the table was turned when the two teams met again. This time the field goal kicking of Bob Waterfield and the passing of Norm Van Brocklin, who tossed a 73-yard scoring pass to Tom Fears, beat the Browns 24-17.

The 1952 and 1953 Detroit Lions emerged under the leadership of the "flamboyant" Bobby Layne. (Layne once told a rookie, "If you want to play quarterback in the National League, you got to drink.") Doak Walker was a do-everything halfback, and Layne could throw to such fine receivers as Lew Carpenter, Jim Doran, Dorne Dibble, and Leon Hart.

The Lions were known for their defensive platoon, which was anchored in the middle by 300-pound Les Bingaman (a writer had once said "Bingaman stops runners the way Pepper Martin used to field ground balls—with his stomach"), anchored at middle linebacker with the formidable Joe Schmidt, and strengthened by a fine defensive secondary starring Jack Christiansen.

In 1952 the Lions triumphed over Cleveland 17-7 despite being outgained in first downs 22-10. The Lions' defense led by the gargantuan Bingaman stopped the Browns' offense at crucial times, and the Lions were able to produce enough offense (including a 67-yard run by Doak Walker which led to a score) to beat the Browns.

In 1953 the score was a closer 17-16, but the results were the same. The Lions, behind 16-10 with fewer than three minutes to play, put on a passing blitz behind the arm of the indomitable Bobby Layne. He hit four of six passes, including a 33-yard bomb to Jim Doran to secure the victory.

In 1954 the Browns finally had their revenge and blew the Lions out of the ball park by a 56-10 score. Actually the Browns only outrushed the Lions by four yards, 140-136, and the Lions had more passing yardage, 195-163. But the Browns had the points, including three scoring passes by Graham.

In 1955 fans saw the last of the three-team domination of the NFL—for two years. In the swan song game, Cleveland met Los Angeles once more and belted them 38-14. Otto Graham was the star as he passed for touchdowns of 50 and 35 yards and scored on runs of 15 and 1 yards. After the game Graham announced his retirement.

The New York Giants came back in 1956. Charlie Conerly at quarterback, Kyle Rote, an all-purpose back, Sam Huff, middle linebacker, Dick Modzewlewski and Andy Robustelli, stalwarts on defense, were the key personnel for the Giants.

Surprise winners in 1956 were the Western Conference Chicago Bears led by the power running of fullback Rick Casares, the pass-catching heroics of Harlon Hill, and the quarterbacking of Ed Brown and George Blanda. Unfortunately for the Bears, the Giants slaughtered them 47-7. The score was 34-7 at half time, and it was a strictly no-contest affair. Alex Webster scored twice, Conerly threw touchdown passes to Kyle Rote and Frank Gifford, and Ben Agajanian kicked two field goals to trigger the Giants' offense.

In 1957 the Detroit Lions and the Cleveland Browns were again matched up in the championship final game. As in the year before, it proved to be a laugher, with the Lions pounding out a resounding 59-14 victory. Five interceptions and the passing of Tobin Rote, who flung 4 touchdown passes including a 78-yard bomb to Jim Doran, sealed the Browns' fate and produced the rout.

The 1958 and 1959 NFL championship games in which the Baltimore Colts and the New York Giants were the opponents have been counted as a major factor for making pro football the number one sport of the sixties and the seventies.

The Colts were an exciting team both offensively and defensively. On defense, Baltimore featured such behemoth linemen as Gino Marchetti, Jim Parker, and Gene "Big Daddy" Lipscomb—a 6-foot 6-inch, 290-pound giant who seemed to have the swiftness of a gazelle while in pursuit of an unlucky ball carrier. On offense, smooth and slick halfback Lenny Moore could run or catch; the peerless Raymond Berry was an elusive, sticky-fingered receiver; Alan "the Horse" Ameche did the heavy duty hauling of the pigskin. At quarterback was the peerless Johnny Unitas, a man who had been cut as a rookie by the Pittsburgh Steelers and who had played for a semipro team, the Bloomfield Rams, for $6 a game, until he received a call from the Colts to try out. Unitas was certainly a Horatio Alger success story if there ever was one.

The 1958 playoff game, which the Colts won in overtime, has been called the "best pro football game ever played." One commentator has noted that "Unitas' plays—the 13 plays it took the Colts to cover 80 yards in sudden death—have been detailed and diagrammed until, through sheer repetition, they have achieved a place in history alongside Roosevelt's 100 days."

Perhaps what made the game doubly dramatic is that the Colts, in order to send the game into overtime, had to drive from their own 14, trailing 20-17. They managed to do this, and with seven seconds left Steve Myhra connected on a 13-yard field goal to deadlock the game at 17-17 and send the contest into overtime.

In the dramatic overtime, Unitas was a master of the situation. After the Giants won the toss and elected to receive, they failed to move the ball and punted to the Colts. In 13 plays Unitas mixed pinpoint passing and the running of Ameche as the means to victory, with Ameche plunging 1 yard for the victory. The Giants could never live down their defeat and resulting image as losers. One comedian cracked to quarterback Conerly while at a dinner he attended as a guest, "I'm sorry I didn't notice you before. I just didn't recognize you without Big Daddy Lipscomb sitting on top of you."

If the Giants were perceived as losers after the 1958 game, the image was enhanced by the results of the 1959 rematch between the two squads. It was a rather strange affair with the Colts taking the kickoff and putting together a 6-play scoring drive orchestrated by the peerless Unitas. The Giants then scored 3 field goals and led 9-7 going into the final quarter. But the Colts exploded for 20 points and the Giants were losers once again.

A number of players deserve to be recognized as outstanding stars during the period, men who often did not play on championship teams. Among these were Ollie Matson, Joe "the Jet" Perry, Hugh McElhenny, and Chuck Bednarik.

Ollie Matson had played halfback for San Francisco and was an All-American in 1951 as he led the NCAA in scoring and rushing that season. Before going on with his pro football career, Ollie ran in the 1952 Olympics, winning a bronze medal in the 400-meter dash and a silver medal as a member of the second place U.S. 1600-meter relay team. He played football for the St. Louis Cardinals until 1959, when he was traded to the Los Angeles Rams, who sent nine men to the Cardinals in exchange for Matson. After four years with the Rams he spent one year with the Detroit Lions and ended his career with the Philadelphia Eagles, retiring in 1967.

Matson possessed blinding speed and was known for his ability to break off long runs. In 1955 he led the league in punt-return average and was the Pro Bowl Player of the game. He was All-Pro for the years 1954, 1955, 1956, and 1957. In 1956 he rushed for 924 yards, but had 350 yards called back in penalties. Matson is a member of the Pro Hall of Fame.

Joe "The Jet" Perry played for fourteen seasons with San Francisco and is considered to be one of the top running backs ever to perform in professional football. A track star in high school, he attended Compton Junior College and then attracted pro scouts while playing for Alameda Naval Air Station. During his pro career Perry accumulated 9,723 yards for a 5.0 average rush and scored 71 touchdowns. Joe won the NFL rushing title in 1953 and 1954 and became the first runner to gain 1,000 yards in two consecutive seasons. He would team with Hugh McElhenny, Y. A. Tittle, and John Henry Johnson, which some called the "million dollar backfield."

Hugh McElhenny was one of the great running backs at the University of Washington from 1949 to 1951. His most productive years were spent with the San Francisco 49ers from 1952 to 1960. In the twilight of his career he would play for Minnesota, New York, and Detroit.

McElhenny played in six Pro Bowls and was All-Pro halfback in 1952 and 1953. He averaged 10.69 yards per carry in his rookie season. He is also in the Pro Hall of Fame.

Chuck Bednarik was the last of the "iron" man two-way players in the NFL. In 1960 Bednarik was still playing center on offense and lineback on defense because of a shortage of personnel. He personally insured victory for the Philadelphia Eagles in the 1960 NFL title game against Green Bay when he tackled the Packers' Jim Taylor on the 9-yard line as time ran out.

Bednarik had played at the University of Pennsylvania after having served in thirty combat missions during World War II. He was eight time All-NFL and played in eight Pro Bowls. The son of an immigrant Czechoslovakian steelworker, Bednarik played with a stocking stuffed with rags as a child in place of a real football. A tough, tenacious player, he played fourteen years and is in the Hall of Fame.

The premier player of the fifties—at least for the last three years—was Jimmy Brown. From 1957 to 1961 Brown was the NFL's leading rusher. An All-American at Syracuse, Brown was also a standout in track, lacrosse, and basketball. In nine seasons playing with the Cleveland Browns he rushed for 12,312 yards and set an individual game rushing record of 237 yards, which he accomplished twice. At 6 feet 2 inches and 228 pounds, Brown had the perfect blend of speed and power, which meant that he could outspeed defenders to the outside and overpower would-be tacklers on the inside. One writer has said about Brown: "Nobody talks about Brown's being 'another Marion Motley' any more. Many think that not even Bronko Nagurski, Ernie Nevers or Jim Thorpe can be compared to him. Brown literally outdistanced all his competitors and played in a class all by himself."

Pro football during the fifties took a long stride toward being the "game of modern America" and a Sunday afternoon habit. However, the sport had its ugly and sinister side because of the violence and injuries involved. Even equipment instituted for protection could be used for maiming or causing injury. For example, the NFL in 1956 had to make grabbing the face mask illegal because of the danger of injury.

In its October 24, 1955, issue, *Life* published an article entitled "Savagery on Sunday: the Nation's Pro Football Players Get Rougher and Rougher." *Life* found that the game was "getting rougher every year" and concluded that "it's war rather than sport." Particularly appalling were the punching and illegal blows that were thrown with knees and elbows, particularly in pileups. Detroit Lion Tackle Bob Miller was quoted as saying, "We're not trying to hurt anybody, but it's no secret that star pro passers are a bad insurance risk. They get hit even after they get rid of the ball."

Yet the violent and aggressive pro game appealed to some. In a lifestyle that was increasingly sedentary, the chance of gaining vicarious thrills while one's favorite team physically annihilated an opponent was too good a chance to pass up. Whatever atavistic qualities that civilized man had sublimated, the predator instincts of human beings still lurked close beneath the surface veneer of what passed for civilized behavior, and identification with the violence of pro football allowed the passive, middle-class average American a chance to safely rid himself of bottled up violence and hostility without getting arrested—most of the time. Thus, for the average fan, the pro players were the new "gladiators" who waged war on the Sabbath and asked or gave no quarter. The game was played by specialist units, and the passing quarterback hero and his receivers opened up the game to make it exciting and unpredictable. The explosive qualities of the pro football game in the fifties stood in sharp contrast to a period of social conformity, the search for security and success, and increasing regimentation of life.

College Basketball

The fifties were a tumultuous time for college basketball. The decade began with revelations of a point-fixing scandal that would lead to the indictment of thirty-three players, including some from the 1950 NCAA championship City College of New York team and the University of Kentucky. In fact, as a result of the scandal, Kentucky did not play basketball during the 1952 and 1953 seasons. Eastern basketball was de-emphasized at such powerhouses as CCNY and Long Island University. The latter, in fact, declined invitations to play in Madison Square Garden. On top of that, *Time* magazine for December 3, 1951, reported that evidence indicated "deliberate fraud and probable forgery in academic admission records at City College of New York, where one player's average of 70.62 percent was raised to 89.4 percent, and another's was raised 10 points to make them eligible for admission, i.e., to play on CCNY's basketball team."

College basketball did not employ a time clock like the pros but still featured a speedier, high-scoring game. Several factors were responsible for the quickening tempo of the game. The introduction of the one-hand shot and then the jump shot meant that despite aggressive defense, accurate shooting while on the move could be done with impunity from the 20- to 30-foot range.

Secondly, taller players who were more mobile and talented than ever before, such as Bill Russell and Wilt Chamberlain, meant better inside scoring and domination of the boards. Fast breaks could be more quickly triggered, often enabling a team to overwhelm the opposition in the first quarter.

Thirdly, an influx of talented black players such as Russell, Chamberlain, Oscar Robertson, and Elgin Baylor would create a fluid, running style of play which emphasized quickness, agility, and jumping ability. Although black players had been playing at predominantly black colleges (the Colored Intercollegiate Athletic Association had its first official champion in 1912) there was little recognition of their play. Black players were in general few and far between at schools with major basketball programs until Catholic schools in urban areas like San Francisco and other schools began recruiting them.

Another reason for the increased recruiting of black basketball players was that many schools dropped football because the sport was too expensive. These schools developed high caliber basketball programs because the sport was cheaper to support; with fewer players, the addition of only a couple of standouts could often transform a mediocre team into one of championship caliber. An outstanding team could produce needed revenues and publicity for the school. In its February 25, 1950, issue, the *Saturday Evening Post* noted in an article by Harry B. Wilson, entitled "They Took the Back Door to the Big Time," that St. Louis University, like some other colleges, had "tired of sinking money into hopeless football teams" and "found a cheaper, quicker path to sports big time" by exchanging a "gridiron for a court and a national reputation." Eight years later, *Business Week*, in its January 4, 1958, issue, featured an article entitled "College Basketball Helps Pay the Bills." According to the article, over a thousand colleges featured basketball teams. Using the University of Utah as an example, it noted that the recent theft from the Utah ticket office of the receipts from games with Washington State and Stanford demonstrated how lucrative the game had become. Thus, the scandals associated with the sport early in the decade did not diminish the financial attractiveness of the game to a majority of colleges and universities.

City College of New York, better known as CCNY, set a precedent in 1950 when it captured both the National Invitational Tournament and the NCAA championships. A team lacking overwhelming height but possessing a good fast break and some astute coaching from mentor Nat Holman, the unranked Beavers beat Bradley in the NIT and then in the NCAA were pitted against Bradley again and eked out a victory, 71-68.

Led by 7-foot Bill Spivey, and by Frank Ramsey, and Cliff Hagan, Kentucky won the NCAA title in 1951 with a convincing 68-58 victory over Big Seven champion Kansas State.

In 1951 a Manhattan College player, Junius Kellogg, reported an attempted bribe of $1,000. Although he was innocent, two of his team-mates were later convicted. As John D. McCallum notes in *College Basketball U.S.A.* (1980), a subsequent investigation revealed game fixing and point shaving involving "at least six colleges, four of them in New York City, and thirty-three players." All told, some thirty-three players in the East and Midwest admitted taking bribes, including Ralph Beard and Alex Groza at Kentucky, although their coach, Adolph Rupp, had been confident that no one on his team had been involved in the scandal.

As a result of the scandals and the manpower shortage produced by the Korean war, college basketball dropped a bit from the limelight. Kansas, Indiana, and LaSalle were the NCAA champions in 1952, 1953, and 1954. In 1955 and 1956 the national champions were the San Francisco Dons, whose style of play captivated basketball audiences everywhere and helped to restore a little glitter to the game that had been tarnished by the fix scandals. Bill Russell, a 6-foot 10-inch center, revolutionized the game because he emphasized defense and shot blocking instead of shooting. Although aware that he could block only 5 percent of a team's shots, Russell said "they never knew which 5 percent." Russell was aided by a quick guard, K. C. Jones, and together they made a virtually unbeatable tandem.

In 1954–55 the Dons allowed only 52.1 points a game—tops in the nation—and won 26 games in a row for a 28-1 record. In the NCAA final game the Dons defeated defending champs LaSalle, with Russell scoring 23 points and Jones 24.

In 1955–56 San Francisco went undefeated in 29 games and beat Iowa in the NCAA championship game 83-71 with Bill Russell again leading the way with 26 points.

In 1957 Wilt Chamberlain was the talk of the college basketball world. A 7-foot high school phenomenon from Philadelphia who averaged 45 points a game as a senior despite playing just half of most games, Chamberlain had been one of the most highly recruited high school players ever. He finally settled on Kansas and led them to the NCAA finals. In the semifinals Kansas, led by the all-around domination of Chamberlain, outclassed the number-one rated San Francisco Dons looking for their third straight title—minus Bill Russell—by a score of 80-68. In the other semifinal, North Carolina outlasted a surprising Michigan State team led by sky high jumping jack Johnny Green, 74-70 in triple overtime. In the final game, North Carolina again played in a triple overtime game, edging Chamberlain's Kansas team 54-53. Unfortunately, Chamberlain would be labeled with a loser's tag that would follow him when he went into the NBA.

In 1958–59 two black athletes would emerge as two of the greatest ball players the game has ever known. Oscar Robertson would average 35.1 points a game and become the first sophomore to win a national scoring title. His team, the University of Cincinnati, also captured the Missouri Valley Conference crown with a 13-1 record.

Elgin Baylor, a 6-foot 5-inch all-around player, led a quick, good shooting Seattle University into the NCAA finals. There they lost to a lightly regarded Kentucky team that had six losses on their season record. The key was getting Baylor into foul trouble, which defused the Seattle offense, and Kentucky eased by Seattle 84-72.

In 1959 California, a slow, ponderous team led by big center Darrell Imhoff, managed to stave off the running, gunning Mountaineers of West Virginia, led by hot-shooting Jerry West. Only last second heroics by Imhoff, who rebounded one of his own misses with 15 seconds left to give the Golden Bears a 3-point lead, allowed them to eke out a 71-70 victory.

College basketball, by the end of the fifties, had weathered the damaging scandals of 1951 as better players, an influx of talented black players, and a more open style of play helped to popularize the game. In 1958 the top five college players—Guy Rodgers of Temple, Oscar Robertson of Cincinnati, Wilt Chamberlain of Kansas, Elgin Baylor of Seattle, and Bob Boozer of Kansas State—were black. Some experts thought that the second team All-American should be all black also and should include Johnny Green of Michigan State, Tom Hawkins of Notre Dame, Gene Brown of San Francisco, Jay Norman of Temple, and Wayne Embry of Miami, Ohio. The changing college game meant that as more poor black youths from the ghetto realized that basketball could be a way out of poverty, they began to concentrate on the game. As college recruiters began to beat a path to their doors, the players found that once they received their scholarships they were merely "hired hands" who were often unprepared for college work and unable to find time to meet the demands of their studies. Schools often did not expect much of these black athletes in terms of academics, letting them drift in their studies and overlooking slow progress as long as the stars stayed eligible. The result was that many of them did not receive degrees. Often, only when they were good enough to make it to the NBA did the college game enhance their economic circumstances in the long run.

Pro Basketball

Pro basketball during the fifties was a sport trying to find itself. It needed to provide a more appealing game than the one that often resembled "roller derby on wheels" or "keep away"—depending on the circumstances. Like pro football, it had to develop perennial stars and stable franchises with which fans could identify. Thus, a number of moves designed to make the pro game more attractive and respectable were instituted during the decade. In the 1950–51 season Chuck Cooper of Duquesne and Nat "Sweetwater" Clifton of the Harlem Globetrotters became the first blacks to play in the NBA, Clifton with the New York Knickerbockers and Cooper with the Boston Celtics. The addition of black players who relied on speed and jumping would revolutionize the game. Also, the college basketball scandals of 1951 cast an ominous shadow on the college game and made the pro game more attractive. The names of stars like George Mikan were also becoming household words.

In 1954 the NBA made several rule changes crucial for its survival. A time limit was established of 24 seconds by which a team had to shoot the ball after achieving possession. A penalty was set on fouls whereby after a certain limit, each foul shot became a two shot foul, and players shooting fouls would be given three attempts to make two. A backcourt foul was also made two shots, and on a charge, no foul shot was given but the offending player was assessed a foul.

The rule changes meant that the game would become a running game and that scores would go up. This formula would prove to be attractive to the paying customers and a developing television audience.

Another crucial year for the NBA was 1957. That year the Fort Wayne Pistons became the Detroit Pistons and the Rochester Royals the Cincinnati Royals. This meant that only one team, Syracuse, was based in a city of less than a million population, whereas three years before half the cities in the NBA were located in smaller metropolitan areas.

Also, the Boston Celtics, with their classy play and outstanding stars such as Bob Cousy, Bill Sharman, K. C. Jones, Tom Heinsohn, and Bill Russell, were attracting a national as well as New England audience. *Life* magazine, for example, published an article entitled "Celtics Climb on Cousy's Clever Coup" in its February 11, 1957, issue. The article stated: "Pro basketball, which for years has been teetering between shoe string vaudeville and respectability has taken on a big league look this winter." According to the article, Bob Cousy more than any other man was responsible for this changed state of affairs in the NBA, and Cousy was described as "the hustling leader of the best pro team in years."

The Minneapolis Lakers, led by the "Babe Ruth of pro basketball," George Mikan, dominated the NBA from 1950 through 1954. Only once in that period did the Lakers fail to win the title, and that was in

1951 when the Rochester Royals challenged the Lakers' domination. Although Mikan was the team star (Philadelphia owner Edie Gottlieb once offered his entire team for Mikan), he was ably aided and abetted by such outstanding players as guard Slater Martin, and front liners Jim Pollard and Vern Mikkelsen. With the retirement of Mikan in 1954, the Lakers became also-rans. In January 1956, Mikan would attempt a comeback, but he was out of shape and would retire for good after the 1956 season.

In 1954–55 the Syracuse Nationals eliminated the Fort Wayne Pistons four games to three and were led by such players as Johnny Kerr, Paul Seymour, George King, Red Rocha, and Dolph Schayes, many of whom would continue on as coaches both on the college and professional levels after their playing days.

In 1956 Bob Pettit, the 6-foot 9-inch pivot man of the St. Louis Hawks, captured league-scoring honors with a 25.7 average and was named the league's most valuable player. Despite Pettit's contribution, the Philadelphia Warriors were the league champions, once again beating the Pistons 4-3 in the finals as they had Syracuse the year before.

In the 1956–57 season, Bill Russell, the All-American from San Francisco and star of the 1956 Olympic basketball team, came to the Boston Celtics. This was the key to the beginning of the Celtic dynasty that would account for nine NBA titles in ten years. Bob Cousy, the backcourt star for the Celtics, said about Russell: "He meant everything. We didn't win a championship until we got him in 1957, we lost it when he was injured in 1958 and we won it back when he was sound again in 1959. This is a team that has always been able to shoot. But when your offense is predicated on the fast break and you can't get the rebound, you haven't got a fast break."

In 1957 the Celtics and St. Louis Hawks played in the finals, and the series was tied at 3-3 when the climactic final game was played on April 13 in Boston. Bob Pettit sent the game into overtime with two free throws. The overtime period ended in a tie, and only in the second overtime was Boston able to beat the Hawks 125-123.

The game had much significance as it was witnessed by a large television audience. With the all-league team featuring such names as Cousy, Sharman, Arizin, Pettit, and Schayes, the NBA possessed stars that fans from all over the country could identify with. No longer did anyone question the league's ability to survive.

The following year the Hawks had their revenge when they beat the Celtics four games to two, winning the fourth game 110-109 with Pettit pouring in 50 points, 19 of them in the decisive fourth quarter. The title was somewhat tainted by the fact that the Celtics lost center Bill Russell in the third game of the series with a sprained ankle.

The 1958–59 season saw the emergence of a new star. Elgin Baylor, a 6-foot 5-inch black ballplayer, would be the prototype of many other black ballplayers entering the league in the fifties and sixties. Baylor placed fourth in the league in scoring, averaging 24.9 and was a good rebounder, scorer, and passer. He had a high game of 55, third highest in league history. Largely through his efforts, the Minneapolis Lakers beat Detroit and the St. Louis Hawks to take the Western Division crown. Against a now healthy Boston team, however, they quickly succumbed 4 games to 0. The Boston backcourt of Sharman and Cousy and the center play of Russell were too much for even the brilliant talents of Elgin Baylor to overcome.

Thus, during the fifties, the NBA had gone through adolescence and survived. It had proven that players over 6-feet 6-inches, such as Bob Pettit and Bill Russell, could do all the things a small man could do and do them better. The big men were no longer "goons" or "freaks." In fact, by the end of the decade, there were only three players under 6 feet left in the league. However, the real revolution in terms of the increased numbers of black players had only begun. But Boston's example of success with a racially integrated team would not be lost on other NBA franchise owners. Never again would a team picture of the NBA title holders, such as that of the Philadelphia Warriors of 1956, feature only one black ballplayer.

Summer Olympics—1952

The XVth Olympiad held in Helsinki in 1952 clearly demonstrated that the Olympic games could not go on oblivious to world events and the realpolitiks of the world. Held while the Korean War still was being bloodily waged, it marked the first time that the Soviet Union would participate. Although eligible for the 1948 Olympics, the Russians had sent only observers and coaches to the 1948 games in London because they knew their athletes were not of world class caliber. In between the London and Helsinki Olympics, the Russians poured millions of dollars into their sports programs. Pjotr Soboleve, secretary-general of the Russian Olympic committee, was quoted as stating that "sports will be a weapon in the fight for peace and for the promotion of friendship among all peoples."

The American public and the American media also conceived of the Olympic games of 1952 as not merely a meeting of individuals in athletic competition but a test of the superiority of two forms of political systems. *Time* magazine, in the August 4, 1952, issue, for example, headlined its report on Horace Ashenfelter's victory in the 3000-meter steeplechase as the "G-Man and the Russian."

Although the Russian track-and-field team was weak, Russian officials believed that the gold medal in the steeplechase would be theirs since Vladimir Kazantsev was the world record holder in the event. Ashenfelter, a 5-foot 10-inch, 145-pound FBI agent, was the 10,000-meter champion in the AAU in 1952 but had run only eight previous steeplechase races. However, when the Russian faltered on the last water jump, Ashenfelter raced away from him for victory in an Olympic and world record time of 8:45.4, indicating that the victory was no fluke. The Russians ended up with no gold medals in track and field but did garner four silver medals.

If the Russian team did not perform up to expected standards, the American team certainly did so and then some, winning some fourteen gold medals, its largest number in thirty years. There were any number of fantastic performances. Bob Mathias repeated his 1948 feat and captured the decathlon, leading an American sweep of the event, with Milton Campbell second and Floyd Simmons third. Harrison Dillard, the 100-meter champion in 1948, grabbed the gold in his preferred event, the 110-meter high hurdles. Mal Whitfield tied his own Olympic mark in repeating his 1948 win in the 800-meter run. Bob Richards captured his first Olympic pole vault victory, and Parry O'Brien led an American sweep in the shotput. Sim Iness, a high school teammate of Mathias, took the discus, breaking the Olympic record on each of his six throws, while Cyrus Young was triumphant in the javelin. Only Josef Csarmak of Hungary, who won the hammer throw, prevented an American sweep in the weight events.

Perhaps the most outstanding performance was by Emil Zatopek of Czechoslovakia, who captured the 5000-meters, the 10,000-meters, and the marathon. Zatopek ran, as some described it, looking like a "man who had just been stabbed in the heart." Zatopek often trained in army boots and could run almost as good times as if wearing normal track shoes. When rivals attempted to emulate him in practice, all they had to show for their efforts were bad cases of blisters.

In the 4 x 100-relay the American team barely edged a speedy Russian team for first. In the 1,600-meter relay the United States took second, while the Jamaican team captured first in an Olympic and world record time.

The only victory in women's track for the United States came when the 400-meter relay team took the gold in 45.9 seconds. On the other hand, Soviet women won medals in two of the four running events and placed in all of the field events.

In other events, American Tommy Kono, Peter George, Norbert Shemansky, and John Davis won gold medals in their respective divisions of weightlifting. American boxers performed well and won five gold medals. Nate Brooks, Charles Adkins, Floyd Patterson, Norvel Lee, and Ed Sanders were the American winners. An ironic side note is that Ed Sanders' opponent was Ingemar Johansson for the heavyweight title. Johansson was disqualified for running away from Sanders. In 1959 Johansson would win the heavyweight crown from Floyd Patterson and then lose it to him in a year. (Patterson had captured the middleweight title in the 1952 Olympics.) Sanders would later die of a brain injury suffered in a ring bout. In swimming the United States men's team garnered six medals, including two first places. The most outstanding performance was by Ford Konno, who slashed 42 seconds off the 1,500-meter freestyle record. The United States also captured the springboard and platform diving titles. The women's team had only a third place in the 400-meter relay, but Pat McCormick won gold medals in both diving events.

The United States basketball team—featuring a nearly seven-foot front line of Clyde Lovellette, Marcus Frieberger, and Bob Kurland—took the gold. The United States team beat the Russian team in a preliminary match 86-58 and then managed to eke out a 36-25 victory over the Russians in the final, as the USSR attempted to slow down the Americans but to no avail.

To those who were keeping unofficial score, the Americans still beat the Russians—614-553½. Obviously the Russians had to be pleased with their performance, and many Americans felt that in the next Olympics the Russian bear would be triumphant.

Black Americans performed exceedingly well in the 1952 Olympics. The *Negro History Bulletin*, in its October 1952, issue pointed out the role that blacks had played in the games. It noted that blacks had been responsible for fifteen gold, six silver, and two bronze medals, and a total of 153 points. The article further stated: "The Negro frequently alluded to as the 'white man's burden,' carried on strong arms and legs the balance of power in the 1952 Olympic Games. In the unofficial contest between the 'Free World of the West' and Soviet Russia the 'burden' pulled the 'superior race' to victory. Without the points contributed by Negroes, Soviet Russia would have been the winner in terms of the unofficial system of scoring." The article also noted the worth of Negroes as "true Americans" and pointed out that those who disparaged the contributions of blacks should consider the cost of "killing the goose that lays the golden eggs" and stressed that "the record of the achievement of Negroes in the Olympic games should be studied and preserved." Obviously the *Bulletin* was stressing that it seemed ludicrous for blacks to make contributions to America's sporting prestige when they could not attain equal rights at home.

1952 Winter Olympics

In the winter Olympics staged in Oslo, Norway, thirty teams and seven hundred athletes competed, and some 700,000 spectators watched the ten days of competition. The Norwegians proved to be somewhat inhospitable hosts as they captured sixteen medals and the United States, demonstrating surprising strength, garnered eleven medals. Hjalmar Anderson and Stein Eriksen were the Norwegian stars. Anderson captured the gold in the 1500-, 5000-, and 10,000-meter speed skating races, while Eriksen was first in the giant slalom and was second in the slalom race.

The United States had a number of stars. Perhaps most unexpected were Andrea Mead Lawrence's victories in the slalom and giant slalom. Her bid for three gold medals ended abruptly when she fell in the downhill contest. The United States hockey team tied Canada in the final game 3-3 played in a furious snowstorm, but the Canadians received the gold medal and the Americans the silver.

Figure skating also provided Americans with another treasure trove of medals. Innovative male skater Dick Button of the United States, executing successfully for the first time in competition a triple loop jump, swept to the gold in the men's competition. In the women's figure skating, Tenley Albright was second and the American pair of Carol and Peter Kennedy also received a silver medal.

In other events, the United States received medals in the 500-meter speed skating contest when Ken Henry and Don McDermott were first and second, and the two- and four-man bobsled team each took a silver medal. Thus, the winter Olympics at Oslo would go down as one of the most productive for the United States in terms of medals. In the succeeding years, it would be difficult to match the performances of the 1952 team.

1956 Summer Olympics

In between the winter Olympics in Cortina in January and the beginning of the summer Olympics at Melbourne on November 22 the world reeled under a series of cataclysmic events. On July 26, 1956, President Nasser of Egypt closed the Suez Canal to Western European nations when a United States offer for help to construct the Aswan Dam had been withdrawn because of continued Egyptian ties with the Soviets. On October 19, 1956, Israel invaded Egypt. On November 5, French and British forces joined the invasion of Egypt. An American sponsored resolution called for a cease-fire and a withdrawal of troops. At first the invaders ignored the resolution, but when Nasser made the Suez Canal unusable by sinking ships and placing obstructions in it, Britain and France agreed to a cease fire. A United Nations force was dispatched to supervise the agreement, and by the end of 1956 French and British troops were gone from Egypt.

Meanwhile in another part of the world, another conflagration had broken out, threatening world peace. Encouraged by Poland's election of Wladyslaw Gomulka, a recent prisoner of the Russians, as secretary of their party, and by the Poles' dismissal, over Soviet objections, of a Russian general as minister of defense, Hungary attempted to divest themselves not only of the Russians, but of communism. In response, Soviet and Warsaw Pact tanks began entering Budapest en masse to crush the rebellion. Brave Hungarians fought back, but bare fists, small firearms, and Molotov cocktails were no match for a modern, mechanized army. The rebellion was soon put down and thousands of Hungarians fled to the West.

Most of the Hungarian Olympic team already had departed or was in the process of departing for Melbourne. Confused by a choice between patriotism and athletics, many of them did not know whether to return to Hungary to fight or to continue to the games. Most of the Hungarian athletes chose to go to Melbourne, making their way by ones and twos, and often lacking equipment. Sympathetic athletes, primarily from the West, helped to equip them.

As a result of these events, there was a large outcry from many countries and famous world personalities who called for a cancellation of the games in protest over the act of Soviet aggression. The International Olympic Committee, led by its president, Avery Brundage, refused to do so because as Brundage stated it: "The Olympics belong to the people. They are contests for individuals and not nations."

Some nations boycotted the games on their own. Egypt, Lebanon, and Iraq withdrew as a protest to the Israeli invasion of Egypt. Spain, the Netherlands, and Switzerland also withdrew because of the Soviet invasion of Hungary. Taiwan withdrew because Red China was admitted and then the Red Chinese didn't show up.

The games were finally opened on November 22 with 104,000 spectators looking on and a final total of sixty-seven nations (six of them for the first time) and 3,539 athletes. Despite a sign on the stadium scoreboard which said "classification by points on a national basis not recognized," most observers were counting to see whether or not the United States or the Soviets would be the dominant athletic power in the world. Rumors had been rampant that the Soviets had been preparing furiously in all sports for a good showing at Melbourne. In particular, there were many stories which claimed that the Russians were going to have some surprises for the American track-and-field team. Even Don Canham, track coach of the University of Michigan, had been convinced of the medal potential of the Soviet track team. Canham had warned that "the Red Machine will stop our athletes as soon as it hits them in Melbourne" (*Newsweek*, Dec. 10, 1956).

The American track-and-field team was not cowed by the Soviets' reputation and responded by racking up fifteen gold medals out of a possible twenty-four, while the Russians won only three. As usual, the American squad was dominant in the short races and the field events. When asked why Americans were good at the short races and not at long ones, one American athlete replied that in America "kids staged races to the end of the block, in Europe, they ran around it."

Sprint star for the American squad was the pride of Texas, Bobby Morrow from Abilene Christian College. In the 100-meter run, Morrow beat teammate Thane Baker in a time of 10.5 and then came back in the 200-meter to edge teammates Andy Stanfield and Baker in Olympic record time of 20.6. (Stanfield and Baker had finished first and second in the 1952 Olympics for the event.) Morrow, who had an incredible nine-foot stride, came back to anchor the 400-meter relay team in an Olympic record time of 39.5.

There were many other stars besides Morrow on the American track-and-field squad. Tom Courtney, after seemingly being beaten, put on a desperate surge which carried him past Britain's Derek Johnson for victory in the 800-meter in 1:47.7, an Olympic record. Lou Jones, the American favorite in the 400-meter, faltered in the home stretch, but Charley Jenkins put on a spurt to secure victory for the United States. Lee Calhoun and Jack Davis came in a virtual dead heat in the 110-meter hurdles, both timed in 13.5. Calhoun was given the nod and for the second Olympics in the row, Davis shared a new record and received a silver medal.

Besides sweeping the 100-meter and 110-meter hurdles, the United

States also won the 400-meter hurdles with Glenn Davis, Eddie Southern, and Josh Culbreath, while Al Oerter led an American grab of the medals in the discus. Fortune Gordien and Desmond Koch took second and third. America took first and second in the long jump, shot put, pole vault, and decathlon with Greg Bell, Parry O'Brien (the world's first 60-foot shot putter), Bob Richards—"the vaulting vicar"—and Milt Campbell the respective gold medal winners. Additional victories went to Charlie Dumas in the high jump, Harold Connolly in the hammer throw and the two American relay teams in the 400- and 1600-meter runs.

The Russian track star was Vladimir Kuts, who won both the 5000- and 10,000-meter runs in Olympic record times. The Russians also captured the 20,000-meter walk, sweeping all three places. In the hotly contested 1,500-meter race, Ron Delaney of Ireland was victorious over an excellent field which included world record holder John Landy, who finished third.

The American press was enthralled by the American domination in track and field. *Time* (Dec. 10, 1956) magazine reported that "the Royal Australian band played the Stars and Stripes so much that wags at Melbourne suggested a switch to "Stars and Stripes Forever." *Sports Illustrated* stated in its December 10, 1956 edition that: "Russia and the United States, the behemoths of sport, have met in heralded conflict in the main stadium—a conflict in which the bear was outdistanced and the United States track and field team proved to be the greatest of all time." *Newsweek* (Dec. 10, 1956) further declared: "For if the sixteenth Olympiad has demonstrated one thing it is this: a country can no more train a man to win an Olympic gold medal than it can train him to write a Nobel Prize novel. There is a most un-Marxian creative aspect to Olympic victory."

Americans did not dominate other Olympic events as they did men's track and field. In women's track and field, for example, Australian women were led by Betty Cuthbert, who captured the 100- and 200-meter dashes and anchored the 400-meter relay team to victory. The Australian women led the way by taking four of the possible nine gold medals. The Russians won two gold while the Czechs, Poles, and Americans each won one. Mildred McDaniel was the United States gold medal winner, high jumping 5 feet 9 inches, establishing both Olympic and world records.

Traditional American dominance in swimming was shattered by a strong Australian squad which grabbed five gold medals in men's swimming and diving and three gold medals in women's swimming and diving. American Patty McCormick was the women's star, repeating her 1952 sweep of both diving events.

The United States basketball team captured another gold medal, maintaining American unblemished record in Olympic competition in that event. The team, led by future Boston Celtics stars Bill Russell and K. C. Jones, crushed the Russians 98-55 in the championship game despite the presence of 7-foot 3-inch center, Yan Kuminisk, a Latvian.

One of the more dramatic United States gold medals came in the eight-oared rowing race. The Yale crew finished third in its heat. It then went into the repechage round and won that race. The Yale crew continued, winning the semifinal heat and then capturing the final heat, surging from behind with about 750 meters to go to beat Canada and Australia, who finished second and third.

The Russians proved strong in boxing, usually an American dominated sport. They picked up three gold medals, one silver, and one bronze. However, in the prestigious heavyweight division, Pete Rademacher battled the USSR's Lev Moukhine, and as William Henry has described it, in *An Approved History of the Olympic Games* (1976) "Pete waded into the Soviet 220 pounder as though the honor and prestige of the free world against the iron curtain were on his shoulders, proceeding to knock him down in the first fifty seconds." Rademacher floored his Russian opponent twice more before the referee stopped the bout with 2:27 gone in the first round.

Cold war conflict, which further spilled out into Olympic competition, was clearly evident in the championship final in water polo between Hungary and the USSR. Many of the Hungarian athletes, who perhaps would have been throwing homemade bombs at Russian tanks if they were in their home country, attacked the Russians as if the match was the battle of Budapest, and the Russians replied in kind. Water polo is a game where fouls of all kinds can occur under water without detection by the officials, and needless to say, numerous uncalled fouls did occur. Before a screaming, partisan crowd, the Hungarians bludgeoned out a 4-0 lead. With about two minutes to go Hungarian player Ervin Zador was butted by Russian Valentin Prokopov, and had to leave the pool severely cut over one eye and bleeding profusely. The crowd screamed like maniacs, and the Russians, in fear of their well-being, exited the pool even though time still remained. The victorious Hungarian team was left to celebrate with their vociferous and vocal fans.

Despite the outstanding performance of the American men's track-and-field team, Russian strength in events which "hold little appeal" for Americans (such as gymnastics, shooting, Greco-Roman wrestling, and soccer) for the first time gave the USSR more gold medals (thirty-seven) than the United States (thirty-two). For those keeping score, the Russians had amassed 722 unofficial points while the

Americans accumulated 593. In retrospect, the United States had won three fewer medals in both swimming and boxing, which was responsible for the United States point deficit. In the meantime, the Russians had continued to improve in all sports. The favored Russian hammer thrower Mickhail Krivonosov, whose best throw in the 1952 games was 150 feet, increased his distance by 60 feet in the four intervening years, having a best throw of 210 feet coming into the 1956 games. *Newsweek,* in its December 17, 1956, issue summed up the athletic confrontation in the 1956 Olympics between the two super powers by stating, ''America had won the big events; Russia had won the big prize.''

During the final procession of athletes in the stadium marking the ending of the games in Melbourne, the athletes did not march as is the custom, by nations, but rather informally, by intermingled groups of differing nationalities, obviously symbolizing the friendship and brotherhood that the games were supposed to foster. But with the realities of fast breaking world events, the confrontations on the athletic field between the East and West and their symbolic meaning were reminders of the deep divisions between the communist and noncommunist worlds, which no brief interlude of cosmetic harmony and felicitousness could miraculously dispel.

1956 Winter Olympics

In 1956 the winter Olympics began on January 22, 1956, while the summer games, which were to be held in Melbourne, Australia would not begin until November 22 in order to coincide with Australia's warm season. It would mark the first time that a city outside of the Western Hemisphere would host the games. Also, the equestrian events were held in Stockholm because of the costs of transporting the animals and because of Australia's strict quarantine laws.

In between the winter and summer games, almost a year apart, the world events ranging from war to revolution would dominate the news and have a profound impact on the nature of the games and their composition.

The Soviets, for the first time, fielded a strong winter Olympic team and ended up capturing six gold medals. They were particularly impressive in speed skating, where they won three of the four events. Yevgeni Grishin of the USSR set a world record in the 500-meter race of 40.2 seconds and then tied for first in the 1,500-meter event with teammate Yuri Mikhailov, both sharing a world record of 2:08.6. Another Russian, Boris Shilkov, got the gold in the 5,000-meters, but Swedish star Sigge Ericsson prevented a Russian sweep by winning the 10,000-meters. In addition, the Soviets picked up a silver in the 500-meter event and bronzes in the 5,000- and 10,000-meter contests. Times had become so fast that forty-two competitors in the 1,500-meter race beat the winner's time in the event in the 1952 games. The Soviets also won the men's 4x10-kilometer relay and two women's skiing events. However, their greatest and most surprising triumph came in ice hockey, long dominated by the United States and Canada. The United States hockey team had a three-game winning streak going when they met the Canadians and upset them with a 4-1 triumph. This set up a confrontation with the Soviet team, which had earlier disposed of the Canadians by a 2-0 margin. The Soviets led by a 1-0 score with but five minutes to go when the American squad collapsed before the fast skating Russian team that blitzed them for three quick goals and a 4-0 triumph.

The gold medal was a significant accomplishment for the Soviet ice hockey program, since Russia did not play the game prior to World War II. Not only did the Soviets win the title but they had also shut out all their opponents, including the so-called hockey powers of the world, the United States and Canada.

American strength in the 1956 winter games was in the figure skaters. American males, obviously influenced by the dynamic style of Dick Button, swept the medals with Hayes Alan Jenkins capturing the gold, Robert Robertson the silver, and the younger brother of the gold medal winner, David Jenkins, the bronze.

American women went 1-2 in the women's figure skating competition with Tenley Albright, the silver medal winner in 1952, edging Carol Heiss for the title. Albright's road to victory was a dramatic one. She was only sixteen when she competed in the 1952 Olympic games. The following year she captured the world championships in Switzerland, but in 1954 while attempting to repeat as champion she took a major fall and lost her championship. Undaunted, she returned to the world championships in Vienna and became the first woman to lose her skating crown and then regain it.

While in practice at Cortina, Albright cut an ankle and it was thought that the injury was too severe for her to continue her quest for the Olympic gold. Her father, a Boston surgeon, arrived to treat her, and although the wound was still raw, she courageously blocked out the pain to put on a stirring performance. Her quest for the gold medal was an example of stamina and bravery in a sport that most observers would not classify as particularly dangerous.

The star of the Olympics in Cortina, however, was a twenty-one-year-old Austrian skier named Toni Sailer, who captured the slalom, giant slalom, and downhill contests to become the first skier ever to win three gold medals in the Olympic games. What was even more significant was that Sailer possessed nearly perfect form and the times of his victories were overwhelming, ranging from 4 to 6 seconds faster than his nearest rival. This was unheard of in a sport that often measured victory and defeat in hundredths of seconds.

Sailer's victory, combined with a gold in the pairs figure skating, gave Austria a total of four gold medals, two fewer than the leading Russians, who garnered six of the possible twenty-four at Cortina. Switzerland and Finland came next with three gold medals followed by Norway and the United States with two each. Of the thirty-two nations represented at the 1956 Winter Olympics, six nations had accounted for twenty-three of the possible twenty-four gold medals. Only Italy's two-man bobsled team could break the domination of the "big six."

The Russians obviously were pleased with their performance at Cortina. They had moved rapidly from being a virtual nonentity in winter sports to being the dominant power, by quickly supplanting the Scandinavian nations and the United States. The Soviet minister of sports, in commenting on the Soviet performance in the 1956 winter games, stated: "We came here expecting triumphs in our strong events and expecting to gain experience in the others. We did both— and we're going to win in Melbourne, too." The games were becoming increasingly politicized and reflected the cold war tensions and ideological competition.

Tennis

Tennis during the fifties—at least what passed for amateur tennis— was dominated by the Australians. In 1950 Harry Hopman, the non-playing captain of the Australian Davis Cup team, led his charges against the favored American contingent, which included such stars as Ted Schroeder, Tom Brown, and Gardnar Mulloy. The Australians were figured to have a weak team since their best player, Frank Sedgman, had lost in straight sets the previous year to Pancho Gonzales and Ted Schroeder. The Australians swept the first two singles and doubles for an insurmountable 3-0 lead and eventually wound up winning 4-1. It was the harbinger of things to come. Australia had replaced the United States as the number one tennis nation.

From 1951 to 1954 the Davis Cup finals were held in Sydney before capacity crowds. The Australians triumphed in 1952 and 1953, but the United States won in 1954 before 25,578, the largest crowd to watch indoor tennis until the 1973 Riggs-King match. The American players, Tony Trabert and Vic Seixas, were determined to revenge the previous year's loss. (Trabert in particular wanted to win since the previous year the United States had been ahead 2-1 in matches when he lost a tough five setter in the rain to Lew Hoad to put Australia back in contention.) Trabert beat Hoad, and Seixas triumphed over Ken Rosewall in the first singles and then lost the second set of singles competition. In the decisive doubles match, the American pair put together a 6-2, 4-6, 6-2, 10-8 win. The following year, however, Australia swept through the Davis Cup finals 5-0.

The triumph of the Australians in tennis illustrated many different cultural and social distinctions between the United States and Australian society. In the United States tennis was still largely a game of the country clubs and drew from a relatively small segment of the population. Other American sports, such as football and baseball, were much more popular and seemed much more "manly." Americans had many more interests as the youth culture and rock and roll revolution in music were occurring, thus providing many youngsters with alternatives to many sports, including tennis. In Australia, on the other hand, young lads of seven or eight trudged to school carrying their rackets. The large Australian cities had hundreds of lighted courts. A well-established youth instruction program, which featured tournaments and introduction to national tennis stars, had produced hundreds of good tennis players.

Many Americans were critical of the Australian system because most Australian youngsters finished their formal education at fifteen and that freed them to become "tennis bums," playing year round. Their American counterparts often went on to high school and college and then were forced to support themselves in a business or profession, which meant that they did not receive the top caliber experience needed to make a world class tennis player.

Another factor which played a role in the development of the Australian tennis stars was the emphasis on general conditioning. Harry Hopman was particularly fanatical in this respect, advocating calisthenics and runs on sandy beaches and in the surf to build up stamina and endurance. Most Americans confined their tennis preparations to playing the game.

Perhaps the Australian method produced good tennis players, but it certainly did not produce well-rounded individuals. In a *Saturday Evening Post* article (September 14, 1957) describing his tennis preparation, Lew Hoad stated: "I was a tennis slave. The association demands that all players going on tour sign a contract which specifies that for travel and other expenses they will compete in tournaments and exhibitions designated by the association. The agreement runs from April, when the team leaves, until the next January 31. The contract makes the player the property of the association. He has no independence. If I go through a rugged tournament such as Wimbledon and say afterwards I am tired and would like a rest, the association says, no, you have commitments to play here and there."

Although perhaps not a thoroughly admirable system, the Australian training and preparation for Davis Cup play aided the Aussie stars in the major tournaments. In the U.S. Open Art Larson, an American, captured the title in 1950. Australian Davis Cup star Frank Sedgman took the crown in 1951 and 1952. The next three years American Davis cup stars held the title with Tony Trabert triumphant in 1953 and 1955, while Vic Seixas earned it in 1954. From 1956 to 1959 it was claimed by the Australians with Ken Rosewall in 1956, Mal Anderson in 1957, Ashley Cooper in 1958, and Neale Fraser in 1959. Thus, for six out of the ten years of the decade, Australians ruled the Open.

Wimbledon victories for Americans were concentrated at the beginning of the decade. Budge Patty in 1950, Dick Savitt in 1951, Vic Seixas in 1953, and Tony Trabert in 1955 composed the American victors in men's singles during the decade. The years 1951 through 1967 were a definite low point in American tennis. During that period the United States won the Davis Cup only three times, the U.S. Open only three times, and Wimbledon only four times. In that time the Aussie "amateurs" were truly dominant.

On the other side of the coin were the tennis professionals. Most officials of "amateur" tennis refused to recognize their contribution to the sport. There were very few professional tournaments, and most of the professional tennis was associated with Jack Kramer's pro tour. Although money could be made on the tour (Pancho Segura was making about $50,000 per year), often it wasn't as much as amateurs were making. The tour was an awful grind, with the players playing as many as five matches a week for fifty weeks of the year plus constant travel.

Often the tour promotion resembled a wrestling match appeal, with Kramer trying to sign a "golden boy" (e.g., Tony Trabert in 1955) to oppose the "bad guy," Pancho Gonzales. Although they were not an effective force throughout much of the decade, more topnotch amateurs had turned pro by the period's end. This denuded Davis Cup

Teams and weakened the draw of major tournaments. The presence of Kramer's tour certainly was one of the major contributing forces leading to open tennis in the sixties.

In the late forties and early fifties the Big Four of American women's tennis were Margaret Osborne du Pont, A. Louise Brough, Doris Hart, and Shirley Fry. Brough had taken the Wimbledon title from 1948 through 1950, while Doris Hart had captured the title in 1951 and was ranked number one in the world. Du Pont was the U.S. Open champion from 1948 to 1950 and was the favorite to retain the title in 1951.

Waiting in the wings in 1951 was a young and determined player who would prevent Mrs. du Pont from capturing her fourth consecutive title at Forest Hills. Maureen "Little Mo" Connolly began a brief but meteoric career. Connolly had captured the National Girls 18 Singles championship at the age of fourteen. A native of California, Maureen was brought under the capable tutelage of "Teach" Tennant. Tennant carefully groomed Connolly, whose game relied on crisp, efficient strokes and deadly marksmanship rather than a serve and volley technique.

In 1951 when Maureen was only sixteen she captured the U.S. Open, disposing of Hart 6-4, 6-4 in the semifinals and struggling to a 6-3, 1-6, and 6-4 decision over Shirley Fry in the finals.

From 1952 to 1954 Connolly was the top player in the world. She beat Hart in the U.S. Open in 1952 and 1953, and took the Wimbledon title in 1952, 1953, and 1954, whipping Brough twice and Hart once. Also in 1953 she achieved what is known in tennis as the Grand Slam, capturing the Australian Open, French Open, Wimbledon, and U.S. Open titles. So dominant was she as a player that she lost only four matches as a world class player and never suffered a loss at Wimbledon.

Connolly's life story had many of the elements of a soap opera melodrama. Her father had abandoned the family when she was a baby. Her mother, who had hoped to be a concert pianist, pushed her daughter in organ playing, dancing, and singing. A poorly performed tonsillectomy prevented Connolly from pursuing a singing career. She thus threw herself into her tennis career with fierce intensity. Once asked what her most humorous moment in tennis had been, her reply was "I never had any."

Connolly's tennis career was tragically cut short when just past her twentieth birthday a horse she was riding collided with a cement truck and her leg was injured so badly that she could no longer play competitive tennis. She died in 1969 at the age of thirty-five from cancer. She provided one of the greatest and shortest rags-to-riches stories in the annals of sports.

Doris Hart captured the U.S. Open in 1954 and 1955, while in 1955 Louise Brough won Wimbledon to be succeeded by Shirley Fry in 1956, who also won the U.S. Open in 1956. Fry's opponent in the 1956 final set a precedent, since Althea Gibson became the first black woman to play in the women's singles finals at the U.S. Open. She had played in the Open in 1950 and lost in three sets to Brough.

Althea Gibson was the other dramatic figure of women's tennis during the fifties. A tall, gaunt, black woman who played a power game, Gibson, like Maureen Connolly, had a life story that sounded like melodramatic fiction. A resident of Harlem, her father was a former boxer who frequently beat her. The family was originally from North Carolina, where her father had been a sharecropper. He moved his family to New York, where Althea Gibson picked up the game of tennis. A schoolteacher saw her on the courts and got her admitted to the Cosmopolitan Tennis Club. She later attended Florida A&M and then taught physical education at Lincoln University in Missouri. In 1955 she was selected to tour with a team of United States women tennis players in Southeast Asia and in 1956 she captured the French Open championship. Althea Gibson lost to Shirley Fry in the quarterfinals at Wimbledon in 1956 but in 1957 she came back and captured the Wimbledon crown. In her autobiography, Gibson would note that "shaking hands with the Queen of England was a long way from being forced to sit in the colored section of the bus going into downtown Wilmington, North Carolina."

Also in 1957 Gibson beat an aging Louise Brough 6-3, 6-2. Brough had beaten Gibson in a second round match in the U.S. Open in 1950. Gibson had not received invitations to play in the Open prior to that time, although she had played in the National Indoors tournament in both 1949 and 1950. Although she did not push the issue because she said she never regarded herself as a crusader, other prominent tennis officials did. Alice Marble, one of the grand ladies of the game, wrote in the July 1950 issue of *American Lawn Tennis*, "If tennis is a game for ladies and gentlemen, it's also time we acted a little more like gentle people and less like sanctimonious hypocrites." Thus, in spite of herself, Althea Gibson was a crusader. Unfortunately, no other black woman has followed in her footsteps.

Gibson repeated her Wimbledon and U.S. Open triumphs in 1958 and then turned professional. She would later also become an outstanding golfer. The title of her autobiography was *I Always Wanted to Be Somebody* (1958). She certainly had become notable, despite the obstacles of poverty and racial discrimination, and she was good for the game of tennis.

Golf

Golf in the fifties was dominated by two contrasting personalities and styles of golf, those of Ben Hogan and Sam Snead. Other notable golfers during the period were Cary Middlecoff, Jack Burke, Jr., Julius Boros, and Doug Ford, each of whom won two major tournaments during the decade.

Sportswriters described Hogan as the "mechanical man" because he played in such a methodical, expressionless way. But his deliberate style of play brought him the U.S. Open title three times in the decade (1950, 1951, 1953), two Masters championships (1951 and 1953), and the British Open in 1953. He was the only American to win a British Open title during the fifties, but that tournament had not yet developed into a prestige event that attracted large numbers of American golfers. However, Hogan could not win a PGA title during the decade, although he had won it in 1946 and 1948.

Hogan was one of the most calculating and disciplined men to play the game, concentrating on his shots in a businesslike manner and anticipating his game as it developed. Because he was not a natural athlete or a long hitter, Hogan made up for these deficiencies by his intense concentration, a skillful irons game that made him a master of the approach shot at green placements, and his functional swing that minimized bad lies or problems on the fairways. Hogan was a businessman on the course; he knew that consistency and discipline were the keys to success. He viewed golf courses as objects to be mastered and controlled, and when he won his second consecutive U.S. Open in 1951 at Oakland Hills, he said, "I'm glad that I brought this course, this monster, to its knees." Hogan had overcome an almost disastrous first round in the 1951 U.S. Open as well as his irritation over how high the rough was left. He literally stalked courses and opponents, a trait that earned him the nickname "The Hawk."

Hogan overcame an almost fatal car accident in 1949 in which he was badly injured with fractured and broken bones. After problems with the veins in his legs developed, doctors had to tie off the principal veins in the legs in order to save Hogan's life. But Hogan overcame these problems, regained the use of his legs despite diminished circulation, and came back within seventeen months to win the 1950 U.S.

Open in a three-way playoff round that taxed his strength and endurance. Possessed by an intense desire to win and to prove himself, Hogan showed that mastery of all phases of the game combined with the intensity of concentration could produce a champion. From 1941 through 1956 Hogan never finished worse than seventh in any tournament, a remarkable achievement. Curiously enough, he never led the tour in money winnings in the fifties, although in the previous decade he had topped the other golfers in winnings five different years. In 1946 he won $42,556 in prize money.

By contrast, Sam Snead was a gregarious, talkative player who had a near-perfect swing that earned him the title "Slammin' Sammy." Snead won the Masters twice (1952 and 1954) and the PGA title once (1951) during the fifties, and overall in his career he claimed three Masters and three PGA titles along with the British Open in 1946. On the course Snead was outgoing and jovial, always distinguished by his wide-brimmed straw hats, his colorful hillbilly slang, and his fluid, strong swing. Snead lacked the concentration that Hogan demonstrated, having trouble with putting, but his long, straight drives made him a tour favorite as did his easygoing style that showed open enthusiasm for the game. In 1950 and 1955 he won the Vardon Trophy for the best PGA average, both times with an average below 70, which no other golfer of the decade could match. Snead's jaunty and relaxed style of play was a dramatic contrast to the mechanical and controlled play of Hogan. Other players like Jimmy Demaret brought jovial and uninhibited personalities to the game, and Arnold Palmer, who turned professional in 1954, would become the most charismatic and popular player of the modern game.

During the fifties golf grew steadily in popularity as tournaments gained prestige and publicity, as prize money steadily grew, and as the tour expanded to give more exposure to the golfing greats. President Dwight D. Eisenhower loved the game and helped to increase its popularity. As leisure time expanded and golf became more of a status sport associated with country clubs and businessmen, golf went through its first real boom period in this decade.

The number of women professionals increased and prestige women's tournaments developed. Patty Berg, Babe Didrikson Zaharias, Louise Suggs, and Betty Jameson were the premier players, and the Babe's comeback from a cancer operation was a story of courage and determination which equalled the recovery and return of Hogan.

Golf in the fifties also saw the arrival of the electric and gas golf cart, the golf "hustler" (Lee Trevino started this way), senior citizen and youth golf, the boom in country clubs, the development of sophisticated golf technology (improved balls and clubs), and more challenging courses, each with a personality and uniqueness of its own. With the arrival of Arnold Palmer and Gary Player, golf was ready for an unprecedented boom that would take place in the next decade.

Boxing

The fifties began with Ezzard Charles winning a fifteen-round decision in Yankee Stadium over Joe Louis, who had retired as champion in 1949 and then come back to challenge Charles. Charles had claimed the vacated title by beating Jersey Joe Walcott on points in fifteen rounds and then beating three boxers before facing the Brown Bomber, now thirty-five years old. After the win over Louis, Charles defended his new title four times, including a win over Walcott.

In July of 1951 Walcott, who was now thirty-seven years old, came back and knocked out Ezzard Charles in seven rounds, avenging his two earlier losses to Charles. Almost a year later Walcott made his only successful defense of the crown by outpointing Charles.

The aging but remarkable Walcott then had the misfortune of coming up against Rocky Marciano, a hungry and bullish fighter who had fought forty-three professional bouts and won them all, before he received his shot at the title. On his way to face Walcott, Marciano had unceremoniously ended Joe Louis's ill-advised comeback by knocking Louis out in the eighth round. In the 1952 title bout Walcott knocked Maricano down in the first round for a four count, but in the thirteenth round Marciano's hard right to Jersey Joe's jaw put him down for the count.

Marciano, the son of an Italian immigrant shoemaker, was a high school dropout who worked as a day laborer to help his family. He gained his first experience as an amateur in the Boston Golden Gloves and in other New England cities. Soon he was ready to turn professional, and after a long string of fights he was matched up with the aging Joe Louis, who needed money to pay mounting debts and tax bills.

Marciano was short, clumsy, and unspectacular as a fighter. Because he had such short arms, he fought out of a crouch and bulled his way inside his opponent's defenses. To offset his liabilities, Marciano had a devastating right hand that he could deliver with awesome force and power. He worked hard in training, and he was at his best in a slugfest that tested endurance. Despite his spectacular success and knockout record (forty-three knockouts in forty-nine professional career fights), Marciano remained modest and unassuming. He was a small town boy at heart and a man who loved his family more than fame and adulation. Over half of his professional bouts were fought in Providence, Rhode Island, near his home state of Massachusetts, where his loyal fans could come to see him fight.

Marciano's reign as champion was relatively short—1952 through April 1956. He defended his title six times, twice against Ezzard Charles, and then announced his retirement. He wanted to go out a winner, which he did, and his dedication to his family won out over his love for the ring. Boxing had brought financial security and a reputation beyond his wildest dreams. Although he was tempted to come out of retirement in 1959 to fight Ingemar Johansson for a million dollars, he had the good judgment to decline the offer. In his retirement he toured the world and refereed wrestling matches. At age forty-six he was killed in a plane crash in Iowa.

In his relatively short life and boxing career, "The Rock" had achieved an American dream of success and fame. He was much loved by his hometown people in Brockton, Massachusetts, and he was a celebrated figure in Boston and Providence. Proud of his Italian-American background and heritage, he evolved from a street brawler into a disciplined fighter and proud family man. His reputation as a class individual was illustrated in the 1951 fight with Joe Louis. After battering Louis and knocking him out, Marciano ran over to the prostrate Louis and helped him to his feet. He then walked, with his head bowed, back to his corner. He never wanted to hurt or humiliate a fellow fighter.

When Marciano retired undefeated, Floyd Patterson claimed the vacated world title by knocking out Archie Moore, who had been Rocky's last victim. Patterson then defended his title four times, winning all the bouts by knockouts. In 1959 Patterson's title was taken away by Ingemar Johansson of Sweden, who surprised the champ by knocking him out in the third round.

The other notable boxer of the fifties was Sugar Ray Robinson. In 1951 Robinson, who held the world welterweight championship, knocked out Jake LaMotta in thirteen rounds to claim the middleweight crown. Less than five months later Robinson lost the middleweight crown to Randy Turpin, an Englishman. In a rematch against Turpin, Robinson clubbed and battered his English foe so badly and brutally that the fight was stopped. After two successful title defenses Robinson tried to win the light-heavyweight championship from Joey Maxim despite the 16-pound weight difference. With the fight easily won on points, Robinson succumbed to heat prostration and couldn't answer the bell for the fourteenth round. The temperature at ringside was 115 degrees.

Before a brief retirement in late 1952 Robinson had fought 140 times and lost only 3 bouts. In 1955 he returned to the ring at the age of thirty-five to knock out Carl "Bobo" Olson and become a three-time champion. After this he lost the title twice and regained it, accomplishing an unprecedented feat of winning a division title five times.

Robinson combined grace, lightning fast hands, speed, and powerful punches to become one of the best all-around fighters of ring history. In all, he fought for twenty-five years from 1940 to 1965.

During the fifties boxing began to suffer from overexposure on television as the Friday night Gillette "Cavalcade of Champions" became a national ritual, and soon Wednesday night fights were telecast. This saturation marketing almost destroyed the local fight clubs that had been the training and proving grounds for aspiring boxers. In 1951 the first movie theater closed-circuit fight was successfully aired to paying audiences in eight theaters located in six different cities. In Pittsburgh 22,000 people jammed a theater to watch Joe Louis's comeback against Lee Savold. This arrangement would eventually prove to be the salvation for boxing. In 1958 when Sugar Ray Robinson battled Carmen Basilio for the middleweight crown at Chicago Stadium and won his fifth title, the bout was telecast to 140 cities and 174 outlets, grossing $1.4 million. The honeymoon between boxing and television ended in 1964 when the weekly shows were cancelled.

During the fifties boxers' names became household words as watching television became an established part of the American leisure-time routine. Thus, boxing became the first sport taken over by the new media and exploited by it to fill prime time. Many have argued that television almost killed interest in the sport, but revenues from sponsors did provide about $4,000 to each fighter for each contest during the peak years of boxing's popularity. Madison Square Garden was the big winner as it made about $15 million in twenty years of television revenues from 1944 to 1964.

7

The 1960s: A Decade of Turmoil and Change

In reviewing sports in the sixties, the *New York Times* in its Sunday, Dec. 28, 1969 edition, called the decade the "Super Sixties"—a decade of the Superstar, the Super Salary, the Super Stadium, the Super Horse, the Super Synthetic, the Super Upset, the Super Controversy." It found that the "little spenders were seeking escape from a tense and tumultuous world" and with "more to spend and more leisure time to spend it, the nation's growing population made the Sixties a roaring bull market for both participant and spectator."

The sixties could also be described as a decade of "expectation and anguish." At the onset of the period a young president issued a challenge to America "to ask not what your country can do for you—ask what you can do for your country." John F. Kennedy's liberal ideas, his New Frontier programs, which were succeeded by LBJ's Great Society, and the unprecedented economic boom from 1961 to 1967, raised the aspirations of many Americans and led them to conclude that "social engineering," coupled with developing technocracy and the emerging "new economics," could solve the majority of society's problems. Many believed that society's afflictions such as unemployment, racial discrimination, urban blight, to name a few, were curable. All that was needed was to discover the right medicinal formula and the correct number of doses.

Many Americans, particularly the nation's youth, responded to the challenge issued to them by their charismatic president. They filled the ranks of the Peace Corps, VISTA (Volunteers in Service to America), and Civil Rights projects. Yet the decade which began with so much promise ended in confusion and disillusionment. The assassination of President Kennedy in late 1963, the escalation of the Vietnam War in 1965, the riots in Watts in 1965 and in Detroit in 1967, the debacle at the Democratic National Convention in Chicago in 1968— all these served to disillusion the idealistic, particularly the young.

In addition, the discovery of the dangers of nuclear power, the hazards of laundry presoaks, massive automotive recalls, power brownouts, the failure to narrow the gap between the rich and poor, seemed further proof that society had foolishly trusted in its own capabilities to solve the complex problems of modern industrial societies.

As a result, young people began to revolt against the "uptight," "plastic," technocratic world. A so-called counterculture began, composed of the "dropouts" from society who gathered in groups to live "alternate" life-styles, such as the "flower children" of the Haight-Ashbury section of San Francisco. College campuses became focal centers for the counterculture movement. Campus enrollment increased from 3.8 to 8.5 million during the period. Some students became politically active and joined such campus groups as the Students for a Democratic Society, in order to humanize the corrupt "bureaucracies of government and business." Others attached themselves to the SDS's radical, anarchical faction, the Weathermen (taken from the Bob Dylan song, "You don't need a weatherman to know which way the wind is blowing"), because they perceived the political institutions to be so far gone that only their total annihilation could bring new hope for humanity.

Others simply turned to hedonistic self-satisfaction. Trendy clothes, unconventional sexual practices, communal living, and drug usage—uppers, downers, "grass," LSD, even "coke" and "smack" (cocaine and heroin)—became characteristic of those trying to find alternative life-styles in the "Age of Aquarius." Although much of the youth culture would prove to be transitory in nature, the "hippie" style in regard to fashion, drug usage, and the exaltation of the individual would leave an indelible influence on American society and culture.

Sports could not long remain unaffected by the throes of a society in convulsive upheaval. President John F. Kennedy was a physical fitness enthusiast, and he challenged Americans, much as Teddy Roosevelt did at the beginning of the century, to abandon high-calorie diets and sedentary habits and to lead a "strenuous life." The president said, "We look instead of play, ride instead of walk." The Kennedy clan set an example for the nation by participating in a number of sports. It was not unusual during Kennedy's presidency to find the Kennedy family engaging in an impromptu touch football game on the White House lawn.

The president's brother, Attorney General Robert Kennedy, submitted statistics that seemed to verify the president's belief that Americans were in poor physical shape. According to figures released by the attorney general in 1961, a good case could be made for Americans being "soft," since forty percent of the American males tested for the Selective Service failed to pass their physicals. The attorney general advocated that less money be spent on varsity sports in high schools and colleges and more on the general student body. Yet later that same year, he would also call upon the nation's coaches to help mold stronger Americans.

So strongly did the president advocate improvement in physical fitness that in August 1963, the *New York Times* could report that by executive order, the president called for the formation of a federal interagency committee on international athletes so that "the United States be constantly informed concerning all events, activities, and conditions that might have a potential effect upon this country's foreign relations." By May 1, 1966, Vice President Hubert Humphrey further emphasized athletic performance as a reflection of a nation's strength when he called for a "great sport effort" to prove that America would surpass the Soviet Union in the development of amateur athletes.

The *New York Times*, however, questioned whether "every area of human activity be subjected to the supposed needs of the Cold War." Undoubtedly, the individual attainments of an elitist corps of trained athletes on an international scale was no real indication of a nation's military and economic strength, but its symbolic value could not be underestimated in the sixties. After the Cuban missile crisis in 1962, when America "stood eyeball to eyeball with the Russians and made them blink" according to one high level State Department official, the nation was ready to respond vigorously to the country that threatened to "bury" us as Khrushchev threatened. Russia had reached nuclear parity with the United States, and a nuclear stalemate was achieved. New symbolic confrontations and shows of readiness were important to this country's international reputation as defender of the free world.

Domestically, athletes changed as they became products of the age. The humble athlete who did not boast of his achievements on the field or in the arena became a vintage memory. "Me too-ism" dominated the sports world. "I am the Greatest," boasted Muhammad Ali, and he went into the ring and proved it. "The Jets are going to beat the Colts," declared Joe Namath unequivocally, and they did. These were just two of the new breed of brash, outspoken, unconventional sports heroes of the decade.

Other athletes wrote books concerning their sports careers, revealing shocking brutality and the prevalence of drugs and unconventional sexual behavior. These inside revelations were a far cry from the previous sports reminiscences that generally presented favorable impressions of the sports world.

The civil rights movement forced integration on sports, both amateur and professional. In 1968 two black athletes with black socks and black gloves gave the Black Power salute during the playing of the National Anthem on the Olympic victory platform in Mexico City. Thus the American sports world in the 1960s was truly a microcosm of radical changes in American society. The sports world was no longer an isolated, special place where American myths of individualism, upward mobility, unselfish team play and spirited cooperation could be played out in a sacred ritual that verified traditional values. Some athletes became more socially conscious and more humanized as they realized that the world beyond sport spoke to personal needs and commitments. Further, athletes found that being controversial could have monetary benefits as sports received increasing television and media coverage.

College Football

College football attendance soared during the sixties, increasing from just over 20 million to nearly 30 million during the decade—a growth rate seven times that of the fifties.

In the previous decade the game was played on grass fields by two-way players who possessed varied skills and superb conditioning. With the gradual liberalization of the substitution rule from 1960 to 1964 and full-scale substitution in 1965, the game became a confrontation between specialists, often on artificial turf. Changes in the clock stoppage rules increased the number of plays per game by twenty-seven.

The sixties also saw the introduction of such innovative offenses as the veer and the triple option that featured a versatile quarterback who could both pass and run and thus placed new challenges to beleaguered defenses, and often led to basketball-type scores.

Several disturbing trends cast a pall on the college game's popularity. The two platoon system meant that double or triple the number of "blue chippers" (athletic recruits who are almost guaranteed to be standouts) were required for gridiron success. In order to attract these players, colleges and universities needed to cough up more money for scholarships and aid, and additional monies needed to be pumped into recruiting budgets. It was not unusual for a football power like Ohio State, for example, to spend from $60,000 to $85,000 per year for recruiting alone.

To attract these players (only 2,000 of the 200,000 high school seniors playing football are tabbed as "blue chippers") for whom the competition was so fierce, numerous blandishments, both legal and illegal, were offered. Jerry Brondfield's book *Woody Hayes and the 100 Yard War* (1974), quotes an unnamed expert who stated: "There isn't a college or university among those listed by the NCAA as major football powers that doesn't bend, break, or fracture the spirit or letter of the rules. Not one. From the football factories to the hallowed and hypocritical Ivies."

Bear Bryant, the legendary Alabama coach, recalled in 1966 that when he coached at Texas A&M he "could hardly get anybody to come to A&M and I think some of our Alumni went out and paid a couple of boys." He indicated that he had to be firm at Alabama since "people begged to buy players."

What Bear did do—without any restrictions by the NCAA—was to build a $1 million brown Italian brick provincial colonial dormitory for athletes, a facility completed in 1963. It contained a library, two study rooms and a 23 inch color TV set. The kitchen had two dietitians, and the athletes were fed steak every night and twice on Sundays. The dorm housed one hundred football players, twenty basketball players, six baseball players, and four track men. According to an Alabama sports publicist, "Golfers, tennis players, or swimmers might qualify if they're winners." Such specialized treatment meant that other schools soon had to follow suit or lose out in the recruiting wars.

As the expenditures for football programs increased astronomically, some schools dropped football, while others valiantly struggled with inferior budgets to compete with the "big boys" for the "golden boys" of autumn whose touchdowns and tackles would keep the turnstiles turning at the campus stadiums in the fall. Generally, the have-nots did not have great success, and the top ten had a familiar look to them. Alabama, Arkansas, Texas, Ohio State, Nebraska, Notre Dame, Southern California, Mississippi, and Penn State and became familiar names on the elite list.

With the amassing of physical talent based on either offensive or defensive positions, and the assembling of an expanding cadre of assistant coaches, each an expert in his particular facet of football, the head coach became more like an orchestra leader or stage personality. Those coaches whom the media deemed particularly colorful or who were designated as personalities, and most importantly, winners—such as Duffy Daugherty, Darrell Royal, Bear Bryant, or Woody Hayes—received special attention and were forgiven such peccadillos as pummeling players, being rude to publicists, or tearing up yard markers. Players come and go, but coaches are always there in the fall provided that they win and don't accept a better job offer. Most alumni could name the head football coach even if the name of the president might escape them.

An Ohio State sports information director once complained that the home media really didn't want to know about the team. He stated, "Hell, I could tell 'em we have a starter out with a broken leg or a case of leprosy for all they'd care. They don't want to know about our football team. All they want to know is what Woody's been up to, what he's said lately, not necessarily about football and how much time can they have with him." Thus not only the athlete's educational needs but ironically even his athletic accomplishments were often overshadowed by "the Coach."

In 1960 nationally televised college games by the ABC network helped to popularize the game, at least for major universities. In 1961, for example, twenty-three games were televised, featuring "nine of 1960 major conference champions, ten of the 1960–61 bowl game participants, and most of the nation's leading powers." Indiscriminate local televising of college games, which had hindered attendance previously, was thus eliminated. Of course, the schools in the NCAA Divisions II and III and those schools who belonged to the NAIA were adversely affected at the gate by the concentration on television coverage at the most successful schools, but their complaints generally went unheeded.

Another impact of television on the college game was that television nominally catered to winners, and although TV receipts generally were split among conference members, the publicity offered by regional or national coverage provided a distinct recruiting boon to those lucky enough to be on the "Game of the Week." Television announcers, like Chris Schinckel and Keith Jackson of ABC, tended to be super boosters of the college game and campus scene, emphasizing youthful vitality and athletic prowess as national virtues.

In 1960 the Big Ten remained a dominant conference. The Minnesota Gophers, guided by Murray Warmath (Warmath sent fifty-seven players to the NFL in eighteen years), rebounded from a cellar dwelling finish to tie Iowa for the conference championship. Press services UPI and AP ranked the Gophers number one, and they received the MacArthur Bowl, symbol of the best team in football. Iowa ranked third and Ohio State was eighth. Other top teams included Mississippi, Navy, Missouri, Washington, Arkansas, Alabama, and Duke. Unfortunately for the Gophers, the Washington Huskies won their second Rose Bowl victory in two years by squelching the Gophers' dreams with a 17-7 score.

Top individual player of the year was Navy's Joe Bellino, who gained the Heisman Trophy, just one of his many awards for his outstanding play. Bellino averaged 5 yards a carry in his college career and was an all-around player as pass receiver and kick returner.

Two unusual circumstances characterized the 1961 season. Ernie Davis, Syracuse's outstanding back, became the first black American to win the Heisman Trophy. Davis rushed for 2,386 yards and scored 35 touchdowns in his college career, and he was scheduled to join Jim Brown in the Cleveland Browns' backfield but Davis died of leukemia before playing in the NFL. The other unusual item was that although Ohio State captured the Big Ten conference title, that university's faculty members, fearing an overemphasis on football, voted not to send the Buckeye team to the Rose Bowl. The second place Minnesota Gophers went in their stead and thrashed UCLA 21-3. In addition Alabama, unbeaten and untied, was named national champion, and Bear Bryant was accorded Coach of the Year honors.

The 1962 Rose Bowl featured the number one and two ranked teams in the nation paired off in one of the most dramatic bowl games ever played—Southern California and Wisconsin. Both teams featured outstanding quarterbacks and ends. Southern California boasted the combination of Pete Beathard and end Hal Bledsoe, while the Badgers countered with quarterback Ron VanderKelen and end Pat Richter. Down by as much as four touchdowns in the fourth quarter, the Badgers rallied valiantly in the final quarter behind the pinpoint accuracy of quarterback VanderKelen's pigskin projectiles. VanderKelen bombarded the Trojans with 48 passes, 33 of which were completed, two for touchdowns, and he also rambled 17 yards for another score. Southern California was forced to stall out the last 1 minute 19 seconds of the game to preserve a 42-37 victory. VanderKelen passed for 401 yards in an electrifying game that is remembered as one of the most wide-open bowl games in history.

The 1963 season saw Texas ranked as the top team in the nation, and Roger the "Dodger" Staubach, Navy's versatile quarterback, captured the Heisman Trophy. Staubach completed .631 percent of his college passes and threw for 3,571 yards and eighteen touchdowns.

The assassination of President Kennedy in 1963 caused over thirty major conference games to be cancelled, including the Harvard-Yale game and the Michigan State-Illinois showdown for the Big Ten title. After the week's delay Illinois captured the Big Ten conference with a

13-0 shutout of the Spartans and then went on to defeat Washington 17-7 in the Rose Bowl.

The year 1964 proved to be an interesting season on the college gridiron. Ara Parseghian, who had resigned as head coach at Northwestern, took over the helm of Notre Dame and parlayed the quarterbacking of Heisman Trophy winner John Huarte to an almost undefeated season with only a 20-17 upset by Southern California to mar an unblemished record. Parseghian shared Coach of the Year honors with Frank Broyles of Arkansas, whose team was one of two major college elevens to go unbeaten and untied for the season. The other was Alabama.

The Big Ten season ended in 1964 in a confrontation between Michigan and Ohio State—starting a trend that would continue with monotonous regularity, particularly in the next decade. Ohio State had been shocked by a 4-4 Penn State team which had embarrassed the Buckeyes by a 27-0 whitewash. Led by 6-foot 4-inch All-American quarterback Bob Timberlake, the Wolverines eked out a 10-0 victory over their Ohio rival. In the Rose Bowl, the Maize and Blue anticipated meeting the Southern Cal Trojans but through an ironic twist of fate, reminiscent of the Ohio State affair two years previously, the Tournament of Roses Committee chose Oregon State for their opponent. Southern California partisans were naturally incensed. Undoubtedly they felt somewhat mollified—and perhaps relieved—when Michigan thrashed Oregon State 34-7.

Other standout teams in the 1964 season included Texas and Nebraska. In the bowl games, Texas upset top ranked Alabama 21-17 in the Orange Bowl, while Arkansas narrowly defeated Nebraska, kingpins of the Big Eight conference, by a 10-7 score in the Cotton Bowl. Of particular note was Alabama's quarterback Joe Willie Namath, who would later star in the NFL for the New York Jets and become a media personality for his exploits both on and off the field.

In the 1965 and 1966 seasons, the Spartans of Michigan State provided many of the headlines for newspaper sports sections. The favorites to repeat in the Big Ten conference were the Michigan Wolverines, who boasted twenty-two lettermen from the victorious Rose Bowl team of the previous season, but it was Michigan State that would claim conference championships in 1965 and 1966. Michigan State, according to one columnist, was "an outsider not only in the national picture but also in the conference." But the Spartan's Irish leprechaun coach, Duffy Daugherty, had shrewdly assembled a stunning array of gridiron talent. He had always been successful in luring black athletes from the South to Michigan State. This was at the time the *New York Times* in 1966 would find it newsworthy "that Duke had signed its first black football player." Such black players at Michigan State included halfbacks Clint Jones and Dwight Lee, reserve quarterback Jimmy Raye, linebackers George Webster and Charlie "Mad Dog" Thornhill, and 300-pound middle guard Harold Lucas. By far the most awesome of this group was Bubba Smith. *Sports Illustrated* had the following to state about Bubba: "Bubba is 6'7", 278 and plays various parts of the defensive line, sometimes simultaneously for Michigan State, and he has been known to boggle opponents just by standing quietly at the door of their locker room. . . ."

"Kill, Bubba, Kill" was the favorite chant of the Spartan student body, but Michigan State opponents who chose to run away from Bubba still had to face such fierce defenders at the opposite end as Bob Viney, only 6 feet 1 inch, who made up in his desire to hit for his lack of size, and explosive linebackers such as Charlie "Mad Dog" Thornhill and the scowling intimidator, 6-foot 4-inch, 225-pound George Webster.

So awesome was the Spartan defense that formidable football powers who traditionally fielded strong ground attacks, such as the University of Michigan, Ohio State, and Notre Dame were held to minus yardage on the ground.

Unfortunately for Michigan State, it played UCLA in the Rose Bowl following its capture of the Big Ten crown in 1965. State had opened up the season by beating UCLA 13-3 and was a heavy favorite to conquer UCLA in their second meeting. However, UCLA, led by the heroics of their outstanding quarterback Gary Beban, upset the Spartans 14-12.

Arkansas, Nebraska, and Dartmouth also garnered undefeated seasons and Notre Dame continued its resurgence under Ara Parseghian. Further modifications in the substitution rules now allowed any number of players to enter the game at the change of team possession and two players at any other time.

In 1966 there occurred what some writers billed as the "game of the century." Both Michigan State and Notre Dame returned powerhouses. The closest Michigan State came to defeat prior to the climactic season-ending game with Notre Dame was the game at Ohio State. Trailing at the half, the Spartans rallied under the leadership of quarterback Jimmy Raye, who ignited a second half rally on a rain-soaked field to pull out an 8-2 decision over the Buckeyes.

On November 19 more than 80,000 crammed their way into Spartan Stadium. Some eager spectators even climbed the ABC scaffolding to get a firsthand view of the contest. The game was the last one on the schedule for the Spartans, so plenty of momentum and publicity had been drummed up by media hypes. Over 30 million witnessed the confrontation on television.

Notre Dame suffered an initial setback when Nick Eddy, their All-American halfback, injured himself stepping off the train. The game was a hard-hitting affair with the rock-ribbed defenses of both teams jarring the ball away numerous times from the jittery offenses. Perhaps the biggest break for the Irish came when starting quarterback Terry Hanratty was smashed to the turf by Spartan defensive end Bubba Smith. Hanratty's substitute, Coley O'Brien, came in and rallied the Irish forces so that late in the game the score was tied 10-10.

The most controversial portion of the game came with 33 seconds to play. The Spartans had previously attempted a desperation drive for victory which failed. The Irish took over the ball on their own 30. Despite the taunts of the Spartan defenders, the Notre Dame players played for a tie under directions from coach Ara Parseghian. Parseghian argued later that "when you're number one and you only get tied, you can't lose it." One disgruntled writer, however, wrote that Notre Dame had "tied one for the Gipper." So much for the argument that the college game was for the boys to have fun and to learn how to become men.

Michigan State was ineligible to repeat for a Rose Bowl trip according to Big Ten rules so second place Purdue, led by passing ace Bob Griese, edged the Trojans of Southern California by a 14-13 margin.

In 1967 Indiana's "Cardiac Kids," so called because of their last quarter rallies when all seemed to be lost, and the unpredictable behavior of their players, shared the Big Ten title with Purdue and Minnesota. John Isenbarger, their punter, would often run instead of punting, often with disastrous results. Isenbarger's mother finally sent her son a telegram, admonishing him to "please punt for Pont," referring to Johnny Pont, the Indiana head coach.

Although beaten by Minnesota, Indiana won a showdown game with Purdue 19-14 to tie for conference crown. The "Cardiac Kids" also won the Old Oaken Bucket, a symbol of victory between the two schools, who were both ranked in the top ten in 1967 polls. Unfortunately the Hoosiers ran into the top ranked team in the nation, Southern California, and its star back O. J. Simpson, and were beaten 14-3 in the Rose Bowl.

Nineteen sixty-seven was a great year generally for collegiate football. Attendance rose for the fourteenth straight year, with over 26.5 million tickets sold for games played by four-year schools. Three schools from the Big Ten—Ohio State, Michigan, and Michigan

State—led the nation's schools in football game attendance. The Big Ten meant big money for athletic programs.

That big-time football often involved cutting corners as far as the NCAA rules were concerned was again made apparent when it was revealed that a slush fund for athletes had existed at the University of Illinois. Peter Elliot, the football coach, and head basketball coach Harry Coombes and his assistant, Howard Braun, resigned as a result of the scandal.

The years 1968 and 1969 saw the emergence of the Big Two and the Little Eight syndrome in the Big Ten Conference—that is—a dominance of Ohio State and Michigan in the Big Ten.

In 1968 Ohio State rambled through its Big Ten foes like Sherman heading for Atlanta. So many Buckeye starters were underclassmen—and many of them sophomores—that the press had dubbed the team "Woody's Kiddie Korps." Ohio State captured the Big Ten and met Southern California in the Rose Bowl. This would be the second time in the decade that the number one and number two ranked teams had met in the Rose Bowl game. After spotting the Trojans a 10-0 lead, the Buckeyes roared back, powered by the passing of quarterback Rex Kern and the bullish thrusts of fullback Jim Otis, with the result that Ohio State decisively defeated Southern California 27-16.

In 1969 Ohio State was favored to win it all, but University of Michigan coach Bo Schembechler (he had played and coached under Hayes) engineered a 24-12 upset of Ohio State to win the Big Ten crown. Unfortunately, Coach Schembechler suffered a heart attack just before the Rose Bowl. This undoubtedly affected the Michigan team, which turned in a lackluster performance and lost to Southern California 10-3. Texas beat Notre Dame 21-17 in the Cotton Bowl and was acclaimed national champion, with Ohio State second.

Thus college football proved increasingly popular during the decade with attendance increasing by about 36 percent. Even President Nixon telephoned Texas after its Cotton Bowl victory to say that in his estimation Texas was the number one ranked team in the nation.

More outstanding players were now being produced. With two platoon football completely in vogue, coaches could now mold specialists who would spend all their practice time on one phase of the game. Players such as George Webster, Jack Tatum, Paul Naumoff, Ted Hendricks, and Tommy Nobis—all of whom became pro stars—could be developed solely on their defensive skills.

Great quarterbacks and runners also dominated the decade. Terry Baker, Ron VanderKelen, Pete Beathard, Roger Staubach, Steve Spurrier, Bob Griese, Jerry Rhome, Joe Namath, and Gary Beban constituted some of the "golden arms." Joe Bellino, Ernie Davis, Gayle Sayers, Donny Anderson, Mike Garrett, Mel Farr, Clint Jones, Jim Grabowski, Floyd Little, Nick Eddy, Leroy Keyes, O. J. Simpson, and Larry Csonka are only a partial roster of the galaxy of star running backs who graced the gridiron in the sixties. Most of these players had at least a fleeting acquaintance with the NFL, raising the serious question as to whether the college gridiron in Division I had become simply a training ground for the pros.

By the end of the decade northern coaches could no longer depend on a pipeline to the South to siphon off the top black players for their teams. Southern and southwestern teams were signing up black players from their states and developing black college football powers like Grambling, Alcorn, and Southern University attracted talented black athletes.

Football players and coaches had also become symbolic of Americanism and discipline—a haven of traditional American values at a time when long-haired draft resisters were burning American flags and their draft cards. The June 10, 1968, *New York Times* took notice of this situation and noted that its November 30, 1959, edition had reported that All-Ivy League tackle, Gordon Batchellor, wore his "hair long and dressed in a black leather jacket and a pair of black leather boots." Batchellor was regarded as weird and strange. The *Times* indicated it wanted to give an update on Batchellor for "those who, then as now, immediately dismiss any young man in shaggy hair as an amoral, un-American instrument of anarchy, nihilism and the devil, regarded Batchellor with scorn." It reported that on January 31 Captain Batchellor was wounded three times in Vietnam with his thigh being so shattered that he would spend one year in a body cast. The *Times'* point was that evidently even longhairs could be heroes.

One could find impromptu demonstrations against the Vietnam War during games and at halftime, especially for the benefit of unsuspecting television cameras. By and large, however, football stadiums did not provide a focus for dissent and antiwar protest. Football was for the hardy and the fit, for the patriotic who were nurtured on fierce competition and the American myth of physical prowess.

The top ten selections for the decade indicated that the rich grew richer and the poor did not appear in the rankings. Ohio State, for example, made the top ten five times. Other teams making the top ten at least four times included Southern California, six times; Notre Dame, six; Penn State, four; Mississippi, six; Arkansas, seven; Alabama, eight; Michigan State, four; Texas, six; and Purdue, four. Alabama was the top-rated team in 1961, 1964, and 1965; Southern California in 1962 and 1968; and Texas in 1963 and 1969. The Big Ten, the

Southeastern Conference, the Southwest Conference, two big independents, and Southern California dominated the college football scene. College football became big business in the sixties, providing a focal point for alumni identification and pride and making the football weekend the exciting highpoint of campus life. Football was "business as usual" during the turmoil of the decade, though much of the conflict centered on college campuses, and college athletics were a healthy and welcomed antidote to the disaffected, angry, and cynical youth who "dropped out, turned on, and tuned out" as drug culture "guru" Timothy Leary urged them to do.

Pro Football

Pro football during the sixties blossomed as never before. At the end of the decade, NFL attendance climbed to 90 percent of stadium capacity, while the upstart challengers of the American Football League drew well over 2 million for a season's play.

Coaches and defense dominated the pro gridiron game during the sixties. Men like Vince Lombardi, George Allen, Bud Grant, and Tom Landry all epitomized the "winning isn't everything, it's the only thing" philosophy. Vince Lombardi was said to have originated that phrase, but he stated that he had been misquoted and what he really had said was "winning is not everything but making the effort to win is." According to some sources, Ted Sanders, former coach of Vanderbilt, was the originator. John Wayne used that line in the movie *Trouble Along the Way* (1953) when he played a coach of a small college football team. Lombardi did say that "as a person I am not well enough adjusted to accept a defeat. The trouble with me is that my ego just cannot accept a loss."

Perhaps George Allen was the best example of a coach consumed by the "winning is everything" syndrome. He once said, "The winner is the only individual who is truly alive. I've said this to our ball club. Every time you win, you're reborn, when you lose you die a little."

While Lombardi and Allen relied on emotion and rhetoric to whip up their charges, Tom Landry, coach of the Dallas Cowboys, and Bud Grant of the Minnesota Vikings reflected a new breed of cold, efficient, aloof men whose players were simply parts of a machine. If the machinery faltered, the parts were replaced. All played according to the master game plan, and the coach replaced the quarterback as the signal caller.

Grant's and Landry's game-coaching techniques clearly manifested a stoic, implacable, cool professionalism. One could not read from the expressions on their stolid faces their reactions to events on the field. Not a flicker of emotion registered either in elation or disgust. Only when victory was assured did perhaps a trace of a smile break the impassiveness of the otherwise stony countenances.

By the sixties defense had become the essential building block for victory. The five- and seven-man lines of the forties and fifties had given way to four-man lines with three linebackers. Of particular importance was the middle linebacker, who by virtue of his position needed to be a super athlete. He had to be big enough to stop rushes up the middle yet quick enough to diagnose the offensive plays. Generally he was well over six feet tall and weighed between 220 and 240 pounds. Joe Schmidt of the Detroit Lions, Ray Nitschke of the Green Bay Packers, and Bill George and Dick Butkus of the Chicago Bears were just some of the stellar standouts at middle linebacker position during the period. Butkus's meanness earned him such terms of endearment as "Animal," "The Enforcer," and the "Maestro of Mayhem."

At the same time, defensive linemen became larger. It was not unusual to see linemen who were 6 feet 4 inches in height and close to 300 pounds. Roosevelt Grier of the Los Angeles Rams was 6 feet 5 inches tall and 270 pounds; Roger Brown of the Detroit Lions was 6 feet 5 inches tall and 300 pounds; and Ernie Ladd of the San Diego Chargers was 6 feet 9 inches tall and weighed 311 pounds.

Not only was this new breed of lineman gargantuan in physical size, but they were remarkably quick in pursuit. Alex Karras, former lineman for the Detroit Lions, in his book *Even Big Guys Cry*, notes that Brown could outsprint most players on the Lions team, and even in a short race outsped a former Olympic dashman. A phrase coined by TV commentators came to describe the pro defenders in the trenches—"mobile, agile, and hostile"—and they were.

The Green Bay Packers were the success story of the early sixties in pro football. Long dormant as a challenger for conference honors (they had won their last division title in 1944), the "Pack" was personally resurrected by the legendary Vince Lombardi. Lombardi took charge as coach and general manager in 1959. In 1960, the Pack won the division title and then captured NFL championships in 1961 and 1962, then in 1965 through 1967. The 1966 and 1967 teams also captured the first two Super Bowl games, winning decisively over Kansas City and Oakland.

Lombardi's teams were superbly conditioned and coached, and his personnel were admirably suited for his offensive and defensive strategy and tactics. The Packers under Lombardi relied less on finesse and more on sheer power. In Fuzzy Thurston and Jerry Kramer Lombardi possessed two of the finest pulling guards in pro football history. In the backfield golden boy Paul Hornung, "Mr. Outside," and crunching fullback Jim Taylor, "Mr. Inside," were two of the premier running backs in the league. When defenses cheated to play the run, cagey and crafty quarterback Bart Starr would exploit the situation with passes to such outstanding receivers as Max Magee and Boyd Dowler.

On defense Bill Quinlan, Henry Jordan, Dave Hanner, and Willie Davis formed a brutally impenetrable front line in the trenches. In linebackers Ray Nitschke, Dan Currie, and Bill Forester, and in Willie Wood and Herb Adderly, the speedy and stylish defensive backs who patrolled the backfield, the Packers had players who could always be called on to make key defensive plays.

Two basic factors made the Packers particularly popular. First, they were located in a small Midwestern city with the franchise's ownership shared by hundreds of individual stockholders rather than by one wealthy family or a relatively small group of rich stockholders. Thus, the triumph of the Packers on the gridiron symbolized for many the triumph of individuals over the masses, of the small town over the big city, of the average Joe over the big-shot entrepreneur. Second, the personality and philosophy of Vince Lombardi demanded discipline, dedication, and hard work to achieve the pinnacle of success. This was particularly satisfying during a period when antiwar riots were breaking out, draft evaders were heading for Canada, and young men were wearing beads, flaunting their long hair, and experimenting with marijuana and other drugs.

Only the Chicago Bears' 14-10 triumph over New York in 1964 and Cleveland's victory over Baltimore 27-0 in 1964 broke the Packer domination from 1961 to 1967. The Packer power often relegated other fine NFL teams to the background. In the Packers' own division—nicknamed the "black and blue division" because of the sheer violence of the blocking and tackling—were the Detroit Lions, who fielded strong teams led by a stout defense anchored by a "fearsome foursome" of Alex Karras, Roger Brown, Sam Williams, and Darris McCord, with Joe Schmidt at linebacker. The Lions usually just fell short of conquering the Packers.

On Thanksgiving day, 1962, in one of the major upsets ever in pro football history, the tables were turned. The Lions, smarting from an earlier loss to the Packers after blowing a 7-6 lead to them in the final two minutes, came out on the field as hungry for victory as their namesakes were when given a scent of Christians in an amphitheater and literally devoured the Packers 26-14, handing Green Bay their only season loss. The Packers' quarterback, Bart Starr, became so frustrated by the relentless Lion rush that he screamed at the referee, "If you give us any more of those lousy calls, I'm going to reach out and bite that big, fat head of yours right off." The referee responded by saying, "Starr, if you do, you'll be the only quarterback in this league with more brains in his stomach than he has in his head."

Perhaps the most dramatic game played during the Packer dynasty years was the NFL championship of 1967 when Green Bay edged Dallas 21-17 on the last day of December in bitter 13 degree below zero weather. Trailing 17-14 with 5 minutes to go, the Packers began a final drive, managing to run the ball down to the 1-yard line with 16 seconds left. Lombardi, eschewing a tie, admonished his troops to go for victory, telling them if they couldn't put the ball into the end zone they didn't deserve to be NFL champions. On a play designed to go to the fullback, quarterback Starr kept it at the last instant and following the block of Jerry Kramer, "ran to daylight" for the winning score.

The NFL was not the only game in town in 1960. That year the NFL domination of pro football in the United States was challenged by a new league, the American Football League, with Lamar Hunt as president. Franchises were awarded to the cities of Buffalo, Boston, Houston, Dallas, Los Angeles, Oakland, Denver, and New York. The League played a fourteen-game schedule, and a five-year contract was signed with ABC to televise selected games, thus providing some financial stability to the fledgling league. To spice up the game, the AFL adopted a two-point option on points after touchdown—that is a pass or run into the end zone resulted in two points, a successful kick, one point. Also, the players' names were stenciled on their jerseys to give more fan identification and to ease the job of broadcasters. Most clubs were composed of older players, marginal athletes previously cut from the NFL, and recent college grads.

Even with the ABC contract, the AFL had to struggle to survive. Part of its problem was that it had a weak franchise in New York, which with the impact of its media and with its huge population, was essential for the AFL's survival. The New York Titans, as they were called, were owned by Harry Wismer, a New York radio personality, and were coached by Sammy Baugh, the former star quarterback of the Washington Redskins.

The franchise drew poorly, Wismer fired Baugh in 1961, and the club became mired in debt. To have the New York franchise club collapse would have tolled the death knell for the new league. A five-man corporation headed by "Sonny" Werblin purchased the Titans. Immediately, Weeb Ewbank, the successful former Baltimore Colt coach, was signed in 1963 as head coach and the name of the team was changed to the Jets.

Werblin believed in the star system and stated that "football is show business. The game needs stars. Stars sell tickets." He immediately signed Alabama's outstanding quarterback Joe Namath, or "Broadway Joe" as he soon would be called. He signed for a then astronomical sum of $427,000.

Namath would prove to be the successful leader the Jets were looking for, and he was a colorful personality who made news both on and off the field. Namath led the Jets to a Super Bowl III victory. Commissioner Pete Rozelle, however, forced Joe to divest himself of interest in an establishment called "Bachelors III" because of the "unsavory" types who frequented the place. Joe's "tell it like it is" attitude and cocky prediction before Super Bowl III of the Jets' victory over the seemingly invincible Colts appealed to a new generation of youth who were turned off by the Vietnam War and who deeply resented the suppression of individualism in a technocratic, bureaucratic society. For them, Namath represented the new jock anti-hero who could thumb his nose at convention and yet at the same time reap the rewards that society usually reserved for its "straight members." Veteran sports writer Tex Maule in a column entitled, "Say It's SO Joe" made the following statement concerning Namath and what he represented: ". . . folk hero of the new generation, a Fu Manchu worth $10,000 to shave off, swinging nights in the live spots of the big city, the dream lover of the stewardi, all that spells insouciant youth in the Jet Age."

Although the bidding war between the AFL and the NFL had ensued since the creation of the junior league, the coffers of the AFL were filled to the brim in 1964 when it signed a $36 million contract with NBC for six years. Each league team was guaranteed $900,000 per year as its share. This meant that the AFL could be much more aggressive in its head-to-head recruiting war with the NFL.

By 1966 the NFL and AFL paid out seven million dollars for the recruitment of new players. This costly competition ended when the two leagues decided to merge that year. Separate schedules were to be played until 1970, but starting in 1966, a Super Bowl would be played between the Leagues. In the first two Super Bowls, the Vince Lombardi led Packers of the NFL easily disposed of the Kansas City Chiefs 35-10 and the Oakland Raiders 33-14. In 1969, however, the New York Jets, led by Broadway Joe Namath, who cockily predicted a Jets victory, beat the Colts 16-7. Namath earned Most Valuable Player honors as he completed 17 of 28 passes for 206 yards and engineered drives that resulted in a touchdown and three field goals. Matt Snell complemented Namath's passing by rushing for 121 yards. Snell was the first number one draft choice to sign with the Jets and had been a prize catch in the AFL-NFL bidding war.

The sixties were certainly a decade of growth for professional football. Television's impact on the sport was enormous. In 1962 CBS televised all NFL regular season games for $4.65 million. The 1966–67 league championship NFL games were televised by CBS for $2 million each, and CBS and NBC signed a $9.5 million contract to televise the Super Bowl for four years. And, of course, the $36 million NBC contract had made the AFL a reality.

Television's impact on Sunday afternoon viewing patterns meant that by the end of the decade, "even the antifootball housewife knew the difference between a blitz and a blintz." Television "gold" was so important that referees signaled for time out to insure that the commercials were run. TV exposure also meant that as more NFL stars received national exposure they became widely sought by companies for commercial endorsements, TV talk shows, and in some cases, film roles. Football stars became corporate entities in their own right. As one writer has indicated, when a football player came on to be interviewed he had to begin by thanking "my attorney, my business partner, my advisor, my theatrical agent, and my publishers."

Not all was positive in the world of pro football during the sixties. In 1963 Alex Karras of the Detroit Lions and Paul Hornung of the Green Bay Packers were suspended and five Detroit Lions were fined for betting on their own teams and other NFL games. Hornung and Karras were reinstated in 1964.

Many felt that the game had become too violent and that the price of broken limbs and scarred bodies was too high a price to pay for a sometimes all too brief place in the sun. Others, particularly women, resented the domination of football on TV on Sundays with sometimes four and five games being available. For many in the sixties, the Sunday drive had been replaced by Sunday afternoon in front of the TV viewing their favorite NFL team. In the sixties football replaced baseball as the most popular national sport, and its television revenues were greatly envied by baseball's management. The violent confrontations on the gridiron captured the popular imagination as fans became more knowledgeable and loyal to a game that was becoming increasingly complex in its strategy. The football pool with its obsession for the point spread became a fixture in offices, factories, and bars across the country. Excitement over the "big game" enlivened the routine of work as football became the favorite of blue collar workers who could idolize former college players.

College Basketball

In recalling the sixties in its "Decade in Review" the *New York Times* remarked that "Superman had changed his skin," a direct allusion to the emergence of black athletes on the sports scene. What began as a trickle in the fifties became a flood during the sixties. Nowhere was this influx of black talent more apparent than in college basketball during the sixties. Jerry Lucas, Bill Bradley, Gail Goodrich, and Pete Maravich were white superstars of the decade; however, the black athletes, like Paul Hogue, Jerry Harkness, Cazzie Russell, Bill Buntin, Walt Hazzard, Dave "Big Daddy" Lattin, Bobby Joe Hill, Charlie Scott, Elvin Hayes, Curtis Rowe, Sidney Wickes, Artis Gilmore, and above all, Lew Alcindor (later Kareem Abdul-Jabbar), were the reasons their respective teams won the NCAA championship or were prime contenders for the crown.

The influx of black players affected the style and execution of the game. Bob Cousy in his book *The Killer Instinct* (1975) has stated that "most black athletes are loose, mobile, quick and have good jumping ability—all things a coach looks for in a basketball player. (Black players sometimes criticize one of the "brothers" for having white man's disease—meaning he couldn't jump very high.) White basketball in contrast is a game of "execution—of mechanical precision." Bob Cousy further had noted that "a black player overcomes an obstacle with finesse and body control, while a white player reacts by overpowering the obstacles." As the decade continued, the black game with its freer, flashier style began to dominate.

The popularity of coaching clinics and the increased exposure of college basketball on TV meant that for the most part, regional differences that had previously characterized the game had virtually disappeared. The popularity of urban playgrounds—with many a city youth aiming for a ticket out of the ghetto via the colleges and the pros, and the numerous driveway baskets in suburbia where endless games of one-on-one ensue—meant the development of players who relied more on individual skills, both offensively and defensively. With improved players who were larger and quicker, with college basketball more popular than ever (attendance was up 5 million in five years), and with more schools boasting huge new arenas, pressure increased on coaches to develop winners. Because a basketball team can employ only five players on the court at one time, the recruitment of one or two key players could transform a poor or mediocre team into a powerhouse. Thus, the intense pressure to recruit these "blue chippers"—players who could quickly turn the program around (a Lew Alcindor, for example)—was enormous. Top high school players would be hounded day and night by coaches and deluged with scores of scholarship offers. The intensity rivaled even that of football recruiting. A Tom McMillen, for example, could have his choice of over two hundred colleges and universities.

Since the popularity of college basketball in the post World War II era, gamblers had been interested in influencing the outcome of the games. In 1961, just ten years after the infamous gambling scandal that had shaken college basketball to its very foundations, another scandal hit college basketball. Former Columbia All-American Jack Molinas, who in 1953–54 had played for the Fort Wayne Pistons and who had been banned for life from professional basketball for betting on games, was now accused of being the "master" fixer. According to charges brought against Molinas and his associates, $70,000 had been used to fix college basketball games from 1957–61. Thirty-two players from over twenty colleges admitted to taking bribes. Molinas drew a ten to fifteen year prison term while others implicated drew lesser sentences. In 1965 three players were expelled from college for having been bribed to fix a game between Idaho and Seattle. In most cases the lure of easy cash for poor boys whose athletic scholarships did not provide for wardrobes and spending money so that they would look like other students and be able to do the things other students did proved too much to resist.

On the courts, basketball during the first three years of the decade was dominated by the state of Ohio. Coach Fred Taylor in 1960 had recruited an outstanding crop of underclassmen, many of them just sophomores. These included such later pro stars as Jerry Lucas and John Havlicek. The Ohio State team averaged 90.5 points a game during the season.

In 1960 Lucas and company defeated previously unbeaten California 75-55 in the NCAA finals at the Cow Palace in San Francisco, as Ohio state shot a torrid 68.4 percent from the field with balanced scoring from the starters. College basketball observers believed that a dynasty had been built and that the Buckeyes would hold the crown for the next two years.

However, another team from the state of Ohio had something to say about that. Ed Jucker, coach of Cincinnati's Bearcats, had been favored to win the NCAA for three years when he had the incomparable "Big O"—Oscar Robertson—as the star. The Bearcats never did. But in 1961, fielding a predominantly black team and emphasizing a defense anchored by 6 feet 9 inch Paul "Oak Tree" Hogue, Cincinnati beat the Buckeyes 70-65. Ohio State entered the championship game with a thirty-two-game winning streak and the nation's top rating.

Mississippi State won the Southeastern Conference title but refused to play in the racially integrated tourney as the South began to take its stand against the developing civil rights movement. In 1962, a repeat of the previous year's matchup, the Bearcats triumphed over the Buckeyes, this time by a 71-65 score as Paul Hogue and Tom Thacker led their team.

In 1963 Cincinnati was expected to defend its NCAA championship and claim a third consecutive crown. The Bearcats fought their way into the final but met their match in the "runnin' gunnin' " Ramblers from Chicago Loyola, coached by veteran George Ireland. Cincinnati was the best defensive team in the country, holding opponents to 52.9 points a game, while Loyola led the nation in scoring 91.8 points per game. Although thwarted in the early game by the Cincinnati defense, the Ramblers rallied when Cincinnati went into a stall while leading by 15 with 12 minutes to go, and tied the ball game to send it into overtime. In overtime, a tip-in of a missed shot by Vic Rouse gave the Ramblers the NCAA title by a 60-58 count. Four of the five Rambler starters were black.

The UCLA Dynasty

From 1964 to 1970 the Bruins of UCLA won six of seven NCAA championships led by their indomitable and often inscrutable coach, John Wooden. A high-school star in Indiana, an All-American guard at Purdue, and a six-year veteran of professional ball, Wooden had only one losing season at UCLA. Wooden became a popular hero to the public not only because he was successful but also because of the way in which he achieved success. He stressed discipline and filled his speech with homilies and epigrams, somewhat like a reincarnated Ben Franklin. Two of Wooden's favorites were: "It's better to go too far with a boy than not far enough," and "If you're not making mistakes then you're not doing anything. I'm positive that a doer makes mistakes." Wooden was also able to win with small men like Walt Hazzard and Gail Goodrich, medium-sized ones like Sidney Wickes and Curtis Rowe, and large ones like Lew Alcindor and Bill Walton.

Some in the coaching fraternity resented Wooden's deaconlike demeanor and homily-filled conversation, pointing out that he needled officials and often opposing players unmercifully. Although Wooden never cursed, he could be capable of a vicious "Goodness, gracious, sakes alive."

Other coaches objected to Wooden's pious "holier than thou" attitude. (Wooden didn't smoke or drink. Critics indicated that he was the type of guy who went to a convention and sat in the lobby and watched everybody else get drunk.) But this was precisely why he was admired—for his midwestern virtues and slightly Victorian attitudes. In a decade where many "hippie" types had rejected the American work ethic and coaches were struggling to discipline long-haired, pot-smoking athletes, or rebellious blacks, Wooden's no-nonsense philosophy struck a responsive chord among Middle Americans who felt comforted that old-fashioned virtues still could bring success.

Wooden's first two NCAA champions were run and gun outfits which featured pressing full court defenses and whose tallest men were only 6 feet 5 inches. In 1964 the Bruins beat a tall and talented Duke Blue Devils squad 98-83, while in 1965 they raced by the powerful Michigan Wolverines, champions of the Big Ten, led by its three stars Oliver Darden, Bill Buntin, and Cazzie Russell. The UCLA team prevailed as Gail Goodrich poured through 42 points, completely overshadowing Russell's 28 tallies.

Only in 1966 were the finals anything other than another edition of the Bruin Invitational. The UCLA five seemed to be waiting for Lew Alcindor to complete his freshman year and failed to make the Final Four. The vacuum was filled by two traditional powers—Duke and Kentucky—and two young upstarts—Utah and an obscure entry from Texas, Texas Western College (formerly the School of Mines, now University of Texas, El Paso). The consensus of the pundits was that the real championship game would be the semifinal between Duke and Kentucky, won by Kentucky for sixty-four-year-old Adolph Rupp. Almost unnoticed, the Texas Western Miners slipped by Utah as the only white player in their playing group, eighth man Jerry Armstrong, stopped Utah's Jerry Chambers (eventually the tournament Most Valuable Player) just enough to provide an 85-78 edge.

The final was a classic of contrasts: Rupp, near the end of a long and brilliant career opposite young Don Haskins, the Texas Western coach; the rich tradition of Kentucky opposite a school entirely new to the limelight of national sports; an all-white Wildcat team, featuring discipline, control and a zone defense opposite a team of black, city players who scratched and clawed on their man-to-man defense and played a free-wheeling, innovative offense. In 1966 the racial contrast was especially poignant. To some, the game looked like a final shootout between basketball's past and its future. The future won fairly handily, 72-65. The game was decided early. With the score at

9-9, little Bobby Joe Hill, Miner guard from Detroit, twice stole the ball and scored and the Wildcats never quite recovered.

The Miners' no-name team, only two of whom ever played in the NBA (Willie Worsley, one year, and David Lattin, four years) and most of whom failed to graduate, took home the trophy—a feat the school has never come close to duplicating (although there have been some NCAA track titles and the exploits of long-jumper Bob Beamon). No Texas Western player made All-American—not top rebounder Harry Flournoy, nor top scorer Orsten Artis, nor Hill, Worsley, nor Lattin—but the team will be remembered at least as a trivia item: the only team to break UCLA's great monopoly of the NCAA championship.

The years 1967, 1968, and 1969 were the Alcindor years at UCLA. With the 7-foot 1-inch center, the Bruins won 90 games, and lost two by a total of 4 points. Johnny Dee, the Notre Dame coach at the time, said that when you played UCLA, all one could hope for was the 3F's: "Foreign Court, Friendly Officials, and Foul Out Alcindor."

Alcindor was a star for Power Memorial Academy in Manhattan. While at Power Memorial, his team ran up a 71-game winning streak. While Alcindor was still in high school, Gene Shue, then a pro coach, said "I'll trade two first round draft choices for him right now." A glimpse of his awesome power came his freshman year when the UCLA freshmen beat the varsity 75-60—the same varsity that had won the NCAA championship the previous season.

In the 1967 NCAA championships the Bruins led 70-46 over Dayton before Coach Wooden pulled his starters and coasted to a 79-64 decision.

In 1968 UCLA participated in a game against Houston at the Astrodome which drew the largest crowd ever to see a basketball game— 52,693. It also drew the largest television audience in sport history— estimated at over 30 million. The UCLA team had defeated Coach Guy Lewis's Houston Cougars in the previous year's semifinals, so the Cougars were seeking revenge. Lewis had assembled an awesome array of talent, featuring six players who towered 6 feet 6 inches and weighed in at well over 200 pounds. They were led by their star, sharp-shooting 6-foot 7-inch Elvin "Big E" Hayes. Hayes had outscored and outrebounded Alcindor in the previous confrontation and had complained that his team had "choked." He was eager to do battle to demonstrate his belief that he was a superior player to Alcindor.

The Cougars' coach and team also contrasted strongly with Wooden's philosophy of coaching and player treatment. Whereas the Cougars could wear beards and mustaches, played more one-on-one ball, were free of restrictions off the court, and held practices that were fairly informal, Wooden forbade facial hair, had strict rules about off-court conduct, and held very organized practices. The Cougars stopped the Bruins' 47-game winning streak 71-69, with Hayes scoring 39 points and seizing 15 rebounds. Alcindor played with an injured eye and scored on only 4 of 18 shots.

Both teams found themselves rematched in the NCAA semifinals and the Bruins, coming out in a diamond and one defense with one player shadowing Hayes, befuddled the Cougar offense and smashed Houston 101-69, holding a 44-point lead at one time. This time Alcindor clearly outplayed Hayes, who scored only 10 points and never was a factor in the game. The Bruins then coasted by North Carolina in the finals 78-55. Four Bruins were named to the all-tournament team.

An interesting postscript to the 1968 season was the introduction of the "no-dunk" rule. Since the dunk was Alcindor's favorite shot, many felt that the rules change was legislated to specifically stop him.

In 1969 a 41-game winning streak was halted in the final Pacific Athletic conference game of the year when a Southern California stall resulted in a 46-44 upset victory. Yet UCLA was favored to win another NCAA, and they did not disappoint their fans. A gutsy and determined Drake team almost derailed the UCLA championship express in the semifinals, but UCLA managed to hang on to an 85-82 victory. In the finals UCLA faced Purdue, an upset winner over North Carolina in the semifinals. Purdue was led by the blond bomber, Rick Mount, a jump shotting phenomenon who sported a 33.8 scoring average and who could seemingly bombard the basket from anywhere.

Coach Wooden, however, had devised a strategy to combat the shooting prowess of Purdue's star player. He had Kenny Heitz cover Mount like a blanket. Mount scored 28 points but made only 12 of 36 shots, which included a streak when he missed 14 straight. Alcindor, on the other hand, sparkled, tossing in 37 points and seizing off 20 caroms. The UCLANs rolled to an easy victory, 92-72.

To the average fan the Alcindor years must have been a time of "bliss and happiness" for coach, star, and team. But was this the case? After the 1969 championship game, Lew stated that he could feel the pressure—for the first time he had had a "fear of losing."

Coach Wooden said of the Alcindor era: "It was not as easy an era as it might have seemed to an outsider." Wooden stated that "It will be fun coaching to win again rather than coaching to keep from losing."

John Valley, a returning guard on the UCLA squad who was interviewed prior to the 1969–79 season said: "We all agree it's a lot more fun now. . . . With Lew, the way he is, once you've seen him hook two or three times, it's over. He used to hook it in a few times and we'd win by 30. What a drag. Now we're running and pressing and all of us are getting into the act—you know, just like in real basketball."

In other words, it wasn't a whole lot of fun for the principals involved. Obviously fans and the media had exerted such tremendous pressure to keep on winning—they were expected to win and no excuses would be accepted—that it was not a very enjoyable experience. The idea that college sports are for the athletes and are for fun proved to be a myth needed by the media who wanted to cover an unbeatable UCLA team led by an unstoppable giant. Alcindor took all the press's attention, overshadowing brilliant play by guards Lucius Allen and Mike Warren.

By the end of the sixties, big-time college basketball had produced tremendous players possessing superb basketball skills. But the game was now big business and often not much fun for the athletes and the coaching staffs, who now carried the burdensome knowledge that losing does not bring happiness (neither does a string of championship seasons).

Bill Bradley, Princeton's three time All-American (30.1 scoring average), Rick Mount (33.8) of Purdue, and Peter Maravich (40.2—of whom a black high school basketball coach after watching films of Maravich play, exclaimed, "He's one of ours"), as well as Jerry Lucas and Gail Goodrich, represented great college ballplayers of the decade who were white. But the handwriting was on the wall—the best ball players were black.

For coaches, the message of the decade was that to be competitive, to keep the dollars rolling into the program, they had to recruit harder than ever in the urban slums for youngsters who could play the "city game."

By the end of the decade, southern colleges who had resisted integration in the fifties and early sixties were featuring all black teams. Whether or not this represented real progress in race relations or a new form of serfdom depended on whether or not you were a college coach or a black activist like Harry Edwards. Certainly, college basketball in the sixties represented a transition period where taller and more talented players, a majority of them black, provided most of the hard court excitement. The 1966 All-American Associated Press team was all black.

Pro Basketball

Professional basketball took off in the sixties. Attracted by an abundant supply of superstars from the colleges, attendance began to soar. In 1960 there were eight teams, and the National Basketball Association became truly national in scope with the Lakers moving to Los Angeles. By the end of the decade the league had expanded to seventeen teams under the able leadership of Walter Kennedy, who became Commissioner in 1963. Kennedy appreciated the influence of television and in 1964 negotiated a five-year contract with ABC to broadcast a game of the week especially selected for fan appeal. Five years later when the NBA inked a three-year television contract it was for $17 million, over 400 percent more than the previous contract.

Attendance by 1965 for the league was 2 million. By the 1969–70 season the league's attendance figures were 5,146,858. The New York Knickerbockers alone attracted over a million spectators.

Like the NFL, the NBA also faced competition during the sixties. In 1961 Abe Saperstein, owner of the Harlem Globetrotters, attempted to form a rival basketball league called the American Basketball League. The league placed franchises in Washington, Pittsburgh, Cleveland, Chicago, Kansas City, Los Angeles, San Francisco, and Hawaii. Despite such innovations as the awarding of 3 points for a field goal outside of 25 feet and the installment of professional basketball's first black coach (John McLendon), the ABL lasted just over a year and then died. In 1967 a better financed attempt to challenge the NBA arose. Calling itself the American Basketball Association and naming George Mikan as its commissioner, the ABA settled in to challenge the established league.

Although Mikan had indicated that the ABA would not compete directly with the NBA in terms of franchises and would not raid the NBA for players, this did not prove to be the case. In reality, the Anaheim Amigos competed against the L.A. Lakers, the New Jersey Americans against the New York Knickerbockers, and the Oakland Oaks against the San Francisco Warriors.

Player raiding began when Oakland owner, entertainer Pat Boone, hired Bruce Hale, former coach of Miami (Fla.), to coach his ABA entry. Hale had been superstar Rick Barry's coach at Purdue and Barry had married his daughter. Hale convinced Barry—then considered a rare commodity, a white superstar—to jump from San Francisco. The owner of the Warriors, Frank Milieui, sued. The court ruled that Barry had violated his contract and could not play for a team other than the Warriors. But he also ruled that Rick could wait out a year and then be placed on Oakland's roster. This is what Barry did, much to the consternation of Milieui and the NBA. Barry's action raised the spectre of the validity of the reserve clause. In football, one could play out the option. In basketball, one could now sit out his option. In baseball, the player could do neither.

The ABA adopted the three-point rule of the defunct ABL and utilized a red, white, and blue basketball, that one cynical critic described as looking like a ''ball on a seal's nose.''

To attain legitimacy and to acquire the financial wherewithal to successfully challenge the NBA, the ABA began to bid competitively for the graduating college stars and even began drafting undergraduates under a so-called hardship clause. Spencer Haywood, the University of Detroit star, was the first to go this route and immediately became a star for Denver averaging 30 points in his first season.

In 1969 the ABA eagerly sought to sign Lew Alcindor, the college player of the decade. His signing would give the league instant credibility. Alcindor and his advisors took bids from both the NBA Milwaukee Bucks and the ABA New York Nets. When the ABA bid proved to be lower than the NBA, Alcindor asked for a bonus. This Mikan refused to allow. Alcindor then accepted the Bucks' offer.

Mikan's inability to secure Alcindor's signing (he would later state that ''the ABA had the inside track'') and the failure to land a national television contract as lucrative as the one secured by the AFL with NBC led to Mikan's resignation on June 14, 1969, and league president James Gardner took over as commissioner.

On the courts the story of the NBA in the sixties was the building of the Boston Celtics dynasty. From 1960 to 1969 the Celtics won every NBA title during the decade except for the 1966–67 season when Alex Hannum's Wilt Chamberlain-led 76ers interrupted the Boston reign.

The Celtics were ably coached by Red Auerbach, who used to antagonize the opposition's fans by lighting up a big cigar when he was convinced that the game was wrapped up. Espousing team basketball and assembling a fine collection of talent whose nucleus was defensive oriented center Bill Russell, the Celtics proved to be unbeatable.

Auerbach helped to break the color barrier in pro sports. With Russell, Satch Sander, and K. C. and Sam Jones—all black athletes—combined with such white stars as Bob Cousy, Bill Sharman, Tom Heinsohn, John Havlicek, and others, the Celtics became the Yankees of pro basketball.

The monotony of the Celtic victory skein was highlighted periodically by the classic confrontations between Bill Russell and Wilt Chamberlain. Chamberlain—the former superstar at Kansas who had also been a fine quarter miler and high jumper—had played previously for the Harlem Globetrotters. In the NBA he began his career playing for the Philadelphia Warriors in 1959. His first confrontation against Russell was a standoff. Wilt scored 30 points and Russell 22 but Russell seized 38 rebounds to Wilt's 35. Russell said afterwards,

"He's the best rookie I've ever seen. He's no freak. By the end of the season he could be the greatest basketball player of all time."

That season Wilt averaged 37.6 points and 26.9 rebounds per game. He was named Rookie of the Year (1960) and Most Valuable Player and was center on the All-Star team. NBA attendance shot up 24 percent that year—much of the increase attributed to Wilt. He had become a superstar in his first year in the League.

On March 2, 1962, Chamberlain outdid himself at Hershey, Pennsylvania, in a game against the New York Knicks when he scored 100 points. This came after a period in February when he had an eight-game string; he scored 78, 61, 55, 52, 43, 50, 57, and 55 points for a total of 451. During the 1961–62 season Chamberlain averaged 50.4 points.

In 1963 Chamberlain and the Warriors moved to San Francisco. In 1965 Chamberlain was sold to the owners of a new ball club in Philadelphia, the 76ers. In 1966–67 Alex Hannum was named head coach of the 76ers. Hannum had coached Chamberlain in San Francisco and had asked him to shoot less and to emphasize passing, rebounding, and defense.

Hannum continued to advocate the same philosophy to Chamberlain in Philadelphia with astounding success. The 76ers jumped out to a seven-game winning streak, including a 42-point romp over Boston. At the end of the season the 76ers had compiled a 68-13 record.

After rolling over Cincinnati in the opening round of the playoffs, the 76ers took Boston in five games. The score card: Russell 117 rebounds, 30 assists, 57 points, while Chamberlain had 160 rebounds, 50 assists, 108 points.

Some attributed Philadelphia's success in 1966–67 not so much to the talent of the 76ers but to the fact that veteran Coach Auerbach had retired after 1037 NBA victories and 9 NBA championships in ten years and turned over the reins of leadership to player-coach Bill Russell, making Russell the first black head coach in the NBA.

Russell, however, regrouped the Celtics in 1967–68 and once again found himself facing Chamberlain and the 76ers in the Eastern Division finals. The series went to seven games with the Celtics winning the deciding game 100-96, and they then went on to take the title over Los Angeles 4-2.

In 1968–69, Jack Kent Cooke, owner of the Lakers, traded three players to acquire Chamberlain from the 76ers. There he was teamed with silky smooth forward Elgin Baylor and hot shooting former West Virginia star Jerry West. With the three superstars it was anticipated that the Lakers were a shoo-in for the title. The end of the regular 1968–69 season saw Los Angeles take the Western Division title with a total of 66 victories, while Boston had limped into the playoffs with a fourth place finish in the Eastern Division.

Yet the Lakers were not a happy team, Coach Butch van Breda Kolff, for whom Chamberlain had little use, wanted Wilt to play high post, while Chamberlain preferred to play the low post. This conflict certainly had an effect on the Lakers' morale.

The series went to the seventh game. The Lakers trailed by 21 points and then rallied to within a one-point deficit. At that point in the game, Chamberlain removed himself from the game because of an injury. When a short time later he indicated to Coach van Breda Kolff that he was ready to go in, van Breda Kolff did not put Chamberlain back into the game, believing he needed a more mobile team on the floor. At the end, Los Angeles missed some clutch shots and the Celtics' Don Nelson scored the winning basket for a 108-106 victory. Jerry West of the Lakers with 42 points, 12 assists, and 13 rebounds in the final game was named the Most Valuable Player.

Chamberlain remained bitter about not having been allowed to re-enter the game. However, Bill Russell later supported van Breda Kolf's position, stating that "any injury short of a broken leg or a broken back isn't good enough. When he took himself out of that final game when he hurt his knee, well, I wouldn't have put him back in the game either, even though I think he's great." In other words, the possibility of suffering a permanent injury should be discounted when questing for a pro championship.

Thus for Chamberlain, despite his accomplishments, the decade ended as it began for him—standing in the shadows of Bill Russell and marked as a loser. But for pro basketball, it was a successful ten years. Attendance had risen, television contracts had substantially helped to increase players' salaries, and the NBA was still "the League" but not the only game in town.

Although the ABA had signed some first-rate talent in players like Dan Issel and Mel Daniels, on the whole it did not have the strength of the NBA, particularly at the crucial center position. As one ABA critic bluntly stated, the ABA "suited up unknowns, second-raters and a bunch of guys named Jones and Brown."

By 1969 most of the NBA teams featured predominantly black stars and already boasted of one black head coach, something the other pro sports could not. The future, however, seemed mixed. Would all-black teams attract white audiences? Would the ABA successfully compete with the NBA? How many franchises could pro basketball support? How high would the salaries soar? Was basketball to be dominated by giants or was there still a role for the small man? Only time would tell.

Baseball

Baseball in the sixties underwent significant changes that were to affect profoundly the future of the game. In the period of 1961 to 1972 baseball decreased in popularity: 34 percent of sports fans named baseball as their favorite spectator sport in 1961, but only 21 percent named it as their favorite sport in 1972. The reasons for this slippage were complex. First, football, especially professional football, was increasing substantially in popularity with the advent of increased television coverage and the development of superstars and super teams. Baseball also suffered from over expansion with its consequent dilution of major league talent and from overexposure on television, a medium not particularly suited to conveying the subtleties and drama of a game that contains multiple points of interest, and that frequently cannot fully capture the quick movement of hits and fielding plays. Baseball revenues from television increased steadily during the decade to hit $27.5 million in 1966, and the A. C. Nielsen Company showed that in 1963 the Sunday World Series game between the Los Angeles Dodgers and Yankees was seen in 20.2 million homes (about 40 percent of the national home television market).

Baseball fortunes were tied to television, but television brought competition from other sports. In the same Nielsen rating the annual baseball All-Star game ranked well below seven individual events of college and professional football. The World Series remained a national event, but fan loyalties were quickly shifting and becoming more diverse with the growth of golf, bowling, tennis, soccer, and hockey.

At President Kennedy's urging for physical fitness, Americans responded by participating in a wider variety of sports. The "New Frontier" mood of the country produced a new optimism and energetic enthusiasms that greatly benefited sports, especially participant sports.

Sports in the sixties would provide an important outlet and diversion from the problems that divided and factionalized a society: racial problems and severe race riots in 1964, 1965, and 1967; the escalating war in Vietnam and Southeast Asia; the decaying cities and problems of chronic unemployment and poverty; the problems related with racial integration and busing; and government corruption and abuses of power. Americans' attention and concern were divided and often diverted from sports as the society seemed, at various times, to be coming apart and losing all consensus and cohesion. The decade was a disconnected one filled with senseless assassinations, constantly upsetting developments, and the increasing commitment to a war that was both militarily futile and humanly unethical.

Confusion and conflict about the society's national goals and purposes could be reflected in its "national game." Baseball seemed irrelevant to many in a time of social ferment and radical change, although the "improbable dream" 1967 Boston Red Sox and the 1969 "Miracle Mets" captured the national imagination in a way that other teams of the period did not do. Baseball has always been politically conservative, serving established national values and patriotic attitudes. With a few exceptions, baseball players have not been socially conscious, or politically active people. The game requires intense concentration, constant physical discipline, and continual travel. Players have sought much-needed diversion in cardplaying, moviegoing, clubhouse antics, barhopping and nightlife, and spent precious little time on families and home life. Owners, managers, and press often looked askance at players who were outspoken, rebellious, or independent minded.

Professional baseball is a self-enclosed subculture with its own rituals, codes, and language. Those ballplayers who had revealed the inside of the game, such as Jim Brosnan or Jim Bouton, were considered violators of the code. In a game where careers can be short and where trades, demotions to the minor leagues, or outright releases are real possibilities, players seek security within the structure even if it means following arbitrary rules and submitting to management. Thus, baseball players in the sixties tried to survive in a sport that personified the country's values and virtues of high professionalism, uncorrupted and pure competition, and high-minded personal dedication to a game with the longest and strongest national traditions. It is little wonder, then, that these athletes operated in a vacuum of stable continuity that became increasingly disconnected from national events. The importance of the game as an ongoing ritual and tradition lessened as people lived from crisis to crisis, saw national leadership become disconnected and unstable, and became disaffected or alienated for various reasons.

The early sixties saw the expansion of the major leagues when the proposed Continental League threatened competition. The American League added two new franchises with the Washington club and the Los Angeles Angels, and the Washington Senators were moved to the Minneapolis-St. Paul metropolitan area. The new teams chose their players from a pool of players made available from other teams and paid $75,000 for each new team member, an investment of over $2 million for each team. The American League operated with ten teams in 1961 and the National League with eight, but in 1962 the other league added the Houston franchise and the New York Mets. The Mets and Houston teams paid $2 million in entry fees, but by 1969 Montreal and San Diego would pay $10 million to join the league. In

1969 the leagues divided into East and West divisions with six teams in each division. A 5-game championship series was instituted to decide the respective pennant winners.

Baseball purists saw this (and the switch to the 164-game schedule) as the end of the organizational coherence of the game. Records were no longer exactly comparable. Roger Maris's record 61 home runs in 1961 had to be noted with an asterisk because the Yankees had played in 164 games, although Maris himself played in just 162 games. But had Maris played in the National League in 1961 and hit 61 homers his record would not have been qualified. The competition between teams within a division could vary from that of the other division, and in the 1969 playoffs, New York swept Atlanta in three games as did Baltimore over Minnesota.

The new franchises struggled for respectability and attendance, seeking to build stability and to escape the stigma of being castoffs and marginal players. The near success of the Minnesota Twins in 1965 and 1969 and the phenomenal triumph of the Mets in 1969 gave inspiration to expansion clubs. Baseball became more of a regional game. As the leagues expanded, the origins and backgrounds of the players became more diverse as the search for talent became more competitive.

The minor league system continued to supply seasoned ballplayers. Maury Wills, the greatest base stealer of the sixties, spent more than eight years in the minor leagues. Willie McCovey played in four different minor leagues in four years. Other black players—Willie Mays, Hank Aaron, and Ernie Banks—played brilliantly in the Negro leagues or with black barnstorming teams such as the Kansas City Monarchs, before having their contracts bought by the majors. Cuba provided a large group of players who achieved stardom and had notable careers: Sandy Amoros, Tony Oliva, Luis Tiant, Tony Perez, and others. Orlando Cepeda came from Puerto Rico as did Roberto Clemente. The three Alou brothers and Manny Mota originated from the Dominican Republic.

The college campuses began to serve as an extension of the minor leagues with universities such as Southern California, Arizona State, and Michigan State providing talent ready for regular big league play. Ron Fairly, who attended Southern California, received a $60,000 bonus in 1958, and Frank Howard, who was enrolled at Ohio State, received $108,000 to sign the same year. Jake Gibbs and Bill Freehan, fresh off the campuses of the University of Mississippi and the University of Michigan, each received over $100,000 in 1961. College baseball coaches such as Danny Litwhiler (Michigan State), Bobby Winckles (Arizona State), and Rod Dedeaux (Southern California), regularly sent players to the major leagues, often having these players for only a season or two before they were lured away. Some players made the jump to the major leagues from high school, with no time or only a short stay spent in the minors. This group included such notables as Pete Rose, Al Kaline, Eddie Mathews, Frank Robinson, and Vada Pinson, and later Bobby Grich and Joe Morgan.

Thus, the major league personnel in the sixties became more racially and socially diversified, and the game retained and even strengthened the myth of upward mobility and success based on raw ability, desire, and innate talent. Talented hitters, catchers, and pitchers could command substantial bonuses and step into regular positions. In this sense baseball has been one of the most democratic of American sports, especially after racial barriers were broken down and after expansion opened up more opportunities and provided for more turnover of personnel. Marginal ballplayers—such as the famous catcher Bob Uecker who averaged .200 for six seasons and had only 74 RBI's in that period—could find a place because their positions were in short supply. Another was the well-traveled, often-traded player Paul Popovich, who shuttled between Chicago and Los Angeles before ending up at Pittsburgh for his last two seasons. He could stay in the majors because he was a utility infielder who could fill spots until a trade was made or new talent developed.

The New York Yankees continued their dynasty into the early sixties, winning their league pennants from 1960 (the last year for Casey Stengel as manager) through 1964. But the Yankee domination of the World Series was to come to an end. In the most unusual Series of the decade the 1960 Pirates' team beat the Yankees in the seventh game 10-9 in the bottom of the ninth as Bill Mazeroski homered as the lead-off man off Ralph Terry. Mazeroski's home run in game one had also provided the margin of victory. The Yankees outhit the Pirates .338 to .256, scored 55 runs to the Pirates' 27, and pounded the Pirate pitching by winning their three games by scores of 16-3, 10-0, and 12-0 with Bobby Richardson setting a Series record of 12 RBI's.

In the 1961 Series the Yankees easily handled the Cincinnati Reds in five games, as the Reds only scored 13 runs and hit .206. This Series saw Whitey Ford record his eighth consecutive World Series victory and extend his streak of scoreless Series innings to thirty-two, breaking a record held by Babe Ruth.

The 1961 Yankees team won 109 games, hit 240 home runs (with Maris powering 61 and Mantle clouting 54), and led the league in fielding average, fewest errors, and double plays. Whitey Ford won 25 and lost only 4 games, Ralph Terry was 16-3, and Luis Arroyo was 15-5 with 29 saves and 65 appearances. This was a remarkably balanced team with solid fielding and power hitting, although the Detroit Tigers led the league in runs scored and batting average while winning 101 games.

The best World Series of the sixties was the 1962 battle between the Yankees and San Francisco. The evenly matched teams went down to the seventh game tied in runs scored (20), and the final game saw Ralph Terry win 1-0 over Jack Sanford as Terry avenged his second game defeat. The game ended with the Giants stranding runners on second and third in the bottom of the ninth. The Terry-Sanford duels in games two, five, and seven were the highlight of the Series.

The Yankees were swept in four games by the Los Angeles Dodgers in 1963 and lost to the St. Louis Cardinals in the seven-game 1964 Series. In the 1963 Series the Yankees scored only 4 runs, 3 of them on 2 home runs, as Sandy Koufax, Johnny Podres, and Don Drysdale baffled the Yankee hitters. In the 1964 Series Bob Gibson pitched two complete games against the Yankees, and Bobby Richardson set an all-time Series record with 13 hits as he hit .406, only to be overshadowed by Tim McCarver's .478 average for the Cardinals. Gibson was to go on to win seven consecutive Series games, winning three in the 1967 Series over Boston and two over Detroit in 1968, losing the deciding seventh game in that Series.

The two most symbolic World Series during this decade were the 1967 Red Sox-Cardinals matchup and the 1969 Mets win over Baltimore. The Red Sox went from a ninth place finish in 1966 to a pennant in 1967, winning it on the last day of the season. Only three games separated the top four teams in the American League, while the Cardinals won by ten and a half games over San Francisco. Boston was down three games to one yet came back to tie the Series before losing to Gibson and the Cardinals. Gibson only allowed three hits and struck out ten while permitting three earned runs in three complete game victories. Gibson struck out twenty-six and walked only five to turn in one of the most brilliant Series performances since Lew Burdette's three wins and 0.67 ERA in the 1957 Series and Harry Brecheen's three victories and 0.45 ERA in the Cardinals' win over Boston in 1946.

The underdog 1967 Red Sox captured national attention and diverted people's attention from the disturbing news of U.S. troop buildup to almost half a million men in Vietnam, the serious outflow of gold from the country along with inflation and devaluation of the dollar in foreign markets, and China's successful testing of a hydrogen bomb. President Johnson and his military advisors assured the country that the escalation of bombing, the search and destroy operations, and the buildup of men and materials would make the "light at the end of the tunnel'' a bright day of victory that would insure an independent and democratic Vietnam. The folly of the war was not yet fully apparent, but the repercussions at home were beginning to be felt. The Newark and Detroit riots in July 1967 were perhaps the most disturbing news as close to a hundred people were killed and thousands injured. These riots erupted in cities where antipoverty programs and urban renewal efforts had been considerable. The dramatic story of the 1967 Red Sox comeback and underdog efforts provided a much needed diversion from the catastrophic news of the day.

Nineteen sixty-eight proved to be a year during which national events and tragedies clearly overshadowed sports. The Tet Offensive of the National Liberation Front of South Vietnam early in 1968 revealed to many antiwar critics the fallacy of those assurances that the war could be won and that South Vietnam could be secured and stabilized. The Democratic Party was wracked by internal struggle and debate, but Eugene McCarthy was not strong enough to prevent Hubert Humphrey, who had avoided the primaries, to take the nomination when he decided he wanted it. Robert Kennedy was gaining strength as a liberal, antiwar candidate when he was killed by an assassin on June 5, 1968, only three months after Dr. Martin Luther King, Jr., was assassinated. The Chicago 1968 Democratic Convention with its police riot against demonstrators radicalized many people as the violence of Vietnam came home. The urban ghettoes were in turmoil and open revolution, mostly as a result of King's assassination, and the Kerner Commission report pointed to the deepening racial gulf and inequalities that could only lead to further violence and anarchy.

The 1969 "Miracle Mets" story also had fortuitous timing. The expansion team, now in its eighth season with a loser's record of 394-734 in seven seasons, won 100 and came from 9½ games behind in August as the Cubs collapsed and allowed the Mets to win the East division by eight games. The Mets then swept Atlanta in the playoffs, and faced the Baltimore Orioles, who had won their division by nineteen games and swept the Twins in the playoffs. After losing the opening game 4-1 the Mets came back to win four straight, with Mets' pitchers holding Baltimore to just five runs in the four games and letting Baltimore average just .146 at the bat.

The Mets had long been underdog heroes, symbolizing futility and inept play that produced a generation of Mets' fans who found excitement in seeing how many ways the team could manage to lose. The 1969 Series excitement should be seen in the more positive mood of the country. In July 1969, United States astronauts landed on the moon, and their explorations were followed by millions of proud Americans. The decade seemed to finally have some continuity and purpose as President Kennedy's goal of putting Americans on the moon first and leading the space technology race was realized. Nixon was enjoying a period in office during which he was relatively free from criticism and seemed to be gaining a national consensus for his quiet and reasonable approach to the nation's ills and the war.

The nation's cities were relatively free of racial violence in the summer of 1969, and the beginnings of detente with the Soviet Union promised hopes of world peace and de-escalation of the nuclear arms race. Nixon's announcement of partial troop withdrawals and his proposal for the "Vietnamization" of the war in June 1969 and his reform of the draft system created many new supporters, and he seemed, at least at that time, to have a concrete, workable program for ending the war.

Thus the mood of the country in the summer of 1969 was quiescent, even optimistic and buoyant to a degree. The story of the Mets fit that mood perfectly, and the Mets players like Seaver, Koosman, Agee, Swoboda, and Clendenon became national heroes, joining Neil Armstrong and Buzz Aldrin as men who overcame great obstacles to bring team victories and the sweetness of long-deserved success. Shea Stadium and the surface of the moon provided lasting television images of the landscape of triumph. The racial and ethnic mixture of the Mets also had its appeal. It was a team made up of players from all over the country, with two Southern blacks (Cleon Jones and Tommy Agee) playing key roles, and the team effort was distributed evenly among no-name players who brought pride to a team that had been the joke of the league. The Mets reestablished the national significance of the game as a focal point for American beliefs and values. Somehow, in a loose and not clearly understood way, their struggles were the nation's struggles to pull itself together, to overcome adversity and disorganization, and to do something with pride and the unselfish team effort of ordinary players rising to the occasion.

In terms of individual performances the decade of the sixties had many individual success stories and remarkable accomplishments. Maury Wills's 104 steals in the 1962 season broke Cobb's record by 8; Wills led the National League from 1960 to 1965 in steals, eventually pilfering 586 bases in fourteen years. He was replaced as the premier base-stealer by Lou Brock, who topped the league in steals from 1966 through 1969, and 1971 through 1974, with a record 118 steals in 1974. Brock also began his steady move toward 3,000 hits during the sixties, and Wills and Brock were the most exciting and daring players of the decade with base-running instincts and speed that put them in a class with Ty Cobb.

The great hitters of the decade were Pete Runnels, Carl Yastremski, and Tony Oliva in the American League, and Roberto Clemente, Tommy Davis, and Pete Rose in the National League. Clemente was in a class by himself with four batting titles, and Tommy Davis's 1962 season with a .346 average, 230 hits, and 153 RBI's was a remarkable individual accomplishment.

The National League continued to be the strongest hitting league as its batting average (except for 1963) was consistently higher, with a 13-point difference in 1967 and 1968. Only two American League players (Bobby Richardson and Tony Oliva) managed 200 hits or more during the sixties, but fourteen different National League players topped that mark with Clemente and Rose doing it four times, and Vada Pinson and Felipe Alou doing it three times. In 1968 Yastremski won the American League batting title with a .301 average, the only bona fide .300 hitter that year in the league. In 1966 that league had only two .300 or better hitters. The American League became the power league, leading the National League in home runs in every year in the decade except 1966, with Maris, Mantle, Harmon Killebrew, Rocky Colavito, Dick Stuart, Frank Robinson, Frank Howard, Norm Cash, and others powering round trippers.

The best pitchers of the decade were Whitey Ford, Bob Gibson, Don Drysdale, Sandy Koufax, Juan Marichal, Denny McClain, and Jim Bunning. Ford pitched up to the 1967 season, but when he realized that his arm was no longer dependable he walked off the mound in Detroit and went to the clubhouse to pack and leave before his teammates returned. Ford was a remarkable performer, especially in the World Series, and his nickname, "The Chairman of the Board," indicated his central importance to the Yankee organization. Ford was a fierce and cocky competitor who personified the confidence and arrogance of the great Yankee dynasty that spanned the fifties and sixties. But after 1964 the pride of the Yankees began to slip, with the team going from first in 1964 to sixth in 1965 and to last in 1966.

Bob Gibson was the premier pitcher in the National League, winning over 20 games from 1967 through 1969, and just missing the 20-game mark in 1963 and 1964. The 1968 season for Gibson was particularly noteworthy as he won 22 games, posted a 1.12 ERA, and led the league in strikeouts with 268. He had nine seasons with 200 or more strikeouts and would amass 3,117 career strikeouts to put him in the same class as Walter Johnson.

Sandy Koufax and Don Drysdale gave the Dodgers brilliant pitching and provided World Series championships in 1963 and 1965. Koufax pitched no-hitters in four consecutive seasons from 1962 to 1965, but his great career was cut short after only twelve years by painful arthritis in his pitching elbow. Before the age of thirty-one he was out of baseball, and at the age of thirty-six he was chosen to the Hall of Fame, the youngest player yet to be elected. Drysdale had stellar seasons up to 1966. In 1966 he and Koufax collaborated on their contract negotiations and divided $225,000, with Koufax reportedly making $135,000 annually.

Other notable pitchers of the sixties included Juan Marichal, who won 191 games from 1960 to 1969, 27 more than Gibson won for the same period. Marichal had a unique style of pitching with his high kick delivery, his variety of pitches and speeds, and his mastery of the high curve and screwball. He finished 244 games in his sixteen-year career, a noteworthy accomplishment in an era of the relief pitcher. The Marichal-John Roseboro incident in 1965 was one of the most publicized of the period. Marichal clubbed the charging Roseboro on the head with his bat, and Marichal's action resulted in an eight-day suspension and a $1,750 fine.

The pitching "phenomenon" of the decade was Denny McClain, who had five remarkable seasons for Detroit. In 1968 he was 31-6 with a 1.96 ERA, although he pitched badly in the World Series and Detroit was led by Mickey Lolich, who had three complete game wins. McClain's career, however, was marred by problems with the local press, with the commissioner's office over allegations of gambling, and with management over his unorthodox and freewheeling lifestyle. He could not handle the limelight and publicity, and the 1970 suspension hurt him as he seemed to lose the conditioning and concentration that had brought success. The 1971 season with the Washington Senators, when McClain lost 22 and won only 10, was the beginning of his demise, and after toiling for Oakland and Atlanta briefly in 1972, he was out of major league baseball. Other free spirits like Bo Belinsky, who "went Hollywood," dated movie queens, and provided grist for the gossip columnists, also showed considerable promise, but the distractions of notoriety proved to be too much.

The sixties also saw the establishment of the Major League Players' Association in 1966 with Marvin Miller as the head of this organization. Baseball players began to realize that collective bargaining was needed to deal with problems of compensation, fringe benefits, a retirement program, expense allowances, grievances, and distribution of receipts from television revenues. The economic picture of baseball had become increasingly more complex, and baseball came under the scrutiny of Congress and the federal government. The 1951 and 1957 investigations of baseball by Emmanuel Celler's congressional committee brought out in the open much-needed information and documentation on the practices of owners regarding player contracts and determination of new franchises. No regulatory legislation came out of these investigations, but the days of arbitrary contract negotiation were coming to an end.

In 1966 the Players' Association boycotted spring training because of a dispute over the pension fund and the owners' contributions to it. An agreement was eventually reached in February 1966 when a three-year contract was signed, with the owners agreeing to pay $4.5 million annually to the pension fund and granting increased benefits, especially the qualifications for eligibility regarding pensions. The pattern of confrontation between players and management was set in 1966, with owners arguing that costs had to be kept in line but being unwilling to offer full disclosure of income and expenditures. As playing careers became shorter and personal expenses increased with inflation, the ball players realized that they needed more control over their financial situations, more flexibility in negotiations, and more job security.

The seventies would bring even further challenges to the baseball establishment with the Curt Flood challenge to the reserve clause as a violation of antitrust laws, a thirteen-day strike in 1972, and the modification of the reserve clause with the development of the free agent market. The sixties represented the last stable period of baseball as a national sport that enjoyed protection from antitrust laws and had special privileges that made it an independent operation, determining its own needs. When Satchel Paige was inducted into the Hall of Fame, he said: "Baseball is too much a business to them [the modern day players] now. I loved baseball. I ate and slept it. But now, players, instead of picking up sports pages, pick up the *Wall Street Journal*. It's different."

Paige was perhaps overestimating the reading habits of baseball players, but he was right in emphasizing the business concerns of modern day players. The seventies would see the advent of the agent as a key factor in contract negotiations and free agentry dealings, and the Players' Association would become a true union that brought the average player salary to $97,500 in 1978, a 62 percent increase from the 1966 season when Drysdale and Koufax collaborated on their salary negotiations with the Dodgers. Baseball attendance would boom in the seventies with 33 million in attendance in 1976. Average ticket prices went from $2.20 in 1970 to $3.45 in 1976, and then to $4.20 in 1980. Add to this the almost $100 million television package signed in 1975 and baseball was ready for multimillionaire players and open-war bidding for free agents. In many ways these economic factors brought more internal changes to the game, its organization, and the realities of players' lives than any other source. Players would argue that one could love the game and seek the big money at the same time, but old timers like Paige had to wonder where these divided loyalties and interests would take the game in the seventies.

Tennis

In the late sixties, tennis began to boom in the United States. Formerly confined mainly to the country club set, the game was attracting thousands of new players, and new public courts became available, provided by cities and towns eager to aid their citizens' improvement of their physical fitness. Many tennis players were drawn from the ranks of golfers who discovered that two sets of tennis took much less time and gave one a lot more exercise than did eighteen holes of golf. Tennis also appealed to those who wanted to keep in shape yet were bored with the monotony and loneliness of jogging. Tennis was still a vigorous activity which strained the cardiorespiratory system yet still was a social activity.

With more people than ever playing tennis (nine million—one million more than the number of golfers) tennis equipment manufacturers began developing new rackets with aluminum, steel, and fiberglass. Indoor courts, both those of the cheaper bubble kind and those of a more permanent nature, began to dot the landscape of the Northeast and the Midwest. The new tennis clubs often offered a number of services usually seen at health clubs, such as saunas and steam baths. Many also included baby-sitting services, making an overt attempt to attract housewives to fill court time during the lightly used daytime hours. And although tennis enthusiasts spent only $24 million annually on equipment compared to $279 million for the golfers, tennis manufacturers were confident that there was a virtually untapped gold mine yet to be exploited.

Tennis attire also changed during the decade. The influence of television on the game meant that TV producers encouraged (or even demanded) that tennis players give up the traditional white clothing for blue, yellow, or even pastel-colored and striped outfits. Suddenly tennis attire was discovered to be trendy, and fashionable court apparel could be seen being worn in the grocery stores and shopping malls. Women who would recoil in horror at the amount of flesh revealed by a miniskirt thought nothing of bending over in public in a tennis dress to reveal frilly panties embroidered with some catchy saying like "love seat."

Tennis balls also changed. The white balls which were difficult to discern on the miniscreen gave way to optic yellow and bright hued orange. White balls became as extinct as the dodo bird, and Americans were purchasing more tennis balls than ever before—15.8 million of them—a 50 percent increase in six years. And 7,000 new tennis courts were being constructed each year.

On the courts in the sixties, tennis was still "shamateur tennis." The players (other than those who belonged to Jack Kramer's tour early in the sixties or George McCall's and Lamar Hunt's groups in the later sixties) were technically amateurs, but most accepted money "under the table."

In 1960 it appeared that open tennis might be approved by the International Lawn Tennis Federation, but the vote on the issue fell a few short. Open tennis would have to wait eight years.

The duplicity of the system was outrageous. Jack Kramer, in his book *The Game: My 40 Years in Tennis*, reported that after he had signed Nicki Pietrangeli of Italy the Italian Tennis Federation made a counter offer which Pietrangeli accepted and thus retained his amateur status. As Kramer noted, other amateur federations were aware of the arrangement. Disillusioned, Kramer dropped out of pro tennis in 1962.

During the rest of the decade a pro circuit featuring established stars such as Ken Rosewall, Pancho Gonzales and Rod Laver played for former Davis cup captain George McCall. In 1967 Lamar Hunt bankrolled the formation of a tour featuring such players as John Newcombe, Tony Rochek, and Dennis Ralston. The name given the tour was the World Championship Tennis or the WCT.

America's male "amateur" players were a somewhat lackluster lot. The U.S. Open, last won by an American in 1955 by Tony Trabert, would be dominated by players from outside the States until 1968. A brief resurgence came in 1963 when Chuck McKinley captured Wimbledon and teamed with Dennis Ralston to wrest the Davis Cup from Australia.

As the decade wore on, many of the players became increasingly disillusioned with the hypocrisy of the amateur game. Among them was America's premier women's player, Billie Jean King. A short, stocky, aggressive player who loved to serve and volley, King had won a doubles title at Wimbledon in 1961 and was ranked second in the nation in 1963 and 1964 and fifth in the world during those years. Starting in 1966 she captured three straight Wimbledon titles, repeating Maureen Connolly's feat of the early 1950s. In her autobiography King attributed the hypocrisy and "shamateurism" to the wealthy people who ran the clubs and tournaments. She asserts that they were the only ones who could afford to be amateurs.

Jack Kramer, in his book *The Game,* stated the following concerning the amateur game: "The people in tennis who ran tournaments preferred having amateur tournaments because the amateurs were then obliged to be social gigolos, to come to the parties, to stay in people's houses, to play games with committee members' children. If they didn't perform these social services, they were not invited back. By and large, the tennis people didn't want the pros because the pros were grown men who did not want great obligations beyond playing." Arthur Ashe would say, "We all deserve Oscars for impersonating amateurs."

King didn't put all the blame on the country club set. According to her, the system could not have operated without the players' cooperation and support. However, many of the players who didn't like the alternatives offered by a refusal to accept the status quo quit tennis, got real jobs, or joined the nomadic pro tour.

Just after winning Forest Hills in 1967 Billie Jean ripped the system. She attacked officials for their interest in parties rather than in the game and the players. She then called for open tennis between amateurs and professionals because she was "ostensibly an amateur who was already a pro."

Under pressure from advocates of honest tennis such as Billie Jean King and Jack Kramer, and with the move of Wimbledon to endorse open tennis in 1968, the latter became a reality by the end of the decade. After Wimbledon opted for open tennis, the rest of the tennis federations fell into line.

The end of the decade saw the emergence of one of the brightest of U.S. tennis stars, Arthur Ashe, who captured the U.S. Open in 1968 and lost an exciting match to Rod Laver in the 1969 Wimbledon, a defeat that was no disgrace since Laver captured the Grand Slam that year.

Ashe was a college graduate, intelligent, well mannered—and black. As Kramer notes in 1968, Ashe represented the following: "After years of American tennis brats, he was an absolute gentleman on and off the court. He was intelligent, he had a good sense of humor, and the press adored him. Remember too, this was 1968; Martin Luther King had been assassinated earlier in the year, there were race riots, whole cities were burning, George Wallace was running for president. And in the midst of all this turmoil, appeared this dignified young black man who seemed to stand for all the good in tennis and America alike. What greater symbol for open tennis could there be than a black hero, signifying that the closed days of country-club tennis were over?"

Arthur Ashe was not the harbinger of developing black tennis stars, and he would remain the only top black tennis star of either sex for the next decade. Tennis had come a long way during the sixties. The seventies would see the dawning of a whole galaxy of new stars—a number of them achieving success before they could legally order an alcoholic beverage. The seventies would see the professionalization of the sport as top seeded amateurs defected to the ranks of the pros, the pro circuits expanded, and prize money expanded to rival golf purses, and television coverage made the game available to a mass audience.

Golf

Golf grew by leaps and bounds in the sixties with two factors contributing to its popularity: (1) television; and (2) the emergence of dynamic, engaging personalities (some called them the "Young Lions"). Chief among them were Arnold Palmer, Jack Nicklaus, and Lee Trevino.

In 1960 Palmer arrived on the scene to become the successor to Ben Hogan. A compact 5 foot 10 inch, 185 pounds, Palmer's major contribution proved to be his appeal to the everyday guy and gal. Palmer had captured the National Amateur in 1954 and the Masters in 1958, but his victory in the Masters in 1960 seized the public's imagination. Palmer was down one stroke to Ken Venturi (who with a 283 score was already in the clubhouse) and had two holes to go. Playing all out on two difficult holes, Palmer birdied both of them to earn not a tie but a dramatic victory. This is what attracted fans to Palmer—his dramatic rallies, his late surges when all seemed lost, and his charges on difficult courses and under extreme pressure. So many spectators followed him that they were soon dubbed "Arnie's Army." What was remarkable was that many of the adoring gallery, such as housewives and teenagers, were in many cases not even golfers. Much like Notre Dame, Palmer developed his own "subway alumni." Palmer was always aware of his following, talking with them and recognizing their importance to his inspired and daring game. The "army" followed their general as he attacked courses and rallied from behind.

Also, Palmer's less than aesthetic golf style distressed purists but made him a darling of the public. Al Barkow, author of *Golf's Golden Grind: The History of the Tour* (1974) has stated the following about the unique Palmer style: ". . . club flailing through the air like wash on the line, his feet almost coming out from under him, his head ducked down and his eyes following the flight of the ball like a man peeking under the table at a lady's lovely legs. It was a fast but not very pretty golf swing but it got the job done. Arnie the ball beater looked like the golfing Everyman. He held out to the masses that they too could play the game without having the inhuman coordinations of Sam Snead or the gear meshing exactitude of a Ben Hogan.''

During the sixties Palmer won one U.S. Open, three Masters, and two British Opens. But by the end of the decade his golf game had slumped. By that time he had become the first pro golfer to win $1 million on the tour, and by January 1, 1977, he had won $1.7 million, second only to Jack Nicklaus's phenomenal $2.8 million career winnings. He was heavily involved in promotions and investment, the start of what eventually amounted to a $60 million empire. Yet in 1969 after not having won a tournament and having withdrawn from the PGA because of injury, he captured the last two tournaments of the year, much to the delight of his many loyal fans. He was named Associate Press Athlete of the Decade.

The second member of the Big Three was the "Golden Bear," Jack Nicklaus. Nicklaus had been a versatile high-school athlete, playing center on the basketball team, catcher on the baseball team, and quarterback on the football team. He had taken up golf to companion his father who played the game for therapeutic reasons (to help rehabilitate an ankle that had been operated on). By the age of thirteen Jack had shot a 69.

Nicklaus attended Ohio State and captured the National Amateur in 1959 and 1961, immediately turning pro after his victory in 1961. In the sixties, Nicklaus won the Masters three times, the PGA once, the British Open once, and the U.S. Open twice.

Nicklaus's approach to the game influenced many club and amateur golfers. He calculated his shots precisely and left nothing to chance. Often, however, Jack took a long time to play eighteen holes. Those who emulated Nicklaus often irritated other golfers who didn't want to take five hours to play a round of golf. Jack's rational approach to the game, combined with a calm disposition and immense hitting power, often made him not only unbeatable but simply an awesome force on the course. Nicklaus was known for his crushing shots off the tee as his massive build and whiplash wrists combined to produce fairway shots that left opponents gasping. In the 1962 U.S. Open he defeated Arnold Palmer in an eighteen-hole playoff, one of the great golf confrontations of the decade. However, Nicklaus did not have the charisma or magnetism that Palmer exuded. He was an unemotional player who rarely showed the intensity or dramatic concentration that Palmer was noted for. Nicklaus dominated the game so completely that his only problem seemed to be concentration and continued interest.

Lee Trevino made his first impact on the national golf scene in 1967, when as a virtual unknown he captured fifth place in the U.S. Open. The following year he won the U.S. Open.

Born in Texas and raised in a house lacking electricity and running water, Trevino dropped out of school in the eighth grade. He was a groundskeeper on a par-3 course and then served in the Marine Corps. He went back to his old golf course job after his stint in the Marines, where he had augmented his income by hustling games, playing with wrong-handed clubs or occasionally with a taped Dr. Pepper bottle, hitting the ball with the fat end and using the bottle as a pool cue for putts.

Lee's behavior on the greens was unorthodox. He laughed, joked, talked with the crowd and gyrated and contorted himself into impossible positions with an electrifying exuberance which thrilled the spectators, who generally were used to golfers who exhibited all the animation of robotized manikins. The TV producers loved Trevino's antics also. Like Palmer, Trevino was known for casting all caution to the wind and charging a hole with aggressive shots that produced birdies.

Other fine golfers during the period were Dow Finsterwald, Julius Boros, Ken Venturi, and Billy Casper. But Palmer, Nicklaus, and Trevino were the big three—not only for the total of their earnings but also because they excited the spectators, and, for television, made a potentially dull game come alive for the television audience.

By the end of the sixties, golf, whose pastoral quietness provided an oasis of solitude in an increasingly frenzied society, was coming in for much criticism. Critics complained that golf was still a segregated sport and that the closest minority type person that could be found in the pro golf ranks was Lee Trevino, a Mexican-American. Charlie Sifford and Lee Elder were the only black golfers to compete successfully on the tour. Sifford was the first black to join the PGA tour, winning his first tournament in 1957. Others said that golf was becoming too expensive and was taking much-needed land away from public and private use. Others indicated that the sport was simply too costly. Indeed, inflation had raised the cost of golf course maintenance over 50 percent in the decade. Increases in the minimum wage had raised labor costs while the tax reform act of 1969 taxed nonmembers' income, and local property taxes which now assessed the clubs' property not on "recreation use" but on "best land use" meant astronomical increases in property taxes—up to 800 percent in the decade for some clubs. Thus a club member might have to pay close to $2,000 per year to enjoy golf privileges at a more exclusive course.

Also during the sixties, the caddy became virtually extinct, being replaced by the electric or gas golf cart. (Young men could make more money at other jobs.) This meant that the exercise value of golf was drastically diminished, thus leaving it open to legitimate criticism from promoters of tennis, jogging, and racketball. These forces appealed to golfers and would-be golfers to join their devotees since their sports improved the cardio-respiratory system while golf did not.

The Olympics

In 1960, an Olympic year, the United States provided a surprise upset in the summer Olympics, while the United States track-and-field team found itself the victim of upsets in the summer Olympics in Rome.

In the winter Olympics at Squaw Valley, California, Carol Heiss won the women's figure skating title. Her victory was particularly poignant because Carol had promised her mother shortly before she died that she would win the Olympic title before she turned professional.

The United States also won the men's gold figure-skating medal when David Jenkins, younger brother of the 1956 winner Hayes Alan Jenkins, put on a flawless free-skating exhibition that earned him at least one perfect 6.0 score from the judges.

But it was the hockey team which garnered most of the headlines. After winning its first four games, the United States edged Canada 2-1, accomplishing a feat that no United States hockey team had been able to do in forty years of Olympic competition. They then went on to upset the favored Russian team 3-2 before a national television audience.

In the final game, the United States faced a powerful Czech team and found themselves trailing at the end of two periods by a 4-3 score. While in the locker room resting for the final period, who should appear but the captain of the Russian hockey team Nikola Sologubov, who indicated by sign language that the Americans should inhale oxygen. Most of the United States players followed the Russian's suggestion, and they went on to crush the Czechs 9-4. Some observers thought the Russian's aid was the epitome of sportsmanship, while the more cynical noted that it was better for the Russians to have the United States win the gold medal than one of the Soviets' satellite countries.

The summer Olympics were held in Rome, where some $52 million worth of new facilities had been built. The United States supposedly was entering its best track-and-field team ever assembled, and most knowledgeable observers felt that the group would surpass the 1956 team's record total of fifteen gold medals. Included in the glittering array of track talent were: (1) John Thomas, who had high jumped 7 feet thirty-seven times; (2) Ray Norton, world record holder in the 100- and 200-meter dashes and unbeaten in two years; (3) Ralph Boston, who two weeks before the Olympics had broken Jesse Owens' long jump record; (4) Don Bragg, world record holder in the pole vault; (5) three excellent shot-putters in Dallas Long, Parry O'Brien, and Bill Nieder; and (6) Harold Connolly, world champion hammer-thrower.

Most of the American track favorites faltered. No one was more disappointed in his performance than Ray Norton. He finished sixth in both dashes—Armin Hary of Germany took the 100-meter dash (the first time since 1928 that the event had not been won by an American) and Livio Berruti drove the home fans wild by capturing the 200-meter dash. To add to his disappointments, Norton, while anchoring the 400-meter relay, took the handoff outside the exchange zone and the United States team was disqualified. In the high jump, John Thomas finished third, beaten by two Russians, one who had never jumped 7 feet before. Harold Connolly never made it to the hammer throw finals.

On the brighter side, Ralph Boston won the long jump while three 1956 champions repeated as champions. These included Al Oerter in the discus, Lee Calhoun in the 110-meter hurdles and Glenn Davis in the 400-meter hurdles. Also Mike Otis Davis, a twenty-five-year-old who had run track only for three or four years, was a surprising winner in the 400-meter run in world record time, and Don Bragg set a world record in the pole vault at 15 feet, 5$\frac{1}{8}$ inches. Nieder won the gold in the shot put, and the 4x400-meter relay was won by the American team.

Perhaps the most dramatic track confrontation occurred between American Rafer Johnson and C. K. Yang of Taiwan, who had trained together at UCLA and were personal friends. Yang had beaten Johnson in the running and jumping events, while Johnson had scored heavily in the weight events going into the 1500-meter final. Yang needed to outrun Johnson by 10 seconds in the 1500-meter to capture the title. Placed together in the same heat, Johnson doggedly clung to

Yang throughout the race, remaining just a stride or two behind him. Yang eked out a 1.2-second victory in the race but it was not enough of a margin to beat Johnson for the decathlon gold medal. Johnson had made up for the disappointment of his second place finish in the 1956 Melbourne Olympics.

Many reasons were offered for the failure of the track-and-field team. The heavily favored Americans who were beaten not only did not finish first, but none finished even second. Some said it was bad food and bad quarters and too many pre-Olympic meets. One communist-oriented Italian newspaper, *Il Paese*, thought it was over-confidence. Commenting on the track results, it pontificated that "this is a lesson in modesty for Americans."

Women's track and field, never popular in the United States, was dominated by the Russians, led by the Press sisters, who grabbed six gold medals between them. United States women had their star in Wilma Rudolph, "la Gazelle" as she was called by the French, who triumphed in the 100- and 200-meter dashes and then anchored the 400-meter relay team to victory, becoming in the process the first American woman to capture three gold medals.

The basketball team, led by such college stars as Oscar Robertson and Jerry Lucas, breezed to victory, averaging 42-point victory margins.

The swimming teams, headed by Chris Van Salza's three gold medals for the woman and Jeff Farrell's two gold medals for the men, dominated their sport.

In both wrestling and boxing Americans captured three gold medals. Most impressive of the American boxers was the light heavy-weight champion, Cassius Clay, who would turn professional and fight under the name of Muhammad Ali.

The Olympics of 1960 revealed that although Americans garnered their share of medals, competition was becoming more intense and the American monopoly was rapidly crumbling. In men's track and field, Americans had won nine out of twenty-four events, with Russia trailing with five gold medals. In addition, the Russians demonstrated strength in such events as weight lifting, gymnastics, wrestling, canoeing, cycling, riding, and fencing for a total of forty-three gold medals to thirty-four for the United States. As in the winter games when the Russians dominated such sports as speed skating, the Russian team had a "gold strike."

Although no national records are officially kept, many observers were wondering, judging from the Olympic results, whether or not America was physically weaker both in terms of the physical health and fitness of its citizens and its ability to defend the free world. The

1960 games helped to promote the emphasis on physical fitness, a major public program of the Kennedy administration. With the U-2 spy plane incident and the Cuban missile crisis, two events that dramatically increased cold war tensions, the Olympics began to assume a national importance as a test of American physical strength and preparedness.

Olympics 1964

The Olympics held in Tokyo in 1964 were the largest held to that day—5,541 athletes from ninety-four nations gathered to compete in twenty sports. The Tokyo Olympics saw a resurgence of American track-and-field supremacy. The men's team gained twelve gold medals and the Russians only two. But the story of the games was the triumph of Americans in two distance events, the 5,000- and 10,000-meter runs. (Peter Snell of New Zealand became the first man to win both the 800- and 1500-meter, two events the United States had previously dominated.) The victors were Bob Schul in the 5,000-meter and Billy Mills in the 10,000. Most American track and field strength was in the field events and the shorter races, and no American had ever won the 10,000-meter run. As one writer said, "to cover any distance greater than 1500 meters, the feeling was, Americans took cars."

Mills's story was the stuff that movies are made of. Part Sioux, born on a reservation in South Dakota, Mills at the time was a twenty-six-year-old marine who had never beaten his teammate Gerry Lindgren let alone come close to the time of Ron Clarke, the world record holder in the event. In the final stretch run, Mills was in a three-man race with Clarke and Mohamed Gammoudi of Tunisia. Mills, who could run a 23.8 in the 200-meter, put on the speed and passed both Clarke and Gammoudi for the victory. Clarke could only say after the race, "I burn off all the regular distance runners and what am I left with? An Ethiopian, a Tunisian, and a half-Sioux Indian."

Mills's victory was no fluke. He had earned his gold medal, running the distance in an Olympic record time of 28:24:44. He had run 45 seconds faster than he had raced previously, and the Russian and Czechoslovakian domination of this distance was ended.

Schul's victory was not nearly as dramatic since he had set a world 2-mile record two months previously. Yet no American had ever won the Olympic event either. Schul outsped Michel Jazy of France and Harold Norpoth of Germany for the victory. Even more surprising was that Bill Dellinger of the United States finished third. The medal victories of Mills, Schul, and Dellinger seemed to indicate that Americans were symbolically at least becoming more physically fit.

In the other track events, "Bullet" Bob Hayes, known as the "world's fastest human," captured the 100-meter and anchored the 400-meter relay to victory, making up a 3-meter deficit and running his leg in 8.6. Henry Carr in the 200, Mike Larrabee in the 400-meter, Hayes Jones in the 110-meter hurdles, Rex Cawley in the 400-meter hurdles, Al Oerter in the discus (third in a row, despite torn rib cartilage), Fred Hansen in the pole vault, Dallas Long in the shot-put, and the 1600-meter relay teams also claimed gold medals.

As usual, the American basketball team led by Lucius Jackson and Bill Bradley, captured the gold medal, beating the Russians for the gold 73-58.

In women's track and field, American women took only two gold medals—Wyomia Tyus in the 100-meter and Edith McGuire in the 200-meter dashes. The Russian women dominated, led once more by the formidable Press sisters.

American swimmers were more overwhelming than ever before, capturing sixteen gold medals in twenty-two events. No woman swimmer was older than nineteen while the oldest male swimmer was twenty-three. The star of the tanker squad was Don Schollander, who would be freshman at Yale in the summer. He captured the 100-meter freestyle in an Olympic record time of 53.4, the 400-meter freestyle in a world record time, and then anchored the 400- and 800-meter relay teams to world record triumphs. Schollander earned four gold medals, a precedent for Olympic swimming that would stand until Mark Spitz won seven gold medals in 1972.

The 1964 Winter Olympics at Innsbruck, Austria, was a fairly dismal affair. The United States Olympic figure skating team had been virtually wiped out by a tragic plane crash in 1961. Thus the figure skating team failed to win a gold medal for the first time since 1956. Lydia Skoblikova of the Soviet Union was the skating star, winning four titles in speed skating, the first speed skater to do so.

The American stars were a speed skater and two skiers. Terry McDermott, a barber from Essexville, Michigan, stunned the world when he recorded an Olympic record time in the 500-meter, going the distance in 40.1 seconds and besting two-time defending champion from Russia, Yevgini Grishin. In men's skiing, Billy Kidd and Jimmy Huega captured the silver and bronze medals.

Between the Tokyo Olympics of 1964 and the Mexico City Olympics of 1970, a new track star burst on the American track scene. For many years America had produced numerous world class milers, but no American had won the Olympic 1500-meter run since 1908 and there had been few world class milers in recent years. In the emergence of Jim Ryun, who in 1964 became the first high-school runner to race the mile in under 4 minutes, America had a genuine distance superstar. In 1966 Ryun established the world record for the mile in 3:51:3, and in 1967 he lowered it to 3:51:1. He would clearly be the favorite for the 1968 Olympics.

However, the 1968 Olympics held in Mexico City would go down as one of the most troubled and spectacular in Olympic history. In 1967 Harry Edwards, a militant black professor of sociology and anthropology at San Jose State College, began organizing an Olympic boycott of black American athletes. Reacting to what he regarded as "racism in American society" and the "exploitation of black athletes," Edwards stated that "I think the time is gone when the black man is going to run and jump when the white man says so and then come back home and run and jump some more to keep from being lynched."

Edwards' boycott effort was aided inadvertently when the IOC moved to reinstate South Africa, which had been barred from the 1964 Tokyo Olympics because of its racial policies. In response to this action, thirty-two African nations along with the Soviet Union threatened to boycott, and Edwards stated that he would increase his pressure on black American athletes to drop out.

Under such attacks, the IOC reversed itself, and then the Edwards' boycott movement began to run out of steam. He then stated that black American athletes would participate in the Olympics but not take part in "victory stand ceremonies or victory marches."

Mexican students began rioting against the government in protest over the gap between rich and poor in Mexico just weeks before the 1968 Olympic games were to begin. Five weeks before the opening of the games, open warfare broke out between a protesting crowd and Mexican soldiers and police. The result was 30 dead, 100 injured, and 300 jailed. The IOC president, Avery Brundage, talked with Mexican officials and decided to continue the games since he had been "assured" that "nothing would interfere with the peaceful entrance of the Olympic flame into the Stadium on October 12." The IOC's official attitude was, "If we stop the Games every time there is disorder in the world, there would never be games. At least there is one place in this troubled world free from politics, from religions, from racial prejudices."

For the American track athletes, the competition was highlighted by Bob Beamon's stunning long jump of 29 feet, 2½ inches (almost 2 feet further than the previous world record), the revolutionary high jumping style of Dick Fosbury, who pioneered the "Fosbury

Flop" whereby he went over the bar backwards, and the failure of Jim Ryun to win the 1500-meter run. However, the event that drew the most media attention came after two of the United States medal winners in the 200-meter—Tommie Smith, who captured the event in Olympic record time of 19.8 and John Carlos, the bronze medal winner—listened to the "Star Spangled Banner" being played while on the victory stand and stood with heads bowed, clad in black socks, giving black-gloved "Black Power" salutes.

Tommie Smith later said that "this was victory for black people everywhere." Carlos explained that he wanted to demonstrate that blacks were not "some kind of work horse," who "can perform and they can throw us some peanuts and say good boy, good boy." He continued: "When Tommie and I got on the stand, we knew we weren't alone. We knew that everyone at home who was watching was up on that stand with us. We wanted to let the world know about the problems of black people and we did our thing and stepped down. We believe we were right. We'd do it again tomorrow." Under pressure from the IOC Carlos and Smith were suspended from the U.S. team and expelled from the Olympic village.

Reaction by American team members was split. Lee Evans, Larry James, and Ron Freeman—who went 1-2-3 in the 400-meter run—wore black berets at the victory ceremony, which they removed when the national anthem was played. When Evans was later asked the significance of the berets, he stated that "it was raining and we didn't want to get wet."

On the other hand, George Foreman, a former Job Corps employee who captured the heavyweight boxing crown, walked around the ring holding a small American flag after his final bout. Foreman said he wasn't making a "demonstration" and that he was just "proud to be an American." After these incidents the rest of the Olympic action occurred in the arenas and playing fields.

The Olympic track events were run for the first time on synthetic turf and in a thinner atmosphere than ever before. Many feared that the high altitude of Mexico City would create major health problems. But although there were some who collapsed after their events, there were no serious injuries.

On the track Jim Ryun, troubled by a number of minor ailments during 1968, could not live up to the favorite's billing. He failed to qualify in the 880 and finished second to Kip Keino of Kenya in the 1500-meters. The men's track-and-field team still managed twelve gold medals. Besides the victories of Beamon, Fosbury, Evans, and Smith, Bill Toomey took the decathlon, Randy Matson the shot-put, Bob Seagren the pole vault, Al Oerter the discus (his fourth), Willie Davenport the 110-meter hurdles, and Jim Hines the 100-meter, clocked in a blazing 9.9 to record the fastest time ever. The relay teams also won gold medals.

Wyomia Tyus led the American women's track effort with a 11.0 victory in the 100-meter dash and anchored the 400-meter relay win. Madeline Manning won the 800-meter run to account for the other women's gold medal.

In swimming, Mark Spitz was expected to be the heavy gold gatherer for the men's tanker squad, but although he received gold medals in the freestyle relay race he finished second and eighth in his individual events, the 100- and 200-meter butterfly.

The star of the women's swimming team was Debbie Meyer, who won three individual events—the first swimmer to do that. Four other women swimmers won two gold medals. Ironically, none of the gold medal winners would be a member of the 1972 team. Swimming had become a young person's sport.

The American basketball team, even without Kareem Abdul-Jabbar (formerly Lew Alcindor) who had passed up the Olympics, were led to another gold medal by two future pro stars, Spencer Haywood and JoJo White. The United States also received gold medals in boxing and yachting.

The winter Olympics at Innsbruck and Grenoble saw skier Jean-Claude Killy become the star with four skiing medals. America's one gold medal was captured by the so-called ice princess, Peggy Fleming. Her performance was highlighted by a 5.9 mark in the free style.

The Olympics in 1968 clearly demonstrated that despite Brundage's claims to the contrary, the Olympics and the sports world could not continue in a vacuum. The problems of the world were the problems of the sports world also. By the end of the decade the battle for Olympic medals had become a cold war struggle. During the sixties the Olympics became more political and controversial than anyone could have imagined, and the games were becoming increasingly more commercialized as sponsors sought to use athletes to display their sporting gear or endorse their products. The issue of professional-amateur status intensified as the Soviet Union provided its athletes with jobs, housing, and subsidies so that they could devote full time to preparation and competition. The 1968 games clearly indicated that American black athletes could show their independence and radicalization, even if it was a symbolic gesture. With the riots in the inner cities, the civil rights push, the militant black leadership and Black Power movement, black people clearly signalled that they would claim their rights and speak for themselves. The sixties saw the increasing maturity of black athletes as they came to the forefront in certain sports and changed the racial composition of sports in a dramatic way. Sports in the sixties were in turmoil and change, and they provided a focus for shifts and changes that could only be accelerated in the next decade.

Boxing

The story of boxing in the sixties revolves around the battles of the heavyweights as three black boxers dominated this sport: Floyd Patterson, Sonny Liston, and Cassius Clay/Muhammad Ali.

The decade began with Ingemar Johansson, a likeable and hard-punching Swede, as the world heavyweight champion. Johansson had won an unexpected third-round knockout from Patterson in June 1959, becoming the first foreigner to hold the title since Primo Carnera of Italy, who briefly held it in 1933–34. An all-around athlete who was also a soccer player and speed skater, Johansson floored Patterson seven times in the third and final round with a powerful straight right punch. The decisive win was unexpected because Johansson's European fighting record looked unimpressive and he had fought only twenty-one times in six years as a professional. Patterson had been the youngest boxer to win the heavyweight crown. He was only twenty-one in 1956 when he knocked out Archie Moore to succeed the retired Rocky Marciano. However, the Johansson win in 1959 was described by one AP correspondent as "pure destruction" and a "slaughter."

Two Johansson-Patterson fights followed in 1960 and 1961. In the 1960 rematch Patterson knocked out his Swedish opponent in the fifth round with a left hook that left Johansson unconscious for several minutes. Patterson became the first former heavyweight champion to regain the title, and in the 1961 bout Patterson knocked out Johansson in the sixth round, even though the "Sockin' Swede" had floored Patterson twice in the first round.

Patterson was a quiet, modest champion who was admired for his discipline, determination, and hard training. He had patiently endured racial slurs, threats, and harassment in Scarsdale, New York, but he was readily accepted by the Kennedys, high-ranking NAACP officials, and Dr. Ralph Bunche. He had rehabilitated his life after a boyhood of truancy and minor scrapes with the law. Like many black athletes he learned to suppress and control his rage against white racism, unleashing his pent-up anger in the ring in the controlled fury

FOOTBALL

The Evolution
of the Game

In 1880 Walter Camp, the "Father of College Football," and Yale University convinced the Intercollegiate Association to limit teams to eleven men. In 1882 Yale and Camp again were able to convince the Intercollegiate Football Association to adopt a set of downs. If a team gained five yards in three plays it was allowed to retain possession of the ball. Equipment was minimal and oftentimes the teams were attired only in stockings, knee pants, jerseys, and caps. In this picture, a nattily attired Michigan Agricultural College 1884 team poses for a picture. This team was undefeated and unscored upon. It also played no outside opponents. (Michigan State University Archives and Historical Collections)

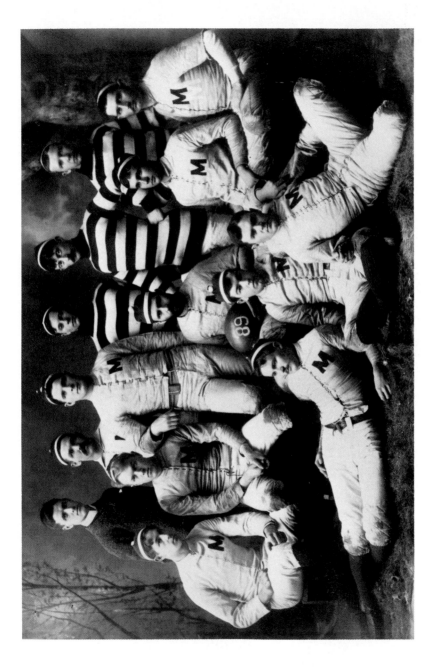

As the years passed, attempts were made to provide some rudimentary protection for players. Padded vests and pants served this purpose. However, the only protection for the head remained a full head of hair. The 1889 University of Michigan team picture clearly demonstrates this mode of dress. (Michigan Historical Collections, Bentley Historical Library, University of Michigan)

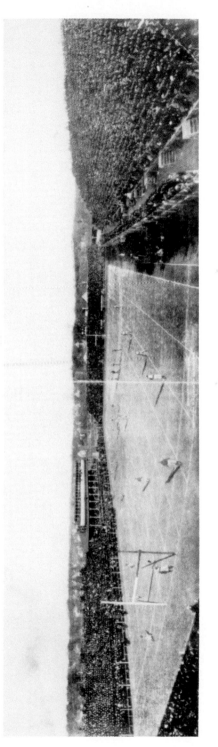

In the early 1900s the football field took on a "gridiron appearance" when 5-yard lines parallel to the sidelines were added in order to aid officials in the enforcement of forward pass rules. According to the current rules, the ball could only be passed forward in a 5-yard zone. In this picture, a kickoff at the Wisconsin-Michigan football game in Ann Arbor on November 18, 1905, this "gridiron appearance" can be discerned. In 1910 the longitudinal lines were omitted because the rules were changed; the pass now could be thrown beyond the 5-yard line zone but had to be passed from 5 yards back of the neutral zone. (Michigan Historical Collections, Bentley Historical Library, University of Michigan)

In the early days of collegiate football, ground plays and mass plays, such as the flying wedge, dominated the game. Innovative and intrepid players such as Yale's legendary Pudge Heffelfinger devised ways to circumvent the offensive tactics. (Pudge would leap at the wedge feet first.) After the Princeton-Yale contest of 1888, the New Haven *Union* reported: "In less than 15 minutes their jackets were frescoed with blood. . . . It was a wonder the players to a man did not have to retire and go home with their bones done up in splints." In 1905 18 boys were killed and 154 drastically injured. Responding to the brutality and violence, President Roosevelt threatened to abolish the game until changes were made. In

1906 the National Collegiate Athletic Association was formed to govern college sports. In the first photo an unidentified but early University of Michigan team demonstrates the compact formation characteristic of early collegiate football. In the second photo, the Minnesota crossbuck play in a 1902 University of Michigan–University of Minnesota contest clearly demonstrates the type of power football that was popular at the time. (University of Michigan Historical Collections, Bentley Historical Library, University of Michigan.)

In the first bowl game, the Tournament of Roses, played in 1902, the University of Michigan trounced Stanford University 49-0. Probably few of those who viewed that contest thought that the annual game between a west coast university and one from the East, Midwest, or South would grow to an extravaganza complete with a three-hour parade and an excess of 100,000 spectators and would be emulated by scores of other communities sponsoring lesser bowls. Yet the Rose Bowl, the so-called granddaddy of them all, still retains a special aura since it was the first bowl. (University of Michigan Historical Collections, Bentley Historical Library, University of Michigan)

In 1909 the flying tackle was still legal, and in that year there were 33 deaths and 246 major injuries resulting from football play. In this 1909 photo the University of Michigan punts from its goal line as Pennsylvania defenders hurl themselves in desperate but vain attempts to block it. (Michigan Historical Collections, Bentley Historical Library, University of Michigan)

In 1934 the passer still had to be 5 yards behind the line of scrimmage, but three changes were made to promote the use of the passing game. First, an incomplete pass in the end zone on first down would not be a turnover. Secondly, the ball was reduced in size, making it easier to grip and throw. Thirdly, the 5-yard penalty for more than one incomplete

pass in the same series of downs was eliminated. These two pictures of unidentified Michigan Agricultural College games of the late 1930s indicate how the aerial dimension had opened up the game. Note the depth of the passer since he had to be 5 yards behind the line of scrimmage. (Michigan State University Archives and Historical Collections)

One of the great college running backs of all times graced the gridiron in the late 1930s. Tom Harmon, "Ole 98," was a genuine triple threat at the University of Michigan during the 1938 to 1940 seasons. As a runner he rushed for 2,338 yards, completed 101 passes (233 attempts), good for 16 touchdowns. His total scoring included 33 TDs, 33 PATs and 2 FGs. He broke the Big Ten records of Red Grange and won the 1940 Heisman trophy. Alonzo Stagg once said, "I'll take Harmon on my team and you can have all the rest." In this photo, Harmon demonstrates his nimble feet and running style, as he follows his blocking to avoid the oncoming defenders. (Courtesy of the University of Michigan Sports Information Department)

In the post-World War II period thousands of ex-GIs thronged to colleges and universities to take advantage of the GI Bill. Many schools were able to use their athletic programs, particularly their football teams, as a means to increase their enrollments and achieve university status. Probably no institution utilized this avenue to success better than Michigan State College, which fielded great teams under coaches Biggie Munn and "Duffy" Daugherty in the postwar era, and subsequently achieved university status and was accepted into the Big Ten conference.

One of the early stars for Munn was Lynn Chandnois, a 6-foot 2-inch, 195-pound running back who rushed for 2,043 yards during his career (1946–49). He also was a stellar defensive back, intercepting 20 passes during his college career. In this picture, Chandnois eludes a tackler in a game against Michigan. (Michigan State University Archives and Historical Collections)

Don Coleman, number 78, was a great two-way player for Biggie Munn's powerhouses at Michigan State College in the early fifties. In this picture Don leads the interference. On defense, he often went up against opponents outweighing him by 50 to 60 pounds, but he was able to use his quickness and agility to bypass them and get at the quarterback or the runner. (Michigan State University Archives and Historical Collections)

Today, there are few three-sport athletes since sports has become so specialized. Ron Kramer, All American at the University of Michigan in 1955 and 1956, not only was an outstanding football player (54 pass receptions, 888 yards for 8 TDs, and 42 PATs), but also played basketball, threw the shot and discus, and high jumped. He later would play as a professional for the outstanding Green Bay teams under Vince Lombardi and would make his position, tight end, a significant addition to the offense in the modern pro game. (Courtesy University of Michigan Sports Information Department)

The 1965 and 1966 Michigan State University football teams were two of the most powerful teams ever to hit the college gridiron, featuring many players of All-American caliber both on offense and defense. Such defensive stars as Bubba Smith, George Webster, Bob Viney, and Charley "Mad Dog" Thornhill stopped offenses cold, often leaving opponents with negative yardage. On offense, running backs Clint Jones and Bob Apisa performed "Mr. Outside" and "Mr. Inside" duties while wide receiver Gene Washington was a constant deep threat. In 1965 the Spartans were Big Ten and national champions but had their season blemished by a Rose Bowl defeat to UCLA, a team they had beaten during the regular season. In 1966 the Spartans went undefeated except for a 10-10 tie with Notre Dame which cost them the "national championship." (Michigan State University Archives and Historical Collections)

In 1966, the so-called game of the century was played between Michigan State University and Notre Dame at East Lansing, Michigan. Both universities featured outstanding squads. Some 80,011 were on hand and an estimated 33 million viewed the contest on television. The ultimate result was a 10-10 tie. Notre Dame ran out the clock to preserve a tie, disdaining a chance for victory out of fear that an errant pass might be picked off and result in a Spartan victory. In the photo, reserve fullback Regis Cavender scores for the Spartans despite the desperate efforts of Irish defenders. (Michigan State University Archives and Historical Collections)

During the 1970s, the Big Ten conference became dominated by the University of Michigan and Ohio State University. One of the surprising defeats of the conference co-favorites came unexpectedly in 1974 at East Lansing when the Michigan State Spartan Levi Jackson on a routine dive play scampered for a long touchdown run with less than 4 minutes left in the game. Note that in the picture, Spartan players and coaches are on the field, which should have caused the play to be called back. Tension was high enough, however, at the end of the game, as Ohio State scored at the end of the game and it was not clear whether or not the score counted. The referees had disappeared, and most of the crowd waited tensely for more than a half hour until word came that Michigan State had indeed pulled the upset. (Michigan State University Archives and Historical Collections)

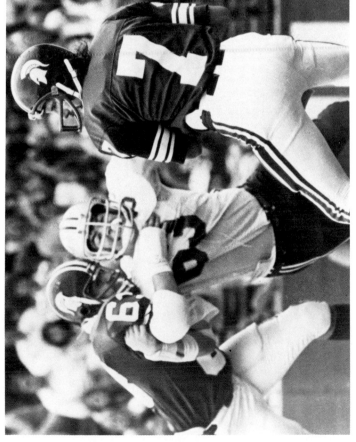

In 1978 Michigan State broke up the Ohio State–University of Michigan domination of the Big Ten conference by tying for the Big Ten crown. The Spartans' key to victory was the pinpoint passing of Eddie Smith (above) shown here coolly looking downfield. His number one target was fleet-footed split end Kirk Gibson (right) who was strong enough to run over linebackers and swift enough to outleg defensive backs to the end zones. (Michigan State University Archives and Historical Collections)

In the early days of collegiate football, bleachers were often on only one side of the field and onlookers ringed the rest of the field. Horses and buggies of citizens perhaps out for a drive clustered nearby to catch a glimpse of the gridiron action, as in this picture of the first Rose Bowl game between the University of Michigan and Stanford. (Michigan Historical Collections, Bentley Historical Library, University of Michigan)

Today the University of Michigan boasts the largest stadium for collegiate football in the nation, with the capacity to seat 101,701. Generally the stadium is sold out. At $10 to $12 per ticket, football Saturdays in Ann Arbor are a million dollar venture and provide revenue for other sports activities. At Michigan and other Big Ten and Big Eight school's, the football Saturday has become a major entertainment spectacle which encompasses tailgate lunches, alumni get-togethers, and long rides in campers and FVs as die-hard fans congregate on the campuses. (Sports Information Department, University of Michigan, Ann Arbor, Michigan)

Expense Accounting Allegheny Athletic Assoc.
Football Club

Game of Oct. 29, 1892 — AAA vs. Washington, D.C.
balance carried over (account) $432.20
guarantee's gross profit (check) $258.00
team traveling expenses (cash) $221.85
net profit $ 36.15
total balance $468.35

Game of Nov. 12, 1892 — AAA vs. Pittsburg A.C.
balance carried over (account) $468.35
game receipts gross profit (cash) $1,683.50
visitors guarantee expense (check) $ 428.00
park rental expense (check) $ 50.00
Donnelly, Malley, Heffelfinger expense (cash) $ 75.00
Schlosser hotel bill for above (check) $ 9.00
game performance bonus to
W. Heffelfinger for playing (cash) $ 500.00
total expenses $1,062.00
net profit $ 621.00
total balance $1,089.85

Game of Nov. 19, 1892 — AAA vs. W.J. College
balance carried over (account) $1,089.85
game receipts gross profit (cash) $ 746.00
visitors guarantee expense (check) $ 238.00
park rental expense (check) $ 50.00
payment to Donnelly for playing (cash) $ 250.00
total expenses $ 538.00
net profit $ 208.00
total balance $1,297.00
This above accounting is hereby certified as
correct by the below signed team manager:
O.D.Thompson.

Traditionally, John Brallier has been considered to be the first professional football player, having received $10.00 to play quarterback for Latrobe, Pennsylvania, against Jeanette. This document displayed at the Pro Football Hall of Fame in Canton, Ohio, reveals that W. ''Pudge'' Heffelfinger received the princely sum of $500 to come from Chicago to play for the Allegheny Athletic Association against the Pittsburgh Athletic Club. In the game, Heffelfinger smashed the ball carrier for the P.A.C., grabbed the football from him, and went 25 yards for the only score of the game. (Pro Football Hall of Fame, Canton, Ohio)

Jim Thorpe, the famous American Indian who helped make Carlisle Indian school a feared college power, was called by the king of Sweden ''the greatest athlete in the world.'' In 1950, Thorpe was voted the greatest football player of the first half of the century in an AP poll. He joined the Canton team in 1915, helping to revive pro football in that town (which had been discontinued almost ten years earlier because of scandal). Other college stars followed him into pro football. In 1920 he was elected president of the American Professional Football Association. (Pro Football Hall of Fame, Canton, Ohio)

George ''Pappa Bear'' Halas was an outstanding college player under the legendary Bob Zuppke at Illinois and later played professional football. Best known for his coaching of the Chicago Bears, his signing of Red Grange in 1925 helped revitalize pro football in the 1920s. He helped create a defensive tradition so that the Chicago team in the thirties was known as the ''Monsters of the Midway.'' The Bears defeated the Washington Redskins in 1940 by a 73-10 score, the largest single game score in league history. Only seven of his many teams finished below .500 (Pro Football Hall of Fame, Canton, Ohio)

Bronislaw ''Bronko'' Nagurski was one of the premier power running backs of all time, and played pro football with the Chicago Bears from 1930 to 1937. He was lured out of retirement to play in 1943. The Bears captured NFL titles in 1932, 1933, and 1943. Strong and punishing as a runner, he often steamrolled over would-be tacklers, leaving them crumpled on the ground as he triumphantly crossed the goal line. George Halas said, ''He's the only man I've ever seen who runs his own interference.'' (Pro Football Hall of Fame, Canton, Ohio)

In 1933, professional football opened up the passing game by making the forward pass legal from anywhere behind the line of scrimmage instead of 5 yards back. Don Hutson, the "Alabama Antelope" as he was known at Alabama where he played as a receiver from 1932 to 1934, became an even more noteworthy pass catcher in the pros. From 1935 to 1945 he starred first with Arnie Herber as the quarterback and then later with Cecil Isbell, who became the Packer flinger. With the legendary Johnny "Blood" (real name, McNally) flanked on one side, the early Packers with their passing attack set a precedent for the wide-open passing attacks of the sixties. Hutson was nine times All Pro.(Pro Football Hall of Fame, Canton, Ohio)

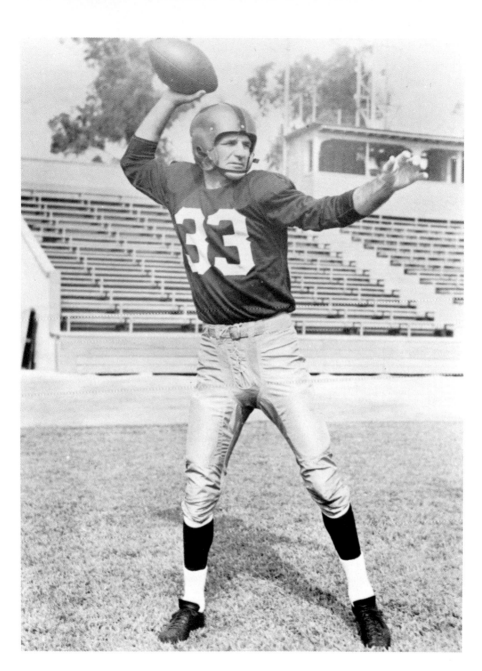

If one had to decide upon the quarterback who played the greatest role in modernizing the game, undoubtedly most votes would be cast for ''Slingin'' Sammy Baugh. A former All American at TCU, Baugh played for the Washington Redskins from 1937 to 1952. Six times he led (or shared the lead) in passing for the NFL. From 1940 to 1943 he also led the NFL in punting. In 1943 he shone as a defensive star, leading the NFL in interceptions with 11. Under his leadership the Redskins won five division championships and two NFL championships while Baugh was All Pro three times. (Pro Football Hall of Fame, Canton, Ohio)

Blacks had not been a part of the NFL since the 1920s. In 1945 the Los Angeles Rams broke the color barrier when they signed Kenny Washington and Woody Strode. In 1945 Marion Motley was the first black to be signed in the All American conference. Motley starred for the Cleveland Browns in both the AAFC and the NFL, winning rushing titles in both leagues. The Browns pioneered the ''Motley trap,'' which he ran with a blend of power and a sprinter's speed. Paul Brown first noticed Motley at the Great Lakes Naval Training Station during the war. In his professional career Motley averaged 5.7 yards per carry and scored 234 points in nine years. In 1968 he was enshrined in the Pro Football Hall of Fame, the second black player (Emlen Tunnell was the first) to be so honored. (Pro Football Hall of Fame, Canton, Ohio)

Joe "the Jet" Perry played for fourteen seasons with San Francisco and is considered to be one of the best running backs ever to perform in professional football. A track star in high school, he attended Compton Junior College and attracted pro scouts while playing for Alameda Naval Air Station. During his pro career Perry accumulated 9,723 yards for a 5.0 average rush and scored 71 touchdowns. Joe won the NFL rushing title in 1953 and 1954 and became the first runner to gain 1,000 yards in two consecutive seasons. (Pro Football Hall of Fame, Canton, Ohio)

Emlen Tunnell was the first black player signed by the New York Giants. He played for them from 1948 to 1958 and then with the Green Bay Packers from 1959 to 1961. He played in 158 consecutive games, a record at that time, and ranks as one of the great all-time safety men. Upon retirement, he held the NFL records for interceptions (79), interception yardage (1,281), punt returns (258) and punt return yardage (2,209). He was an All Pro four times. (Pro Football Hall of Fame, Canton, Ohio)

The premier player in the NFL from the late fifties to the early sixties was Jimmy Brown. From 1957 to 1961 Brown was the NFL's leading rusher. An All American at Syracuse, Brown was also a standout in track, lacrosse, and basketball. In nine seasons playing with the Cleveland Browns he rushed for 12,312 yards and set an individual game rushing record of 237 yards, which he accomplished twice. At 6 feet 2 inches and 228 pounds, Brown was the perfect blend of speed and power, which meant that he could outspeed defenders to the outside and overpower would-be tacklers on the inside. One writer has said about Brown: ''Nobody talks about Brown being 'another Marion Motley' anymore. Many think that not even Bronko Nagurski, Ernie Nevers, or Jim Thorpe can be compared to him. Brown literally outdistanced all his competitors and played in a class all by himself.'' The contributions of black stars such as Joe Perry, Emlen Tunnell, Marion Motley, Jimmy Brown and numerous others certainly provided a convincing testimony that the NFL had been avoiding an impressive pool of talent during its ''unofficial'' boycott days. (Pro Football Hall of Fame, Canton, Ohio)

Frank Gifford, All American quarterback at USC, was one of the last triple threats to play in the NFL before two platooning became the order of the day. He played for the Giants from 1952 to 1960 and 1962 to 1964. Gifford appeared in eight Pro Bowls and in five NFL championship games. When he retired he held Giant records for scoring points and TDs and gained more yards catching passes and caught more passes than any other Giant. He also kicked 10 PATs and 2 FGs. Gifford has for years been part of the ABC broadcast team on Monday night football. (Pro Football Hall of Fame, Canton, Ohio)

Many consider the 1958 NFL playoff game between the Baltimore Colts and the New York Giants, won by the Colts in overtime, as the game which popularized pro football, made it a Sunday afternoon ritual, and propelled it into the most popular professional sport of the sixties and seventies. Of all the heroes of the Colts, none stood out more than their quarterback, Johnny Unitas. His gridiron success was an American Horatio Alger story. Turned down by Notre Dame because he was too small, he attended the University of Louisville, where he grew two inches and added forty pounds. Upon graduation in 1955 he was drafted and cut by the Pittsburgh Steelers. After playing semi-pro ball, he was picked up by the Baltimore Colts. Known for his coolness and leadership, Unitas was at his best in the 1958 title game. He drove the Colts from their own 14, trailing 20-17. They moved upfield and scored a field goal with seconds to go to tie it 20-all. In the overtime, Unitas engineered a drive of 80 yards in 13 plays with Alan ''the Horse'' Ameche covering the last yards for a 23-20 victory. He threw touchdown passes in 47 straight games, was AP's player of the decade for the sixties and in 1969 was named by the AP greatest quarterback ever in the NFL. (Pro Football Hall of Fame, Canton, Ohio)

The "Bald Eagle," Y. A. Yelberton Tittle, had the misfortune until the end of his career to play in the shadow of someone else. In college he threw for 2,576 yards but the publicity went to glamour boys Johnny Lujack (Notre Dame), Charlie Trippi (Georgia), and Charlie Conerly (Mississippi). Tittle played with the Baltimore Colts, San Francisco, and New York. At New York he led the team to three division titles but not to an NFL championship. He once threw for 7 touchdowns and 505 yards in one game. Tittle was All Pro three times. (Pro Football Hall of Fame, Canton, Ohio)

By the 1960s, seven-man lines had given way to the four-three defense. The key defender became the middle linebacker, who, by virtue of his position, needed to be a super athlete. He had to be big enough to stop rushes up the middle yet quick enough to diagnose the offensive plays. Generally he was well over 6 feet tall, weighing between 220 and 240 pounds. Joe Schmidt of the Detroit Lions, Sam Huff of the New York Giants, and Dick Butkus were some of the premier linebackers of the period. However, if winning denotes excellence, then an argument can be made that Ray Nitschke of the famed Green Bay Packer juggernaut of the sixties was the greatest of them all. He was named All First Year NFL Middle Linebacker and the All Pro Squad of the 1960s by Pro Football Hall of Fame. A fierce competitor, he was known as a ''hitter.'' (Pro Football Hall of Fame, Canton, Ohio)

With three men playing in the backfield, increased pressure was felt by the four down line-men. Such gargantuan players as 6 foot 6 inch, 285 pound Eugene "Big Daddy" Lipscomb of the Colts; Ernie Ladd, 6 feet 9 inches and 311 pounds and Buck Buchanan, 6 feet 7 inches and 275 pounds, of the Kansas City Chiefs; and Roger Brown, 6 feet 5 inches and 300 pounds were just some of the "mobile, agile, and hostile" giants who roamed the defensive perime-ter. Identification of the down four as a unit with their own trademark became a characteristic of winning teams in the sixties. Setting a precedent in this area was the Los Angeles Rams' awesome "Fearsome Foursome," composed of Roosevelt Grier (6 feet 5 inches, 290 pounds), Deacon Jones (6 feet 4 inches, 272 pounds), Lamar Lundy (6 feet 7 inches, 235 pounds), and Merlin Olsen (6 feet 5 inches, 270 pounds), perhaps the most devastating of these defensive units. In this picture, Deacon Jones leads his playmates to the prey. (Pro Football Hall of Fame, Canton, Ohio)

The Green Bay Packers were the success story of the early 1960s in pro football. Long dormant as a challenger for conference honors (they had last won their division in 1944) the ''Pack'' was resurrected by the legendary Vince Lombardi. Lombardi took charge as coach and general manager in 1959. In 1960, the ''Pack'' won the division title and then captured NFL championships in 1961, 1962, 1965, 1966, and 1967. The 1966 and 1967 teams also captured the first two Super Bowl games, winning decisively over Kansas City and Oakland. Lombardi's teams emphasized execution and hard hitting. He was a strict taskmaster who supposedly adhered to a ''winning isn't everything—it's the only thing'' philosophy. (Pro Football Hall of Fame, Canton, Ohio)

Pro football is a dangerous game, and a career can end quickly and prematurely. Most vulnerable are the runners who must run with reckless abandon and stretch for the precious extra yardage. One of the greatest halfbacks ever to play in the NFL and to have a spectacular career ended by knee injuries was Gayle Sayers of Speed, Kansas. As a rookie with the Chicago Bears, Gayle streaked for 22 touchdowns, and in one game, scored 6 TDs. However, he injured his knees in 1968 and 1970. Sayers once held eight NFL and fifteen Chicago records. He was All NFL in 1965, 1966, 1967, 1968, and 1969. (Pro Football Hall of Fame, Canton, Ohio)

of boxing. Patterson was never completely accepted by the boxing public because of his enigmatic behavior, his failure to defend his crown against major opponents and contenders, and his sensitive, nice-guy side that did not seem to fit a heavyweight champion.

Patterson's downfall came at the hands of Sonny Liston, who during the fifties had compiled a respectable record with only one loss from 1953 to 1962. Liston had dynamite hands that measured 15¹⁄₂ inches and a reach that extended 84 inches. When he fought Patterson in September 1962, Liston was twenty-eight years old (some say older), and had spent two terms in prison. But Liston was honest and open about his past. His childhood had been difficult. Raised in Arkansas on a cotton farm, he was one of twenty-four children. Liston preferred to consort with known criminals, hoodlums, and low-life types. His values were those of the street—survival and tough behavior—and he developed the image of a menacing, mean, angry black who battled his way through the world with his fists and powerful body.

He dispatched Patterson in the first round of the 1962 bout, pounding his rival with two long left hooks that finished off the champion in 2:06. In losing, Patterson took home over a million dollars, while Liston gained $282,015. In the July 1963 rematch, the "Big Bear" ended Patterson's comeback hopes as Liston knocked out his opponent in the first round. Patterson could never come back from such a quick and devastating defeat, even though he would continue to fight.

Liston's scowling, powerful presence was finally challenged and broken by Cassius Clay in February 1964. After trying to quit the fight in the fifth round because he was partially blinded by sweat and resin, Clay was shouted back into the ring by Angelo Dundee, his trainer, and quickly pounded Liston into submission. The champion knew he was whipped and that Clay's fury and superior speed and punching power would only inflict more punishment. Claiming a shoulder injury, Liston refused to answer the bell for the seventh round, presenting a picture of dejection and submission as he sat on the stool and conceded the fight. Clay, who had recently taken the name Muhammad Ali, was jubilant. He had shown that he could jab, dance, and move so quickly and easily that Liston's flat-footed power punching was useless. Liston was demoralized.

In the 1965 rematch, fought in a high-school hockey rink with only 2,434 onlookers, Ali put Liston down in the first round with a punch that few saw. There was confusion over the count in the knockdown as well as the time of the knockdown, and Liston managed to gain his feet after being down for 22 seconds. The confused referee was ready to let the fight continue, but the timekeeper intervened, and Ali was declared the winner. In all the confusion many cried "fake" and "fix" over the alleged nonpunch and Liston's apparent willingness to remain down. Liston's brief career as champion was over. A new champion—colorful, controversial, and brash—had emerged to dominate boxing until he was stripped of his title in 1967 for refusing to accept induction into the army.

While the media had found Patterson and Liston difficult to know and fathom, Ali played up to the press and used them for his own purposes. Ali sensed that his verbal personality and his exhuberance were appealing to the press. Relying on a quick wit and his brash defiance of white expectations regarding a black champion, Ali quickly became controversial and therefore a hot item in the mid-sixties, a time of racial tensions and ghetto riots. Ali declared his independence of the white man's control with his emergence as a Black Muslim and Islamic believer, with his change of name, and with his refusal to accept the power of the government over his future. When Ali returned in 1964 from well-publicized visits with Gamal Abdal Nasser in Egypt and Kwame Nkrumah in Ghana, he said "I'm not no American, I'm a black man."

Ali knew the power of international publicity and fame, and his controversial reputation at home seemed to make him more popular in Europe. During 1965 and 1966 Ali had eight title bouts in defense of his crown, with two of the bouts fought in London, one in Frankfurt, Germany, and one in Toronto. At home Ali was subjected to almost daily criticism of his bragging and predictions of the round in which he would dispatch with his opponent. His response to a question about the Viet Cong ("The Viet Cong ain't done nothing to me and I ain't mad at them") was widely publicized and condemned as unpatriotic.

Few whites took seriously Ali's claims for draft deferment because he was a conscientious objector or a Black Muslim minister. Ali refused to step forward for induction, but many blacks had been drafted or enlisted to fight in Vietnam, and their casualty rate was quite high. With highly paid lawyers, Ali was in a position to fight his sentence for draft evasion with lengthy and complicated appeals and legal maneuverings. Many felt that his unwillingness to serve showed a "sissy" and unmanly side to a man who claimed to be "the greatest" and who could "whip anyone" for the right price. The press criticized Ali further because he was always surrounded by a phalanx of Black Muslim bodyguards, who took pleasure in muscling out reporters and looking with menace on those who sought to interview the champ.

Ali was, in fact, a man in search of his own identity, pulled one way by those who wanted to make him a champion that white fight fans could accept and the other way by a group of black militant activists, like Elijah Muhammad, who wanted Ali in their camp as they pursued their goals of black separatism with heated denunciations of the "evil whites." Ali enjoyed the mental, spiritual, and physical discipline of the Muslims because it fit his needs as a boxer in training and because it made him resist the temptations that any champion could succumb to: women, alcohol, and dissipation. Ali kept his religious beliefs quietly in the background, or at least tried to, but reporters and even other fighters (like Floyd Patterson in 1965) made an issue of it. When cornered and pressed on the question, Ali responded by lashing out and puffing up his own reputation. It was a defensive reaction of a proud and independent black man who was suspicious of whites as well as contemptuous of them, an attitude not unlike that of many blacks who lived in a racist and prejudiced society.

Ali had come a long way from the Olympic Gold medal in 1960 to the draft induction center in Houston in 1967, and he knew the serious consequences of his refusal. His simple, personal act was again his own way of declaring his independence in a symbolic way. The war in Vietnam did have racial implications, as black leaders like Dr. Martin Luther King, Jr., clearly perceived; morality and racial improvements were being undermined by the conflict. Ali had found an identity that transcended his commitment to his country. Accepting his race and color as his first identity, he used his position and visibility to defy the control that others, especially fight promoters and gamblers, sought over him. Bringing color, controversy, and notoriety to the fight game, he symbolized the emerging militant black spirit of the sixties that found its expression in the Black Power movement under Eldridge Cleaver, H. Rap Brown, and Stokely Carmichael; the Black Muslim movement with Elijah Muhammad and Malcolm X; and the more popular and commercialized "Black is Beautiful" movement symbolized by black magazines like *Ebony* and *Jet*. Ali was the focus of black individualism and militancy, and the press should have taken him more seriously and listened to what he was really telling them in his jive talk, impromptu poetry, and boasting. Under the "hyped" surface was a man coming of age and maturity, a man who spoke for the blacks' situation and condition in his own unusual and special way. Ali was, and still is, an incredibly complex person who loves the limelight and the sport of boxing. His verbal taunts and chastisements of his opponents in the ring during the fights, notably in the Patterson and Ernie Terrell fights, have been seen as displays of cruel arrogance and a violation of the code of boxers. But in another context, his humiliations of other fighters can be seen as the outbursts of a provoked man who insisted that his Muslim name was his new identity and that his convictions be taken seriously. Ali also knew that many hoped to see him fail, and this increased his determination to prove himself as well as escalated the level of his prefight boasting.

After being stripped of his title, Ali was out of boxing for three-and-a-half years. In 1968 Joe Frazier, who had won a gold medal in the 1964 Olympics, was declared the world champion in New York and five other states, Mexico, and South America after defeating Buster Mathis. The World Boxing Association recognized Jimmy Ellis as champion when he decisioned Jerry Quarry in the title fight of a tournament to decide Ali's successor.

In 1970 the title picture became less confused as Frazier knocked out Ellis in the fifth round to claim both versions of the title. In 1971 Ali, after winning a court decision that upheld his right to refuse induction, returned to the ring and met Frazier. The seventies would be dominated by dramatic fights involving Frazier, Ali, and George Foreman (all Olympic gold medal winners) as boxing became a multi-million dollar business. The 1971 Frazier-Ali fight was telecast to more than 300 million people who watched at closed-circuit television sites in forty-six countries, and total revenues were almost $20 million. Boxing would become an international, satellite-assisted media sport.

8

The 1970s: The Modern Era in Sports

The 1970s were a bifurcated decade. The first part of the period saw Americans still grappling with the impact of the Vietnam War. By 1970 many administration officials began to believe the war was a mistake. In December 1970, Congress repealed the Gulf of Tonkin Resolution. In 1971 a former employee of the Pentagon, Daniel Elsberg, released classified information which shed new light on the Vietnam involvement. Although the government attempted to prevent the *New York Times* and other newspapers from printing the so-called Pentagon Papers, it was unsuccessful. With more people convinced, after having read documents such as the Pentagon Papers, that the war was a mistake and needed to be terminated as quickly as possible, the administration gradually began moving on negotiations which would lead to United States withdrawal from Vietnam. In January 1973 an accord was signed by the governments of North and South Vietnam and the United States. U.S. military personnel were gradually withdrawn, and the long and costly war which had taken 57,000 American lives and physically wounded thousands more had ended.

The end of the war did not mean a return to normalcy. At home the presidency of Richard Nixon and his attempts to strengthen the executive office created a great deal of opposition to his administration. In fact, the release of information that Nixon had secretly bombed Cambodia and Laos for over a year without authorization or congressional knowledge galvanized the war protest movement in the streets as well as in the national assemblies. The administration was also haunted by the burglary of the office of the Democratic National Committee, specifically Chairman Lawrence O'Brien's office at the Watergate apartments in Washington on June 16, 1972. The burglars were detected by a night watchman who called police and apprehended the intruders. The five were really employed by the Committee to Reelect the President, headed by Jeb Magruder and then Attorney General John Mitchell.

The White House began a long strategy of suppression and cover-up as Nixon and his two chief lieutenants, H. R. Haldeman and John Erlichman, attempted to "keep the presidential lid on." However, pressure exerted by Watergate Trial Judge John Sirica forced confessions from several of the accused. Most damaging was the testimony of John Dean, who accused the president of complicity and prior knowledge of the break-in. When it was revealed by Alexander Butterfield, former deputy assistant to the president, that the president had taped and recorded all Oval Office conversations and phone calls, pressure was exerted to have access to the tapes. It took a full year from the time of this disclosure, July 24, 1974, for the Supreme Court to issue a ruling that Nixon would have to release the tapes. By this time Vice President Agnew had resigned because of income tax evasion and acceptance of bribes while governor of Maryland. Eventually the release of the so-called smoking gun conversation and the beginning of impeachment proceedings forced Nixon to resign on August 8, 1974.

Under Nixon, inflation had risen to 11 percent by 1974 and unemployment reached close to 6 percent. An oil shortage created by OPEC (an organization of countries that produced and exported oil) created a temporary oil shortage and made people concentrate on energy conservation.

Nixon was succeeded by Gerald Ford. Ford had been House minority leader and had been nominated by Nixon to replace Agnew. At first a popular man, Ford soon earned the disapproval of many when he pardoned the ex-president. He vetoed many bills to aid the unemployed as the recession of 1973–1974 continued. By 1976, the bicentennial year, there was new cause for hope as the economy recovered. By the end of the decade, however, the United States was mired in another recession even more severe than six years earlier. Oil prices had gone up 300 percent, and the Japanese were outselling the domestic automakers. At the same time inflation galloped to near 15 percent. Strict credit restrictions on consumer lending and a tight federal reserve policy brought inflation somewhat in check but at the cost of thousands of small businesses going bankrupt and with thousands out of work.

The seventies were a time of transition and a time of testing. Even the validity of its government and the strength of its constitutional system had been challenged. In addition, Soviet incursions in Afghanistan and the bungling of an aborted rescue attempt of United States embassy hostages held by Iranian militants led many to believe that America had lost its sense of purpose and its military strength. The mood of the country turned conservative.

At the beginning of the decade college students had taken to the streets for various causes. By the end of the decade they were concentrating on taking "practical courses" such as accounting so they could land good jobs and avoid the growing unemployment lines. They seemed more interested in a good time than in solving society's problems. Student volunteers for such programs as VISTA or the Peace Corps began to grow scarce. With the pressure of the military draft removed, a generation of males developed who never thought about selective service or patriotic duty.

The spirit of "look out for oneself" came to be the slogan of the athletes of the decade. This outlook was particularly true in terms of the professional athlete, who saw his salary escalate to unbelievable heights. For example, Nolan Ryan—who at the beginning of the decade saw his salary double from $12,000 to $24,000—was earning a million dollars a year by 1980, setting a new record for an individual player. But Ryan was not unusual. The average player in baseball in 1969 earned $25,000. By 1979 the average baseball salary was $121,000. In football the average in 1969 was $28,000. Ten years later it was $62,500. Basketball salaries increased even more astronomically, rising from an average of $43,000 in 1969 to $180,000 in 1979.

Yet as early as July 5, 1971, *U.S. News and World Report* could headline an article entitled "Pro Sports: A Business Boom in Trouble," indicating that although attendance was up in many sports, revenues were down. It pointed out that in baseball twelve of twenty-four teams lost money, and in basketball only three of twenty-eight franchises made money. But pro sports "boomed" instead of "busted" during the decade despite such failures as the World Football League and World Team Tennis. Although the development of free agency meant higher salaries, attendance rose and higher prices were charged for tickets. Financial backing for sports franchises was not difficult to find. Many wealthy pro sports enthusiasts eagerly sought an opportunity to be a part of the action—to share in the fallout from the media pyrotechnics associated with the pro sports world. Even if a team was not profitable, depreciation and other tax write-offs helped sustain the owners' total profit picture. Sports teams became part of business conglomerates or the playthings of multimillionaires who loved the publicity and power over athletes that ownership brought.

Even losses and profits in the sports business are difficult to define.

For example, in buying and selling a player's contract, the buying team can depreciate the player acquisition cost, while the selling team does not have to count money earned from the sale as income revenue. Despite public financial statements many times to the contrary, Roger C. Noll in a chapter entitled "The Team Sports Industry: An Introduction" from a Brookings Institute publication, *Government and the Sports Business* (1974), has found that almost all professional sports teams make money, and although they are not overwhelmingly profitable, "very few teams actually lose money."

Television continued to play an increasingly important role in the expansion of sports as big business. Early in the decade television seized on tennis as the sport of the seventies, and by 1973–74 the three networks were televising a total of 100 hours of tennis. Yet tennis began to suffer from overexposure. As one TV critic has stated, "Television embraced tennis for its upbeat audience and then almost destroyed the sport by sometimes programming live and taped events on the same day with the same players and falsely advertising big money 'winner take all' matches." By the end of the decade, NBC had cut down from a high of fifteen televised tennis matches to one, Wimbledon.

In its end-of-the-decade analysis of sports, the *New York Times* called television the "big daddy" of nearly all sports, not just tennis. In 1970 the networks televised 787 hours of sport. At the end of the decade sports telecasting hours totaled 1,356, an awesome 90 percent increase. So important was television money that CBS's $18 million contract with the National Basketball League was labeled by the *Times* as "survival" money.

"Trashsport," as some cynical critics called it, arrived on the scene during the decade. This new media concept featured competition among pro athletes for a "Super Stars" competition, media personalities in athletic competition for network athletic supremacy, or the exploitation of such obscure physical feats as cliff diving and arm wrestling. By the end of the decade the Public Broadcasting Service and cable television were providing sports alternatives to the commercial networks for television viewers. PBS, for example, was televising 100 hours of tennis, and the Madison Square Garden cable network was televising the French Open. Most interesting was the creation in the fall of 1979 of the Entertainment and Sports Programming Network (ESPN), a cable company which hoped to telecast, when fully developed, sports of various kinds twenty-four hours a day, enough to satisfy the craving of even the most avid sports junkie. Although cable TV was available to less than 50 percent of the population by 1979, a CBS spokesman stated that when the country was 50 percent cable connected, he believed that cable companies would be very competitive with the three major commercial networks and that "it'll be fascinating because then Madison Avenue will call the tune."

Those who found tennis was not the answer to physical fitness because the game, despite the designer clothes, was not easy to learn and "who really knew how to hit a topspin backhand anyway," turned to racquetball. Soon racquetball centers began dotting the landscapes, much as indoor tennis courts had at the beginning of the decade.

For many others, jogging became the "in" sport and jogger's knee replaced tennis elbow as the chic injury. A combination of the popularity of marathon runners such as Olympic champion (1972) Frank Shorter and Boston Marathon champ Bill Rodgers (three times) along with the influence of the "very substantial meditative movements" in the late sixties aided its popularity (in ten years, the number of runners in the New York Marathon increased from 126 to 11,533). Books about running proliferated on best seller lists, and journals devoted to running and jogging soon hit the newsstands.

Some gurus of running, such as George Sheehan, author of *Running and Being* (1978), reached metaphysical heights in describing the joys of running. He stated, "Like most distance runners, I am still a child. And never more so when I run. Like most children, I think I control my life. I believe myself to be independent. Like most children, I live in the best of all possible worlds, a world made from running and racing where nothing but good can happen." Others painted a darker picture of the running addict. Stanton Peele, a faculty member of Columbia University and author of *Love and Addiction* (1975), has stated the following: "Overall, I'd say that running can be more dangerous to physical well being than heroin. Assuming that the heroin user has sterilized needles and pure drugs and is on a good diet, I'd say that heroin would do a lot less physical damage to a drug addict than running does to a running addict."

For those who preferred something less strenuous, slow pitch softball proved to be equally addictive. Both women's and men's teams increased in number. So popular was the sport that in Detroit, where the famous Little Caesar's team became one of the original members of a pro softball league, investors were able to profit by creating Softball City, a commercial enterprise which provided softball diamonds for teams—for a fee, of course. The venture was an instant success.

The expansion of women's sports was perhaps the most revolutionary sports development during the decade. The sports explosion was fueled by such feminist sports advocates as tennis star Billie Jean King, who sees "competition . . . as the cornerstone of . . . society," and by the impact of Title IX of the Education Amendments of 1972, which provide that "no person in the United States shall, on the basis of sex, be excluded from participation . . . under any education program or activity receiving federal financial assistance."

Women turned to sports in increasing numbers. Despite the lamentations of athletic directors who insisted that RPS (Revenue Producing Sports) could not support women's programs, high schools and colleges struggled to provide better facilities. By the end of the decade 33 percent of all high school athletes were female, a 600 percent increase in ten years. For universities and the colleges the increase was 30 percent, an increase of 250 percent. In college tennis in 1970 there were only 231 teams affiliated with the Association of Intercollegiate Athletics for Women. By 1977 the number was 701, with 244 at the junior college level.

Women's pro sports also grew. In 1970 the Ladies' Professional Golf Association tour total prize money was $435,000. By the end of the decade it was $5.1 million. Similarly, the women's tennis purse grew. In 1970 purses totaled $200,500, while by 1980 it was in the vicinity of slightly over $9 million.

Women are now running marathons, and some of the top women runners could beat all but a handful of top male runners. Some doctors were suggesting that in Ultramarathons, women had an advantage because of their additional fat supply. In 1979, Lynn Lemaire, a twenty-eight-year-old woman and Harvard law student, participated in the Iron Man Triathlon, a 140.6-mile endurance contest of swimming, cycling, and running. The running event came last and consisted of a 26-mile race around the Hawaiian island of Oahu. Lynn finished fifth among twelve competitors.

Dr. K. F. Dyer, an Australian scientist, has shown that the differences between men's and women's records in track and field and in swimming have been drastically reduced since the 1950s. For example, the difference between the 800-meter record for men and women was reduced from 19.4 percent to 11.2 percent, while the 800-meter swimming record was slashed from 12.6 percent to 7.4 percent.

Women had proven during the decade that they could perform outstanding athletic feats, often to the chagrin and astonishment of some of the more "sedentary, unathletic, spectator-oriented men." As one critic has said about women's sports in the seventies, "the changes will affect not only the athletic system but society as well."

The politics of society certainly pervaded the sports world. The May 25, 1970, issue of *Sports Illustrated* reported that seventeen members of the Princeton varsity baseball squad distributed brochures seeking to clear up the "misunderstanding and perhaps indignation about what is occurring on the nation's college campuses today. We are interested in doing whatever we can do to dispel these confusions.''

At the same time it noted that a football player and navy veteran, 6-foot 3-inch Bill Pierson, refused to allow the lowering of the American flag during an antiwar demonstration at San Diego State. He stated, ''I was born under that flag and I'm going to college today because of what it represents. No one is going to desecrate it as long as I can defend and protect it.''

Yet the burning issues of the day raised challenges even to the necessity of competition, seeing it as continuation of the hostile spirit and aggression of the national leaders who were characterized by some as warmongers. Peace groups developed ''noncompetitive games,'' and in 1970 David Smith, a self-styled ''Super Hippie'' (whose hairdo made Joe Namath look like ''Mr. Clean''), participated in what he termed the World's Peace Pentathlon—swimming, parachuting, running, sky diving, and trail biking—''a six-hour statement on the absurdity of competition.''

On the other hand, Vice President Gerald Ford made a long statement in the July 1, 1974, issue of *Sports Illustrated*, reasserting the validity of athletic competition and its implication for society. He objected to the fact that Americans had been ''asked to swallow a lot of home-cooked psychology in recent years that winning isn't all that important anymore, whether on the athletic field or in any other field, national and international!'' He asserted, ''I don't buy that for a minute. It is not enough to just compete. Winning is very important. Maybe more important than ever. . . . Broadly speaking, outside of a national character and an educated society, there are few things more important to a country's growth and well being than competitive athletics. . . . Being a leader, the U.S. has an obligation to set high standards. I don't know of a better advertisement for a nation's good health than a healthy athletic representation. Athletics happens to be an extraordinarily swift avenue of communication. The broader the achievement the greater the impact. There is much to be said for Ping-Pong diplomacy.''

Carrying his argument further, Ford said, ''with communications what they are, a sports triumph can be as uplifting to a nation's spirit as, well, a battlefield victory.'' Certainly in Ford's view, sports and politics, both national and international, had striking similarities in the seventies.

The seventies was a period of increasing violence in sports, both on and off the field. One LA psychiatrist declared that the ''old fan yelled, Kill the Umpire'' while today, the new fan ''tries to do it.'' On

June 17, 1974, for example, in a game between the Texas Rangers and the Cleveland Indians on Beer Night (beer was ten cents a cup) the baseball song could well have been changed to "Take Me Out to the Brawl Game," and it would have adequately described the activities on the field. Fans spilled on the field in the ninth inning and fights broke out among players and the fans. Even the Indians raced on the field to aid their beleaguered opponents. Umpire Nestor Chylak called the fans "uncontrolled beasts." The Indians forfeited the game because order could not be restored. A similar incident occurred in Chicago in 1979 between the games of a doubleheader played by the White Sox and the Tigers. A local radio DJ sponsored a disco record burning and breaking contest that got out of hand. The rampaging fans tore up the outfield and made the grounds so unplayable that Chicago forfeited the second game.

Violence became a part of the game even in the so-called noncontact sports. *Sports Illustrated* featured an issue devoted to the "Enforcers," players in pro basketball who make sure their teammates are not intimidated by the opposition. One of the featured enforcers, Kermit Washington, proved to be such an enforcer that he almost ruined the career of Houston Rocket Rudy Tomjanovich when he shattered his jaw in a court confrontation. The allowance of hand contact (disallowed later in the decade) and of discretionary calls meant that pro basketball was often more dangerous than football.

College coaches like Al McGuire, former coach of the Marquette Warriors, Bobby Knight of Indiana, and Jud Heathcote of Michigan State specialized in violent outbursts against referees and often against their own players. Coaches stalked the sidelines, came out on the court during play, defied referees, and challenged them to call a technical foul. This kind of behavior by coaches encouraged team members to insult referees and act in an unrestrained manner. Coaches openly admitted that they behaved this way in order to intimidate referees and to "control" the game.

On the professional football field injuries were rampant, and quarterbacks were constantly undergoing surgery. Viciousness was deemed an admirable quality, and Pittsburgh Steeler defensive lineman "Mean" Joe Green could earn a lot of money and recognition for being nasty—an attribute not universally admired off the football field.

Jack Tatum, former Ohio State defensive standout, in his book *They Call Me Assassin* (1980), describes in gleeful detail how he and another Oakland defensive back competed to knock out their opposition. Tatum was so proficient that he ended the career and almost the life of Darryl Stingley. In an exhibition game Tatum caused such damage to Stingley's spine that he became a paraplegic for life with only limited use of one arm and hand.

For some, the seventies was a time when the "fun went out of fun and games." Dr. Thomas Tutko, cofounder of the Institute of Athletic Motivation at San Jose State University, has found in pro sports that victors are ruthless and unhappy because "most Americans truly believe that they're going to walk on water if they win. But winning is like drinking salt water. It's never saleable." Tutko believes that sports in America is a "chronically stressful, neurotic environment."

In an editorial in the September 5, 1973, issue, the *New York Times* uttered a nostalgic wish concerning sports: "In the roseate years when sports for youngsters and even professionals were regarded as fun and games and not simply spectaculars between commercials. . . Grantland Rice wrote the starry-eyed but nevertheless inspiring lines: 'When the One Great Scorer comes to write against your name, He marks not that you won or lost—but how you played the game.' " Of course, Mr. Rice never heard of the free agent system.

College Football

Collegiate football attendance records were shattered at the dawn of the new decade as a total of 29,465,605 spectators viewed the college game at all levels of competition. This was an increase of 1,839,444 from 1969.

Spectators were treated to aerial shows as such fabulous flingers from the West as Jim Plunkett, Don Bunce, Sonny Sixkiller, and Joe Theisman of Notre Dame performed during the early part of the decade. By the end of the decade, even the ground-oriented Big Ten was turning into an aerial circus. New coaches, such as Darryl Rogers at Michigan State and Jim Youngs of Purdue, installed passing attacks with great success. Such passing quarterbacks as Eddie Smith of Michigan State, Mark Hermann of Purdue, and Art Schlicter of Ohio State set school and conference records and ranked among the top ten in passing statistics.

Great running backs also abounded. Southern California fielded a succession of fleet backs in the O. J. Simpson tradition, such as Anthony Davis, Charles White, Ricky Bell, and fullback Sam "The Bam" Cunningham. Other outstanding runners of the decade included such luminaries as Johnny Rodgers of Nebraska; Billy Sims of Oklahoma; Tony Dorsett of Pittsburgh; Charles Muncie of California; Earl Campbell of Texas; Rob Lytle and Gordon Bell of Michigan; Pete Johnson, Champ Henson, and Archie Griffin of Ohio State; and Lydell Mitchell and John Cappelletti of Penn State.

In terms of tactics and strategy, the emphasis on the rushing game, popularized by such offenses as the veer and the wishbone, which were developed in the mid-sixties, continued until 1975. From that year on, rushing attempts and rushing yardage declined as more teams turned to speed and aerial attacks to open the way for the running game instead of vice versa. So effective was the college air game that *Sports Illustrated* in its September 5, 1977, issue could report that college quarterbacks were completing 47.44 percent of their passes. A change in the rules which allowed linemen to block downfield if a pass was completed at or behind the line of scrimmage also helped to open up the air game.

For many, the college football game provided a superior entertainment product. The offensives were more innovative with often four backs involved in the offense rather than the two back offenses of the pros, bringing to the college game more deception and an emphasis on speed and stealth rather than brute power. One college football enthusiast commented that he preferred the college game over the pro game because the college coaches ''are not so wrapped up in precision and technical efficiency that they forget the name of the game is to make yards and points, not to keep from making mistakes.''

But all was not rosy for college football during the seventies. Galloping inflation kept raising the cost of outfitting a player. In 1974 the *Chicago Tribune* indicated that it cost approximately $300 to outfit a football player with the proper equipment and uniform. Also numerous lawsuits relating to head injuries had reduced the number of companies making helmets down to three by the end of the decade. One study of sport injuries done in 1973 indicated that Americans suffered 17 million sports injuries, with football averaging one injury per participant.

Again during the decade, football recruiting scandals and illegal aid to football players caused major investigations at various schools. Oklahoma State was hit with probation twice for providing illegal aid. Oklahoma received probation and was prohibited from television for forging a high school transcript. The athletic director and football coach at the University of Montana were investigated by a federal grand jury for the possible misuse of a $227,000 government scholarship fund. In 1976 Michigan State University of the Big Ten was placed on a three-year probation, charged with thirty-four violations of the NCAA code in its football program. The penalties assessed the Spartans were some of the harshest ever meted out by the NCAA. Besides the three-year probation, the Spartans were prohibited from playing in a bowl game for three years; they could only recruit twenty freshmen the first year of probation and twenty-five the next two years (all other Big Ten teams could recruit thirty); seven members of the football team lost their eligibility. In addition, one assistant coach was fired, and, eventually, head coach Denny Stolz resigned. Michigan State's effort to regain a competitive edge and to repeat the glory years of 1965 and 1966 ended in disaster and a complete housecleaning in the athletic department.

By the end of the decade college recruiting problems had not decreased. Over one hundred athletes at about two dozen schools had been implicated in "various transcript scandals." *Sports Illustrated* in an editorial commenting on these unsavory disclosures commented that: "These imposing numbers raise a serious question about the fundamental assumption underlying big-time, big-money college sports: that there are enough quality athletes to be found who can fill arenas and stadiums and also are capable of making the grade in the classroom. Without cheating, that is."

College presidents and football coaches still had not faced up to the problems that a year-round football program run by professional coaches (most big-time college coaches do not have faculty appointments) creates for an educational institution. In 1972, for example, *Sports Illustrated* interviewed a University of Nebraska quarterback who indicated that he didn't attend class since he didn't "need a degree to play football." One disgruntled football player who suffered permanent injury playing college football while hurt wrote in the November 26, 1978, *New York Times;* "Playing college football is like signing up for the Marines. The first thing coaches do is break everyone's individual spirit in the interest of achieving some sort of equalitarian spirit. . . . I was a football player and I will pay for it the rest of my life."

Yet various athletic officials have widely differing views concerning recruiting. Don Canham, the highly successful athletic director at the University of Michigan, was reported by the *New York Times* on March 13, 1974, as making the following statement: "Recruiting is a justified pursuit without question. Let me put it another way. It's a necessary evil. For instance, if we did not recruit and have great football teams, we wouldn't have any money. It's absolutely essential in our system of amateur athletics today." Yet Canham's position ignores many of the problems that are associated with his statement. At many schools basketball, not football, is the moneymaker. At some schools sports programs are a drain on available resources. All sorts of illegal (as noted previously) and even immoral activities are condoned in order to recruit. For example, one western coach stated in the January 26, 1976, edition of the *New York Times* that he was able to recruit kids from New York because "we send them across the border into Mexico to shackup for a few days. Every one of those kids signs on the dotted line when he gets back."

Former NBA star and former college and professional basketball coach Bob Cousy, reflecting on recruiting in the same issue of the *New York Times* that featured Canham's statement, remarked, "You recruit a kid by licking his boots. Once you've begged like that, there can never be a player-coach relationship. The kid is boss."

In commenting on the Michigan State penalties, John B. Fullen, who from 1928–1967 was a director of the Ohio State University Alumni Association and editor of the alumni magazine, effectively summed up the dilemma of college recruiting, and his words in light of the recent revelations seem hauntingly prophetic. He stated: "The Western Conference is no longer the Big Ten. In football, it's the Big Two and the Little Eight. The Big Two not only dominate their brethren, they also murder them. So now you have to win, you have to win big to get those turnstiles clicking. The rich get richer while the poor drain off legitimate scholastic revenues to try to hang in there. All of which is why Big Time college football bears as much relation to higher education as the Mafia does to legitimate business."

On the gridiron itself during the decade the disturbing trend noted in the sixties—that of a small number of teams dominating the top ten rankings—continued during the 1970s. In its September 16, 1979, edition the *New York Times* headlined a column entitled "An Appeal to Break Up That Ol' Gang of Nine." The paper's contention was that the so-called Big Nine—which included Oklahoma, Alabama, Southern California, Michigan, Notre Dame, Ohio State, Penn State, Nebraska, and Texas—had "dominated college football polls" from 1969 to 1978. According to the *Times*, the Big Nine "occupied 66 of 100 available spots in the top 10; 42 of 50 available spots in the top 10; 42 of 50 available in the top five and 9 of 10 No. 1 ratings." (Pittsburgh in 1976 being the only exception.)

The *Times* further noted that "although 139 teams play football on the major level, only 28 have been ranked in a final A.P. top 10 since 1969. Of these 28, 10 have been ranked just once, while four others have been listed only twice. The members of the Big Nine, on the other hand, have each been ranked after at least six consecutive seasons." In 1978 the paper found that the Big Nine were all in the top ten. They had also been in the top ten in 1973 although not in the same order.

The *Times* article concluded that television perhaps bore the greatest responsibility for this situation. According to the *Times* a ''dispro-portionate number of network appearances have gone to, you guessed it, the Gang of Nine. Since 1966, when the American Broadcasting Company began the current series of NCAA broadcasts, the Big Nine had 136 coast-to-coast appearances, or approximately 48 percent of the total.'' Also the TV revenues ($266,700 currently for each school appearing) certainly aid the scholarship coffers and of course provide important exposure to potential recruits and wealthy alumni.

Nowhere was this dominance by a select number of teams more evident than in the Big Ten Conference and the PAC Ten. During the decade, only Michigan State's surprising 1978 tie with Michigan for the Big Ten crown broke the Ohio State-Michigan monopoly. Michigan was frustrated from 1971 to 1973, posting a 31-1-1 record, and ranked in the top ten throughout the period yet did not go to the Rose Bowl. Particularly vexing was the 1973 season when both teams tied in the standing and tied each other 10-10. A vote of the conference's athletic directors by a 6-4 margin sent the Buckeyes to the Rose Bowl. (University of Michigan backers blamed jealousy for its sister school Michigan State casting the deciding vote to Ohio State. A 5-5 tie would have sent Michigan.)

The Big Ten athletic directors must have been possessed of some prophetic ability since Ohio State ripped the USC Trojans 42-21. This was the only time that the Big Ten was able to win a Rose Bowl victory during the decade. Undoubtedly the Buckeyes were happy to avenge their previous Rose Bowl defeat by Southern California by a 42-17 margin. West coast writers in particular lambasted the 1973 Ohio State team's performance. Acerbic tongued Jim Murray of the *Los Angeles Times* chortled that USC could have beaten them with the faculty. He continued, ''In fact, coach John McKay did everything but suit up an English Lit class to hold down the score. And when Tom Lupo intercepted a pass and ran it into the end zone, John was eying the gal cheerleaders. The tipoff on Ohio State came when the water boy beat them to the bench, carrying two pails full. He could have had a hod on his back, too, it turned out. These guys couldn't catch a standing bus. Women move faster getting ready to go to a party. You could lay sidewalks faster than they could move the ball. Watching you kept hoping they could do bird imitations. They acted as if they had a five year contract to make a touchdown. They put 17 passes in the air. Their players caught three of them. Meanwhile, back at Ohio State, Wayne Woodrow Hayes is going to have to do some reevaluating on the relative importance of brute strength. Unless they start handing out the Grantland Rice award for overturning street-cars, his teams ain't going to win any for a while.''

For sheer frustration no one could match the record of U of M's Bo Schembechler, whose Michigan teams appeared in the 1970, 1972, 1977, 1978, and 1979 Rose Bowls and came away without a win. His most frustrating loss was in 1979 when USC won 17-10. TV cameras seemed to reveal and most spectators seemed to agree that Trojan back Charles White had dropped the ball on the one yard line before scoring his controversial "phantom touchdown." The referee ruled otherwise and the Trojans had their victory.

Some critics felt that the militaristic attitude of Bo and Woody, who treated the game as war and hid their troops in a monastery, contributed to the string of defeats suffered by the Big Ten teams in Pasadena. Quarterback Don Bunce, who played on the Stanford teams that defeated Michigan and Ohio State in the 1971 and 1972 Rose Bowls, commented that "Hayes and Schembechler wouldn't let their players do anything. In fact, Schembechler took his players to Bakersfield to get away from the extracurricular activities."

Bunce also said that he remembered that the "Ohio State players came marching down Main Street [of Disneyland] in their military style, very stern and rigid. We were running all around, eating cotton candy, having a good time. Kim Kauffman, one of our defensive backs, was doing cartwheels and wearing his Mickey Mouse ears, and taking pictures of Ohio State players. Woody Hayes only let his players stay a short while we had most of the afternoon there. It was such a contrast of philosophies." Hayes, of course, had established the "three yards and a cloud of dust," grind it out style of football that relied on possession and direct handoffs. West Coast teams played a fast and loose game of multiple formations, wide running plays, surprise plays, and frequent passing.

Woody Hayes's militarism and violence finally cost him his job. In 1971 ABC TV cameras had captured Woody tearing up yard markers in the Michigan game. Don Canham, Michigan's athletic director, was nonchalant about Woody's behavior. He said he was willing "to buy all the sideline markers Woody wanted to rip up." Canham justified his attitude by stating, "When Ohio State comes to Michigan, who do you think our fans come to see—the players? No sir, they come to see Woody Hayes. He's worth an extra 30,000 tickets. The men take their children down the field and point him out. I've seen it."

Woody was even violent against his own players. Former star lineman Doug France said of his coach, "You leave his practices with scars on your helmets. There are always wars. The helmets are proof of that. . . . Really we hate him. But we don't let that hatred get in the way of winning football games."

In 1976 Hayes refused to talk to newsmen when his team was beaten by UCLA 23-10. The last straw was in the 1978 Gator Bowl game against Clemson. Charlie Bauman of Clemson intercepted a pass, and after running out of bounds, Bauman was punched by a frustrated and uncontrollable Hayes. Hayes was subsequently fired. Another notorious player abuser, Frank Kush of Arizona State, was also forced to resign at the end of the decade for striking a player, this time one of his own.

One critic made the following comment with regard to college football coaches: "One of the problems with big time college football is the reverence in which coaches are held. Coach Jones, Coach Smith, and Coach Hayes, investing them with almost priestly eminence and inviolability. It goes to the head; and Hayes isn't the only coach who regards himself as omnipotent and beyond criticism and football as something separate from the University."

The annual showdowns between the PAC 10 and Big Ten leaders in the Rose Bowl overshadowed the play of many fine teams. Nebraska ended up ranked number one in both the 1970 and 1971 seasons, led by speedy Johnny Rodgers. In 1971 Nebraska seemed a surprising choice, but after the bowl games concluded—Notre Dame surprised number one Texas, Stanford upset Ohio State, while Nebraska beat LSU 17-12—the Nebraska Cornhuskers emerged with the national championship. During those two years Nebraska posted win skeins of 23 straight victories and 32 games without a defeat. A particular coup for the Big Eight conference was that the final top ten Associated Press standings for the 1971 season revealed a 1-2-3 sweep for conference teams with Oklahoma and Colorado following Nebraska in the ratings.

The most surprising college gridiron story was the emergence of Pittsburgh as the number one team in the nation in 1976. Pitt became the first major team from the East to win a national title since Syracuse in 1959. Sparked by a fantastically fleet-footed running back, Tony Dorsett, the Panthers set fifteen NCAA records. Included among these were Dorsett's records for the most yards rushing (6,082) by a player in his career and the most yards in a season (1,948). A 27-3 win over Georgia in the Sugar Bowl convinced even the most hardened cynics among sports aficionados that Eastern football was once again "for real."

History repeated itself in 1971 when Notre Dame and Texas again were foes in the Cotton Bowl. But this time the Irish emerged the victors by a 24-11 score. (This was a repeat of the 1970 bowl game.) After the game, Coach Dan Devine of Notre Dame quipped that he had better have won since he had received "moccasins for Christmas" from

Chicago alumni—"water moccasins"—after the 1970 defeat by Texas. In the Sugar Bowl of 1979, Alabama's 14-7 triumph over Penn State earned them the national title.

College football in the seventies thus saw familiar names and teams dominate the standings. Costs had risen astronomically so that in the early 1970s most teams moved to an eleven-game season. By the end of the decade even the staid Big Ten had relaxed its rules and allowed its teams to be eligible to participate in other bowl games besides the Rose Bowl. Television revenues and conference media exposure ruled the day.

With the end of the Vietnam War by 1975, the latter part of the decade saw little protest against football from the student body. As the economy faltered, students grew more conservative—fraternities and sororities revived, panty raids came back (it was no accident that the film *Animal House* was the big box office hit of 1978), and college football was the thing to do once again on campus on Saturday. The fifties seemed ready to repeat themselves. College officials became increasingly concerned about problems of crowd control as students became rowdy and unpredictable, largely due to large quantities of alcohol and marijuana as well as a carnival atmosphere. Crowds could become abusive and even dangerously violent, as the Notre Dame team found out at Georgia Tech or the Minnesota team discovered at Michigan State. In the guise of good fun losing fans could be unpredictable and ugly in their frustrations.

Pro Football

The story of pro football during the 1970s was centered on the fortunes of the Pittsburgh Steelers, truly the dominant professional team of the decade. According to the *Detroit News*, the Steelers justified this accord because a "record three Super Bowl championships, a record-tying eight straight playoff appearances and ninety-nine regular season victories in ten seasons are proof that Pittsburgh was the National Football League's dominant team of the decade." Once the joke of the league, the Steelers were transformed into Super Bowl champions by Chuck Knoll, who was named head coach in 1969. Prior to Noll's assumption of the leadership of the Pittsburgh club, the Steelers had won only thirteen games in four seasons. Craftily utilizing the draft, Noll brought in the players who were to be the cogs of the winning machine. These included: quarterback Terry Bradshaw;

defensive line terrors, "Mean" Joe Green and L. C. Greenwood; outstanding linebackers, Jack Ham and Jack Lambert; offensive stars Franco Harris and Lynn Swann. Twice All-Pro defensive back Donnie Shell was merely a free agent.

In fact, to state that the Steelers won three Super Bowls is something of a misnomer. Since they won the 1980 Super Bowl with a 31-19 triumph over the Los Angeles Rams, they were the victors of the 1979 NFL season. In 1975 Pittsburgh defeated Minnesota 16-6 in Super Bowl IX (thus champions of the 1974 season); Pittsburgh defeated Dallas 21-17 in Super Bowl X in Miami (thus champions of the 1975 season); and again defeated Dallas 35-31 in Super Bowl XIII in 1979 (thus champions of the 1978 season). Truly the Steelers dominated the 1970s and could be accurately described as a dynasty.

If Pittsburgh was the glamour team of the seventies in pro football, certainly the Minnesota Vikings were the hard luck team of pro football, earning the dubious distinction of being the Super Bowl bridesmaid four times in the seventies, having lost to Kansas City 23-7 in Super Bowl IV in 1970, 24-7 to Miami in Super Bowl VIII in 1974, 16-6 to Pittsburgh in Super Bowl IX in 1975, and 32-14 to Oakland in Super Bowl XI in 1977. This perennial failure to win the big game was excruciatingly painful for coach Bud Grant and the Viking players, but undoubtedly no one was more keenly disappointed than scrambling quarterback Fran Tarkenton, who was the NFL lifetime leader in passing attempts, completions, total yards, and touchdown passes.

Two other teams dominated the NFL in the 1970s. Dallas, always a strong team and commanded by the stoical Tom Landry, lost in the 1971 Super Bowl when Baltimore got a 32-yard field goal by Jim O'Brien with five seconds to go to edge the Cowboys 16-13. Dallas would win Super Bowls in 1972 and 1978 when they defeated Miami 24-3 and Denver 27-10, respectively. They were also bridesmaids in 1976 and 1979, victims of the Steelers.

Miami, led by the brilliant coaching of Don Shula and powered by the glamorous backfield of Butch Cassidy and the Sun Dance Kid, alias Larry Csonka and Jim Kiick, also were a team to be reckoned with. Miami lost to Dallas 24-3 in the 1972 Super Bowl, edged Washington in the 1973 Super Bowl 14-7, and bombed Minnesota 24-7 in the 1974 Super Bowl. An expansion team, Miami won the 1971 American Football Conference title in the club's sixth year, the earliest title for any expansion club. Bob Griese, a cool-headed signal caller and smooth passer, combined with Paul Warfield to produce one of the best passer-receiver combinations in the game.

If Pittsburgh was the team of the seventies, certainly O. J. Simpson was the premier running back of the decade. The Heisman Trophy winner of the 1968 season and runnerup in 1967 had an eleven-year career in the NFL, playing nine seasons with the Buffalo Bills and his last two with the San Francisco 49ers. His last game was in December 1979. Behind him he left an impressive trail of statistics. Although falling short of Jim Brown's total career yardage of 12,312, O. J. did compile 11,236 career yards, six 200-yard games, and 273 yards in one game. He also held the NFL career records of 2,003 yards and 23 touchdowns in one season. Aided by his "Electric Company" line, O. J. was a galloping demon who was the terror of NFL defenses. Unfortunately, Buffalo was never able to surround O. J. with the type of players who could make Buffalo a title contender, so O. J. would never be able to sport a coveted Super Bowl ring.

The 1973 season was O. J.'s premier season. That year he gained 2,003 yards to eclipse Jim Brown's single season record of 1,863 yards rushing. Enroute he would gain 250 yards in a game, breaking both Cookie Gilchrist's American Football League record of 243 and Willie Ellison's NFL mark of 247. Later O. J. would have a 273-yard game.

During that same season, Simpson rushed 332 times, breaking Brown's record of 305, and he rushed 11 times for over 100 yards— three of them were for over 200 yards. For his efforts that season, O. J. was awarded the prestigious S. Rae Hickock "Professional Athlete of the Year" Award, emblematic of being the finest professional athlete in America.

Perhaps more important were O. J.'s activities off the field, which had even greater significance. O. J., a tall, handsome, articulate man, was able to parlay his athletic accomplishments on the field into even greater business success. His Hertz commercials in which he was seen racing through airports became one of the most popular commercials ever carried and made him one of the most recognized personalities in America. Soon he gave other personal endorsements for shoes, boots, sunglasses, and, naturally, for orange juice. He became a sports commentator on ABC and started a motion picture career. Joe Namath had demonstrated the product power of a pro football star by the success of his endorsement, but this had primarily benefited white football stars. O. J. was the first black NFL star to become a "commercial" hit. In addition, he was regarded as a star and a hero not only to black kids but to white kids and white audiences also. O. J. was popular because he was O. J.—an American football hero—not simply because he was another quick black running back. (Jim Brown had a modestly successful career as a movie actor, but he never was able to convert his fame and name to business success in commercial endorsements.)

Although there were numerous heroes and stars during the 1970s, two performances by individuals stand out. In 1970 forty-three-year old George Blanda, in his 21st season of play, ''led five frantic finishes in a row for Oakland: throwing two touchdown passes against Pittsburgh; kicking a 48-yard field goal with three seconds to go, tying Kansas City 17-17; kicking a 52-yard field goal with three seconds left, beating Cleveland 23-20; driving the Raiders to a winning touchdown against Denver 24-19; kicking a field goal with four seconds left, beating San Diego 20-17.'' Certainly George had defied the adage that pro football was a young man's game. Blanda and Earl Morrall, who led the Miami Dolphins to a Super Bowl win, were survivors and gracefully aged warriors in a game that did not promote longevity.

Also in 1970 Tom Dempsey, the field goal kicker for the New Orleans Saints and a man who played with half of a foot, kicked a 63-yard field goal to beat the Detroit Lions. So confident were Alex Karras and the other members of the strong Lions defense that Dempsey would miss, they did not attempt to block the kick. Much to their chagrin and embarrassment, they could only wait helplessly as the ball curved over the uprights. With one blow of his foot, Dempsey had clearly demonstrated that a determined individual could overcome a handicap and be successful in pro football.

Television continued to play an important role in the popularizing of pro football. In 1978 Commissioner Pete Rozelle announced that a four-year agreement had been signed with the three major networks to telecast all NFL games and postseason games, plus selected preseason games for four years. This was considered by the television industry to be the largest single television package ever made. Each team received about $5.1 million per year as their share.

An A. C. Nielsen study of television viewing of Super Bowls indicated that the 1980 viewing of Super Bowl XIV was the most watched sports event of all time and viewed in 35,330,000 homes. It was followed by Super Bowls XIII, XII, XI, X, and IX as the next most watched sports events. In addition, a 1978 Harris Sports Survey poll revealed that 70 percent of the sports fans of America followed football, contrasted with 54 percent who said they followed baseball. The poll also indicated that football was considered to be the favorite sport of 26 percent of those polled, while 16 percent indicated that baseball was their favorite sport.

Despite these impressive statistics, the NFL had its problems in the seventies. In 1974 a rival league, the World Football League, was started with entries with such intriguing names as the Chicago Fire and the Detroit Wheels. Although the league quickly folded, the signing of such standout stars as Jim Kiick, Larry Csonka, and Paul Warfield of Miami helped to destroy the possibility of what seemed to be a Miami dynasty begun with consecutive Super Bowl wins in 1973 and 1974.

During the early part of the decade, many fans became disillusioned by the sameness of the pros. The increase in size of the players and the dominance of the defenses—using three down linemen and the so-called nickel defense with a five man backfield—neutralized the passing game which most fans came to see. As a result, stadium attendance declined from a record level of 95.5 percent of capacity in 1973 to 87.8 percent in 1977. In 1977 the NFL had over 1.5 million unsold seats compared to fewer than one-half million in 1973.

To open the offenses and make the game more popular, the NFL made several rules changes. In 1978 the so-called chuck rule was revised. Defensive backs were restricted to one hit of pass receivers within five yards of the line of scrimmage. Also, offensive linemen were allowed to open their hands while fighting off charging behemoth defensive linemen, lessening the amount of holding penalties and allowing the quarterbacks additional time to pass. The result was that from 1977 to 1979 average points per game increased by 17 percent, and 286 more touchdowns were scored in 1979, the majority via the air route. In addition, the Super Bowls, which in many cases turned out to be anything but super, also reflected the impact of the rules changes. In 1979 Pittsburgh beat Dallas 35-31 with a total of 66 points scored. In 1980 Pittsburgh beat Los Angeles 31-19 with a total of 50 points scored.

Contrast these scores with the totals of the previous Super Bowls.

Super Bowl	Total Points
1970	30
1971	29
1972	27
1973	21
1974	31
1975	22
1976	38
1977	46
1978	37

Another vexing problem is that the realignment that resulted with the merger of the American Football Conference with the National Football League has produced an imbalance in favor of the American Conference. The Super Bowl champion has been from the American Conference for the eighth time in the ten years since the merger realignment. During the 1979 season the AFC teams dominated the

NFC in head-to-head encounters, triumphing in thirty-six of fifty-two contests.

The conference alignment that was agreed to was no plan made in heaven or through some divine computer. It was merely one of five plans that were placed in a bowl, and plan three, the current alignment in the NFL, was drawn out by the commissioner's secretary. So there is nothing sacrosanct in maintaining the status quo. Geographic realignment establishing natural rivalries would, according to one writer, make sense, particularly in times of energy crises. However, any realignment proposal encounters owner opposition, since as Commissioner Pete Rozelle has noted: "Each owner wants his team to be in a division with at least one warm-weather site or a domed stadium, with teams with large season-ticket sales and with teams that are pigeons."

Pro football has also had to contend with the problem of free agency. The old Rozelle Rule, declared unconstitutional because it violated antitrust laws, permitted the commissioner of the NFL to judge the amount of compensation for teams who lost players through the free agency route. Article XV of the players Representatives and NFL's Management Council collective-bargaining agreement provided that once a player's contract expired on February 1, he could examine offers from other clubs. The player's current ball club was given the right, however, to counter new offers and keep him or let him go for an agreed upon amount of compensation.

If the player receives no offers by April 15, he has to wait until June 1, when he must be notified in writing whether or not his former team desires to retain his services. If the team wants the player, the player is offered a 10 percent raise or the best written proposal made by the ball club. If the ball club does not want the player, he becomes a "free agent." The problem is that by August 1979 only 15 of a possible 260 free agents have received offers from other teams.

Ed Garvey, executive director of the National Football League Players Association, believes that there are a number of reasons why this has happened. Writing in the August 12, 1979, *New York Times,* Garvey indicated that an informal gentlemen's agreement exists not to upset other owners by going after their players; the television contract for the NFL insures $5.6 million to each team yearly so that stars cannot affect the gate or purse as in other pro sports, and thus there is no "economic incentive" for them to acquire these players. No additions to the lineups would create larger profits for the owners. Also, the sixteen-game season has put a premium on versatility and longevity, and few teams are willing to shell out big bucks for an oft-injured veteran no matter what his credentials. Garvey concludes that "players in the NFL are getting a smaller and smaller percentage of gross revenues because winning is less and less important to the owner's profit picture; therefore, more and more older veterans are cut for less expensive rookies. . . . The NFL owners make the greatest profit by far in all organized sports. The NFL players' salaries represent the smallest percentage of gross revenues. Something is wrong and we are going to try to correct that wrong. But not by losing a grievance. Rather by exposing the NFL owners for their refusal to play by the rules, their refusal to bid on free agents and their bad-faith bargaining.'' Obviously, the Players' Association is unhappy, and in 1982 when the current contract expires, the Players' Association will seek additional clarification in regard to free agency and the sharing of profits.

One of the greatest threats to pro football and football on any level is the number of injuries related to the sport. Numerous quarterback injuries, for example, have often decimated squads and changed the complexion of league races completely. In 1979, for example, an injury to quarterback Gary Danielson of the Detroit Lions changed the Lions from title contenders to also-rans. To help combat injuries, the NFL has attempted to develop safer equipment and rule changes. Don Pastorini, for example, in 1978 pioneered in the wearing of a ''flak'' type jacket during the 1978 season, and since then many other quarterbacks have taken to wearing this device as a preventive measure. In regard to rule changes, the elimination of the ''crack back block'' and the quicker whistle when a quarterback is being tackled have been aimed at preventing unnecessary injuries.

The required NFL injury list, published and released each Monday after Sunday's battles, grew in length throughout the decade. It also assumed importance to opposing coaches planning game strategy, as well as to the big-time gamblers and point-spread predictors. The connection between pro football and gambling grew closer, and ''Jimmy the Greek'' of Las Vegas became a respectable part of the CBS pro football broadcast team.

Pro football will always have its share of injuries because it is a contact game and there is a violence inherent in the game itself. However, pro football's image suffers not so much from the ''accidental'' injuries, which are not deliberately induced, but by the injuries suffered because some players violate the spirit if not the letter of the rules— those who need to maim and injure their opponents as a means of achieving victory. No greater example of this type of viciousness has been demonstrated than the paralyzing of the New England Patriots wide receiver Darryl Stingley from a tackle by Oakland Raider defensive back Jack Tatum. If there was any doubt as to Tatum's attitude it was quickly dispelled by the subsequent publication of his book *They*

Call Me Assassin (1980). In his book, Tatum describes his enjoyment of hitting a receiver and then emitting a train whistle. Bob Sudyk, of the *Cleveland Press*, writing in the *Football Digest*, comments that Tatum "salivates at the sound of a bone cracking, oxygen being squeezed from the lungs, the snap of an Achilles' tendon. A groan or the sight of a tear only means a job well done according to Tatum's Tome." The NFL commissioner will have to take steps so that such sordid and vicious behavior is reduced and condemned. The mayhem is bad enough in pro football without the legitimizing of sheer butchery. The players themselves have ways of curbing or discouraging such outlaw behavior, and the press can certainly downplay or condemn the outright violence that is beyond clean, hard play. Unfortunately, the "bad ass," mean image has prevailed and has even been romanticized and glamorized.

Another development that bears watching in the future is the increasing business competency and intelligence of pro players who can see the shortness of their careers. With the aid of business agents, lawyers, and advisors, players are becoming shrewder in contract negotiations. Many are successfully establishing business ventures and enterprises based on their local name recognition and professional image. The smarter ones are becoming more financially secure sooner so that they can end their playing careers of their own choice before permanent injuries burden their lives. One NFL center has recently indicated that he will negotiate to play only a certain number of quarters per game. Others have left football after only a few seasons because they enjoyed business enterprises more than head knocking. These developments can only serve to enlighten other players and make them realize that life beyond and after football is more important than their all too brief careers.

College Basketball

College basketball during the seventies continued to increase in popularity. With more schools dropping football because of financial losses (the *New York Times* would report that in 1974 forty-one colleges had dropped the sport in the previous ten years), added emphasis was placed on recruiting the "blue chip" ballplayers since just the addition of one or two key players could turn a previously mediocre team into a national contender. The emphasis on recruiting also meant that NCAA rules violations often resulted. Probably the most famous case in the decade was Long Beach State, which was placed on probation for numerous violations. Head coach Jerry Tarkanian (or Tark the Shark as he was known in coaching circles) did not deny many of the allegations, explaining that he was helping poor athletes who didn't have any alternate resources. Tarkanian moved on to the University of Nevada-Las Vegas, which he quickly built into a national power. An attempt to prevent him from coaching was halted by court injunction filed by Tarkanian, and the case is still pending.

The college game became dominated by black players even in the South. Willie Morris, writer in residence at the University of Mississippi, in an article entitled "The Ghosts of Ole Miss" in the May 31, 1980, issue of *Inside Sports*, commented extensively on the investigation of varsity sports not only at Ole Miss but also at the other Southeastern schools. Morris noted that it was not until 1971 that the color barrier was broken at Ole Miss. The school was playing Grambling, an all black team, in an NIT preliminary round and won the game when a black guard from Mississippi popped in a jump shot. He noted also that Alabama had one white on its traveling squad, Florida had three, Mississippi State four, LSU played only black players, and Auburn "was not far behind."

The combinations of urban blacks thrown into college work, which they were in many cases ill-prepared for, the pressure of big-time basketball, and the disciplined team approach of white coaches proved to be an explosive combination of forces that could erupt into "unpleasant" situations. In 1975 Michigan State was forced to start four of its reserves against Indiana because the black varsity players were boycotting over the starting of a local area white player who was a crowd favorite. The incident created a great deal of racial animosity, and the white player subsequently transferred and starred at another state institution. Four years later, with five of its top six players black, Michigan State University captured the NCAA championship. Few if any MSU rooters complained about the "blackness" of the team. Winning has a way of curing a lot of problems.

The signing of a basketball recruit did not necessarily mean that colleges and universities were guaranteed four years of his "services." The recruiting war between the NBA and the American Basketball Association made it lucrative for a college player to jump for the "big" bucks when the leagues started bidding for him. With the merger of the two leagues, opportunities still abound for outstanding college players to be grabbed off by the pros before they finish their college eligibility. Earvin Johnson, star of the Michigan State University NCAA champions of 1979, joined the Los Angeles Lakers after his sophomore year and led them to the NBA championship. In hopes of similar success, Red Auerbach attempted to lure Ralph Sampson, 7-foot 1-inch center of the University of Virginia, to the Celtics after a highly successful freshman year. Sampson turned Red down, and Auerbach bitterly denounced university authorities who had counseled Sampson not to accept his offer. Education was hardly mentioned.

College basketball on the courts witnessed two distinct trends during the seventies. UCLA continued to dominate the scene, capturing five of six NCAA crowns from 1975 to 1979 with only North Carolina State in 1974 breaking the UCLA hegemony. From 1976 to 1980 the collegiate basketball powers were situated in the Midlands and the Midwest. In 1976 Big Ten powers Indiana and Michigan dueled for the title in the championship game, with the Hoosiers triumphing. In 1977 the Marquette Warriors led by free-spirited coach Al McGuire earned the crown. Tall and talented Kentucky beat back North Carolina in 1978. In 1979, the number two ranked Spartans of Michigan State, sparked by their dynamic duo of 6-foot 8-inch guard-forward-center Earvin "Magic" Johnson and Greg "Sky King" Kelser (who according to some commentators "talked to God" at the apex of his leaps), combined to upset the number one ranked Indiana State Sycamores led by the nation's premier white player, Larry Bird. And in 1980 the Louisville Cardinals, with "Dunking Demon" Darryl Griffiths as its catalyst, wrested the crown from a surprisingly resurgent UCLA squad led by former Denver Nuggets coach, Larry Brown.

In 1971 the UCLANs were powered by forwards Sidney Wicks and Curtis Rowe (6 feet 8 inches and 6 feet 6 inches, respectively) and quarterbacked by elusive and pesky guard, Henry Bibby. In the NCAA finals, the Bruins found themselves opposed by a formidable foe, the Jacksonville Dolphins. Led by 7-foot plus players, Artis Gilmore and Pembrook Burrows, and aided by 6 foot 10 inch Rod McIntyre, the Dolphins' front line averaged an awe-inspiring 7 feet.

The confrontation reminded many of the clashes between UCLA and Houston during the sixties. Once again, the Bruins were the established basketball power led by the staid John Wooden, who had imposed a ban on his players from talking with the press and media. Jacksonville, on the other hand, was a brash upstart, only recent Division I team, coached by the "flashy and flamboyant" Joe Williams. Williams imposed few restrictions on his team both on and off the court. When asked about his attitude toward discipline, Williams responded by saying, "They do what they want to do." One commentator called the game "the Establishment vs. the Age of Aquarius."

Unfortunately, the Wooden style and strategy prevailed. Sydney Wicks, giving away 6 inches to the towering Gilmore, who could touch the rim standing flat-footed, blocked four of Gilmore's shots, forced Gilmore into a 9 for 29 shooting night, and out rebounded the Jacksonville star 18 to 16.

The 1971 championship road for the UCLANs was a precarious one. They were almost derailed in the Western regional finals when they edged Long Beach State, led by their star Ed Ratleff, 57-55. In the finals the Bruins broke out into an early lead mainly on the contribution of 6-foot 9-inch center Steve Patterson's 20 points (he would have 29 for the game). A stall by the Bruins, who were hoping to bring Villanova out of their zone, almost proved disastrous. Villanova's man-to-man held the Bruins to three layups, while the Wildcats Howard Porter was dumping in jumpers to cut the UCLA margin (he would wind up with 25 points). In the end, UCLA held on for a 68-62 victory.

From 1972 to 1974, UCLA once again possessed the dominant player in college basketball as they did from 1967–1969 when Lew Alcindor dominated the game. Bill Walton was a 6-foot 11-inch redhead who passed, shot, and rebounded with ferocity. Walton represented a change for Wooden also, for Walton was outspoken, dressed in lumberjack style with a bandana around his head, and ate his own vegetarian meals. Walton more closely reflected an image of the youth counterculture movement than any other player who had played for Wooden previously.

Yet when it came down to the bottom line Walton could play the game. And this was at a time when there was no dearth of centers such as Marquette's Jim Chones, North Carolina's Tom McMillen, and Ohio State's Luke Witte. In 1972 "the Walton Gang" crushed their victims by a 32-point average winning margin. There was so much depth on the Bruins' team that Walton's backup, 6 foot 11 inch Swen Nater, would earn a starting position in the NBA. Their closest challenge came in the finals when an upstart Florida State team, just coming off probation for NCAA violations, gave UCLA all they wanted until they succumbed by an 81-76 margin. This was the closest game of the seven consecutive NCAA championship contests that UCLA was involved in. In 1973 the Bruins were just as dominant although they had to surge in the closing minutes to down Indiana in the NCAA semifinals 70-59. Against Memphis State in the finals, Walton dominated the boards and the final score was 87-66.

Though 1974 was a tough year for the Bruins, most other teams in the country would have gladly accepted their record. The Bruins' eighty-eight game win streak was broken by Notre Dame 71-70 at South Bend, although UCLA would win the rematch at Pauley Pavilion by an 18-point margin. Also Dean Smith's North Carolina State team, led by the leaping David Thompson, put an end to the UCLA victory skein in a dramatic 80-77 double overtime triumph in the NCAA semifinals. Seven-foot center Tom Burleson, who battled Walton to a draw, and diminutive 5 foot 5½inch tall Monty Towe, who quarterbacked the Wolfpack, aided and abetted Thompson whose forte was sailing high above the rim to take the alley oop pass for a basket.

In the finals technicals called on the coaching histrionics of Marquette coach Al McGuire helped the Wolfpack to a 39-30 halftime lead, which they never relinquished as they went on to a convincing 76-64 victory.

In 1975 the Bruins, led by forwards David Meyers and Richard Washington, fought their way past stubborn Michigan, Montana, and Louisville to reach the finals. Just prior to the final game, Wooden announced to his team that he was retiring on doctor's orders. Buoyed by the desire to give the old master one more victory and another NCAA crown, the inspired Bruins edged an imposing Kentucky team 92-85.

If the first half of the decade belonged to UCLA, the second half belonged to teams playing in the Midlands and Midwest. In particular, the Big Ten, noted for its football prowess, began to flex its basketball muscle. In 1975 the number one ranked Indiana Hoosiers had been upset by Kentucky 92-90, which shattered a thirty-four-game winning streak and their chances at NCAA. Led by former Army coach and Ohio State player, Bobby Knight, a rigid disciplinarian and perfectionist, the Hoosiers were hankering for the national title in 1976. Knight had his players keep their hair short, wear neat clothes, and refrain from any confrontation with the coach. So obsessed was the Hoosier state (which is basketball crazy anyway) during the 1975–76 season that Indianapolis clubs only met on Indiana's nonplaying nights and the state legislature adjourned early so legislators could attend the Hoosiers' games.

Although pressed a number of times, Indiana managed to go through the Big Ten undefeated. Led by quarterback guard Quinn Buckner, behemoth center Kent Benson, and smooth shooting forward Scott May, Indiana fought their way past Alabama and Marquette in a tough Mideast regional. They easily disposed of UCLA by 14 points (Indiana had beaten UCLA by 20 earlier in the season) and ended up facing Michigan, a Big Ten foe they vanquished twice during the Big Ten season. Michigan meanwhile had disposed of Eastern power Rutgers, which had been riding a thirty-one-game winning streak, whipping the Scarlet Knights by an 86-70 score.

The confrontation between Michigan and Indiana was the first time that two teams from the same conference had faced each other in the

NCAA finals. The game was close until center Kent Benson asserted himself, scoring 15 of his 25 points in the second half, leading the Hoosiers to an 86-68 score.

In 1977 Al McGuire in his last season of coaching went out in a blaze of glory by capturing the NCAA championship. McGuire, a street tough Irish kid from New York, specialized in bringing black city kids primarily from the East to play a surprisingly slow, disciplined game based on shot selection and tough defense. With only a 20-7 season record the Warriors were not the favorites to go all the way. However, they found themselves in the semifinals facing unheralded North Carolina-Charlotte, whose star 6-foot 8-inch Cedric "Cornbread" Maxwell was used to taking the ball down the court against the press. With three seconds left and the game tied 49-49, the Warriors called time out and McGuire strode on the court to look at the clock, fearful that an inbound pass might deflect off it. A deflected pass went through the opposition and the Warrior's Jerome Whitehead scored at the buzzer for the Marquette victory.

In the final, Marquette was opposed by the University of North Carolina, which had managed to survive the helter-skelter, run and gun attack of the "running Rebels" of Nevada-Las Vegas, edging them on a foul shot with seven seconds left, for an 84-83 victory.

Again, the coaching contrast in the finals was interesting. McGuire was an eccentric, riding his motorcycle, and enjoying the Atlanta nightlife incognito. When asked about problems with his ball players, he responded candidly, "I never had a problem with a ball player. I'm the only problem at Marquette."

Dean Smith, a cool, organized, and popular coach, who was a constant innovator in basketball tactics and strategy, featured the four corner offense when his team was ahead. Against Marquette, the four corner offense backfired. North Carolina had gone in front 45-43 with about 14 minutes left. Marquette, however, was prepared for this tactic and sagged to take away the back door play. Marquette edged to a lead and began their own stall. In a period of two minutes the Warriors sank 14 straight foul shots to secure a 67-59 victory.

The victory found the tough alley fighter in tears, proclaiming that "an alley fighter . . . don't usually get into silk lace situations." But McGuire was not an alley fighter in the sense that he would do anything to win. In the final game, when Phil Ford had ended in the fans section under the basket after driving for a layup, McGuire held his team up until Ford could regain his defensive position. No mere alley fighter ever did that. McGuire had an enthusiasm and love of the game that was infectious, and his knowledgeable coaching helped many a player to develop a disciplined game.

For Dean Smith and the North Carolina team, it was another frustrating tournament loss. Smith's teams had been in the Final Four five times in eleven years and reached the finals twice but never had captured the coveted NCAA crown.

The pressures of college basketball on coaches and teams certainly were evident. Kentucky, a team loaded with talent and perennial Southeastern Conference champs, was picked by most experts to be the cream of the crop during 1978. Kentucky found themselves in the final four only after fighting off tenacious Big Ten champs Michigan State 51-48 in the Mideast regional. In the semifinals the Wildcats edged a quick Arkansas team 64-59 and then cruised by the Duke Blue Devils 94-88 in a game which was not as close as the final score might indicate. Coach Joe B. Hall of Kentucky could finally smile. He and his team had played all season not to lose the championship, since they had been virtually overwhelming choices by the media and basketball experts to win the crown before the season began.

The final basketball season during the seventies, the 1978–79 season, would be one of the most dramatic during the decade. Rated number one during the season was an unlikely team, the Indiana State Sycamores, largely overshadowed in its state by the feats of Indiana University. The Sycamores were led by the finest white ball player in some time, 6-foot 9-inch giant Larry Bird, and a smooth shooting guard, Carl Nicks. Derided by critics for not playing a tough schedule, the Sycamores, powered by the shooting, passing and rebounding of the "Amazing Bird Man," fought their way to the final four.

The Michigan State Spartans, Big Ten champions the year before and losers to Kentucky in a close Mideast regional game in 1978, had been odds on favorites to recapture the Big Ten crown. But Purdue, Ohio State, Indiana, and Michigan all possessed formidable teams, and at one point in the season after an upset loss to Northwestern, the Michigan State team found itself 4-4. Regrouping, they tied for the Big Ten championship, fought their way past perenially tough Notre Dame in the regionals, and joined the select group in the NCAA finals.

The Spartans were led by Earvin "Magic" Johnson. A hometown player from Lansing Everett who had led his team to the state class A championship his senior year in high school, Johnson had to call a press conference because so many in the state were interested as to whether he would choose Michigan State or Michigan.

Johnson was unique, because at 6 feet 8 inches he could play any position on the floor. He was an adept ball handler who repopularized the pass, often gaining spectacular assists when he lofted them into the skies above the basket where 6-foot 7-inch Greg "Special K"

Kelser would hover above the rim, for a spectacular jam dunk. Yet Johnson could flick hook shots in from the pivot or post up for bank shots from a forward position. Johnson had a real sense of the court and tremendous anticipation for his teammates' moves. He took as much joy in an assist as he did in scoring.

The Spartan coach, Jud Heathcote, was a screamer who was adept at acquiring technical fouls. He also was a master defensive strategist who had developed a suffocating match up zone defense which had stifled most high scoring offenses during the year.

In the semifinals, the Spartans had a much easier game than the Sycamores. Playing the University of Pennsylvania Quakers, who were hoping to prove that Eastern basketball was making a comeback, the Spartans quickly shattered the upset dreams of the players from the Keystone State. Roaring out to a 50-17 lead, the Spartans coasted to a 101-67 point victory. *Sports Illustrated* reported that when Johnson (29 points, 10 rebounds, 10 assists) came out of the game with a little over five minutes to go, he whispered to Greg Kelser (28 points, 9 rebounds) that "if we keep playing like this, its' going to be worth a couple of million dollars for us in the pros."

Indiana State faced a much tougher semifinal test in a young but talented and resurgent DePaul Blue Demon squad coached by wily veteran coach Ray Meyer. The Sycamores managed to eke out a precarious 76-74 victory as Larry Bird had 35 points, hit in 16 of 19 from the field, collaring 16 rebounds and dishing out 9 assists.

In the finals, the Spartans had too many guns for the Sycamores. The Spartans' zone defense collapsed on Bird, who went 7 for 21, had 6 turnovers, and only 2 assists. A fine Indiana State defense prevented the Spartans from running rampant as they had in their other tournament games. The outside shooting of guard Terry Donnelly, who fired in 15 points, was the key as he loosened up the Sycamore defense so that the Spartan big guns, Kelser (19 points) and Johnson (24 points) could get untracked. Earvin Johnson, nicknamed the "Magic Man," had certainly performed a feat of legerdemain for Michigan State basketball fortunes. The success of the Michigan State basketball team helped to rebuild and revitalize an athletic program that had been devastated by scandal and a punitive NCAA probation.

The seventies saw college basketball more popular than ever before. The 1979 national college basketball attendance reached 30 million for the first time, boosted by enormous increases in Division I attendance—976,190. (Major college attendance increased by 1.2 million in 1978 and by 1.1 million in 1979.)

Over 100 major college arenas were constructed in the decade and 124 arenas in Divisions II and III. More than 100 teams played half their games in arenas seating 10,000 or more. In 1959 only 22 teams did and in 1969 only 51 teams did.

The Big Ten conference, although boasting only one arena built in the seventies, in 1979 established all-time national attendance records of 12,238 per game and 1,713,380 overall. Eight of the Big Ten teams averaged over 10,000 a game (28 Division I teams did so in 1979). The Southeastern conference ranked second, and 11 Division I conferences recorded increases in total attendance. In addition, televised NCAA games were popular with viewers. NBC could report that the 1977 NCAA championship game between Marquette and North Carolina was the second time that over 42 million had viewed an NCAA championship game, the first being the 1975 title game between UCLA and Kentucky. The featuring of nationally ranked teams in intersectional contests on Sunday afternoon, going head to head with pro basketball telecasts, had been an overwhelming success, particularly since former Marquette coach Al McGuire added his colorful commentary.

By the end of the decade college basketball officials could be proud of the caliber of players and the skills demonstrated by college basketball players. The 1979 NCAA finale had been a dream matchup which featured spectacular superstars, one black and one white, who could score but who emphasized passing and the team game instead of shooting—which helped to deflect the knock by critics that the game was just one of running up and down the floor and flinging up jump shots. The records during the seventies clearly show that the team that won the NCAA championship rarely had a player who was an overwhelming scorer or featured players who were not well schooled in the fundamentals of both offense and defense.

But university officials had to be concerned with the role basketball played at a college or university. Many players were not completing their education as they were often selected by the NBA draft after they had demonstrated their superior ability as a college freshman or sophomore. Some would have good pro careers, but others would be cut and have nowhere to go since they were no longer amateurs. Michigan State's Earvin Johnson was signed after his sophomore year by the Los Angeles Lakers and led them to the NBA championship in his rookie year (1979–80). But for every Earvin who debuted spectacularly there were dozens of other black ball players who would go back to the ghetto with their dreams shattered. Colleges and universities had to face the fact that they had perhaps simply become the minor leagues for pro basketball.

Colleges and universities also reflected a desire to accumulate more revenues from basketball's popularity. Most conferences had traditionally decided their NCAA tournament representative by electing their conference champion. By the end of the seventies, many of the conferences chose to follow the lead of the Atlantic Coast Conference and staged postseason tournaments for that purpose. Coming after a long—perhaps as many as thirty games—season, such a tournament certainly does not take into consideration the academic well-being of the players. This is an area where colleges and universities must seriously reexamine their consciences and priorities.

Pro Basketball

The NBA at the end of the seventies seemed stronger than ever. Its 240 players averaged $158,000 a year. The league was in the second year of a $74 million contract with CBS. The American Basketball League had essentially folded in 1976 with four of its teams becoming members of the NBA.

By the end of the decade, superficial prosperity could not hide the fact that the NBA was a league in trouble. For years attendance had soared and TV ratings were high. But since the 1977 championship round between the Philadelphia 76ers and the Portland Trail Blazers, NBA ratings had declined and attendance, particularly in the major markets such as New York and Los Angeles, had also slipped. Each team received about $800,000 per year from television and in the final year of the contract would receive $1 million. Without increased television ratings, the NBA might find it difficult to procure a similarly lucrative contract.

Numerous reasons have been offered for the dip in the NBA's popularity. Some suggested that lack of winners in important media areas such as New York and Boston hurt the league. Others pointed out that the league is composed of 75 percent black players and that much of the white public will not support a predominantly black sports franchise. (In 1979–80 sports history was made when for the first time two all black NBA teams, the New York Knicks and the Detroit Pistons, met in a regularly scheduled NBA game.) Yet some say it is really the ticket prices that have caused attendance decline. Four tickets to an NBA game could cost close to $50.00.

Veteran Paul Silas, commenting on the price of tickets, has said "It's a lot of money just for one night. If the buying public stops coming to games, then I guess the owners will have to decide what they want to do about the big salaries."

Another major criticism of the NBA is the amount of pushing and shoving—allowable violence—which has made the game less aesthetic to watch and has triggered incidents such as the slugging of center Kent Benson by Kareem Abdul-Jabbar and Kermit Washington's attack on Rudy Tomjanovich which shattered his face and almost ruined his basketball career.

To reduce the incidence of violence the NBA used three referees and made hand checking illegal in the 1978–79 season. For the 1979 season, the NBA went back to two referees. Also in 1979, a three point basket from a distance ranging from about 23 feet in the corners to 25 feet straight out from the basket was introduced. The reason for such an innovation was that it was believed that putting a premium on outside shooting would force teams to avoid clogging the middle where most of the contact and injuries occur. Critics contend, however, that the three point shot would just give added incentive to "gunners" to launch their shots from anywhere on the courts and only make the game an even more "run and gun affair."

Whatever the reasons for the NBA's fall from grace, the ending of the decade left the league with new challenges. Many identifiable stars such as Walt Frazier had retired, and team rosters seemed to change overnight, making it difficult for a fan to identify with a team, even if he had the predilection to do so. The NBA also had to live with the criticism from many educators who argued that although millions dream of NBA glory and work for that goal, only 200 players are drafted each year and only 40 remain for a full season. For those who didn't make it, their basketball skills are not the skills needed to provide a living in the normal world, and these rejected aspirants often "are frequently left without the skills to do anything more than become economic and social derelicts." A real question for the Players Association and the League owners and officials was to decide whether or not it was guilty of offering a largely illusory road to achieve success, particularly for the average black youngster for whom basketball often played such a large role in his life.

The ABA league managed to linger on until 1976 with varying degrees of success. Franchises folded and went under, players switched back and forth, and only the red, white, and blue basketball and the three point play seemed constant. The ABA could never procure the lucrative television contract that would have enabled many of its marginal franchises to maintain operation. However, the ABA with its drafting of University of Detroit star Spencer Heywood for the 1969–70 season began the somewhat dubious practice of signing college undergraduates. Soon other undergraduates such as Ralph

Simpson of Michigan State and George McGinnis of Indiana were induced by lucrative contracts to forego their collegiate eligibility and join the ABA.

Although unable to secure the rights to Lew Alcindor and Bill Walton, the ABA did offer big money, some of it not wisely spent. The league signed such varied individuals as Artis Gilmore, Johnny Neumann, John Roche, Jim McDaniels, and Collis Jones. And of these, only Artis Gilmore could be said to have been a superstar in the ABA. (He would go on to star with the Chicago Bulls of the NBA after the merger.)

In the first several years of the decade, Indiana, led by George McGinnis and other home state talent such as Rick Mount, and Kentucky, led by former Kentucky stars Dan Issell and Louis Dampier, were probably the premier ABA teams and generally drew the best attendance. The signing of Julius Erving from the University of Massachusetts before he completed his senior year was a coup for the ABA. He was signed by the Virginia Squires for the 1971–72 season. In 1973, Dr. J., as he became known, took his high flying act to New York, where he starred with the Nets, leading them to their first title, capturing the scoring crown with a 27.4 average and also earning MVP honors.

By 1974–75 the ABA was still changing franchises. Still seeking to survive, the league hired former Knick star Dave DeBusschere as a commissioner, the seventh and last commissioner of the league. The league also set a precedent by signing 6-foot 11-inch center Moses Malone right out of high school. Others had signed while in college but none had been added to either league straight out of high school. The ABA record seemed ready to raid any territory for available talent.

By the 1975–76 season, with the folding of the San Diego and Utah franchises, the ABA was down to seven teams. Although Denver, led by David Thompson, and New York, with Dr. J., were strong franchises, the ABA was evidently on its last leg. New York beat Denver for the final ABA championship. On June 17, 1976, a treaty was made with the NBA whereby four ABA teams—New York, Denver, Indiana, and San Antonio—would join the NBA. The nine-year rocky existence of the ABA had come to an end. Pro baseball and football had successfully expanded and opened new sports markets, but basketball could not match this success. Two leagues stretched the available talent too thin, and the increasing competition with the college game could not be matched by the ABA.

The NBA during the seventies escalated in popularity during the first six or seven years but declined, as previously noted, in the last several years. The addition of the two premier college stars, Larry Bird and Earvin Johnson, for the 1978–79 season helped to stem somewhat this tide of disaffection. Among the problems plaguing the NBA not already mentioned were the lack of a team dynasty and the overemphasis on individual play. The fascination with one-on-one matchups had diminished.

During the decade the New York Knickerbockers and the Boston Celtics were the only NBA teams to take the championship twice and neither did it in consecutive years: the Knicks in the 1969–70 and the 1972–73 seasons and Boston in the 1973–74 and 1975–76 seasons. A dynasty like the Yankees in baseball or the Celtics in basketball creates an interest for their respective leagues. Their superiority denotes a specialness which makes other teams' victories over them an achievement meant to be treasured rather than just another pit stop in the eighty-one game grind.

Secondly, although NBA champions during the seventies reflected team play and a reverence for the passing game (the inability of the Philadelphia 76ers to win a title despite a gaggle of superstars demonstrated clearly how important team play was), much of the NBA play had become a mirror image of the inner city playgrounds where many of the NBA players had first practiced their skills. More interest in flinging "in your face" jumpers at every opportunity than in scoring totals, innovating new dunks, and making spectacular blocked shots (no matter that the opposing team often got the ball right back) caused individual play to dominate and left the other players standing and watching. It was an ironic twist that instead of the pro game influencing other levels of play, it was the playground game of the legendary playground stars such as Helicopter Knowings, Joe Hammond and Earl Manigault that had come to dominate NBA play. Earl Monroe, commenting in a 1980 issue of *Basketball Digest,* placed much of the blame for the "demise of team play" on the NBA team owners. He stated, "Basically, management brought this about. They started showcasing guys. Every team has a guy who is the designated superstar. The star has to play more minutes and have a big game because he is the show. Basketball should be the show."

The New York Knickerbockers, NBA champions in 1969–70 and 1972–73, became one of "the country's most popular sports teams." Unlike previous pro basketball teams, the Knicks were not built around a gargantuan and dominating center such as a Mikan, Russell, Chamberlain, or Abdul-Jabbar. The fans could more readily identify with "the more ordinary people"—according to pro basketball standards—who played for the Knicks. Willis Reed, the 6-foot 10-inch center, was merely the "hub" of the attack.

The Knicks featured an interesting blend of players, white and black, with varying styles yet who melded together to play the epitome of the team game. Dave DeBusschere, the strong forward, played tenacious defense, boarded well, and was a good outside shot. Bill Bradley, former Princeton All-American and Rhodes scholar, flitted around picks to fling up one-handers and cut constantly for the open basket while looking for the pass from the center. Reed could shoot from the outside, set tremendous picks, and hammer the boards. Dick Barnett, the penultimate "fall-back in your face" fade away jump shooter, added another dimension to the varied Knick attack.

The man who proved to be the catalyst of the Knicks was Walt Frazier. Frazier in 1967 had led his unheralded Southern Illinois team to the championship of the NIT. Playing in New York for the Knickerbockers, Frazier became the epitome of the guard who can do it all—pass, shoot, set up plays, and turn defense into an art form. Called "Clyde," for his smoothness on the court and for his image as a well-dressed man about town, and seen frequently attired in "Superfly" fashion, Frazier became the dream guard of both coaches and youngsters seeking a hero to emulate. Willis Reed once said about him that "the ball belongs to Frazier, he just lets us play with it—sometimes."

Red Auerbach, the president and general manager of the Boston Celtics, and certainly a man who knows the NBA, said of Frazier: "Walt Frazier was unquestionably one of the great guards of his era. He was a premier player because he understood that basketball is a team game and he used his abilities within a team context. As a result, the Knicks were winners. He did not have great speed, but when the moment called for it, he was very tough to catch. He was an outstanding pure shooter who hardly ever forced a shot because he understood what the Knick system would give him and played within those limits. . . . But what stands out about Frazier is that no matter how furious the action or how tense the situation, he was always Mr. Cool, always seeming above the pressure."

In 1970 the Knickerbockers won 60 and lost 22 in the regular season and then rolled into the finals with the Los Angeles Lakers as their opposition. In the fifth game of the series, Willis Reed hurt his leg and did not play the sixth game. In the seventh game, Reed hobbled onto the court and made two baskets. His courage inspired his team and they bowled over Los Angeles 113-99. In 1970–71, the Milwaukee Bucks, powered by Kareem Abdul-Jabbar and crafty Oscar Robertson, rang up an even more impressive victory skein than had the Knicks the previous season, compiling a 66 and 16 record and sweeping the Baltimore Bullets in four straight.

In 1971–72 the Los Angeles Lakers even surpassed the outstanding records of the NBA champs of the two previous seasons by posting a 69-13 record and at one time hitting a 33 game win streak. Milwaukee had a not so shabby 63-19 record. However, the Central Division winner Baltimore posted a 38 and 44 record, a winning percentage of only .463.

In the playoffs the Lakers beat Chicago in four games, Milwaukee in six, and the Knicks in five, posting a final record of 81-16 including the playoff games. Finally, the Los Angeles super combination of Jerry West and Wilt Chamberlain had paid off.

In the succeeding year, Willis Reed, spelled by former Ohio State star Jerry Lucas, who looked and played a lot like Dave DeBusschere, again sparked the Knicks to a title. Although finishing in second place in the East, the Knicks edged Boston in seven games for the Eastern conference championship and after losing the opening game to the Lakers won the next four for the championship.

The Boston Celtics, led by their versatile and fiery center Dave Cowens, beat Milwaukee in seven games in 1973–74. In 1975–76 an aggressive San Francisco Warrior team, spearheaded by the leadership of Rick Barry and the coaching of Al Attles, surprised all by making the finals and sweeping by the Washington Bullets in four games, making it six years in a row when a defending champion had not repeated, a feat unprecedented in the NBA. One analyst stated, ''The days of dynasties, built on supercenters were indeed ended. The team player era had arrived, and the Warriors, with their endless flow of substitutions, were its prophets.''

In 1975–76 Kareem Abdul-Jabbar decided he wanted to leave Milwaukee because he found the Midwestern city too confining for his life-style. Subsequently, he was traded to Los Angeles for four players. This trade did not guarantee instant success for the Lakers. The surprising Phoenix Suns, led by Rookie of the Year Alvan Adams and by Ricky Sobers, a big, tough guard from Nevada-Las Vegas, fought their way to the finals where they confronted the Celtics for NBA supremacy. After splitting the first four games, the Suns and Celtics played an exhausting triple overtime game won by the Celtics, 128-126, setting a record for the longest game in the NBA finals. Less than forty-eight hours later, the Celtics wrapped up the title with an 87-80 win.

An interesting sidelight to that season was that when Commissioner Walter Kennedy retired Lawrence O'Brien, former Democratic party official and a close friend and advisor to the late President Kennedy, as well as a man without much basketball expertise, was selected to replace the commissioner.

In 1976–77, another significant trade was consumated when Julius

Erving went from the New York Nets to the Philadelphia 76ers, an attempt by new owner Fitz Eugene Dixon to assemble a galaxy of stars in an effort to gain an instant title. The attempt fell just short as a fluid and team-oriented group of Portland Trail Blazers sparked by the rebounding and passing of a healthy mountain man, Bill Walton, and the astute coaching of Jack Ramsey, edged the 76ers in six games, winning the final one 109-107. Although Dr. J. had demonstrated his own prowess, other 76er stars such as George McGinnis were ineffective and Portland teamwork prevailed.

The 1976–77 season was complicated by the fact that it was the first season under the merger. This meant not only the addition of four completely new teams, but the shuffling of players from the three now defunct ABA teams throughout the NBA. This situation necessitated a "dispersal" draft and often numerous personnel changes which created problems for fan identification.

In addition, a new playoff format had to be developed. According to the new rules, the four division winners would receive a first round bye. The other four qualifiers in each conference would be selected on the basis of their win-loss records and then they would be matched against each other in a miniround playoff. The two teams emerging from these contests would then take on the division champs and the winner would play for the division championship. The eastern and western champions would then play off for the NBA title.

In 1977–78 and 1978–79, the Washington Bullets and Seattle Super Sonics were the NBA finalists. The Bullets were coached by Dick Motta, former Chicago Bulls coach, and were led by aging superstars Wes Unseld and Elvin Hayes. Seattle was coached by former star Lenny Wilkens and sparked by blond, 6-foot 11-inch strong boy Jack Sikma and the guard play of Dennis Johnson and the outside shooting of "Downtown" Freddie Brown. The two teams traded championships, with Washington winning in 1977–78 and the Super Sonics gaining revenge in 1978–79.

In 1979–80 the NBA was buoyed by the signing of the biggest white college basketball star since Bill Walton, Larry Bird, and the signing of Earvin "Magic" Johnson, who had two years of college eligibility remaining, by the Los Angeles Lakers. Coached by former Cleveland Cavaliers coach Bill Fitch, Boston previously had added Detroit stars Chris Ford and M. L. Carr in exchange for point productive but temperamental Bob McAddo. With a rejuvenated Dave Cowens, the Celtics easily won their division. Having dumped George McGinnis, allowing Julius Erving more freedom to play his free-lance game, and getting improved all-around playing from towering Darryl Dawkins and his awesome, often backboard shattering dunks, the Philadelphia team triumphed over the Celtics, who looked weak and ineffective in the playoffs against Philadelphia.

In the West, people worried whether the enthusiasm of Magic Johnson and his friendly demeanor would be well received from the laid back players and fans of the Lakers. They need not have worried. With Johnson passing, scoring, and rebounding, pressure was taken off Kareem Abdul-Jabbar so that he responded by having one of his best seasons ever. Although he only averaged 25 points a game, almost the lowest in his career and did not grab 1,000 rebounds for the third time in his career, Kareem, thanks to numerous assists from Magic, shot an amazing 60 percent from the field, blocked the most shots in the NBA, and ranked second behind Sam Lacy in assists by a center.

The Lakers fought their way into the finals, downing Seattle 111-105 in the final game of the Western Conference playoffs. In the finals against the 76ers, the Lakers held a 3-2 edge, but Kareem injured his ankle and was left home when the Lakers traveled to Philadelphia. It looked gloomy for the Lakers, but rookie Magic Johnson responded by playing all three positions and leading the Lakers to a 123-107 triumph. In three years the irrepressible "Magic Man" with the million dollar smile had won high school, college, and professional basketball titles—a feat unparalleled in the annals of basketball history. For the NBA, the quick emergence of Johnson and Bird as true stars in the NBA, renewing their collegiate rivalry, meant that the new stars for the '80s had arrived and NBA accountants could only be drooling over the piles of money fans would be paying to see these extraordinary ballplayers display their skills in the decade ahead. Johnson's identification with the Lakers was sealed when he signed a 25 year $25 million pact, creating a new kind of "exclusive services" contract.

Baseball

Baseball in the 1970s saw a resurgence in popularity and fan support as well as internal changes that would revolutionize the sport as a business and a game. In 1979 attendance at major league games was 43.5 million fans, a jump of almost 3 million from 1978. A Gallup poll released in 1973 showed that 24 percent of the people interviewed named baseball as their favorite spectator sport, still down from the 34 percent that claimed baseball as their special sport in 1961. However, baseball continued to have solid fan support at the box office, and with rising ticket prices and lucrative television revenues baseball was ready for a decade of prosperity and rapid change. The switch to night games in the World Series made in 1972 opened up a vast new television audience. When the fourth game of the Baltimore-Pittsburgh Series in 1971 was experimentally scheduled for a night contest, an estimated audience of 61 million viewers tuned in, three times the daytime audience that saw the Sunday game of the 1963 World Series. The seventh game of the 1975 classic series between Boston and Cincinnati commanded an estimated audience of 70 million viewers. Television coverage helped to "showcase" baseball and to whet fan appetites for pennant races, new and colorful player personalities, and the promise of new levels of achievement (seven players reached or surpassed the milestone of 3,000 hits during the 1970s).

The decade featured remarkable individual accomplishments. Henry Aaron and Willie Mays surged beyond the 3,000 hit mark in 1970, and Willie Mays and Aaron would join Ruth and Cobb as the greatest hitters and run producers the game had seen. Aaron would break Ruth's lifetime home run record in 1974 with his dramatic seven-hundred fifteenth home run. Aaron's chase of Ruth's record inspired a popular song ("Move Over, Babe, Here Comes Henry"), spot television coverage of Atlanta Braves' games as Aaron moved in on the record, and scores of journalists and writers waiting on every word from the slugger. For all the media hype, Aaron handled the situation with cool aplomb and restrained pride. Aaron knew that his own personal accomplishment was being exploited to boost baseball as it approached its centennial year, and perhaps he resented the belated attention that came after years of nonrecognition and neglect. Commissioner Bowie Kuhn even ordered the Braves to play Aaron in Cincinnati when he was close to breaking Ruth's record, with Kuhn uncaring whether Aaron tied and broke the record in Atlanta or not. This order angered Aaron, but the record-breaking round tripper did rightly come in Atlanta. Later, after his retirement, Aaron would speak more openly about racism in baseball and prejudice against black players when it came to endorsements and television broadcasting jobs.

The same year of Aaron's famous home run, Lou Brock stole a remarkable 118 bases, as he pushed his career steals to over 900, breaking Ty Cobb's career mark and Maury Wills's single season record. Brock would also reach the 3,000 hit mark in 1979, as would Pete Rose and Carl Yastremski. After the 3,000 hit Brock was congratulated by Stan Musial, another member of that exclusive group of only fifteen men.

The 1970s also saw the ends of the careers of two of the American League's best players: Al Kaline and Brooks Robinson. After a twenty-two-year career with Detroit Kaline retired in 1974 with 3,007 hits, nine seasons of a .300 or better batting average, and fifteen All-Star appearances with a .384 average. Having never played a game in the minors, Kaline won the batting title in 1955 at the age of twenty, and in 1968 he helped lead the Tigers to a World Series win over St. Louis with a .379 average and 8 RBI's. Kaline overcame several serious injuries in his career to play with consistency and the calm competitive pride of a true professional. As a television announcer of Tiger games with George Kell, Kaline displays the insights and sound baseball knowledge that have made him one of the great students of the game. Kaline represented a dedication to the game and a degree of personal discipline that earned him the respect and love of Detroit fans.

Brooks Robinson retired in 1977 after twenty-three consecutive seasons with the Baltimore Orioles. When he left the game, Robinson held major league records for the most games played by a third baseman, most assists, most total chances, most double plays, and most years leading the league in fielding average. His fielding gems in the 1970 Series against Cincinnati were memorable moments as the "human vacuum cleaner" showed how quick reflexes, brilliant body control, instant recovery, and a strong arm could make fielding as exciting as hitting or pitching.

Like Kaline, Robinson was the disciplined professional who played with an intensity that was often understated. Both were fielding specialists, and both were men who loved playing the game more than amassing money or garnering publicity. In an era of outspoken egotists, these two men were players who let their play speak for their talents and professionalism. Few modern players would enjoy the length of the careers that Kaline and Robinson had or the distinction of being with only one team and becoming respected symbols of their town's pride. Carl Yastremski, with nineteen consecutive years at Boston, and Lou Brock, with fifteen seasons for St. Louis, could make the same claims of such stability and endurance. When Yastremski finally retires, as well as Pete Rose and Rod Carew, baseball will be without the greatest hitters of the modern day era.

These players were unique because they underwent the changes from day baseball to predominantly night baseball, from the traditional league organization to expansion, from train travel to plane travel, and from natural grass to artificial turf. The future possibility of 3,000-hit players seems increasingly remote, although Steve Garvey and Amos Otis could join that select group if their careers last close to twenty years. More than likely, new standards or milestones of achievement will have to be developed for the modern day player as the older standards of 3,000 hits, 400 career homers, .300 or better career average, and 300 wins for pitchers become increasingly inaccessible. Extended careers seem to be the exception rather than the rule, as night baseball, the demands of jet travel, the decreased emphasis on physical conditioning, the increasing specialization of careers, and the impact of free agentry with more trades and personnel changes all taking their toll on careers and endurance.

The 1970s saw major legal and financial developments that would produce a new breed of professional baseball players. The first development was the Curt Flood lawsuit in 1970, filed against the St. Louis Cardinals. The Cardinals decided to trade Flood to the Phillies after he had spent twelve years with the St. Louis team, hitting over .300 in six of those seasons and playing a steady centerfield. Flood charged baseball with violating the antitrust laws and asked for a court injunction that would nullify the "reserve clause" that bound him to report to the Phillies if he wanted to continue his career. He wanted to become a free agent, even though the Philadelphia team tried to dissuade him with a $110,000 contract for 1970. Flood was out of baseball during the 1970 season, although he returned from Europe to play thirteen games for the Washington Senators in 1971 before he left the team, pocketing the $100,000 annual salary that owner Bob Short had assured him. Finally reaching the Supreme Court in mid-1972, Flood's case produced a ruling that upheld the reserve clause and indicated that jurisdiction in this area rested with Congress, not the courts. Baseball was still exempt from antitrust laws, and Flood's argument that he "was not a consignment of goods" but "a man, rightful proprietor of my own person and talents" was set aside. Flood's career was ended, but his challenge to the absolute authority of owners had been supported by the Major League Baseball Players Association.

Players were becoming more militant as the 1972 thirteen-day general strike proved. The immediate issue was the pension plan contributions of the owners, but the real issue came out in the threatened 1973 strike. At this time the owners were forced to agree to outside arbitration in salary negotiations and a clause that would allow a player with ten years of major league experience, the last five with the same club, to nullify a trade. The baseball world was no longer a special place of financial negotiation where owners held the upper hand and could be as arbitrary as they liked. Players wanted and needed more security and bargaining power in a sport in which economics, owners' whims and power brokerage, and instability of players' careers were increasing realities.

By 1974 the sacred reserve clause lost its hold over players' fates and futures. Andy Messersmith, Dave McNally, and Jim Hunter were declared free agents by a labor arbitrator, Peter M. Seitz. Players who refused to sign contracts and who played for a year without a contract could become free agents and then offer their services to other ball clubs, creating a seller's market where teams would bid competitively. Or if a club violated or failed to fulfill the terms of a contract, as in the case of Jim Hunter and the Oakland A's, the player could become a free agent. Of course, the player could negotiate with his current team and remain with it if he so chose.

From this point on contract negotiations were to become more complex, and the professional agent, representing the players' interests, became a new face on the scene. The important thing was that now the individual player decided his options. Declaration of free agent status was a calculated risk, but most athletes seemed to benefit from it and many players who stayed with teams received a sizeable boost in salary to keep them from looking elsewhere. The average salary went from $25,000 in 1969 to $37,000 in 1973, to $121,000 in 1979. In 1973 only 5 percent of all major league baseball players made $100,000 or more a year, but six years later the average salary was well over that mark.

In July 1976 the owners and Players Association reached an agreement regarding free agentry. Players without 1976 or 1977 contracts could become free agents and players with six or more years in the majors could declare free agent status immediately. The owners also reluctantly agreed that no compensation would be paid to the free agent's former team. By November 1976, twenty-five players who did not sign 1976 contracts were available for the re-entry draft, and the Oakland A's had seven free agents as players sought to escape the arbitrary and whimsical owner, Charlie O. Finley. The re-entry draft brought long-term contracts along with more complicated means of remuneration, all which favored the bargaining athlete. Free agent status also brought pressures of immediate production and stardom to measure up to the fantastic salary. A team filled with carpetbagger free agents who were unproductive could quickly lose fan support, as was the case at first with the California Angels, San Diego Padres, and Texas Rangers, teams that went into the free agent market heavily. The New York Yankees came back to respectability in 1977 and 1978 by means of the acquisition of free agents and intelligent trades. They rightly deserved the appellation "the best team money can buy," and the $70 million spent to renovate and modernize Yankee stadium gave them the posh surroundings befitting a team that was called a "millionaire's club."

The free agent system made baseball less profitable for the owners, but with the increase in attendance and other income sources from concessions and parking, baseball was still profitable for most clubs. Club owners claimed that the free agent development threatened the "competitive balance" of the sport, introduced financial uncertainty, and caused average ballplayers to be greedy and unrealistic in salary demands.

It should be noted, however, that in 1973 the players were paid only 17 percent of the income from the game, which then had a gross annual income of about $130 million. Commissioner Bowie Kuhn claimed that baseball operated at a deficit from 1975 to 1977 and in 1978 had a total profit of a mere $4,000. Others estimate that owners' profits range as high as $80 million annually. With these disparities in the estimated profits from the game, it is little wonder that there is confusion about how financially solvent the game is and whether it can afford the annual inflation factor of the free agent re-entry draft.

Another point to consider is that television revenues make up one-third of baseball's total income, and one has to wonder what would happen if that level of sponsorship was cut because of a lengthy recession or a shift in fan interest that sent commercial money elsewhere. A number of the franchises seem shaky enterprises, notably San Francisco, San Diego, Oakland, and Atlanta. Another question is whether fan interest and support can remain high or adequate with the two American League expansion teams—the Seattle Mariners and the Toronto Blue Jays—when the prospects of a contender or winner seem remote and the "miracle" of the 1969 New York Mets seems unlikely to be duplicated. One has to wonder further how many new markets can be developed if franchises have to be moved or whether increasing costs may necessitate a complete realignment and merging of the two leagues with the old National and American League designations disappearing.

The bottom line is that the free agent situation has brought major changes to the game with the stars being paid the lion's share of the new revenues. The average salary has gone up dramatically, largely because of the multimillion dollar contracts enjoyed by Jim Hunter, Nolan Ryan, Dave Parker, Dave Winfield, Don Gullet, and others who have been paid over a million for a multiyear contract. Many players are making below the average salary as certain teams refuse to enter the free agent market and are holding the line on salaries, notably Detroit and Boston.

Still, labor arbitrators are playing a key role in affecting the salaries of these clubs, as Detroit found out when Lou Whitaker, Alan Trammel, and Steve Kemp all won sizeable boosts in their pay via this arbitration route. Players now have more options open to them in influencing their careers and remuneration, but the free agent situation has not brought financial chaos to the game. As long as the gentleman owner is the game's bankroller who has diversified assets and other resources, and as long as these men consider the game an amusing diversion and ongoing interest, baseball can survive increasing costs and a greater percentage of revenues paid out to players.

It remains to be seen whether the Yankees or any other major league team will produce another dynasty that dominates the game and monopolizes available talent. The free agent system seems more to have redistributed talent rather than concentrating it, and most of the players have not chosen to go this route with its attendance pressures and problems. Additionally, the free agent system seems to have decreased the number of trades and thus will perhaps bring some much needed stability to the sport with a continuity of playing personnel that is the basis for ongoing fan interest and support. Fans support players who feel loyalty to a club, as the local popularity of Yastremski, Burleson, Evans, and Rice attested to in Boston, one of the most stable franchises.

The 1970s also saw the American League expand to fourteen teams in 1977, with the National League staying at twelve teams. Canada now had two teams, making the game a North American game and opening up a new fan and television market. Montreal's near success in 1979 brought pennant fever to that city and offered promise of a future international division playoff and possible World Series.

Another major development was the American League's option of the designated hitter rule in 1973 on a three-year experimental basis. The experiment provided such a success that the DH was a permanent fixture by 1975, and the rule extended the careers of great hitters who had slowed down in the field as well as provided a means of further platooning. In the 1976 Series between Cincinnati and New York, the Reds' designated hitter, Dan Driessen, hit .357 including 3 hits and scoring 4 runs, embarrassing the two Yankee DHs, Carlos May and Lou Piniella. In the 1978 Series Reggie Jackson hit .391 as the DH with 8 RBI's and 2 home runs as the Yankees defeated the Dodgers in six games. By agreement, the leagues accepted the use of the DH in alternate years of the World Series. The new position made Rico Carty, Willie Horton, Ron Fairly, Lee May, Rusty Staub, Hal McRae, and Richie Zisk the new specialists of the game. The existence of the DH rule introduced new strategy to the World Series as American League managers had to forego a potent offensive weapon, and use pitchers differently, and make difficult decisions about the use of pinch hitters in the Series where the DH was disallowed.

The 1970s was an era of great baseball teams as the Oakland A's established a minor dynasty with five division titles between 1971 and 1975 and three consecutive World Championships (1972, 1973, 1974); the Cincinnati Reds had powerful teams in 1975 and 1976 with consecutive world championships; the Yankees returned to prominence with convincing Series wins over Los Angeles in 1977 and 1978; and the Pirates defeated Baltimore in the 1971 and 1979 Series.

In the 1970 Series Baltimore pounded Cincinnati pitching for 50 hits in five games, including 10 home runs, and amassed a .292 team batting average, which was the highest team average since the Yankees hit .338 and had 91 hits in their losing effort to the Pirates in the remarkable 1960 Series. Baltimore overcame three run deficits in games one, two, and five to take the Series in five games. The Orioles of 1970 were one of the hottest stretch drive teams in baseball, winning the last eleven in the regular season, sweeping three in the divisional playoffs, and winning the first three games of the Series.

Baltimore repeated in 1971 as divisional champion, featuring four pitchers with twenty wins: Mike Cuellar, Pat Dobson, Jim Palmer, and Dave McNally. The pitchers led the league in complete games and earned run average. After defeating Oakland easily in the playoffs, Baltimore faced Pittsburgh in the Series. The Orioles were hot again, winning sixteen consecutive games, including the first two games of the Series. The fourth, sixth, and seventh games were all decided by one run as the Pirates came storming back to win a closely contested Series. Steve Blass pitched brilliantly for the Pirates, winning the key third and seventh games, pitching complete games, and allowing only 2 runs. Baltimore hit an anemic .205 compared with their .292 Series average in 1970, and the Oriole fielders committed an uncharacteristic 9 errors.

In 1972 the Oakland A's won the first of three straight World Championships, defeating Cincinnati in seven games. The Series featured six games that were decided by 1 run, as only 37 runs were scored and pitching dominated. Rollie Fingers appeared in six games as a relief pitcher, being credited with 2 saves and a win. The hitting star of the Series was Gene Tenace, who hit 4 home runs and had 9 RBI's while hitting .348. Oakland scored only 16 runs but won all four games by 1 run as manager Dick Williams used his starting pitchers brilliantly in relief.

In 1973 Oakland defeated the New York Mets in another seven-game Series, hitting only .212 as a team and striking out 68 times.

However, Oakland again won the close games on the basis of brilliant relief pitching by Rollie Fingers and Darrell Knowles, who each had 2 saves. Fingers again appeared in six games and Knowles in all of the contests. The weak hitting A's had only 2 home runs in the Series, and those came in the third inning of the seventh game to give Oakland pitchers a 4-run cushion to work with. After the Series, manager Dick Williams quit, fed up with the intervention of Charley O. Finley in the running of the team.

The 1974 Oakland Series win was much easier, with the A's prevailing in five games over Los Angeles. Three of the wins were by 1 run as Oakland relief pitching again rose to the occasion. Fingers was credited with 3 saves and a victory in this first all-California World Series. Mike Marshall pitched brilliantly in relief for the Dodgers, allowing only 6 hits and 1 run in five appearances, although Joe Rudi's seventh inning home run in the fifth game off Marshall proved to be the margin of victory.

The Oakland team was rife with discontent, conflict, and player feuds. Finley was constantly stirring up controversy, as he treated managers with contempt and dealt with players in a paternalistic way, playing one against the other in a perverse game of power and control. In the 1973 Series Finley tried to fire Mike Andrews, the A's second baseman, after Andrews made two costly errors in the twelfth inning of the four hour, thirteen-minute second game, won by the Mets 10-7. Andrews, under pressure, signed a paper that admitted that he had a bad shoulder injury and should be placed on the disabled list, which would have allowed Finley to add another player to his roster. Bowie Kuhn intervened and disallowed the results of the hasty medical examination. The A's players threatened to boycott the rest of the Series if Andrews was not allowed to play. Andrews appeared only as a pinch hitter in the fourth game at Shea Stadium, grounding out to third in the eighth inning, but the Mets fans gave him a standing ovation when he came to the plate. The next year Andrews was out of baseball, his taste for the game soured by the Series humiliation.

Finley later drove seven key players to declare free agent status in 1976 after he tried to sell three players for $3.5 million, with Bowie Kuhn disallowing the deals in the "best interest of the game." Finley traded away or forced away a remarkable collection of talent because he could not deal with the new freedom and militancy of the players as they sought higher salaries and better contract terms. Unwilling to pay for the genuine stars he had assembled, Finley preferred no-name players who would accept his authoritarian and unpredictable rule, as well as his meddlesome interference. As a result, a once proud franchise steadily declined, with attendance and fan support reaching new lows in the 1979 season. Finley has also blocked the sale and transfer of the club to Denver, a move that seemed promising. The players on the team took pride in winning in spite of Finley, and Dick Williams' tenure as manager from 1971 to 1973 certainly contributed to the team's success, since he was a steady, calming influence on a team constantly in disruption. Also, few teams have been blessed with such a strong and reliable starring rotation as Ken Holtzman, Vida Blue, and Jim Hunter or with such strong, consistent relief pitchers as Rollie Fingers and Darrell Knowles.

The 1975 World Series between Cincinnati and Boston was perhaps the most dramatic Series and the most closely contested. Five of the seven games were decided by one run, and the sixth game proved to be one of the most thrilling games in Series history. Down 6-3 in the eighth, Boston tied the game on a home run by Bernie Carbo, and in the tenth inning Boston loaded the bases and failed to score. Finally, in the bottom of the twelfth, Carlton Fisk homered, and baseball fans were given one of their most memorable images of dramatic excitement as Fisk jumped with excitement, following the flight of the ball and using body English and arm waving to assist its flight into the stands. The ball rammed into the foul pole, and Fisk began his joyous canter around the bases while the Boston fans poured on the field. It was an exhausting and tension-filled game that saw the Reds use seven pitchers to try to stem the Boston comeback.

In the deciding game of the Series Boston had a 3-0 lead going into the top of the sixth, but Tony Perez hit his third round tripper of the Series to make the score 3-2. Cincinnati tied the score in the seventh as Pete Rose singled in Ken Griffey. Griffey also scored the decisive run in the ninth as Joe Morgan singled to center. The 1975 Series was baseball at its dramatic best as the "underdog" Red Sox faced the Big Red Machine that had won its division by twenty games and rolled past Pittsburgh in three games. The Red Sox team of 1975 included two venerable carryovers from the 1967 comeback team: Carl Yastremski and Rico Petrocelli.

The 1976 Cincinnati team has been called the best team of the decade. This talent-laden squad had five hitters above .300, the best fielding in the league, the top hitting team with a .280 average, and the top run scoring team with 857 runs (the high mark of the National League during the 1970s). The Reds easily disposed of the re-emerging Yankees in a four-game sweep as the Yankees managed only 8 runs and gave up 22. The Reds stole 7 bases in the Series, having copped 210 steals during the regular season with Joe Morgan accounting for 60 of these. Seventeen of the 42 Reds' hits were for extra bases, and Johnny

Bench powered 2 home runs and 5 RBI's in game four, while hitting .533 for the Series. Cincinnati had more than avenged its embarrassing defeat to Baltimore in 1970 and its painful loss to Oakland in 1972 by its back-to-back World Championships in 1975 and 1976. Joe Morgan, Peter Rose, George Foster, Johnny Bench, and Ken Griffey provided a run-producing lineup and a defense that was unmatched for consistency.

The Yankees quickly recovered from their 1976 embarrassment in 1977 and 1978, winning these two Series over the Los Angeles Dodgers in six games each time. In the 1977 Series Reggie Jackson hit 5 home runs, drove in 8 runs, and scored 10 times while hitting .450. In game six Jackson hit 3 successive home runs, each on the first pitch. Ironically, the Dodgers scored two more runs than the Yankees in the Series and hit 9 home runs, but all their power was concentrated in the two games they easily won 6-1 and 10-4. In the 1978 Series the Yankees lost the first two games but came storming back to sweep the next four and pounding Dodger pitching for a .306 average as Bucky Dent, Brian Doyle, and Reggie Jackson accounted for half the team's RBI's.

The new Yankees were built around a smooth fielding infield, a veteran outfield, and a pitching staff built around Ron Guidry and Ed Figuero with two great bullpen stoppers in Rich Gossage and Sparky Lyle. Before his tragic death in an airplane crash Thurman Munson was asserting his claim to being, along with Johnny Bench, one of the greatest modern day hitting and defensive catchers. George Steinbrenner, owner of the Yankees, helped to re-establish the pride of the club by making key trades, buying wisely in the free agent market, and making the team a first-class organization. He also became famous for his firings of Billy Martin and the Lite beer commercials featuring the two feuding. Like the Oakland A's the Yankees were a controversial team, loaded with superstars and outspoken individuals who quarreled off the field but played with pride and harmony on the field. Like Charley O. Finley, Steinbrenner overshadowed the Yankee manager, taking an active hand in the running of the team and often alienating players. But Yankees had truly returned to prominence as the club became one of the richest collections of free agents.

In 1979 Pittsburgh met Baltimore in a rematch and won in seven games after being down three games to one. Pittsburgh won the last three games handily. Kent Tekulve saved three games, and Pittsburgh set a team batting average record with a .323 average. Five Pirate players had 10 or more hits, with Willie Stargell having a record 7 extra-base hits. Baltimore, which averaged .261 during the season, hit only .232 in the Series and made 8 key errors and a number of mental lapses. The Pirates were helped by a hype of "We Are Family," a popular song played regularly at their home park. Willie Stargell was the venerable patriarch of the team, handing out his Stargell's "stars" that players put proudly on their caps in profusion and dispensing with wisdom that befitted his eighteen years of veteran experience, all with the Pirates.

Chuck Tanner, a veteran manager who had endured a year of Charley O. Finley at Oakland, provided a calm image of a confident man and brilliant strategist, even putting baseball above the mourning he felt when his mother died during the Series. The play in the 1979 Series seemed hampered by the miserable weather and difficult playing conditions, raising the question whether the Series should be played so late when weather can adversely affect performances. Howard Cosell appropriately noted that the two teams represented cities that had experienced a rebirth of civic pride with the renovation and reconstruction of inner cities badly decayed and aged.

Baseball teams could provide a vehicle for local pride and civic enthusiasm, as they frequently have, helping to provide a focus for improving racial relations and bettering social conditions. The Pirates' "family" image provided just such a focus for Pittsburgh's revival as a blue collar workers' city that valued teamwork and harmony to get the job done. The enthusiasm of the Pirates and their team harmony provided a dramatic contrast to the discontented and disturbed Oakland and Yankee teams of the 1970s. Stargell also has involved himself in a personal mission to fight sickle-cell anemia disease and set up his own foundation for that purpose, and other baseball players have been involved with special causes to show they care about the local community and the kids who idolize them.

The 1970s produced a number of free spirits who livened up baseball and produced a new carefree image of the ballplayer. Bill Lee, the "spaceman" as he was called, was known for his unconventional behavior, particularly his admission that he freely used "grass" and was unrepentant. But if Lee was unconventional, he was also one of the best read and most intelligent men in baseball, an articulate man of wide-ranging interests. Mark "the Bird" Fidrych also brought excitement and novelty to the game as he moved from pumping gas in Massachusetts to talking to baseballs and carefully landscaping the mound in Detroit. In his rookie year in 1976 Fidrych won nineteen games, and he led the league in earned run average and complete games. He was a naive innocent who won the hearts of fans as they filled ball parks to watch his clown antics, his fresh, unsophisticated approach to the game, and his contagious enthusiasm. He soon lost his fastball due to arm problems caused by his unconventional deliv-

ery and by overpitching as the Tigers management sought to capitalize on his popularity and box office draw.

"The Bird" was a personality phenomena, the first pitcher who really generated fan excitement since Dizzy Dean. After several attempted comebacks and extensive reports on the condition of his arm,
he continued to toil at the Tigers' Evansville farm club. His future
seems dim, although few players have had so many fans anxious and
hoping for a comeback.

Other ballplayers preferred the designation as the team "flake" or
cutup, such as Ron Pruitt of the Indians, who is known for his unpredictable and obnoxious behavior to break the monotony of long road
trips and clubhouse waits. Baseball players have always enjoyed the
status of boy-man, frequently acting like adolescents full of great enthusiasm and comraderie.

The 1970s brought out the "boy side" of the men just as the decade
matured them as men in control of their own careers and financial situations. "Flakes" were sports personalities who made good press,
and the "inside" revelations like Jim Bouton's *Ball Four* (1970) and
Sparky Lyle's *The Bronx Zoo* (1979) brought to life the off the field
antics, conflicts, and locker room personalities. These books were attacked because they revealed too much, but they have actually provided a healthy antidote to the puffery of much baseball writing and
have made players more human and even more interesting. Lyle's
book also is about baseball as a game with complex strategy and about
individuals as team members. It has the on the field and off the field
balance that Bouton's *Ball Four* lacks. *The Bronx Zoo* is probably the
best insider's book written about baseball since Jim Brosnan's *The
Long Season* (1960).

The new breed of ballplayer also included individuals like Mike
Marshall, a rebel against the establishment. A well-traveled relief
pitcher, Marshall has set numerous records for relieving, the most notable being his appearance in 106 games for the Dodgers in 1974 when
he won 15 and saved 21 contests. Marshall has had problems with all
of the eight teams he pitched for in twelve seasons, although he has
been happiest when pitching for Gene Mauch, a manager Marshall re-
spects for his knowledge of the game. However, during the 1980 season Marshall was released outright by the Minnesota Twins. Marshall
contended that he was released because of his union activities as
player representative and that the release violated his contract and
Federal Labor law. Taking a militant role as player representative,
Marshall filed a number of grievances against the Twins management
when it apparently violated the basic players' agreement or when it
was arbitrary about team rules. The outcome of Marshall's case

against the Twins will be important in terms of determining the limits of free speech, union activity, and active opposition to management over working conditions by player representatives (the counterpart of the union steward).

With Marvin Miller reportedly retiring in 1981 as the Players' Association executive director, the future of the association and its leadership are important upcoming developments. After threatening to strike during the 1980 season, the players signed a new basic agreement, but many crucial issues were unresolved and will surface again, particularly problems that the owners see with the free agent system (escalating salaries with no ceiling or maximum salary, the question of compensation for the loss of a free agent, and the complex problems of contractual terms demanded by star players).

Baseball faces other problems in the 1980s. Fan violence and rowdiness, fed by the tradition of beer and cheap bleacher seats, have introduced new problems of crowd control. There has also been an alarming rise in player violence rising from the increased use of the brushback pitch and more aggressive base running and physical contact on the bases. The authority and role of the commissioner need further clarification and definition, as Bowie Kuhn has taken many actions that are unprecedented and smack of arbitrary decisions rather than balanced and judicious management of the game's "best interests." The question of television overexposure is once again raised by the increasing coverage of baseball on such cable networks as Madison Square Garden, which now broadcasts a doubleheader on Thursday evenings; and the future of pay television, with unlimited access to local and even national broadcasts of games, will be important to watch.

Baseball's formal recognition of the talents and achievements of black players in the Negro Leagues has reached a critical stage. The special Hall of Fame committee set up in 1969 named nine former black stars to the Hall before disbanding, and now the Veterans Committee will consider past Negro players for possible induction along with all other potential candidates. According to Joe Black, who pitched in the Negro Leagues and six years in the majors in the 1950s, the abolition of the special committee represents a retrenchment on baseball's commitment to make up for years of neglect and prejudice. Baseball has long depended on blacks for fan support and attendance, and Bob Gibson and the eleven black Hall of Famers (with Rube Foster admitted in 1981) still represent tokenism. More recognition and inductions of black stars are needed, and the contention that records of the Negro Leagues are incomplete and unreliable is insubstantial and unconvincing.

Baseball in the 1970s underwent dramatic and extensive changes as traditional elements of the game changed radically, notably the control of players by owners and management. Ballplayers gained more freedom and asserted their individualism, and the game took on new dimensions of competition and team play. With threatened and actual strikes, with tough negotiation for the basic players' agreement that promised and caused disruption of the game (the fifty day players' strike in 1981), and with players' discontent with each other and managers as well as the press, the game changed significantly. It no longer had the stability and continuity that had been the basis of its enduring appeal. Its dimensions as big business became more apparent in the 1970s, and it lost its special considerations, protections, and exclusions as "the national game" that did not need legislative and judicial interference. It was no longer a pastoral, rural game that found a special home in the urban environment. Baseball was now part of the business marketplace with the courts, labor negotiators, business agents, and the Players' Association determining its future. Free agency, player militancy, the more complicated financial picture of the game, and the response of ownership to these all made the game more complex with its future situation more difficult to predict.

Tennis

In the early years of the decade the tennis boom that had begun in the last years of the sixties continued unabated. In 1972, some 14 million adults claimed to play the game. By 1976 the number had escalated to 26 million. By 1979 a major news weekly could feature a column entitled, "Net Loss: The Tennis Boom Fades." Citing the end of team tennis, the cutback on television coverage, the reduction by one-third of sponsors for the U.S. Open, and a 60 percent decline in racquet sales in three years from its high point in 1976 as evidence, the article concluded that many of the new tennis converts had switched allegiance and moved on to jogging, racquetball or other racquet sports.

Obviously, those concerned about tennis were worried about the state of the game. The two major tennis publications, World Tennis and Tennis, both featured articles early in 1979 evaluating the uncertain state of the game. In its January 1979 issue, World Tennis printed an article by Neil Amdur, entitled "Has the Tennis Boom Lost Its Bloom?" accompanied by a one-page article entitled "Who Plays Tennis? Some New Answers" by Geoffrey Godbey.

Amdur's analysis was basically positive on the state and future of tennis. He found that from 1968 to 1976 the number of male high school tennis teams had increased from 6,221 to 8,421 with 143,970 males on organized teams. For women there were only 26,010 playing on 2,648 high school teams. By 1976, there were 112,616 women on 6,999 teams. Women's growth in collegiate tennis was even greater. In 1971 only 231 women's college teams played varsity tennis. Six years later that number had increased by over 300 percent to 701 with 244 teams at the junior college level.

Amdur cites Al Alschuler, director of Tennis Planning Consultants in Chicago, who estimates that in 1979 there were 160,000 tennis courts in the United States with 5,000 being built each year. Alschuler estimates that by 1985 the number will have increased to 200,000. The Tennis Education and Research Center indicates more beginner certificates (22,990) in the first six months in 1978 than it had for the entire previous year. The National Junior Tennis League also is continuing its expansion.

Bob Briner, executive director of the Association of Tennis Professionals, believes that tennis needs a "sane television policy." "How television covers the sport in the future could determine the long-range impact of the professional games," is his analysis.

Godbey in his article, "Who Plays Tennis? Some New Answers" analyzed the results of a nationwide telephone survey taken by the Heritage Conservation and Recreation Service of the United States Department of the Interior. Its sampling included over 12,000 individuals. The results indicate that 25 percent of the American public age twelve and over play tennis more than four times a year. Another 9 percent play from one to four times per year, double the number who play golf. Those who play tennis in excess of four times a year "are just as likely to be female as male and just as likely to be black as white."

The survey also found that people with more education play tennis. Of those with more than seventeen years of education, 42 percent played tennis, while only 2 percent of those with nine years or less of education played more than four times a year.

Godbey made the following conclusions concerning the telephone survey: "From these results it is clear that tennis has become a sport of the mainstream, part of the middle class. Women and minorities participate as much as white males and may, in fact, determine the future growth of the game."

In *Tennis*, associate editor Robert Cubbedge in an article entitled "Beyond the Boom: Where is Tennis Headed Now?" in the February 1979 issue, also examined the tennis situation. He sought to examine whether the "bubble had burst" and whether or not 10 million tennis players have been lost. After months of interviewing equipment makers, club owners, tournament sponsors, teaching pros, resort owners, camp directors and players, the following conclusions were made.

According to Cubbedge, the tennis boom was over if one meant the 20 to 30 percent annual growth rate that tennis had been expanding at for a number of years. As he indicates, "No sport—nor anything else—could have possibly continued to grow at such a phenomenal rate." But despite some "softening up" in some areas, his general assessment is just as positive as Amdur's. According to Cubbedge: "Tennis, in short, is alive and well in America; it has developed and matured into a stable force in the American economy; it's probably healthier today than in all its previous history. And you don't have to take our word for that; all you have to do is to listen to the people on the front lines in the thick of the action."

Some of those who were interviewed by *Tennis* included the following: Sam Briscoe, national sales manager for Penn Athletic Products; Jack Murray, president of Prince Manufacturing; Joe Carric, president of the United States Tennis Association; Gil de Botton, president of All American Sports; and Bill Tym, retired executive director of the United States Professional Tennis Association (USPTA).

Briscoe indicated that although there may not be the number of beginning players, those playing tennis buy more balls and racquets. Murray, the president of Prince Manufacturing, said his company ran about 11 percent ahead of the same month last year compared to a 150-200 percent rate but indicated that this was still phenomenal. Westervelt, a tennis court builder, indicated courts for private homes had increased, and Botton indicated that in 1978 more people attended his company's tennis camps than ever before. Also, like Amdur, *Tennis* magazine found the National Junior Tennis Association growing by leaps and bounds and found that serious players during the decade increased. Figures compiled by the National Sportsmen's Consumer Audit and the National Sporting Goods Association indicated that the number of serious players (defined as those who play twice a week or more in the outdoor season) had grown from 2 million in 1970 to over 7 million in 1979. Thus, both *Tennis* and *World Tennis* were optimistic about the state of the game and its future.

On the courts in the 1970s almost anything could and did happen. Great matches, petulant performances, childish tantrums, male-female matches, tie-breakers, team tennis, and a transsexual enlivened the tennis world.

With the demise of the "shamateurism" the tennis world seemed a "whole new bag" during the seventies. Stan Smith, Arthur Ashe,

Jimmy Connors, and John McEnroe were the American tennis players of the decade. Stan Smith was the number one ranked player in 1971 and 1972 in the United States (number two in 1970). Jimmy Connors was top ranked in 1973, 1974, 1976, and 1977, with Arthur Ashe breaking Connor's success streak in 1975. The Swedish sensation, Bjorn Borg, winner of five straight Wimbledon titles from 1976 to 1980, became the most dominating figure in the game. Yet Borg for all his skill could not capture the U.S. Open, which Connors did in 1974, 1976, and 1978. Connors also copped the Wimbledon title in 1974. By 1979, John McEnroe, a precocious twenty-year old, looked like the American male tennis star of the future, winning the U.S. Open in 1979 at the tender age of twenty.

Two matches highlighted the seventies—Ken Rosewall's fifth set tiebreaker for the 1972 World Championship of Tennis title and the Bobby Riggs' match against Billie Jean King in 1973, since they symbolized so much more than merely the game on the court. Rosewall emerged the victor in a 4-6, 6-0, 6-3, 6-7, 7-6 marathon (52 million watched on TV) for $50,000 and the world pro championship only after coming back from a 5-4 deficit in a tie breaker in the final set with Laver. Rosewall returned screaming Laver serves for points and then served out the final point for the match. The effort demonstrated the skills of perhaps the two premier players of the game who had been denied exposure because of the previous system of tennis organization.

As one writer indicated, "at a time when women's lib and women's lob were almost inseparable," the winner-take-all match between Bobby Riggs and Billie Jean King in 1973 had a great impact upon women and tennis in general. Although the confrontation was largely a media hype and had been billed as a "grudge" match, Ms. King whipped Riggs by a score of 6-4, 6-3, 6-3 before a crowd of 30,472, the largest crowd ever to witness a tennis match, striking a blow for womankind and avenging Margaret Court's earlier loss to Riggs.

Women's tennis during the seventies was dominated by Billie Jean King, Chris Evert, and a new star, Tracy Austin, at the end of the decade. Billie Jean was the top ranked United States woman from 1970 to 1973, while Chris Evert was ranked number one from 1974 to 1977. Billie Jean took the U.S. Open title from 1971 to 1973 and the Wimbledon title in 1972, 1973 and 1975. Chrissie captured the U.S. Open title from 1975 to 1978 and the Wimbledon title in 1974 and 1976.

Billie Jean and Chris were different types of players. Billie Jean played serve and volley and rushed the net. Evert, particularly effective on clay, was a methodical player who relied on a flawless two-handed backhand to wear down her foes. By the end of the decade,

Chrissie, after an abortive romance with Jimmy Connors, married John Lloyd of Great Britain. As Chris said, "For the first time in my life, there's something that's more important to me than tennis. For the first time in my life, I'm really happy."

The most notable new star was Tracy Austin, a precocious fourteen-year old who first played at Wimbledon in 1977. She turned professional in the fall of 1978 about a month prior to her sixteenth birthday. Within a year she was one of the three top ranked women in the world and in 1979 captured the U.S. Open crown by dethroning Chris Evert 6-4, 6-3, preventing Chris from taking her fifth straight Open title.

The Women's tour made big money. Although the addition of a former male, transsexual Renee Richards, in 1977 caused some concern, the Women's Tennis Association increased its prize money from $900,000 in 1974 to $8 million in 1979. Bigger prize money did not necessarily mean more happiness. In a particularly perceptive column entitled "Why Women's Pro Tennis Is Letting Everybody Down" in the April 1976 issue of *Tennis*, Catherine Bell analyzed the role of professional tennis and professional sport and its impact on the quality of life. The writer notes that when the women's tour was put together, "no great attention was paid to the quality of life or such side issues. . . . The state of the game has been assessed so far on how much the top players receive. The more money people are collecting, then the better the world is." However, as Bell points out, "beyond a certain psychological place, money in itself no longer makes up for a task that is seen to have no object but money. This is playing tennis in a wilderness and it becomes meaningless. As meaningless as the most degrading factory work."

She found that many women on the tour ignore politics, geography, and the different sites they travel to and just talked to each other—which becomes boring since most of them know only tennis. She found that the Billie Jean King victory over Bobby Riggs notwithstanding, women's tennis throughout the decade had "abandoned pretense of being the adoptive sport of the movement and drifted into its role as a conventional American professional sport."

Although the tennis tour was a monetary success, Bell believes that women in tennis have to "address themselves to the issue of how to give sport its proper place in society, how to remove tennis from the sports section and restore it as recreation for everybody. . . . Change must happen. If it is radical change that is proposed, so much the better; radical arguments usually produce moderate solutions."

One area where tennis did attempt to demonstrate social responsibility and awareness was the National Tennis Development Program aimed at inner city youth. A ten-week program with vans sponsored by Pepsi Cola went through the ghettos encouraging black youngsters to take up tennis. With an emphasis on immediate participation, the program introduced many underprivileged youngsters to a game that was largely white and suburban. As the eighties dawned tennis faced problems, particularly for the pro tour in terms of a uniform surface, player attitudes, and television.

During the early seventies, grass was replaced by clay. Even Forest Hills' surface was changed to Har-Tru in 1975. The game then saw a lot of marathon matches which were won by endurance. In 1978, when the U.S. Open moved to Flushing Meadows, a hard surface, Deco-Turf was installed. Jack Kramer believes that a hard surface will mean that players who have a complete game will be the victors and that the surface will no longer have such a radical determination on the outcome.

Rude behavior by players has caused anguish and embarrassment to tennis purists. Jimmy Connors, John McEnroe, Vitas Gerulaitis, and Ilie Nastase are only a few of the top stars who resorted to boorish and outlandish behavior. The Detroit *Free Press* of September 4, 1979, entitled an editorial, "Tennis? The next backhand we see may be a fist to somebody's jaw." The article stated that "tennis is becoming a mass-spectator sport and any day now we shall be treated to the spectacle of Nastase or Jimmy Connors climbing into the stands to punch a heckler in the nose, as Rocky Colavito used to do. Tennis . . . uh . . . mayhem, anybody?"

In 1979 after Wojtek Fibak's second round win over Vitas Gerulaitis, Gerulaitis stalked off the court and refused to shake hands. The young Pole's reaction was to state: "I have never said this before, but now I can say that I really feel that young people, young sportsmen in America, are only taught to win. They do not know how to lose." To combat irregularities the ATP is now experimenting with three professional officials paid by the tour who will have all final determinations concerning tournaments rather than local officials.

Also the ATP has to make sure its stars show up for the numerous stops on circuit and not play simply winner-take-all special tournaments. As Arthur Ashe and Jack Kramer have noted publicly many times, "This can only have a detrimental effect upon the growth of tennis and cause sponsors to pull out of backing of tournaments." Bob Briner, executive director of the Association of Tennis Professionals (ATP) and chairman of the Men's International Professional Tennis Council, wrote in the *New York Times:* "A sponsor of a golf tournament on the PGA may not know exactly who will be in his tournament, but he does know that if a professional golfer is playing that week he will make the appearance in that tournament. He does not have to worry about top players participating in an exhibition in competition with his event.''

Commenting on this matter and the problem of multiple television showings of tennis matches, Jack Kramer has stated "The game is headed for a great depression unless we resolve the problems." Again Bob Briner has cited the need for a saner television policy. In 1979 he commented that "Right now, there is no sportwide policy for television. Everybody is taking their shots, and you're getting a mixed bag that has muddled the whole picture. TV can be a boon, but you need some consistent policy."

In a decade that has seen many things happen to tennis, including the application of eastern mysticism (see Tim Galloway, *Inner Tennis*), perhaps the most regrettable failure has been the failure of World Team Tennis. Largely initiated by Billie Jean King and her husband, Larry King, much of the initiative behind the effort was to popularize the game and to democratize the game. Billie Jean has always maintained that she was not a country club player and that she sought to "combine the best parts of tennis with the best parts of traditional team sports." Team Tennis operated from 1974 to 1979 and featured a five-set format with three doubles and two singles, with each game scoring a point. Team Tennis struggled along for five years and then collapsed in 1979. With it ended an admirable attempt to democratize tennis and take it out of its middle-class surroundings.

Golf

Jack Nicklaus continued to be the dominant figure on the PGA tour in the 1970s, winning eight major tournaments from 1970 to 1979, including two Masters, two British Opens, and three PGA titles. "The Golden Bear" was the leading money winner from 1971 to 1973 and again in 1975 and 1976. After a disappointing year in 1969, his worst year on the tour since he started in 1962, Nicklaus shed twenty pounds, changed to a stylish and tailored mode of dress, and concentrated on his game with renewed dedication to excellence. In the 1970s Nicklaus became more popular with tour galleries as he relaxed more, showed more emotion, and became more accessible. He also continued his reputation for a high level of sportsmanship and class behavior in losing.

In 1980 Nicklaus claimed his fourth U.S. Open title and his eighteenth major tournament victory. With renewed discipline and determination, he revamped and changed all phases of his game, and in the 1980 U.S. Open he shot an 8-under-par 272 and shattered his old scoring record for that tournament set in 1967 and tied by Lee Trevino the following year. After Nicklaus birdied the seventy-second hole and claimed a major title that had eluded him for two years, the fans broke through the ropes surrounding the green and almost overran the putting surface. This spontaneous and spirited display of enthusiasm had not been seen on the tour since Arnie's Army followed their leader. The Baltusrol Golf Club scoreboard read ''Jack Is Back'' on its message board, and Nicklaus, who had earlier contemplated retirement, was inspired to announce that he would remain on the tour. It should also be noted that the last two of the four major tournaments in 1979 had been won by foreigners; David Graham, an Australian, won the PGA in a sudden death playoff over Ben Crenshaw, and Seve Ballesteros, a Spaniard, won the British Open. Ballesteros also won the 1980 Masters, finishing four strokes ahead of the Australian Jack Newton and the American Gibby Gilbert. Thus, Nicklaus ended a string of three major championship titles by foreigners and came from a thirty-third place finish in the 1980 Masters to triumph in the 1980 U.S. Open. It was the kind of dramatic recovery that Arnold Palmer's loyal fans had hoped for but been denied throughout the late 1960s and all through the 1970s.

The 1970s also saw the continuation of the brilliant careers of Lee Trevino and Gary Player, two of the most consistent golfers on the PGA tour. Trevino had brilliant years in 1971 and 1972, and in three dramatic showdowns with Nicklaus, Trevino came out on top. In 1971 Trevino won an eighteen-hole playoff in the U.S. Open against Nicklaus. In the 1972 British Open Trevino edged a charging Nicklaus by one stroke, and the 1974 PGA was claimed by ''Super Mex,'' with Nicklaus finishing second again. Trevino also claimed three Canadian Open titles in the 1970s, and from 1970 through 1972 and in 1974, he won the Vardon Trophy for the best PGA average on the tour. Trevino brought color and excitement to the game, and his generosity to charities, devoting a share of each purse to a needy organization, is noteworthy.

Gary Player, a South African, won the Masters in 1974 and 1978 as well as claimed a PGA title in 1972 and a British Open crown in 1974. Only Nicklaus, Trevino, Player, and Tom Watson could claim two major titles in the same year during the 1970s as the ''Grand Slam'' escaped their efforts. The U.S. Open had nine different winners in the decade, with only Hale Irwin as a two time winner. Sometimes playing with a cordon of police and under death threats, Player was identified with South Africa's apartheid government as politics intruded on the golf course. Player, Palmer, and Nicklaus formed the "Big Three" of golf in the 1960s to make the sport successful and popular. Steady and quiet in his style of play, Player continued, along with Nicklaus, as one of the most consistent craftsmen of the game. Trevino joined Player and Nicklaus to constitute the new "Big Three" when Palmer faded quickly after enjoying only two big years of success and dominance.

The 1970s brought the emergence of new faces and instant stars, young men who had played college golf and gained publicity as amateurs. Johnny Miller, Tom Watson, and Hale Irwin were the most successful of this group. Watson claimed three major titles in the 1970s, winning two of them in 1977. Watson won the most tour money in 1977 and 1978, amassing $362,429 in 1978, quickly moving into the select class of men, including Trevino and Nicklaus, who have amassed over $2 million in career earnings. Watson seemed to offer the promise of becoming another Nicklaus, but he has failed to win a major tournament since 1977, even though he is a consistent high finisher and big money winner.

Other "young lions" of the present day game are Ben Crenshaw, John Mahaffey, Jerry Pate, Tom Kite, Hubert Green, Lanny Wadkins, Andy North, and Fuzzy Zoeller. The substantial purses have brought more competitive talent to the game. In 1978 twenty-four players won over $100,000 in prize money, with the fiftieth top money winner taking $62,621. In 1980 Tom Watson was averaging over $25,000 in winnings per tour event and won over $376,000 with a number of tournaments still remaining. The Kemper Open in 1980 offered a total purse of $400,000 with John Mahaffey winning the $72,000 top prize. It remains to be seen whether one of these newcomers will achieve the stardom of Nicklaus or Trevino, or whether one of them will become the kind of popular favorite that Palmer became. Competition from foreign players will undoubtedly increase as players like Seve Ballesteros, David Graham, and Isao Aoki make their claims to international fame. The tour has also seen a number of black golfers join it to integrate what has been a sport almost entirely white. Lee Elder won $152,198 in 1978 at the age of forty-three and claimed the Westchester Classic that year.

With so many talented young golfers joining the tour and presenting different faces in the winner's circle, the PGA began to issue weekly statistics that list the top ten leaders in nine categories. Now tour fans could learn who was the longest driver, the most accurate driver, the putting leader, the sub-par specialist, and so on. These statistics have helped to enliven fan interest and to break down individual performances to show that final score and finish are not the only measures of excellence. In the 1979 PGA Championship a Detroit computer firm distributed a computerized analysis of the previous rounds with a statistical breakdown on how each hole played and what scores were made.

Women's golf in the 1970s came into its own as a major sport. Kathy Whitworth, the leading LPGA money winner from 1965 through 1968, garnered the most prize money from 1970 through 1973 and reached a career high of over $87,000 earned in 1973. By comparison, in the same year Jack Nicklaus led the PGA with over $320,000 in winnings. However, women's professional golf did not enjoy the kind of television coverage and earnings, the sponsorship, or the level of fan support that the men's game had developed. The women's game lacked the long hitters and power drivers, and the ladies played a finesse game that relied on a combination of shots and consistency. The women had only two major tournaments to shoot for, the LPGA Championship and the USGA Open.

In 1976 Judy Rankin became the first woman golfer to win over $100,000 in a year as she wound up with well over $150,000 in prize money. Donna Caponi Young and JoAnne Carner also won over $100,000 in 1976, and twelve women had over $50,000 in earnings. In 1978 Nancy Lopez would garner $189,813, winning nine tournaments, five of them in a row. Up to 1980 no woman had won over a million dollars in her career, although Kathy Whitworth, Judy Rankin, JoAnne Carner, Donna Caponi Young, and Jane Blalock are approaching it. The women's tour is gaining more sponsors, and purses are well over $100,000 for each event. The women's tour in 1980 has thirty-nine tournaments. The most consistent winners on the women's tour have been Donna Caponi Young, Kathy Whitworth, Sandra Haynie, JoAnne Carner, and Judy Rankin. Judy Rankin has been a professional since 1962, the same year Jack Nicklaus turned pro. After over ten years of hard work and struggle she found her golfing identity in 1972.

As in the men's ranks, younger women golfers have emerged and are more dedicated to the game as purses grow. These newcomers include such fine talents as Hollis Stacy, Sally Little, Nancy Lopez Melton, Amy Alcott, and Beth Daniel. As women's sports at the collegiate level expand and improve due to more equitable funding, more talented women golfers will join the tour, and many will make a profession of it. Veteran women golf stars like Kathy Whitworth, JoAnne Carner, and Judy Rankin have been largely ignored by the media and their skills underestimated. But Nancy Lopez Melton's smile and engaging personality, combined with skill and almost instant success, proved that a woman golfer can attract national publicity and media interest that almost equalled that of the men golfers.

Golf matured as a national sport in the 1970s even though the Arnold Palmer legend faded and television coverage became more selective. The increasing sophistication of the television coverage of golf is one of the unheralded developments of the decade. Coverage was expanded beyond the finishing holes to include most, if not all, of the back nine; mobile cameras and on-the-course commentators provided more dynamic action and close-up shots; former golfing greats became part of broadcast teams, giving informed insights into the game; multiple camera locations allowed for the dramatic simultaneity of the game played in foursomes with staggered starts and finishes. Networks wisely avoided overexposure that might have killed the sport public's interest. Frank Beard, a well-known tour golfer, has proposed that providing microphones to the fifteen or so players who are in contention the final two rounds would bring more interest and more of a personal element to the telecasting. Beard has noted that many players are entertainers and that vocal interaction between the player and the gallery is an important part of the spirit and color of the game.

As long as the quality of telecasting improves, as long as courses are redesigned to make them challenging potential for drama and the big golf shots, and as long as journalists like Dan Jenkins of *Sports Illustrated* continue to write such high quality journalism on golf, interest in the sport will remain high. The main danger is possibly that the equipment manufacturers and the golf course ownership, in the interest of high profits, will make the game inaccessible to youngsters just beginning it. And golf could certainly use a new superstar of the caliber of Palmer, Nicklaus, Trevino, or Player to galvanize interest and media coverage.

Boxing

In October 1970, Muhammad Ali returned to the ring after a three-year enforced absence. During that time Ali dubbed himself "The People's Champion" and kept himself in the media limelight with his activities on behalf of the Black Muslim movement. In Atlanta Ali quickly disposed of Jerry Quarry, a white pretender in a sport now dominated by black boxers. Ali's opposition to United States involvement in Vietnam now seemed less controversial, as mainstream Americans belatedly realized the mistake and costs of the war.

The inevitable happened in 1971 when Ali signed to fight Frazier, the reigning champion, in what was called the "Fight of the Century" or just "The Fight." Frazier was a powerful, devastating boxer who always came out "smoking" and who could pound his opponents into submission with a relentless attack that was always moving in to punish. In contrast to Ali, Frazier said he didn't "need a cause to fight because I fight for my family, for myself, and for my pride." Frazier was financially backed by a corporate syndicate in Philadelphia with about two hundred investors, and thus he had no taint of underworld connections. Having come from the South to Philadelphia as a teenager, Frazier took up boxing to lose weight, and within a short period of time he won an Olympic gold medal in the 1964 Tokyo games, fighting his bouts with a fractured thumb that only he knew about. He was the pride of Philadelphia.

Frazier and Ali were given a guarantee of $2.5 million each, and the fight would produce revenues of over $20 million. The prefight buildup was exciting and colorful as veteran boxers and sports writers exchanged opinions about each man, and Ali's running commentary on Frazier made excellent press. The bout itself lived up to the media hype and expectations. After nine close rounds with Ali keeping away from the charging and relentless Frazier, Frazier almost knocked out Ali in the eleventh round. In the last round Frazier floored Ali with a left hook and had Ali reeling around the ring for the rest of the round. Frazier won a unanimous decision, and Ali did not crawl across the ring at Madison Square Garden and say to Frazier, "You are the greatest, you are the true champion," as Ali had said he would do if he lost. Both fighters ended up in the hospital, Frazier for a lengthy stay with kidney problems. Ali's much publicized comeback had to wait until 1974 when he would defeat George Foreman and reclaim the crown after seven years of waiting and talking.

Frazier was soon challenged by George Foreman, whose delinquent youth in Houston had brought him constant trouble with the police and caused him to drop out of school in the ninth grade. However, Foreman's life was turned around by the Job Corps, where he learned the value of hard work and was motivated to make a legitimate success of himself. Like Frazier, Foreman was overweight and out of shape, but with guidance and encouragement he disciplined himself into a skillful boxer. In 1968 he won a Gold Medal at the Mexico City Olympics, and his walking around the ring waving a small American flag was a welcome sight to viewers disturbed by the

"Black Power" salute and the apparent disrespect shown for the flag by sprinters John Carlos and Tommie Smith. Foreman took a business-like attitude about turning professional, just as Frazier had done earlier, and Foreman won twenty-six straight professional fights, twenty-three by knockouts.

The 1973 confrontation between Frazier and Foreman took place in Kingston, Jamaica, in January 1973. The money was hardly the quantity Ali and Frazier had received, with Frazier getting $850,000 and Foreman $375,000. Foreman went toe to toe with the aggressive Frazier, and knocked Frazier down six times before the fight ended in the second round. Frazier's manager mercifully stopped the fight, although Frazier had gamely risen to his feet after each knockdown. After his shocking but convincing victory Foreman said he wanted "to publicly thank God and all the people who have supported me." He was a welcomed champion who was supported and advised by Joe Louis and Archie Moore, and he was trained by Sandy Saddler, a former featherweight world champion.

Ali was now free of his legal problems and had been vindicated in the courts, but his boxing career seemed to be in trouble when in 1973 Ken Norton won a decision over Ali after breaking his jaw. In a rematch six months later Ali won a close split decision that would have gone to Norton if he had won the last (twelfth) round. Ali now set his sights on Frazier. The two giants of the ring, now reduced to the role of contenders, met in Madison Square Garden in January 1974, with Ali showing the quickness, boxing skills, and concentration that had earlier brought him to the top and made him one of the most graceful and balanced boxers to ever enter the ring.

In Zaire, Africa, Ali reclaimed the title by devastating George Foreman in the predawn setting of a soccer stadium with 70,000 Africans watching. Ali was thirty-two years old and had been guaranteed $5 million for facing Foreman. Ali attacked Foreman and wore him down with an unorthodox strategy, as he allowed Foreman to pound away at him and sapped his opponent's strength as well as demoralized him. In the eighth round Ali came off the ropes and threw a long right hand to Foreman's head, sending him down for the count. "The Greatest" claimed the heavyweight championship he had never really lost, and Ali joined company with Jack Johnson and Joe Louis as one of the greatest black American boxers of all time. He had finally put to rest the criticisms that he could not stand up under a heavy hitting attack, that he could not throw the knockout punch, and that he lacked the "killer instinct" to put his opponents away.

Ali had persisted in the fight game for ten years, coming back from setbacks that would have discouraged most fighters and caused them to quit. In 1964 he had left Sonny Liston on his stool, unable and unwilling to answer the bell, and in 1974 he left Foreman groping and vainly struggling to regain his feet. In reclaiming the title, Ali had shown that he could back up his rambling, hyped oratory with the skills required to survive in a brutal sport. He had brought grace and style to a game dominated by ponderous, stalking behemoths who relied on punching power and relentless physical assault to overcome opponents.

Ali went on to continue his tradition of being a fighting champion who fought all potential challenges, American and European. He had four title defenses in 1975, with three of them knockouts. His October "thriller in Manila" against Joe Frazier went fourteen rounds as the two giants fought a memorable match that featured all-out punching and awesome punishment to each boxer. Ali pummeled Frazier almost at will after the twelfth round, closing his left eye tight and landing unanswered blows on the challenger's head. Frazier's manager finally realized the extent of the damage and ended the fight after the fourteenth round. The Frazier fight left little doubt that Ali could punch or stand up to the punishment that a power fighter like Frazier was capable of dealing out.

In 1976 Ali fought four times in eight months, knocking out two European opponents in the fifth rounds and claiming unanimous fifteen-round decisions over Jimmy Young and Ken Norton. The decision over Norton was controversial with many sportswriters believing that Norton won the fight handily, and Norton had returned to his corner jubilant with what he thought was a championship and even taunting a downcast Ali. At age thirty-four Ali was subdued in his victory and defensive about the decision. A few days after the fight he announced his retirement. Jim Murray had called Ali a "clumsy, flat-footed bum," and Dick Young accused the judges of being "victims of the Ali syndrome," perpetuating Ali as champ because they believed boxing would die without him. But in fairness to Ali he had fought a grueling schedule of title defenses with eight bouts in nineteen months. The money was the biggest take of Ali's career, as he was guaranteed $6 million and 50 percent of all revenues over $9 million. With the assurance of this kind of money, he could afford to be complacent, and Ali had perhaps tired of the media attention and his role as self-promoter.

The February 1978 fight against Leon Spinks, who was twelve years younger than Ali and twenty-seven pounds lighter, saw Spinks upset Ali in fifteen rounds. But Ali came back eight months later to claim his crown from Spinks in a fifteen-round decision. Thus, Ali now was a three-time champ, and he soon retired and let other fighters contend for his crown. In 1980, after almost two years out of boxing, Ali decided to make another comeback, even though his weight had ballooned to 251 pounds. Irrepressible and loquacious as ever, Ali takes pride in shocking the fight world with his ability to discipline and train himself, and he is blessed with a powerful pair of legs that seem to defy the ravages of time and constant training. Ali has seen two generations of heavyweights come and go, and he sees the current generation as one which he can still challenge. In a recent interview he attributed his endurance and condition to his Muslim beliefs, which have served to discipline his life and gain him the respect of many of those who doubted his initial identification with the Muslim faith.

Beyond the ring Ali has become an international figure with well-publicized visits to the Soviet Union, to China, and to African countries as President Jimmy Carter's personal envoy. The final chapter in the Ali story has yet to be written, but it is safe to say that none of the current champions or contenders seem able to generate the excitement and interest that Ali has created since 1964.

The media attention has, in fact, shifted to the welterweight class with the emergence of Sugar Ray Leonard, Pipino Cuevas of Mexico, Roberto Duran of Panama, and Thomas Hearns. Undefeated in twenty-seven professional fights before he lost to Duran in Montreal and gave up the welterweight crown, Leonard stood to make $8 million for one fight, with Duran making almost $2 million. Leonard had won a gold medal at the 1976 Montreal Olympics and gained a television-made reputation, greatly assisted by Howard Cosell and the ABC network. When Leonard beat Wilfred Benitez, the two boxers were the first nonheavyweights ever to fight for $1 million each, and the shrewd Leonard parlayed his success into a financial security that has even escaped Muhammed Ali. Both Duran and Leonard have shown the ability to bargain and negotiate intelligently and sensibly, thus avoiding the fate of many boxers who are at the mercy of promoters, backers, and managers. This also means that once retired they will be secure and satisfied, not tempted by promises of big guarantees to come back to the ring past their prime.

The welterweight class has become the heavyweight class of the moment, as the welterweights show the punching power, muscle, and intense physical violence that once was only attributed to the heavyweights. Leonard and Duran both talked about "killing" each other, and the 1980 fight in Montreal saw Duran, who resembles Joe Frazier with his relentless, aggressive attack, pummel the classy Leonard into submission and win a unanimous decision. The "dream fight" between those two welterweights received as much media attention and generated as much fan interest as "The Fight" between

Ali and Frazier in 1971. Leonard came back to reclaim his title from Duran. Duran quit the bout and his reputation as the man with "fists of stone" was considerably tarnished.

The media found that it could "hype" the welterweights in the same way that it had the heavyweight class. Boxers like Leonard, Duran, Hearns, and Cuevas have proved to be more interesting to fans because of their agility, speed, and reputations for devastating knockout punching. In an August 1980 issue of *KO Magazine* article entitled "The Best Punchers in the World," the top ten punchers were listed, and only two were heavyweights. The welterweight class has also gained more attention because it is more international. Of the top ten welterweight boxers in April 1980 six were from countries other than the United States, but in the heavyweight class only Gerri Coetzee of South Africa was listed with nine Americans. Ali had kept the heavyweight class interesting and international by fighting a number of European champions and staging many fights in foreign countries. By the end of the 1970s the heavyweight class had lost this international flavor.

Boxing in the 1970s went through a tremendous boom, as did other sports, and the multimillion dollar gate and the million dollar plus guarantees became standard demands of boxers for the big fight. The level of physical violence also increased substantially as the big knockout or the damaging blow became the standard of success for almost all classes of fighters. Ring deaths and serious injuries increased to an alarming rate, and there have been calls for reform of rules regarding the licensing of boxers, the certification of injured boxers to fight again, the refereeing of fights, the outlawing of certain kinds of punches (behind and on top of the head), and the role of ringside physicians in stopping fights before fatal damage is done. It appears that little will be done, since no uniform rules or codes exist and since individual states vary so much in licensing practices. With the increasing use of closed circuit and cable television, aided by international satellite communications, boxing could well be ready for a period of an even greater boom. But the spectre of boxing-related fatalities and debilitating injuries lurks in the background to haunt the popularity and media hype of the sport.

Track and Field and the 1972 Olympics

There was a lot of the old and new during the decade concerning track and field. In order to tap the open commercial market, professional track and field was attempted in the United States. After several years the International Track Association (ITA) failed and its most lasting consequence was to make such premier athletes as Al Fuerbach, Brian Oldfield, and Steve Smith outcasts in the "amateur" circuit. (Oldfield and Smith were able to compete in the 1980 United States trials only because of ruling by federal and state courts.)

The loss of Dwight Stones' amateur status (America's best high jumper during the decade) for winning $33,633 in a 1978 Superstars competition struck many as farcical when under the table payments for athletes are common. In 1975 Frank Shorter, the 1972 Olympic marathon champion, told the President's Commission on Olympic Sports, "We're all professionals, rules don't mean anything." Yet the concept of open competition supported by many in track and field circles is given little chance of success because unlike tennis, which remains out of the Olympic movement, track and field is caught up in the increased politicization of the Olympics. Winning medals is very important for Russia and the Eastern European countries of the Soviet bloc. As Emil Zatopek of Czechoslovakia has stated, "The Olympics, it means too much for East Germany, Russia and these countries. For them, it is everything. They want the medals, not the money."

In the United States the conflict between the NCAA and the AAU over domination of track and field seems to have ended when a new organization was founded, the Athletic Congress (TAC). Yet the July 1, 1980, *New York Times* could report that track athletes had attended a meeting to form a union. However, the *Times* analyzed, such a union "faces an uphill battle" since "college athletes have prior responsibilities, and postcollege ones often have short careers before responding to society's demand to quit playing and get a job."

The glamor event of American track and field, the mile, almost faced extinction with "the growing use and acceptance of metric distance," the explosion throughout the United States of long distance running, and the absence of a dominant American such as Jim Ryun to sustain public interest. As a result few world class American milers came on the scene during the decade. John Filbert Bayi with a 3:51.0 and John Walker of New Zealand with a 3:49.4, both times recorded in 1975, broke Jim Ryun's record of 3:51.1. Tony Waldorf, perhaps America's most promising miler during the period, ran nine sub-4 minute miles in 1973 and then faded into obscurity.

American sprinters did not dominate the racing world as they had in the past. Harvey Glance was probably the most consistent, while Houston McTear, a sub-6 second runner for the 60-yard dash, lacked the stamina to be a world beater at the longer distances. Perhaps the most unusual sprinting story to evolve during the decade was that of

Dr. Delano Merriwether, a twenty-seven-year-old hematologist who studied leukemia cells in mice at the Baltimore Cancer Research Center. Merriwether became convinced after watching track meets on TV that he could sprint also. The January 18, 1971, *Sports Illustrated* reported that this unusual athlete, after having gone into training, began to show up at track meets wearing gold swim trunks, a hospital shirt and striped suspenders, and began beating established sprinters such as Mel Pender and Ivory Crockett in the 60, posting a 6.0. Merriwether was only on the professional indoor circuit for a couple seasons, but he certainly provided a fine human interest story.

The Olympics held in Munich in 1972 resulted in a mixed bag for the United States. Mark Spitz won a record seven gold medals in swimming and promptly gave up the thoughts of dental school to go the commercial endorsement route. The men's basketball team lost on a questionable last second basket by the Russians, who were given three chances to inbound the ball under the American basket. The team decided to refuse to accept its silver medal as a protest and thus did not officially receive medals. Eddie Hart and Roy Robinson were disqualified from the 100 meter dash after their coach, Stan Wright, had misread the time for the 100-meter trials. (As a result a Russian, Valery Borzoi, won the 100- and 200-meter dashes.) Rick DeMont lost his 400-meter freestyle medal because a prescription drug he took contained a prohibited ingredient and United States medical officials had not notified IOC medical officials. After pounding Valery Tregubov of the Soviet Union almost into a bloody pulp, boxer Reginald Jones was declared the loser to the Russian, one of the major injustices of the games. And probably most disappointing was the tripping of Jim Ryun in a preliminary heat of the 1500-meter which prevented his qualification for the finals, an action that one commentator said, "cast a pall over American track and field for the decade."

But the pall that hung over the Munich games was not the failures of American athletes but the attack by terrorists, members of the fanatical Black September group, on Israeli athletes at the games. Eight terrorists captured nine Israeli athletes and presented a number of demands. ABC kept the world informed by transmitting live telecasts of the event via satellite to the world. The German government pretended to accede to the terrorists' demands, but when a bus taking the terrorists and the hostages to a waiting Lufthansa 727 was being readied, trained marksmen opened fire. The Arabs killed all nine hostages. In the ensuing gunfight five terrorists were killed as well as one German policeman.

Many called for the cancellation of the games because of the slaughter. The IOC contended that "an end to the Games would mean a victory for terrorism," and instead held a memorial ceremony. There in a quavering voice, eighty-four-year-old IOC leader Avery Brundage stated that, "I am sure the public will agree that we cannot allow a handful of terrorists to destroy this nucleus of international cooperation and good will we have in the Olympic movement. The Games must go on and we must continue our efforts to keep them clean, pure, and honest, and try to extend the sportsmanship of the athletic field into other areas." So the games continued.

The American track-and-field team garnered only six track and field medals: Dave Wottle, taking a dramatic 800-meter victory with an astonishing kick; Vince Matthews, the 400-meter; Rod Milburn, the 100-meter hurdles; Frank Shorter, the marathon; Randy Williams, the long jump; and the United States team the 400-meter relay. Such traditionally American dominated events as the pole vault, shot put, and discus were all claimed by East German, Polish, and Czech competitors. American chances to take the 1600-meter relay were lost when Vince Matthews and Wayne Collett were disqualified for not standing at attention during the ceremonies honoring the 400-meter winners.

Women's track and field was a disaster for the United States. No gold medals were won. Kathy Hammond's third place finish in the 400-meter and Kathy Schmidt's third place finish in the javelin were the high points. West Germany won four gold medals and the East Germans six so that ten of the fourteen gold medals in track and field remained in Germany.

The darling of the games was the dimunitive Russian gymnast, Olga Korbut. An alternate on the Russian team, she was a competitor because of the illness of another Russian gymnast. Her style and grace and smile captured the crowd and the television audience. Not only did she win two gold medals but she made gymnastics a popular sport for girls instantaneously in the United States.

In the winter games at Sapporo, Japan, the United States won three gold medals, all by women. Annie Henning and Dianne Holum from Northbrook, Illinois, won gold medals in the 500- and 1500-meter speed skating events, while Barbara Cochran won in the slalom event. Janet Lynn, a popular favorite in the figure skating event, could only come away with a bronze.

The most controversy at the games came when veteran Austrian skier Karl Schranz, thought to be a candidate for the Alpine triple crown, was disqualified for commercialism. Although the Austrian team talked of boycotting, at the insistence of Schranz they continued in the games, while Schranz flew home to a hero's welcome.

The 1976 Summer Olympics

Political controversy once again overshadowed the games. African countries refused to participate in the Olympics unless New Zealand was expelled, because New Zealand had played South Africa. (African nations were reacting to bloody uprisings in Soweto, South Africa.) New Zealand was not expelled, and many African nations boycotted.

The Montreal Olympics were conducted under tight security as there was a desire to prevent any of the tragic violence experienced at Munich. The IOC did not want any memorial made to the slain Israeli athletes. However, praise was given to the eleven workers who lost their lives in the construction of the Olympic facilities—their families were given free tickets to Olympic events.

The 1976 Olympics reflected how times change and how people change. Olga Korbut was replaced as the darling of the Olympics by another gymnast, Nadia Comaneci of Romania. Nadia's routines were bold and innovative. She received seven perfect scores, and with her elfin beauty became the crowd's favorite much as Olga had been four years before.

In women's swimming, previously an American domain, the East German team, led by the fabulous Kornelia Ender (four golds and a silver), won eleven of the gold medals. The United States could salvage only the 400-meter freestyle relay.

Shirley Babashoff, the American favorite, had to settle for three silvers and a share of the gold relay medal. Babashoff was a less than generous loser. Her classic (if not so classy) comment on the swimming results was "at least we look like women."

The men's swimming team captured eleven gold medals. The United States swept all three medal places in the 200-meter backstroke, 200-meter freestyle, 200-meter backstroke, and the 200-meter butterfly. John Naber was the individual men's star, winning four gold and a silver in both individual events and relays.

In track and field the women's team could salvage only Kathy Schmidt's bronze in the javelin and a silver in the 100-meter relay. The men's track-and-field team did not have a good year either. The highest finish for an American in the 100-meter was a fourth by Harvey Glance. The United States garnered silvers and bronze in the 200-meter.

Alberto Juantorena, a tremendous athlete from Cuba, put down the challenges of Americans Fred Newhouse and Herman Frazier in the 400-meter and captured the 400-meter. He then came back to win the

800-meter with American favorite Richard Wohlhuter finishing third.

Lasse Viren of Finland took the men's 5,000- and 10,000-meter amid charges that he was "blood doping" (having blood drawn out and old, more highly oxygenated blood put in). No one could question his world shattering records, or the fact that he had repeated as champion in both events.

Probably the most memorable American performance was by Edwin Moses, who won the 400-meter hurdles, with Michael Shine of the United States finishing second. In exaltation Shine grabbed Moses and they danced around the track. Moses was black and Shine was white.

Arnie Robinson captured the long jump and Mac Wilkins the discus, but once again the men's pole vault, high jump, and shot put went to competitors other than Americans. Most surprising was the defeat of Dwight Stones, the world record high jump holder from the United States, who had to settle for third behind Poland's Jacek Wzsola and Canada's Greg Joy.

The most glamorous athlete of the games was Bruce Jenner, who triumphed in the decathlon. Jenner, who had trained for four years supported by his wife, celebrated his triumph by waving a flag. Like Mark Spitz before him, Jenner would be able to transform his Olympic championship into a springboard for monetary success. After all, as someone said, he had the "looks of Robert Redford and the body of Tarzan."

In basketball, the Americans avenged their bitter loss in 1972 by capturing the gold with Yugoslav's finishing second and the USSR a surprising third. The Olympics had become an East European and Russian showcase as medals were piled up in cycling, wrestling, Judo, gymnastics, canoeing, kayaking, fencing, and handball—sports in which Americans did not participate.

The 1976 Winter Olympics

The winter Olympics of 1976 were held in Innsbruck, Austria, with 1,040 athletes from thirty-seven nations participating, and were viewed by perhaps twice that many security people. This would be the first Olympiad in more than a quarter of a century without the presence of Avery Brundage. Brundage had resigned his office at the

Munich Olympics and died in May 1975 at the age of eighty-seven.

Traditionally, the winter Olympic sports were not America's forte. Other than medals in figure skating, and the gold medal in 1960 for hockey, United States medals in the winter Olympics had been few and far between. Skiing, luge, bobsledding, and the like had been traditionally the strengths of the Scandinavian countries, and in recent years, the Russians and East Germans had also figured quite prominently. One sport in which an American had never won a medal was cross country skiing. This would change in 1976. Bill Koch, a twenty-year-old Vermonter, placed second in the 300-kilometer race. He then finished sixth in the 15-kilometer race and skiied the third fastest leg in the 40-kilometer relay race in which the United States placed sixth.

Koch's effort was no fluke as he was a product of two years of training instituted by America's cross country ski coach, Marty Hall. Behind Bill Koch's medals lay some 5,000 miles of practice, hiking, running, and skiing. Koch also revealed that he possessed some of the fabled New England dry wit. When asked whether or not he had lived all his life in Vermont, he replied laconically, "not yet."

Both men's and women's speed skating also proved to be medal events for the United States. The star of the women's team was Sheila Young, daughter of a traffic department worker at Budweiser in Detroit. Sheila captured three speedskating medals: a gold in the 500-meter, a silver in the 1,500-meter, and a bronze in the 1,000-meter. A teammate, Leah Poulos, finished second in the 1,000-meter race.

In men's speed skating, Peter Mueller of the United States took the gold in the 1,000-meter event, while Dan Immerfall won a bronze in the 500-meter.

The United States hockey team demonstrated a lot of team spirit and enthusiasm and soon became the crowd favorites. When the team upset Finland, there was some hope of a bronze medal. They finished tied with two other teams with a 2-3 won-loss record, but West Germany took the third place bronze because they had scored more goals.

American figure skater Dorothy Hamill was another star of the 1976 Olympics. Not only her flawless style but her beauty and her stylish hairdo (which inspired thousands of women to imitate it) captured the hearts of the live audience and the millions watching throughout the world on television. Her performance was capped by a distinctive and innovative maneuver called the "Hamill camel," a combination of a leaping camel and a sit spin. All nine judges gave her first place votes. In ice dancing Colleen O'Connor and Jim Millns took a bronze.

Another surprise placing by an American was Cindy Nelson's third place in the women's downhill. One of the most dramatic events occurred in the men's downhill run when Austria's great skiier, Franz

Klammer, the favorite, was forced to make an extraordinarily fast run if he wished to win a gold medal. In a slam-bang, reckless run, approaching speeds of 70 mph, Klammer grabbed the gold. His almost out of control, on the edge run was one of the most memorable and often replayed events of any Winter Olympics.

Rosi Mittermaier of West Germany was the star of women's alpine skiing, almost winning all three alpine events. She captured the gold in downhill and slalom, and received the silver in the giant slalom after a virtual unknown, Canadian Kathy Kreiner, came out of nowhere to seize the gold. Mittermaier had been skiing competitively in World Cup and Olympic events for ten years, but in 1976, at the age of twenty-five, she provided the finest performance ever in the history of the three major women's ski events.

Near the end of the meet, one East German official commented to reporters that "contrary to what we sometimes read in the West, we don't shoot our athletes at dawn if they fail to win. Socialism is identical with competition." Obviously, even in this statement which attempted to deflect criticism of East German athletic training and success, it had ironically revealed how important that sport was to the East German political system.

The 1980 Winter Olympics

The 1980 winter Olympics were held at Lake Placid, the village in the Adirondacks that had hosted the 1932 games. Unlike Denver, which had rejected its selection as the site for the 1976 Winter Olympics because they saw the games as a threat to the environment and a stimulus to rapid growth and real estate development without proper planning, Lake Placid officials welcomed the chance to host the games. They built the Olympic village and new sports facilities outside the small village so as not to disrupt its unique character and charm.

The competition produced numerous heroes and unforgettable moments, as the whole nation focused its interest and hopes on the United States hockey team. Coached by Herb Brooks, the team jelled together during a long exhibition season in Europe and the United States and learned to play as a team that relied on passing, deliberate offensive plays that insured puck control, and unselfish play to set up other players for an open shot. The players were not the best collegiate players in the country, but Brooks had chosen them because he could see in these players the team traits and dedication that he wanted to develop.

The hockey team had won all of its 1980 Olympic games and tied one before beating the mighty Soviet team 4-3 on Friday night. The win over the Soviet team was dramatic and unexpected, as a team of collegians outplayed the best team in the world, a Russian hockey unit that was professional in every sense of the word.

The Americans were led by goalie Jim Craig, who played every minute of the seven games and allowed only 15 goals. Craig was particularly tough in the third periods, allowing only three last period goals and making unbelievable saves that ignited his team. The defense was incredibly tough and tight as Ken Morrow, Bill Baker, and Bob Suter played with an intensity and efficiency that astounded the opposition. They played brilliant defensive position hockey and controlled the puck behind the net and around the boards. The offense was spearheaded by Mike Eruzione, who scored the winning goal against the Soviets, Buzz Schneider (four goals and three assists), Dave Christian (leader in assists), and Mark Johnson (five goals, two against the Russians). The Americans carried and controlled the play with sharp passing, sure puck handling, and alert passing to the open men.

When the American team beat Finland 4-2 to take the gold medal, they were down 2-1 going into the final period but scored three goals, the last one while killing off a penalty. The victory produced a frenzy of celebration and shows of patriotism as fans chanted "U.S.A., U.S.A." in the rink and the proud chant was picked up all over the nation in living rooms, taverns, and wherever people watched the game. It was an electric moment, one of those few times in history when a nation feels unity and pride in its best effort. A group of young Americans playing on pride and inspiration had proven itself the best in the world. It beat the Russian machine because it believed in itself. The youthful enthusiasm of the team inspired people to believe in America at a time when the Iranian crisis, the Soviet invasion of Afghanistan, and the attacks on American embassies abroad left people bewildered and doubtful of national prestige. To their credit, the Soviet squad, which included seven players from the 1976 Olympics, showed true sportsmanship and dignity in defeat, upholding the traditions that the games have established. Perhaps they recognized that the Americans needed a lift and resurgence of pride, and they accepted defeat stolidly but gracefully.

Another big story at the Lake Placid games was the performance by speed skater Eric Heiden, who won five individual medals in an incredible show of speed, power, and endurance. In the 25-lap, 6.2-mile race he bettered the world record by over 6 seconds.

Competing in the shadow and glory of her older brother, Beth Heiden, who had been touted to win a number of gold medals, could manage only a bronze medal in the four events she skated. Leah Mueller won two silver medals in speed skating to claim her share of glory.

Phil Mahre, a slalom racer, won a silver medal, just losing to Ingemar Stenmark of Sweden. Mahre had come back from a multiple left ankle fracture that he had suffered on the same Adirondacks Whiteface Mountain less than a year before the 1980 Winter Olympics. Overcoming pain and fear of injury, Mahre showed a rare courage in the way he attacked a dangerous course and became the first American man in sixteen years to win an Alpine Olympic medal of any kind. His courage was not as celebrated as that of the hockey team, but it was as personally satisfying and inspiring.

In ice skating American hopes were dashed when Randy Gardner and Tai Babilonia had to withdraw from competition because of Gardner's injury. They were the favorites to win a gold medal in pairs figure skating, but Gardner reluctantly withdrew because he was afraid that he could not lift his partner and that she might be injured in a fall. The sight of Gardner falling repeatedly in the warmups as he tested his injured leg was painful to watch, and Tai Babilonia's tears revealed the dashed hopes of a graceful and beautiful skater. Linda Fratianne won a silver medal in figure skating, losing by a fraction of a point to East Germany's Anett Potzsch. The final programs by each skater were dazzling, all-out performances in one of the most dramatic confrontations in the history of the event. The women's figure skating far overshadowed the men's competition, in which Charlie Tickner of the United States took a bronze medal.

Overall, the United States won twelve medals, half of them gold. As expected, the Soviet Union and East Germany dominated the games, but the games provided memorable moments that Americans will long remember for their inspiration and uplift at a time when these qualities were in short supply.

The 1980 Summer Olympics

The 1980 Olympics in Moscow were ill-fated and controversial before they even began. When the Russians moved into Afghanistan in order to prop up and solidify their choice of a Marxist leader and government in Kabul, the United States, led by President Jimmy Carter, promoted a boycott against the Olympics that would give considerable media exposure to the Soviet way of life. The Soviets, of course, claimed that they had been invited into Afghanistan to resolve internal problems, and the Kremlin argued further that decisive action in their neighboring country was necessary to protect the Russian border and insure national security. But the invasion and occupation were viewed differently, and many saw Soviet actions in the historical context of the earlier treatment of Czechoslovakia, Hungary, and Poland.

President Carter was obviously surprised and shocked by the Soviet incursion, for he had been strongly pushing the ratification of the SALT II agreement as well as expanded trade and cultural exchanges with the Soviet Union. He felt betrayed by the Soviet's sudden shift to militarism, and the president's strong stand on human rights was also called into question and challenged. Carter responded with strong denunciations of the USSR's military actions and with an impassioned appeal to the American athletes and Olympic committee that they should sacrifice competition and participation for principle.

The athletes did not all fall into line and enthusiastically endorse the boycott. Many felt that we should send a strong team that would challenge and triumph over the Russians on their own home turf. Others proposed that American athletes could participate without the trappings of nationalism and patriotism, that is not marching with our flag and not allowing the national anthem to be played or flag to be raised at gold medal award ceremonies. Instead, the athletes would use the Olympic flag and anthem. Another group proposed that the athletes be sent but that spectators forego their trips and that the viewing public forego the planned 152^1/$_2$ hours of NBC programming so that the Russians could not use the media for its intent of promoting the Soviet way of life and accomplishments. These restrictions would also prevent the Russians from gaining hard currency and thus profiting from their sponsorship of the games.

President Carter's total boycott position prevailed; only a few Americans attended the games (only 3,000 out of the expected 18,500) and television coverage was scant and spotty. From what Americans were able to see, they missed a spectacular opening and closing ceremony and truly memorable athletic performances. Thirty-five countries joined the boycott (including China, Canada, Japan, and West Germany) and kept their athletes home. This scale of nonparticipation prompted some reporters to call the 1980 games the Eastern European Olympics, and *Time* called them "A Warsaw Pact

Picnic.'' The top six medal winning countries were all Warsaw Pact countries, with the USSR winning 80 gold medals and 196 total medals while East Germany garnered 126 total medals, including 47 golds. Only Great Britain offered competition to the little four (Bulgaria, Hungary, Poland, and Rumania) that finished well behind the big two winners.

Although many argued that the medals won were tarnished by the absence of the Western nations, many remarkable performances were recorded. World records were set in the pole vault (Wladislaw Kozakiewicz of Poland with 18 feet 11½ inches) and high jump (Gerd Wessing of East Germany, who cleared 7 feet 8¾ inches). The 800- and 1,500-meter races between Britain's Sebastian Coe and Steve Ovett (with each winning one race) produced the most interest in America, largely because of the news media's coverage of the alleged animosity and fierce competition between the two talented middle-distance runners. Another memorable confrontation involved Lasse Viren of Finland and Miruts Yifter of Ethiopia in the 10,000-meter race. Viren had won both the 5,000- and 10,000-meter races in 1972 and 1976, and Yifter had missed the 1976 Montreal games because of the African boycott. In Moscow Yifter won both races convincingly, although Viren's 1972 and 1976 records in the events easily remained intact and were never really in danger. Lutz Dombrowski, an East German, became the second man in Olympic history to exceed 28 feet in the long jump, but Bob Beamon's 1968 record was also never threatened.

Many Americans also saw Nadia Comaneci fall during her routine on the uneven parallel bars, an event she had dominated in Montreal with perfect scores. With a badly infected hand and with increased height and weight, Nadia missed her grip and fell to the mat. Undaunted and game, she finished her exercise, but Romania had to settle for a silver behind the Soviet women gymnasts in the all-around competition. The all-around women's title went to Yelena Davydova of the USSR. Like Olga Korbut, Nadia Comaneci had become a media favorite and television personality. Both had brought grace, daring, and youthful vitality to women's gymnastics, making it popular by combining animation and personality with the most disciplined of sports. Both also accepted defeat with grace and dignity, maturing into women from the pixielike sprites that had first captured the interest of television audiences.

American athletes had to content themselves with receiving special gold-plated congressional medals at the Capitol, bestowed by the president who kept them home. Or they competed against the already established Olympic times during the U.S. National Championships in Irvine, California, where times indicated that American swimmers would have captured more than their share of medals and honors in Moscow. The U.S. Olympic basketball team played teams of NBA professionals in a series of games held at four sites and won three of the games in convincing fashion. In the Golden Gala track meet in Rome, held just after the Moscow games closed, American athletes beat gold medal performances in the 400-meter (Edwin Moses), the 100-meter dash (Stan Floyd), and the discus throw (Ben Plunckett). These events, however, were some consolation for the Olympic hopefuls, but they could not replace the drama and challenge of Olympic competition.

The 1980 Olympics illustrated the increasing need to depoliticize and denationalize the games within reasonable limits. The games are costly, and security problems can only increase in the future. The 1984 Olympics scheduled for Los Angeles will perhaps be the key test for the relevance and meaning of the games in the context of their ideals of international competition.

The Olympics provide a focus for national pride and spirit as well as supply the occasions for remarkable and memorable athletic performances. The competition has also provided significant moments when differences of race, national identity, political ideology, and arguments about amateur status and training programs are forgotten and prove insignificant in the exultation of determined effort and proud performance, win or lose. The Olympics have often provided moments or images, however brief, of an international community or sense of fellowship based on shared values of the Greek ideal of a sound mind in a sound body. If only for those moving moments, the Olympics deserve their place in the world community. Perhaps the 1984 games scheduled for Los Angeles will restore an international event that has been plagued by controversy and disrupted by power politics.

9

The Future of Sports in America

The 1970s was a decade of dramatic changes and developments in sports, especially the development of the free agent situation in professional baseball, with its impact on player salaries and concepts of team loyalty or identification, and the rulings involved in Title IX (1972), which have promoted the growth of women's sports programs and brought about the faint beginnings of more equal opportunities and funding. More and more Americans became actively involved in sporting activities as joggers, runners, paddleball players, aerobic dancers, and weight reducing exercisers all sought to shed excess pounds and escape the negative effects of aging and poor eating habits. As fashion designers emphasized the slim look with designer jeans and tight, form-fitting clothing, people responded with a flurry of activity and a determined search for the diet that would magically transform middle-age spread into the desired look. The 1970s was an age of diet soft drinks, diet foods, and diet regimens that became acceptable topics of social conversation.

Thus, sports or sporting activities became, for many, a means to an end. Sports began to be analyzed for their relative value in terms of calories burned, body fat reduced, or the cardiovascular system strained. Promoters of such exotic theories as biorhythms could claim to explain and chart the cycles of the body and mind so that athletes or business people could understand their "highs" and "lows" and adjust accordingly. Even Transcendental Meditation could be pressed into service in order to put athletes in tune with their inner consciousness and prepare them for competition.

Americans have always tended to judge the value of anything in practical and utilitarian terms, and sports and physical activity are no exception to this general rule. During the 1970s Americans became increasingly interested in levels of performance as well as the process by which the athlete trains and prepares. Numerous books have been written on the psychology of winning and the mental preparation for competition, whether on the playing field or in the business conference room. Success was becoming "number one," the best in one's field or the one who could command and demand a compensation package that insured absolute future security. Athletes were now executives and were equally at home in uniforms and business suits. Their deals and negotiations were widely reported in detail and assumed a significance beyond whether they would report to training camp or begin the season on time.

The new sports "hero" is a wheeler-dealer who is increasingly free to sell his or her skills and name to the highest bidder, within the limits established by the owners' willingness to increase expenses and make concessions on an individual basis. With his agent, his business counselors, and his lawyers, the big-name athlete can negotiate intelligently and shrewdly for the big contract.

Or the athletes could use name recognition and popularity to land lucrative endorsement contracts that would keep their image before the public long after careers had ended. "Broadway" Joe Namath could sell anything from pantyhose to an assortment of Brut products, and Bruce Jenner could enhance such diverse products as Wheaties and a 35mm camera.

The public's fascination with the details of these negotiations and final contract arrangements can be explained by the fact that athletes, recently liberated from the control of the reserve clause and belatedly realizing the need for strong unionization, represent a kind of economic freedom that most people do not enjoy. In an age of continuing recession, rampant inflation, decreased job mobility, and unprecedented white collar unemployment, the athlete symbolizes the individual who can control and dominate the situation because he or she is convinced of the value of physical skills and abilities to perform.

Many people have criticized modern athletes for being greedy and unreasonable in their demands as they threaten to bankrupt a sport or as they display an arrogance stemming from selfishness and egotism. In response, athletes argue that they are only "cashing in" on a relative short career, that they have been previously underpaid and are only "catching up," or that they individually bring fans to watch and should be paid more of the game receipts. They want some security to compensate for the possibilities of injury or the whims of an owner who can send them packing in a trade or exiting in the disgrace of an outright release. These defenses often find public sympathy and understanding in a society and economy where average people struggle with the same kinds of haunting job insecurities.

The modern professional sports "hero" is viewed ambivalently. The big-name players are often distant from fans, disdaining their adulation and worship as well as avoiding direct contact with them. Athletes often seem to lack a visible enthusiasm for the game or an appreciation and knowledge of their sport's heritage. Sports have become business or highly skilled professional work rather than spontaneous play or a celebration of the physical effort. Accused of being pampered, vain, selfish, and uninspired, modern day athletes respond by becoming more private and more restrained in their approach to the sport. The individual performance becomes the measure of their relative value to a sport. The personal career becomes more important than the records of the teams played for or the game's ongoing heritage.

The professional athlete is still envied and admired for his or her "place in sun" as well as for the talents and skills required by a level of sport that has so many measures of excellence. The pro athlete remains a success story, and in a society of automation and routine services, sports still provide moments of excitement and transcendence when the human body and its controlled, directed performance provide the focus of attention and appreciation. Sports form a core of shared interests and values as well as provide a community feeling and identification. The athlete enables all of this to happen and is therefore valued and honored. Teams can come to symbolize the collective identity and pride of a city, as the Pittsburgh Steelers and Pirates do, or can even represent the unique qualities of a neighborhood as the Chicago Cubs and Wrigley Field do.

Modern sports heroes tend to be more momentary, incidental, and situational as they rise out of specific occasions or are made into media stories to fulfill the needs of television or the press. The consistent, steady performers are often ignored, and conflicts or clashes of personalities behind the scenes make bigger news than reporting the game. Sports telecasting, notably on the major networks, has become the art of reporting rumors as fact and penetrating the surface story to reveal the "real" or "inside" story that contradicts appearances. Thus, sports becomes entertainment and diversion that go far beyond the experience of the game itself.

As a consequence, sports heroes are creations of the moment, quickly discarded for a bigger story or soon put aside to let another situational hero emerge. With the increasing sports saturation of the television market by cable television networks, it becomes harder and harder to separate the significant from the insignificant, the truly heroic or memorable from the hyped. Few lasting or durable heroes have been created in the past decade, men or women who give new stature and honor to a sport. No one person has come to symbolize or incorporate the meanings of a specific sport: constant dedication to excellence, excitement and potential for great moments, superiority of skills and the ability to meet the changing demands of the game. Only Jack Nicklaus in golf, Henry Aaron and Lou Brock in baseball, Bill Rodgers in the marathon, Billie Jean King in tennis, and O. J. Simpson in football have become modern day legends.

The television hype for sports creates levels of expectation that often cannot be fulfilled or realized. Super Bowl week is a prelude to what has been, in the recent past, a dull game or a runaway. Pretty faces like Phyllis George Brown or Jane Kennedy have been used to introduce the women's point of view or simply to provide nice looking camera shots. The baseball All-Star game has become something of a joke, with players refusing to play and during-the-game interviews becoming comical routines for self-indulgent players.

Sports have become further adulterated and cheapened by the promotion of "trash" sports on television, contests that settle nothing and are pointless. A series like NBC's "Games People Play" relies on sensationalism and daredevil stunts that have resulted in some serious injuries and lawsuits. Women's arm wrestling, motorcycle jumping over operating helicopters, jumping over speeding cars, or trying to escape from a straight jacket while suspended upside down on a burning rope are not games since they do not involve play or developed physical skills. Huge football players look ridiculous trying to excel at sports like bicycling, swimming, and tennis.

Too often players begin to "play up" to the television exploitation of their sport and become controversial or act "flakey" simply to amuse themselves or to show their contempt for the unwanted intrusions. Sportscasters and journalists often seem more interested in how "badly" Reggie Jackson is behaving or how many fights he is having with the manager or Yankee owner than with his performance in the ball park. Controversy and conflict produce better ratings, and reporters become gossip mongers and unwanted intruders who will easily betray confidences for the "big story." Athletes are often shown to be immature boys rather than maturing adults. Their attentions and energies are diverted away from the sport that they should learn to master and play with developing dedication and consistent skill. Those who refuse interviews or jealously protect their privacy are branded as loners or "pouty" losers who cannot deal with the realities of the sports media industry. Rabid fans drive their teams to outbursts of violence or unsportsmanlike behavior as they expect them to prove their macho image or "destroy" the opposition, thus violating codes of play and camaraderie that form the core of sports among those who perform. Cheap shot "artists" and bad boys or "enforcers" are encouraged in their mayhem and often injurious play.

The future of sports in America will be decided by the athletes themselves as they attempt to deal with pressures put on them by the media and fans who seek novelty and circus-type excitement rather than the beauty of play that comes from consistency, professional dedication and pride, and adult maturity. Willie Stargell of the Pittsburgh Pirates expressed this idea well when he said that the "real heroes" were the men and women who worked hard, supported their families and loved them, and lived with dignity and honor among their friends. Professional players gain respect when they are socially involved in the communities they play for, when they show that they have commitments, sensitivities, and interests beyond winning and making money. They demonstrate maturity when they can face personal problems like alcoholism or drug use and overcome the easy temptations or excesses that have corrupted the game and its players. The final stage in this increasing maturity will come when players rid the game, on their own volition and initiative, of dangerous practices such as the bean ball in baseball or the dangerous crippling hit in football.

Professional sports are faced with serious problems that demand short and long range solutions. Levels of player violence have steadily increased and have resulted in such infamous cases as Daryll Stingley, now a paraplegic after a vicious hit from "Assassin" Jack Tatum; Rudy Tomjanovich and Richard Rhodes, who both had their jaws shattered by punches thrown in NBA basketball games; Henry Boucha, seriously injured with permanent eyesight damage in an NHL hockey game; and a number of boxers who have been killed in boxing matches. League officials have tried to control the situation with rules changes, stiffer penalties that include suspensions and fines, and greater discretionary power to referees. By and large, these have not effectively reduced violence levels or provided needed discouragements. Perhaps the problem will be solved only by the threat of legal prosecution and actual arrest and punishment, or by the courts, which may have to intervene and police the sports. A number of multimillion dollar lawsuits and damage cases might also make club owners reassess the profits or box office appeal of violent, aggressive teams or individual players. League commissioners have to take uncompromising positions on such potentially lethal and disruptive behavior, even if it may mean banning players for a season or even for life. The 1980s may well prove to be the decade of reform, and if sports enterprises and the athletes themselves do not lead the way, they will probably be forced to institute reforms by the courts, law enforcement officials, and even local governments.

Violence on the field has spilled over into the stands, presenting serious problems of crowd control, especially when fans are loaded with alcohol or high on marijuana. The use of ball parks and sports arenas for rock concerts has caused problems because people do not view the facility in the way that loyal sports fans do, treating it with some degree of respect and observing a code of behavior.

Professional sports also face serious problems related to drug use and injuries that are caused by or worsened by drug use. Rumors and charges multiply about the level and incidence of the use of "uppers" and pain-killers. The National Basketball Association has recently faced the reality of widespread cocaine use by its players by announcing that a "solid" drug program would be developed to educate players in the dangers of cocaine and to discourage usage. A number of prominent professional players have been arrested for possession of hard drugs, so finally league officials are going to have to do something to turn the tide of scandal and exposé.

Spokesmen for professional sports say that they are suffering from an "image problem," and to a certain extent this is true. However, the real crisis is in the fans' image of the athlete as a hero worthy of admiration and emulation. Modern day athletes have tended to promote images that may evoke envy and temporary identification but do not produce ongoing esteem. These ambivalent images include: the "outlaw" figure, the "bad ass" dude, the "enforcer," the mod man about town and trend setter, the "flake," the hustler, and so on. The clean, good guy All-American type, like Steve Garvey, is discredited as being too "straight" or "nice," and the Garveys have been disparagingly described as a "Ken and Barbie" doll couple. Players become confused about their media images and even fight among themselves over whose image is hotter. The media exploitation of sports has, in many cases, proved divisive and caused identity problems for athletes who had always been pampered, cajoled, and treated as special.

The professional sports scene can be aptly described as an uneasy marketplace that faces pressures from within and without. Racial tensions and problems still exist despite statistical evidence that integration and salary equality have become realities. Blacks resent the endorsements and advertising perks that usually go to white athletes, and there are few black professional managers or coaches. Athletes have to wonder when the boom in salaries will taper off and high-priced free agents will go begging for a contract as new cost cutting measures are taken by ownership. The impact of a continued recession, double-digit inflation, and an uncertain energy supply has yet to be fully felt or encountered. Further, as the national population shifts away from the Northeast and Midwest to the Sun Belt region, and as those states become richer and more influential, sports franchises will be shifted there, existing league alignments will have to be readjusted, and new arrangements of ownership and franchise control will be introduced. All these conditions produce uncertainty and anxiety in those in the sports world as traditions and continuities give way to new exigencies. Sports, to a large extent, are no longer that special place with its own protections, laws of operation, interests, and exemptions. Their meaning and value have come under increasing scrutiny and questioning, as have other cherished American institutions like the presidency and the Supreme Court.

This tendency toward investigation and examination is particularly evident in collegiate sports, particularly football. University and college sports programs and athletic departments have long been almost sacrosanct functions that did not have to justify their operations or bear close scrutiny. As available public funds diminish, as operating costs rise dramatically with inflation, and as the available supply of college-age students declines, sports programs are moving into a new era of accountability and self-justification. A number of smaller schools have already dropped "minor" sports or are curtailing expenses and retrenching.

Collegiate football has been sorely hurt by widespread recruiting scandals and financial corruption in athletic departments that for too long have been able to dictate the terms of their operations. Two of the former paragons of tough, no-nonsense winning football, coaches Woody Hayes and Frank Kush, have resigned in disgrace and dishonor.

The problem of the place of sports in higher education is anything but new. As the following quotes indicate, periods of economic success and widespread popularity have brought internal problems that threaten to undermine the integrity and assigned values of college football. "The result is that today, notwithstanding many statements to the contrary, the colleges and universities of the United States are confronted with acute problems of recruiting and subsidizing, especially with respect to intercollegiate football."

"External competition from professional sports, selective treatment by the media, as well as pressure from alumni and the public have put big time collegiate athletic programs into competition with each other, not only on the playing field, but in the market for entertainers/performers/athletes."

The first quote is from the famous 1929 Carnegie Foundation for the Advancement of Teaching on College Athletics Report. The second is from the American College on Education Committee study report published in 1974. Obviously, not much has changed.

If anything, the problems of collegiate sports have gotten worse. A number of recent published works have examined the nature of recruiting and college athletics. These include (1) John F. Rooney, Jr., *The Recruiting Game: Toward a New System of Intercollegiate Sports;* (2) Kenneth Denlinger and Leonard Shapiro, *Athletes for Sale: An Investigation into America's Greatest Sports Scandal— Athletic Recruiting;* (3) Joseph Durso, *The Sports Factory: An Investigation into College Sports.* Recruiting and its evils are the central concern in Neil D. Isaacs' *Jock Culture U.S.A.,* with Isaacs calling an athlete the "high-priced whore of our society." Rooney, Denlinger and Shapiro not only point out and document the evils but offer a solution that is not entirely new—let the colleges adopt a professional approach—or at least a semiprofessional approach—and keep things aboveboard. Denlinger and Shapiro conclude: "It is a time for a wave of realism to wash away the hypocrisy in collegiate athletics. Let the recruiters bring their offers above the table, at last. Let them continue to tell the athlete that he means so much to the university. But let him know how much." Whether or not this is the ultimate solution, only time will tell. However, some reforms must be instituted.

During 1978–80 new revelations of chicanery involving universities and their athletes repeatedly hit the headlines. Arizona State was accused of providing phony course credits for football players. This was on November 15, 1979. Within five months of that date officials at New Mexico, Purdue, Oregon State, California State Polytechnic at Pomona, the University of Oregon, UCLA, the University of Utah, and the University of Southern California had to admit to similar violations of NCAA rules. However, these admissions were serious in the sense that they involved not just money or goods for players, but tampering with the integrity of the universities as dispensers and certifiers of knowledge.

In response to these revelations, *Sports Illustrated* (May 19, 1980) featured an article by John Underwood entitled "Student-Athletes: The Sham, the Shame," which thoroughly examined the sorry situation. Underwood admits that one way would be to professionalize college athletics, but he concludes that "such a move would only be an anathema to the academic community, but also, while proving that college athletics are no more than a business would do the business in. The rich get richer, the poor would go bankrupt. And it would do nothing to help get anyone educated." Underwood's solution is "caring." Of course, this is only a start, not a definitive program.

But will needed changes come? Recently the PAC Ten Conference revealed that five conference schools will be ineligible for the 1981 Rose Bowl and other postseason play. Oregon, Oregon State, and UCLA were also forced to forfeit twenty-one victories over the past three seasons. Glenn Terrell, president of Washington State University and chairman of the conference's presidents and chancellors, said the sanctions would "certainly act as a deterrent" against future improprieties.

Michigan State University in the 1970s was put on three years NCAA probation, allowed no television appearances, and had its grants-in-aid reduced by twenty over a three-year period. The school's most glaring violation was the unauthorized use of a credit card by an overzealous alumnus. In addition, there were some temporary suspensions of players and one permanent suspension. MSU's violations were mere peccadilloes compared to the improprieties of the five PAC Ten schools. The whole educational process was being subverted, and yet the penalties were relatively minor. Undoubtedly this disparity in punishments can be explained by the big money involved and the television audience that the USC and UCLA games attract. The NCAA has remained notably silent on the affair.

No one would deny that college coaches are under heavy pressure to win. Some of the more vociferous cheerleaders are college presidents themselves who see the media attention given to athletic winners as a means of popularizing their school and insuring enrollments. Legislators are made happy with free tickets and choice seats so larger appropriations may be garnered. In addition, school administrations have, in many cases, made the coaching profession a very insecure one. At one Big Ten school the president mandated that coaches could no longer hold dual appointments as coaches and as professors of physical education with tenure. This prohibition was done obviously to facilitate elimination of unwanted coaching staffs.

What must be remembered is that even if an athletic program is on the up and up, the way big-time college athletics are being run, the athlete is being cheated and done a disservice anyway. He does not have time to choose the discipline that he wants since he has little time for it. He has to take "voluntary" running and weight-training classes and "God help him" if he doesn't. Not being able to choose and train for the career that he desires will adversely affect his entire life. This is one of the gravest injustices that is being done. Further, if he does attempt to choose tougher courses, he will be strongly advised to take safe driving courses or more physical education courses—anything to keep the athlete eligible. With fall practice and games, films on Sunday, running and weight classes in the winter, spring practice, and a take-home summer training program, the athletes are truly full-time employees. Yet they continue, trapped into the belief that they're going to make the pros or that they are receiving a "free," quality education. Seldom do they realize that they are poorly paid gladiators who are often forgotten as soon as their eligibility is used up.

It remains to be seen what impact this growing number of abuses, illegalities, and legal prosecutions involving coaches, athletic directors, and players will have on public attitudes toward college football. The current list of schools involved and the severity of the charges would seem to demand a wholesale cleanup of the kind that Teddy Roosevelt demanded earlier regarding violence and fatalities. A number of major universities have been tainted and discredited by these scandals, but public opinion is a fickle and unpredictable factor.

What seems certain is that college sports, like their professional counterparts, will come under increasing scrutiny from legislators and the courts. No longer can athletic departments, schools, conferences and associations like the NCAA be depended upon to "police" themselves and regulate their own affairs. Perhaps the real financial costs of football will become evident, and internal allocations of financial resources will be readjusted so that so-called non revenue sports do not have to beg for a subsistence or go under the budget axe.

Like the nation and the economy, sports are going to face a future of more limited resources, more reasonable expectations, and scaled-down levels of operation. With these certain future realities, perhaps sports will lose some of its glamour and glitter. Athletes may regain the physical joy of sport and come to accept it as a temporary diversion and challenge rather than an end-all and be-all. Dramatic and even radical changes will come, perhaps with no immediate discernible pattern. America has been and will always be a sports oriented culture and a sporting society. We look to sports for the youthful vigor and mental readiness that participation can provide, and we still look for values and hero models in the sports world. Those cultural needs remain strong and valid. Many hope that our sports can continue to fill those requirements and revitalize a nation now looking for stability and an American identity that will endure.

Bibliographic Essay

Hundreds of books and articles have been consulted by the authors, but in this bibliography the aim is to present reference sources which are generally the major works in the area and which may prove to be an aid and guide to further reading in the field.

Valuable general reference sources concerning sports per se are: Ralph Hickok, *New Encyclopedia of Sports* (1977); *The NFL's Official Encyclopedic History of Professional Football* (1974); Zander Hollander, *The Modern Encyclopedia of Basketball* (1979); Roger Treat, *The Encyclopedia of Football* (15th rev. ed., 1977); Joseph L. Reichler, ed. *The Baseball Encyclopedia* (4th ed., 1979); and Paul Soderberg, ed., *The Big Book of Halls of Fame in the United States and Canada* (1977); Donald Steel and Peter Ryde, *The Encyclopedia of Golf;* Thomas C. Jones and Buck Dawson, eds., *The Hall of Fame* (1977); U.S.T.A., *Official Encyclopedia of Tennis* (1979); Gene Karst and Martin J. Jones, Jr., *Who's Who in Professional Baseball* (1973); Ronald L. Mendell and Timothy B. Phares, *Who's Who in Football* (1974). Robert J. Higgs' bibliographical essay on sports in *Handbook of American Popular Culture*, vol. 1 (1979) provides useful information and critical insights on major works.

Works on Social and Cultural History

Some general works concerning American culture and society include: Arthur M. Schlesinger and Dixon Ryan Fox, eds., *A History of American Life*, 13 vols. (1927–48); Dixon Wecter, *The Saga of American Society* (1937); and Ashley Montagu, *The American Way of Life* (1967).

On American heroes and their role, see Dixon Wecter, *The Hero in American Society* (1941); Leo Gurko, *Heroes, Highbrows and the Popular Mind* (1953); and Richard M. Dorson, *American Folklore* (1959).

In regard to leisure, Eric Larrabee and Rolf Meyersohn, eds. *Mass Leisure* (1958); Sebastian de Grazia, *Of Time, Work and Leisure* (1962), and James F. Murphy, *Concepts of Leisure: Philosophical Implications* (1974) contain stimulating observations on the topic. Thorstein Veblen, *The Theory of the Leisure Class* (1899) was one of the original critics of the use of increased leisure.

For the late nineteenth century period, the best single brief survey is Samuel P. Hays, *The Response to Industrialism, 1885–1914* (1957). Robert H. Wiebe, *The Search for Order 1877–1920* (1968); Ray Ginger, *The Age of Excess: The United States from 1877 to 1914* (1965); and John A. Garraty, *The New Commonwealth* (1968) are more detailed analyses. Glenn Porter, *The Rise of Big Business, 1860–1910* (1973) and Edward C. Kirkland, *Industry Comes of Age: Business, Labor and Public Policy, 1878–1898* (1961) are good accounts of business development. Matthew Josephson, *The Robber Barons* (1934) and Stewart H. Holbrook, *The Age of Moguls* (1954) contain dated but colorful portraits of entrepreneurs. William Miller, ed., *Men in Business* (1952; revised editions, 1962 and 1979) contains more scholarly studies of the business leadership.

Zane Miller, *The Urbanization of Modern America: A Brief History* (1973) is a good introduction to urban history, and Blake McKelvey, *The Urbanization of America, 1860–1915* (1963) is a good survey of the period. There are many works on urban history, but Raymond A. Mohl, *The Urban Experience: Themes in American History* (1973), and Sam Bass Warner, Jr., *The Urban Wilderness: A History of the American City* (1972) would be most useful for further exploration.

John Higham, *Strangers in the Land* (1955), and *Send These to Me: Jews and Other Immigrants* (1975) provide good coverage of the problems of immigrants. Aaron I. Abell, *The Urban Impact on American Protestantism* (1943) covers this topic well.

Gerald N. Grob, *Workers and Utopia: A Study of Ideological Conflict in the American Labor Movement 1865–1900* (1961) is a good coverage of the labor movement. Norman Ware's *The Industrial Worker 1840–1860: The Reaction of American Industrial Society to the Advance of the Industrial Revolution* (1924, new edition 1964) and *The Labor Movement in the United States 1860–1895: A Study in Democracy* (1929) should not be overlooked. John A. Garraty, ed., *Labor and Capital in the Gilded Age, Testimony taken by the Senate Committee upon the Relations between Labor and Capital—1883* (1968) contains prime source material concerning the workers' problems during the period. Daniel T. Rodgers, *The Work Ethic in Industrial America 1850–1920* (1978) is an important analysis of the subject. Henry Nash Smith, *Popular Culture and Industrialism*

1865–1900 (1967) is a good compilation of documents relating to industrialism's impact on the common person's life.

Richard Hofstadter, *The Age of Reform* (1955); Eric F. Goldman, *Rendezvous with Destiny* (1952), and J. D. Buenker, *Urban Liberalism and Progressive Reform* (1973) all give good treatments of the progressive period.

For the twenties, William E. Leuchtenburg's *The Perils of Prosperity, 1914–1932* (1958), Frederick Lewis Allen's *Only Yesterday* (1931), and George Soule's *Prosperity Decade from War to Depression: 1917–1929* (1947) are interesting reading on the period.

Dixon Wecter, *The Age of the Great Depression* (1948) and Frederick Lewis Allen's *Since Yesterday* (1940) are surveys of social history during the thirties and should be read with Broadus Mitchell, *Depression Decade From New Era through New Deal, 1929–1941* (1947).

Eric Goldman's *The Crucial Decade and After: America, 1945–60* (1960) provides an engrossing look at the life and times of those years. Douglas T. Miller and Marion Nowak, *The Fifties: The Way We Really Were* (1977) is the most comprehensive and thorough study of that decade.

David Burner et al., *A Giant's Strength: America in the 1960s* (1971) has a chapter on the meaning of the fifties as well as an analysis and survey of the sixties.

Theodore Roszak, *The Making of a Counter Culture* (1969), and William L. O'Neill, *Coming Apart: An Informal History of America in the 1960's* (1971) are studies of the social tensions of the modern era.

Erik Barnouw's *Tube of Plenty: The Evolution of American Television* (1975) is an examination of television's impact on America.

Journals and Sports

Many journals throughout the time period covered in the book carried articles on sports. During the 1865–1900 period such magazines as *Scribners, Atlantic Monthly,* and *Popular Science Monthly* carried articles about the impact of sport. *Outing* (published under various titles from 1882 to 1923) was the most useful journal containing the most comprehensive coverage of sports for our use.

During the twentieth century, *Colliers* and *Saturday Evening Post* consistently carried articles on sports topics. With the development of *Time* and *Newsweek* coverage of important sports was provided almost every week. With the advent of *Sports Illustrated* in 1954, a consistent source of America's sports activities was provided. Since references to specific articles have been carried out throughout the text, references will be made only to whole books on sports topics. *Football Digest* and *Baseball Digest* are indispensible sources.

Sports Books

General Works

Older general works on sports include John A. Krout, *Annals of American Sport* (1929); volume 15 in *The Pageant of American Sport*, Foster Rhea Dulles, *America Learns to Play* (1940); Frederick W. Cozens and Florence Scovil Stumpf, *Sports in American Life* (1953). John Durant and Otto Bettman, *Pictorial History of American Sports from Colonial Times to the Present* (1952); Associated Press Sports Staff, *A Century of Sports* (1971); and Wells Twombly, *200 Years of Sport in America* (1976) are useful for reference. Roger G. Noll, ed., *Government and the Sports Business* (1974) contains a number of essays concerning the impact of sports on the society as a whole.

John R. Betts, *America's Sporting Heritage: 1850-1950* (1974) is the finest work on sports and society. John A. Lucas and Ronald A. Smith, *Saga of American Sport* (1978) is a useful synthesis and is particularly good for the 1865–1900 period. Betty Spears and Richard A. Swanson, *History of Sport and Physical Activity in the United States* (1978) gives a concise treatment of sport as well as concerning itself with the larger topic of physical education. Robert H. Boyle, *Sport: Mirror of American Life* (1963) contains useful information on the cultural impact of sports as does James A. Michener, *Sports in America* (1976) and Robert Lipsyte, *Sports World: An American Dreamland* (1975).

College Football

John McCallum and Charles H. Pearson, *College Football U.S.A.*, *1869-1972* (1972) is the official book of the National Football Foundation; Allison Danzig's *Oh How They Played the Game: The Early Days of Football and Heroes Who Made It Great* (1972) and *The History of American Football* (1956) are informative and well written. John D. McCallum, *Big Ten Football Since 1895* (1976) is a comprehensive study of the Big Ten Conference. Ivan N. Kaye, *Good Clean Violence! A History of College Football* (1973) presents a less than unified history of the game. John Underwood, *The Death of a Game* (1979) looks at some of the unpleasant aspects of the game. Richard I. Miller, *The Truth about Big-Time Football* (1953) covers the scandal of the early fifties.

Pro Football

Harold (Spike) Claussen, *The History of Professional Football* (1963) gives a coverage of the game's development. Bill Wallace, *Nelson's Encyclopedia of Pro Football* (1964) provides useful but more scattered coverage for those years. David S. Neft, et al., *The Complete All Time Pro Football Register* (1975) is a useful reference. Robert Smith, *Pro Football: The History of the Game* (1963) is a comprehensive look at the game from its inception. Mike Holovak and Bill McSweeny, *Violence Every Sunday* (1967) tells the agony of a pro football coach. William Henry Paul, *The Grey Flannel Pigskin: The Movers and Shakers of Pro Football* (1974) gives a look at the men in the front offices of the NFL. Vince Lombardi and W. C. Heinz, *Run to Daylight* (1963) and Jerry Kramer and Dick Schaap, *Instant Replay: The Green Bay Diary of Jerry Kramer* (1968) give personal insight into the Green Bay "Glory Days." Jack Tatum and Bill Kushner, *They Call Me Assassin* (1979) is a revealing portrait of violence in the NFL. *The Official National Football League Manual* is a handy reference guide. The development of the Professional Researchers Association in 1980 and the subsequent publication of an annual journal promise scholarly research into the area. Alex Karras, *Even Big Guys Cry* (1977) is a personal account of a pro football career. Arthur Daley, *Pro Football's Hall of Fame* (1963) contains well-written, concise career summaries of some of the more outstanding members of that select group.

College Basketball

Three excellent works on college basketball that give insight into the game and past feats on the court include: John D. McCallum, *College Basketball U.S.A. Since 1892* (1978); Ken Rappoport, *The Classic: The History of the NCAA Basketball Championship* (1979); and Neil D. Isaacs, *All the Moves, A History of College Basketball* (1975). Charles Rose, *Scandals of '51* (1978) provides a thorough history of the basketball scandals of the early fifties. Herb Michelson, *Almost a*

Famous Person (1980) tells the tragic story of one player for whom the "Big Time" was too much.

Pro Basketball

Zander Hollander, *The Pro Basketball Encyclopedia* (1971) includes complete coverage of the pro-game since the post World War II era. Pete Axthelm's *The City Game* (1970) is an analysis of pro basketball and the impact on its players. Wilt Chamberlain and David Shaw, *Wilt* (1973) gives Chamberlain's views on basketball and life. Phil Berger, *Miracle on 33rd Street* (1970) is a personalized view of the New York Knickerbockers' rise to a championship.

Tennis

Will Grimsely, *Tennis: Its History, People and Events* (1971) is a comprehensive look at tennis in the United States but is not well organized. Paul Metzler, *Tennis Styles and Stylists* (1969) covers the game worldwide, but American tennis is well covered. Jack Kramer, *The Game* (1979) is a first-hand analysis by one of the giants of the game. Pancho Gonzales, *Man with a Racket* (1959) is a first-hand look at one of the first professional stars. Billie Jean King and Kim Chapin, *Billie Jean* (1974) is the biography of the woman who has had the greatest impact on women's sports in the last twenty-five years. Elizabeth Wheeler, *Tennis Superstars* (1980) is an update on stars of the women's circuit.

Track and Field

Standard histories of track and field include J. M. Coherty, *Modern Track and Field* (1953) and R. L. Quercetani, *A World History of Track and Field Athletics 1864–1964* (1964). Histories of the Olympics include: Arthur Daley and John Kieran, *The Story of the Olympic Games* (1969); Bill Henry, *An Approved History of the Olympic Games* (1976); Wolfgang Girardi, *Olympic Games* (1972); and John Durant's *Highlights of the Olympics* (1961). Accounts of specific games are Neil Allen's *Olympic Diary Tokyo 1964* (1965) and Christopher Brasher's series that includes *Tokyo 1964—A Diary of the XVIIIth Olympiad, Mexico 1968—A Diary of the XIXth Olympiad,* and *Munich 72* (1972). *The Olympics 1972* (1972), by James Coote and John Goodbody, provides a detailed account of those tragedy marred Olympic Games. David Anderson's chapter on the Olympics in *Sports of Our Times* (1979) deals with the 1976 Montreal Games. Zander Hollander's *Great American Athletes of the 20th Century* (1966) includes chapters on Glenn Cunningham, Rafer Johnson, Bob Mathias, Jesse Owens, Don Schollander, Jim Thorpe, and Johnny Wiesmuller.

Baseball

Basic primary sources are *The Baseball Encyclopedia: The Complete and Official Record of Major League Baseball*, edited by Joseph L. Reichler (4th ed., Revised and Expanded, 1979) and *The World Series*, compiled by Richard M. Cohen, David S. Neft, and Roland T. Johnson with text by Jordan A. Deutsch (1976). Solid general histories include David Q. Voigt's *American Baseball: From Gentleman's Sport to the Commissioner's System* (1966) and *American Baseball: From the Commissioners to Continental Expansion* (1970). Lee Allen's *The American League Story* (1962) and *The National League Story* (1961) are helpful although sketchy and spotty in coverage. *Who's Who in Professional Baseball*, compiled by Gene Karst and Martin S. Jones, Jr., is a treasurehouse of anecdotes, biographical information, and relevant facts. Harold Seymour has also written a multivolume survey history with two volumes completed, *Baseball: The Early Years* (1960) and *Baseball: The Golden Age* (1971). Other notable histories include Arthur Daley, *Times at Bat: A Half Century of Baseball* (1950), Fred Lieb, *The Story of the World Series* (1965), and Glenn Dickey, *The History of National League Baseball Since 1876* (1979) and *The History of American League Baseball since 1901* (1980). David Q. Voigt's *America Through Baseball* (1976) is a stimulating sociological and cultural look at the sport. Recent oral histories have provided a much needed individual and personal perspective on the national game. Lawrence S. Ritter's *The Glory of Their Times: The Story of the Early Days of Baseball Told by the Men Who Played It* (1971) includes the edited transcripts of twenty-two interviews. Visual Education Corporation Sourcetapes offers a package called "Black Diamonds: An Oral History of Negro Baseball," which includes three cassettes. The best bibliographical source is Anton Grobani's *Guide to Baseball Literature* (1975), a reference work that has become the standard bibliography. Ken Smith, *Baseball's Hall of*

Fame (1975) and Martin Appel and Burt Goldblatt, *Baseball's Best: The Hall of Fame Gallery* (1977) are the best sources of information on that select group.

Golf

Numerous survey histories of golf are available. Some of the best include Herbert Warren Wind, *The Story of American Golf* (3rd ed., rev., 1975), Henry Cotton, *A History of Golf Illustrated* (1975), Will Grimsley, *Golf: Its History, People and Events* (1966), and Mark McCormack, *The Wonderful World of Professional Golf* (1973). The official history of the Professional Golfer's Association is *The PGA*, by Herb Graffis (1975), an informative, well-illustrated, and readable book. Dave Anderson's *Sports of Our Times* (1979) contains a chapter on golf, and Glenn Dickey's chapter "Palmer, Nicklaus and Miller" in *Champs and Chumps: An Insider's Look at America's Sports Heroes* (1976) should not be overlooked.

Boxing

The history of professional boxing is ably covered in Harry Carpenter's *Boxing: A Pictorial History* (1975), which also has a chapter on "The Olympic Games 1896–1972." Two excellent histories of the heavyweight division are John D. McCallum, *The World Heavyweight Boxing Championship: A History* (1974) and Stanley Weston, *Heavyweight Champions from Sullivan to Ali*, rev. ed. (1976). Glenn Dickey's *Champs and Chumps: An Insider's Look at America's Sports Heroes* (1976) contains a chapter on Muhammad Ali, as does Robert Lipsyte, *Sports World: An American Dreamland* (1975) and Dave Anderson, *Sports of Our Times* (1979). The Lipsyte chapter contains the most insights for understanding a complex man. Muhammad Ali, with Richard Durham, tells his own story in *The Greatest: My Own Story* (1975). The best biographies of boxers to date are, Finis Farr's *Black Champion: The Life and Times of Jack Johnson* (1964), Al-Tony Gilmore's *Bad Nigger! The National Impact of Jack Johnson* (1975), Randy Roberts, *Jack Dempsey, the Manassa Mauler* (1979), and Barney Nagler, *Brown Bomber* (1972), a biography of Joe Louis. Louis's *Joe Louis, My Life*, done with Edna and Art Rust (1978), is revealing and moving and should be read with Muhammad Ali's *The Greatest*.

Blacks in Sports

Standard works in this field include such pioneering books as Ocania Chalk, *Pioneer of Black Sport* (1975) and two books by A. S. "Doc" Young, *Great Negro Baseball Stars and How They Made the Big Leagues* (1953) and *Negro Firsts in Sports* (1963). Other notable books are Wally Jones and Jim Washington, *Black Champions Challenge American Sports* (1972); Robert Peterson, *Only the Ball Was White* (1970) on the Negro baseball leagues; William Brashler, *Josh Gibson: A Life in the Negro Leagues* (1978); and the chapter entitled "A Minority Group: The Negro Baseball Players" in Robert H. Boyle, *Sport: Mirror of American Life* (1963). Art Rust, Jr., *Get That Nigger Off the Field!* (1976) is an important book on race relations and integration in baseball. The article on black athletes in Ralph Hickok, *New Encyclopedia of Sports* (1977) is a good beginning point. Biographies of the great black boxers Jack Johnson, Joe Louis, and Muhammad Ali are listed in the biographical section on boxing. The chapters on blacks in sport in John A. Lucas and Ronald A. Smith, *Saga of American Sport* (1978) are well researched and reliable.

Index

85-1294

GV   Noverr, Douglas A.
583
. N68   The games they
1983   played
C.2

DATE		
AG2 4'87		
AUG 0 4 1987		
MAY 2 0 1998		
MAY 2 0 1998		

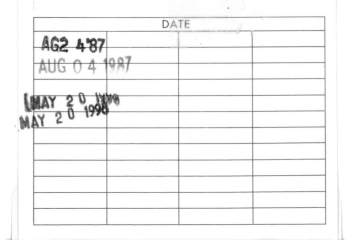

85-1294

WITHDRAWN

PJC LEARNING RESOURCES CENTER